THE ISRAELI COOK BOOK

by the same author

MY PROMISED LAND

WOMEN IN ISRAEL

THAT'S THE WAY IT IS WITH US

The Israeli Cook Book

MOLLY LYONS BAR-DAVID

International Cook Book Series
General Editor: Charlotte Adams

CROWN PUBLISHERS, INC.   NEW YORK

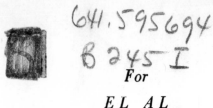

For

EL AL
ISRAEL AIRLINES

who, without so planning, made this book possible. As their culinary adviser, I began to collect old Jewish recipes at all of El Al's European stops. From then on, spurred by the wealth of dishes and the food legends about them, I began to interview immigrants from seventy lands in Israel, all of whom are contributing to the new culinary melting pot of this ancient land. Most of the dishes that have come to stay in Israel have been gathered into this book. El Al is the eagle upon whose wings this festive food has come to us, and today the best of it is served on its flights to and from the Holy Land.

Library of Congress Catalog Card Number: 63-21117

ISBN: 0-517-50667X

Printed in the United States of America

Fourth Printing, November, 1973

Acknowledgments

To give due credit to all who helped me with this book, I would require more pages than this volume contains. Every one of the five hundred cook books in my library, which I use constantly, has through the years taught me things which ultimately in some form have found their way into this book.

As wave after wave of new immigrants arrived in Israel from all over the world, dishes we had once considered foreign became familiar fare in every community. They were adapted to Israeli products, seasoned to local tastes, and became distinctively Israeli. And all this happened as quickly as the ingathered communities themselves were absorbed into the country. My late editor of the *Jerusalem Post*, Gershon Agron, coined the saying, "Israel's melting pot is a pressure cooker," and this is as true of its culinary practices as of its population, two-thirds of whom have come here since the birth of the State, hailing from almost a hundred countries.

For information on the lore of food and its preparation, the books to which I owe most are the Bible and the Talmud. I have also consulted the following works many times and have found them helpful:

Maurice Samuel: *Prince of the Ghetto*
Peter Gray: *Mistress Cook*
Helena Frank: *Yiddish Tales*
Nathan Ausubel: *A Treasury of Jewish Humor*
Nathan Ausubel: *A Treasury of Jewish Folklore*
Sholom Aleichem: *The Old Country*
Leah Leonard: *Jewish Cookery*
Savarin: *Real French Cooking*
Brillat-Savarin: *Physiology of Taste*
Fannie Engle and Gertrude Blair: *Jewish Festival Cookbook*
Helen Morganthau Fox: *Gardening for Good Eating*
Lilian Cornfeld: *Ani Mevashelet*
Wizo Education Department: *Kach Nevashel*

For direction of and patience with my own book, my gratitude to my editor, Charlotte Adams, and my business guide, Herbert Michelman, of Crown Publishers.

v

For insisting that I write the book, and for the neglect he suffered during my three years of work on the job, a kiss for my husband.

To my children, who plead that I never, but never, again write another book, an apology for writing this one.

To the following organizations whose staffs and services and even kitchens I imposed upon—my sincere thanks:

El Al Israel Airlines, for my experience through them.
The Foreign Office of the Israel Government and all its embassies in Western Europe which I visited.
Malben, J. D. C., in whose institutional kitchens I saw the cooking of so many communities where the aged are under their care.
The Israel Folklore Society, who directed me to so many sources of information on ancient lore of food.
The Hebrew Language Academy, for culinary terms and sources.
The Hebrew University, for archaeological information on food.
The Israel Government Tourist Department, who sponsored the Queen of the Kitchen Contest and the Wizard-Chef Contest.
The *Jerusalem Post*, whose culinary column is my potboiler.

My gratitude for encouragement and assistance in the food and folklore research involved in writing this book, particularly in translating from the many foreign languages used in Israel, to the following:

Professor Andrieux, president of the World Gastronomic Society, Paris
Professor Michael Avi-Jonah, archaeologist
Rabbi Barzilai, chief rabbi of Greece, Athens
Ehud Ben-Yehuda, translator
Rachel Yanait Ben-Zwi, wife of the late President of Israel
Dr. Hillel Blondheim, leading specialist on diets
Etta Chalfon, translator
Rabbi Harry Cohen, Biblical lecturer at Bar-Ilan University
Zipora Dak, wife of Israeli consul, Vienna
Miriam DeLeeuw, pioneer folklore of Israel and nutritionist
Esther Frankenburg, translator and nutritionist
Yehezkel Friedmann, Russian folklore
Marlyn Frisch, American folklore, New York
Leah Hellner, American folklore
Reuven Kashani, folklore of Afghanistan and Persia
Yona Kempel, translator
Lyla Lefkovitz, translator
Hassia Lev-Er, translator
Judge Seymour Levine, Yiddish folklore, New York
Tereska Levine, French folklore
Gania Lubinsky, translator
Golda Meir, foreign minister of Israel, Jewish folklore

Varda Mor, translator
Dora Moss-Morris, Lithuanian folklore
Dr. Oehler, ancient folklore, Vienna
Professor Raphael Patai, Biblical folklore, New York
Rebecca Perlman, English-Yiddish folklore
Daphne Plotkin, translator and nutritionist
Dr. Meyer Pratt, psychiatrist and Biblical scholar
Rabbi I. L. Rabinowitz, Biblical and Talmudic folklore
Helen Rossi, editor of woman's page, *Jerusalem Post*
Reuven Rubin, painter, Romanian-Jewish folklore
Medad Schiff, Israeli folklore
Rabbi Shilli, French-Jewish and ancient folklore, Paris
Dr. Elio Toaff, chief rabbi of Rome, Italian-Jewish folklore
S. Tolkowsky, citrus folklore and seafaring legends
W. A. van Gelden, Dutch consul at Tel Aviv, lore of Dutch food
Dola Ben-Yehuda Wittman, Israeli folklore
Dr. Geoffrey Wigoder, Talmudic folklore
Professor Yigdal Yadin, archaeologist
Dvora Zadikoff, translator

My thanks to the following friends who gave me unusual or newly created Israeli recipes born of traditional Jewish cooking in some far-off land:

Rose Amity (Russian)
Mrs. Arouk, Athens (Greek)
Mina Atoun, London (Greek)
Mrs. Bar-Yosef (Sephardic-Spanish)
Bayta Lancet (Hungarian)
Hilda Bendan (honey dishes)
Rebecca Bergman (citrus dishes)
M. Berlowitz, Zurich (Swiss and Alsatian)
Rosalie Berman (South African)
Arona Berold (South African)
Shomrona Bigger (Old Tiberias)
Shula Braudo (vegetarian dishes)
Sarah Cohen (Swiss)
Max Cymbalista, chef of the S.S. *Herzl* (Israeli)
Rivka Dabid (Yemenite)
Dr. Eckerling (Israeli)
Hanan Ephraim, chef of the ORT Cooking School, Nathanya (Israeli)
Phil Freeman, London (Russian and English)
Judy Friedgut (Russian)
Emma Gantoni, Florence (Italian)
Nehama Goldsmit (Old Jerusalem)
Judy Goldwasser (American)
Otto Gromer, chef of the Sheraton, Tel Aviv (Israeli)
Eugene Hochman, Toledo (Hungarian)

Rosa Kipnis (Old Jerusalem)
Melvina Klausner (Romanian)
Mrs. Krell, Vienna (Austrian)
Levana Madrassi (Moroccan)
Mrs. Isaac Nahoum, Istanbul (Turkish)
Nicolai, chef of Government Hotel School (Israeli)
Jeanne Pierre, Paris (French and Belgian)
Mrs. B. Polak, Amsterdam (Dutch)
Simcha Rahamim (Syrian)
Jean Rosenbaum, New York (Far Eastern)
Trudy Rosenberg, Rome (Italian)
Miriam Rosov (American)
Sally Rothberg, Melfort (Canadian)
Malka Royzen (Brazilian)
Judith Russo, Istanbul (Turkish)
Marjam Sabhalah (Ethiopian)
Mary Sachs (Lithuanian)
Fanya Shechter (Polish)
Helma Shepherd (German)
Geulah Shmueli (Georgian and Caucasian)
Jane Slone (South African)
Mrs. Soffher (Iranian and Iraqi)
Baroness Cecile van Tuyl van Sorenkerken, Holland (Dutch)
Susan Strugow (Turkish)
Pnina Swartz (Chilean)
Hady Traceman (Danish)
Dr. Corina Troestler (Romaniar.)
Werner, chef of Hotel Accadia, Herzlia (Israeli)
Dorothé van Karneebeck van Busslo van Wijenberg, Holland
(Dutch)
Mathilda Yokowlewitz (Yugoslav)
Shoshana Zelter (Algerian)
Yehudit Zuckerman (Egyptian and Middle Eastern)

Contents

On Friday night at the Sabbath board
I sing the praises of my wife
"A virtuous woman, noble, true"
And a wonderfully good cook too.

In moments between the stew and brew
She writes books and reads the Bible too
And, oh, at her pace, with time to race
She oft mixes, and stirs in the two.

So, dear reader, please control your wrath
When her active imagination
Doth in error sacrifice a lamb
On the altar of conversation.

If Abigail's five sheep did go
Not to feed King David's men at war
But astray to celebrate—oh ho!—
A *kumzits* at Dizengoff *Kikar!*

For hoary fable or good food pun
Make table talk such a lot of fun.
Even harsh curses and history bleak
Are savory, served with tongue in cheek.

—JAAP BAR-DAVID

*The holidays for which recipes are appropriate are indicated
beside the recipe title.*

APPETIZERS

FELAFEL—SPICY TIDBIT   *Independence Day*

In Israel these deep-fried tidbits are put into halved pita (see Index), the pancake bread of the Middle East, covered with spicy salad and peppery chili-cumin sauce. They are sold on the streets from kiosks, and are also used today as a cocktail tidbit.

½ pound chick-peas
3 tablespoons burghul
   (cracked wheat)
2 cloves garlic
1 teaspoon cumin

1 teaspoon salt
2 tablespoons flour
   dash of chili pepper
   dash of coriander

Soak the chick-peas overnight and then grind through the meat chopper. Soak burghul one hour, then grind it. Mix with the remaining ingredients. Form into small balls and fry in very hot deep fat until golden brown. May be reheated.

TAHINA (SESAME PASTE)   *Independence Day*

Tahina is a sesame paste that is akin to a mayonnaise in texture and color. It can be made of 1 cup sesame seed and 1 cup water, in a blender. The dish was introduced to Israel by Jewish refugees from Arab lands.

1 cup tahina
2 cloves garlic, crushed
½ cup water
   dash of cayenne
1 teaspoon salt
   juice of 2 lemons

3 tablespoons olive oil
2 tablespoons chopped
   parsley
   olives and vinegar
   pickles

Mix the tahina, garlic, water, cayenne, salt, and lemon juice until creamy. Add a little more water if the tahina is too pasty. Serve like homos, on small plates with a swirl of olive oil, a sprinkling of parsley, and a garnish of olives and vinegar pickles. This dish is eaten as a dip for pita (*see* Index) the pancake bread of the Middle East.

Independence Day

HOMOS AND TAHINA—CHICK-PEA AND SESAME PASTE

Homos is a spicy pulse paste made of chick-peas, often mixed with tahina, a sesame paste. It is served as an hors d'oeuvre with a garnish of olive oil, olives, chopped parsley, and cayenne pepper, and is eaten by dunking with pita (see Index*), the Arabic pancake bread. Used also as a dip at cocktail parties, it is a Middle-Eastern treat now internationally popular.*

2 cups chick-peas	*1 cup, 4 tablespoons tahina*
1 teaspoon baking soda	*olive oil*
1 or 2 cloves garlic	*dash of cayenne*
juice of 1 large lemon	*olives for garnish*
dash of black pepper	*1 tablespoon chopped*
salt to taste	*parsley*

Cover the chick-peas with water and add the baking soda. Soak overnight. Rinse the chick-peas and cook until tender and the skins begin to come off (2–3 hours). Put the cooked chick-peas into a blender with the garlic, lemon juice, black pepper, and salt. Blend, adding tahina gradually, until you have a smooth paste. Flatten servings of homos on small plates with a swirl of olive oil in the center of each. Garnish with cayenne, olives, and a sprinkling of chopped parsley.

FILLED AVOCADOS *Succot*

4 small or 2 large avocados	*salt to taste*
1 clove garlic	*filling (see* NOTE, *below)*
juice of 1 lemon	

If the avocados are small, serve one half to each person; if large, quarter them lengthwise. Do not peel the fruit. Crush a clove of garlic into the lemon juice and drizzle over the cut avocado. Sprinkle with salt, fill the cavity, and serve chilled. (Serves 8.)

NOTE: A popular filling in Israel is "gezer hai," Israel carrot salad (*see* Index) which makes an ideal taste, color, and texture combination. Tuna fish salad or chicken salad are fine, too. A quartered egg or quartered tomato are also effective as filling.

ENSALADA GUACAMOLE—AVOCADO SALAD *Succot*

The quickly growing community hailing from the South American countries of Chile, Argentina, and Brazil have introduced this appetizer into Israel. Often used as a spread for bread or as a salad on a lettuce leaf or sectored tomato, it has become popular at parties as a dip.

1 tomato	*lemon juice to taste*
1 onion	*salt to taste*
2 avocados	*chili powder to taste*

Blanch and peel the tomato and chop to a pulp. Grate the onion. Peel and mash the avocados with a wooden spoon and add to the tomato and onion. Add seasoning to taste: it should be pungent. Usual amounts are 1 tablespoon lemon juice, ½ teaspoon chili powder or ¼ chopped fresh chili pepper. But this may be too high a flavor for Northern or Western palates. (Serves 4–6.)

ROSSEL COCKTAIL   *Passover*

4 cups rossel (beet sour)	*1 teaspoon grated onion*
(*see* Index)	*salt and pepper*
2 teaspoons horse-radish,	*4 tablespoons sour cream*
grated	

Boil up the rossel and strain through a fine sieve. Add the horse-radish and grated onion. Chill very well. Stir in the sour cream to a smooth consistency and add salt and pepper.

TUICA—BEAN HORS D'OEUVRES (TAMIA)   *Hanuka*

The Passover Seder points to the long-standing custom of appetizers, for the various herbs and nibblers offered from the Seder dish during the service preceding the dinner are all of the hors d'oeuvres family. The ancient Romans and Greeks may have learned the custom when they invaded Palestine, and they eagerly introduced it to excite their appetites before tackling their fabulous feasts. The custom spread through Europe centuries ago. This appetizer has been brought back to Israel by Romanian immigrants. In Arab countries the dish is called tamia.

1 cup cooked white beans	3 tablespoons olive oil
1 clove garlic, crushed	salt and pepper
juice of 1 lemon	

Press the beans through a sieve. Add the garlic and beat in the lemon juice, oil, salt, and pepper. Serve as a dip or on canapés with a drink of slivovitz or vodka.

WHOLE HOMOS—NAHIT—NAHUT—CECCI—
GARBANZOS—CHICK-PEAS   *Shabbat*

The wide range (and these are not all) of names for the whole chick-pea proves how much it is loved in many lands. This legume was used in ancient days (archaeological evidence dates it back more than two thousand years in Israel) and has never lost its hold on the Middle East. Kadmoniot HaTalmud (Antiquities of the Talmud) tells of grains, pulses and legumes (such as chick-peas) being boiled and eaten dry with the fingers in the Maccabean period. Prepared in the following way, chick-peas are eaten like salted nuts, particularly on a Sabbath afternoon.

Soak chick-peas overnight and change the water in the morning. Cook for about an hour until tender. The skins will come off. Rinse in cold water and drain. Salt and pepper well.

CHOPPED EGG APPETIZER   *Hanuka*

6 *hard-cooked eggs*	3 *tablespoons chicken fat*
½ *cup finely chopped onion*	*or chopped greben*
1 *teaspoon salt*	*(cracklings)*
dash of pepper	

Chop the eggs and add the finely chopped onion. Add the remaining ingredients and serve on lettuce with tomato slices. (Serves 4–6.)

IKRE—JEWISH-STYLE CAVIAR   *Succot*

In Bible times pickled roe was imported from Egypt. The dish was so well liked that later it was prepared in Palestine, both pickled and salted, and known as "tarichea." Real caviar comes from a nonkosher fish (Jewish dietary law commands that fish for food must have both fins and scales) and therefore cultivated new "pearls of the Caspian" are made in Israel of carp roe. The following is a Romanian-Jewish substitution for caviar.

½ *pound fresh carp*	*salt and pepper to taste*
(or other fish) roe	2 *white rolls*
cooking oil as required	½ *cup lemon juice*
(about 2 cups)	

Put the fresh roe in a bowl, cover with a layer of oil and let stand for 24 hours. Remove the membrane from the roe and stir up.

Add oil slowly (use oil in which roe was soaked, plus enough to make 2 cups), beating constantly as you do for mayonnaise, until an emulsion is formed. Add salt and pepper. Remove the crusts from the rolls, dip in water, and squeeze out excessive moisture. Then crumble and beat into the emulsion. Add lemon juice slowly and stir well. Serve with a little finely chopped onion and black olives on the side. (Serves 4–6.)

CALF'S BRAIN PATTIES   *Rosh Hashana*

Brains are served on Rosh Hashana in some Eastern communities, not only because the brain symbolizes wisdom, but as a token of esteem to the head of the house, who of course sits at the head of the table. The most honored guest, in East European Jewish tradition, sits at the foot, or the other head, of the table.

2 *calf's brains*	1 *egg, slightly beaten*
flour	*breadcrumbs*
salt and pepper to taste	3 *tablespoons margarine*
dash of nutmeg	*juice of 1 lemon*

Parboil the brains and remove the membrane. Cut into thick slices. Sprinkle with the flour, salt, pepper, and nutmeg. Dip in beaten egg and roll in breadcrumbs. Fry in the margarine until golden. Sprinkle with lemon juice and serve with lemon wedges as an hors d'oeuvre. (Serves 4.)

ANCHOVY SALAD

1 *can anchovies*	1 *tablespoon lemon juice*
white wine to cover	1 *onion, sliced*
2 *oranges, without rind*	*dash of pepper*
2–3 *slices lemon*	1 *head of lettuce*
2 *tablespoons olive oil*	

Drain the oil from the anchovies and keep for the salad. Cover the anchovies with white wine and allow to marinate for a few hours. Cut up the anchovies, thinly slice and quarter the oranges and sliver the lemon slices. Mix the anchovy oil, wine, olive oil, lemon juice, onion, and pepper. Arrange the crisp lettuce in a wooden bowl with bits of anchovy, orange, and lemon throughout. Use the oil-wine-lemon juice mixture for a dressing. Serve as an hors d'oeuvre. (Serves 6.)

COCKTAIL ELATH *Shavuot*

The red snapper is fished out of the Red Sea at Israel's port of Elath. This fish cocktail can be made of other fish such as pike, salmon, trout, whitefish. The cocktail is from the Dan Hotel, in Tel Aviv.

3 large onions	*½ cup ketchup*
3 carrots	*1 tablespoon tomato*
salt and pepper	*purée*
2 bay leaves	*1 teaspoon grated horse-*
8 cups water	*radish*
2 pounds red snapper	*1 teaspoon brandy*
1 cup white wine	*lemon and parsley or*
1 cup mayonnaise	*mint, for garnish*

Cut up the onions and carrots, add the salt, pepper, bay leaves, and water and bring to a boil. Put in the fish and reduce the heat immediately. Add the wine. Simmer on as low heat as possible. When the fish can be lifted from the bone (about 20 minutes), remove it and cool. Dice the fish (it should be chunky). Mix the mayonnaise, ketchup, tomato purée, horse-radish, and brandy and pour over the fish. Serve very cold, with a garnish of lemon and parsley or mint. (Serves 6–8.)

ONION AND EGG APPETIZER *Shabbat*

Don't confuse this with the "Egg and Onion" appetizer, which is the reverse of this dish. It must have chicken fat and reminds me of Sholem Aleichem's story about Berl who was called "Barrel" because he was so fat and was so fat because he so loved chicken fat.

6 large sweet onions	*salt to taste*
4 hard-cooked egg yolks	*pepper aplenty*
4 tablespoons chicken fat	

Dice the onions fine. Mash the egg yolks and mix with the chicken fat. Add salt and pepper and stir into the onions. (The egg and fat are only a dressing.) Stay home alone after you eat this dish. (Serves 8.)

NOTE: You must have sweet onions for this dish.

BRAIN APPETIZER   *Yom Kippur*

1 pair brains	*juice of 2 lemons*
2 teaspoons salt	*1 onion, chopped fine*
2 tablespoons vinegar	*lettuce*
water to cover	*black olives*
5 tablespoons olive oil	*tomatoes, cut in sections*

Pour boiling water over the brains, drain, and remove membrane. Add salt and vinegar with water to cover and cook brains for about 20 minutes. Cool, then slice. Dress with olive oil, lemon juice, and chopped onion. Serve cold on lettuce garnished with black olives and tomato sections. (Serves 4.)

JELLIED FOOT—PITCHA, FISNOGA, OR PILSA   *Shabbat*

1 calf's foot, cut up	*¼ teaspoon pepper*
8 cups water	*½ cup white wine vinegar*
2 cloves garlic, crushed	*2 hard-cooked eggs, sliced*
2 teaspoons salt	

Cover the foot with the water, bring to the boil, and simmer for a few hours until all the gristle comes off the bone. Remove the bones and cut up the gristle. Add the garlic, salt, pepper, and vinegar to the liquid in which the foot was cooked and cook a few minutes more. Put the egg slices into the bottom of a mold. Cover with the gristle and pour part of the liquid over. Chill until firm. Pour in the remaining liquid and chill again until firm. This dish is also very good hot as an appetizer. (Serves 6.)

CHOPPED LIVER—GEHAKTE LEBER   *Shabbat*

1 pound chicken livers	*½ teaspoon salt*
2 large onions	*dash of pepper*
3 tablespoons chicken fat	*tomatoes on lettuce,*
4 hard-cooked egg yolks	*for garnish*

Dip the livers in ice-cold water and then grill them until all the blood has dripped off. Chop the onions and fry in the chicken fat. Put the livers, onions, and hard-cooked egg yolks through the meat chopper. Add the seasoning and the fat from frying. Serve with a garnish of tomatoes on lettuce. (Serves 4–6.)

FRIED ONIONS AND CHICKEN LIVERS *Succot*

20 *chicken livers*
3 *tablespoons chicken fat*

6 *large onions, sliced*
salt and pepper

Grill the livers. Meanwhile heat the fat and add the sliced onions. When the onions are golden, add the grilled livers and season with salt and pepper. Serve on toast or with mashed potatoes or boiled rice. (Serves 6–8.)

CHOLODNY OR DRELIES OR JELLIED GIBLETS *Shabbat*

Cholodny or Drelies or just Jellied Giblets is served at the third Sabbath meal known as "Seudah Hashlishit." Calves' or chicken feet are used to jell the dish.

10 *chicken feet*
1 *pound giblets (necks,*
gizzards, hearts, livers)
½ *pound celery root*
water to cover
2 *egg yolks*

2 *tablespoons mild vinegar*
1 *clove garlic, crushed*
salt and pepper to taste
2 *hard-cooked eggs, sliced*
lettuce

Cook the chicken feet with the giblets and celery root in water to cover about 1 hour. Add water from time to time to keep the giblets covered. When the meat is very tender, remove from heat and strain. Cut up all the giblets as well as the meat from the necks and feet, and return to the sauce. Beat the egg yolks and stir into the hot sauce. Add the vinegar, garlic, salt, and pepper. Lightly grease 10 individual molds and put a slice of egg in each. Fill with the meat and sauce. Chill. Unmold and serve on lettuce as an appetizer. (Serves 10.)

STUFFED KISHKE (DERMA) *Succot*

The Scotch have many things in common with the Jews, and one of them is the intense love of intestines. However, the preparation of the Scotch haggis and the Jewish kishke are as remote from each other as shortbread and kichel.

beef casings (if thin
about 18 inches, if
thick, 12 inches)
1½ *cups flour, sifted*

1 *large onion, chopped*
1 *teaspoon salt*
¼ *teaspoon pepper*
½ *cup chopped suet*

Have the shiny side of the casings thoroughly cleaned and scraped. Turn out the casings so the suet side is exposed. Remove excess suet and chop up for the filling. Mix with the remaining ingredients for the filling. Sew up one end of the kishke and proceed to fill the casing, pushing it back as you go along, so that finally the shiny side is exposed. Do not overstuff. Sew up the second end. Place in a pot on a bed of onions next to a roast, or in cholent (see Index). Cover with water. Most of the liquid will be absorbed and the kishke will roast. This should be done on low heat for about two hours. Serve hot with horseradish.

NAKAHNIS—SYRIAN KISHKE (DERMA)   *Shabbat*

½ *yard beef or goat cas-*
    ings, 1 inch in diameter
2 *cups ground meat*
½ *cup pine nuts*
½ *cup chopped green*
    peppers

dash of cinnamon
salt and pepper to taste
cooking oil
grape juice as desired

Proportions depend on the thickness and length of the derma. Add the chopped green peppers, dash of cinnamon, salt, and pepper to the meat and stir in the pine nuts. Fill the derma. If you like, tie with threads like tiny sausages and when done, pull the thread out. Brown in oil and pot roast with a little grape juice and water. (Serves 6.)

STUFFED TOMATOES NANA   *Shabbat*

Émile Zola's name is familiar to almost every teen ager and adult in Israel because of his "J'accuse" and his courageous role in the Dreyfus affair in France in 1895. His books, moreover, are widely read and Nana, heroine of the novel by that name, has an appetizer named for her.

6 *large firm tomatoes*
1½ *cups diced chicken*
¼ *cup blanched almonds*
½ *cup sliced celery*

salt and pepper to taste
mayonnaise to taste
lettuce

Rather than scoop out the tomatoes, cut them into sixths, leaving the bottom uncut. Push the sixths apart and you can fill them without cutting away any of the vegetable. Mix the chicken, almonds, celery, salt, pepper, and mayonnaise to taste, and fill the tomatoes. Serve on lettuce leaves. (Serves 6.)

UNLAID EGGS *Shabbat*

*In Israel one gets unlaid eggs frozen, and I put them into the
Sabbath soup en masse, instead of dumplings, or serve them in
this way:*

½ *pound unlaid eggs*	*2 tablespoons chicken fat*
1 cup water	*salt and pepper*
2 onions, chopped	

Simmer the unlaid eggs in the water until they are done
(about 30 minutes). Fry the onions, in the chicken fat. Add salt
and pepper and stir in the cooked eggs. Serve as an hors d'oeuvre.

STUFFED TOMATO MEDYAS *Shabbat*

*When the early pioneers came from Russia to Palestine, some
fifty years ago, they were enchanted with a vegetable they had
never seen—the Arab* bandura! *Today the tomato is used more
than any other salad vegetable in the settlements. Whole tomatoes
are piled high on every breakfast table in the* kibbutzim, *and the
settlers cut them up, cube, slice, or section them like culinary
experts, mixing them with cheese, onion, peppers, or hard-
cooked eggs or just salting them and eating them with olives.
For festive occasions housewives—particularly the Sephardic
women—make it thus.*

6 tomatoes	*2 eggs, well beaten*
2 cups chopped beef	*dash of coriander*
1 onion, chopped	*(optional)*
1 tablespoon olive oil	*salt and pepper*
1 tablespoon breadcrumbs	*1 egg, beaten, for dipping*
1 tablespoon chopped	*3 tablespoons flour for*
parsley	*dipping*
1 tablespoon water	

Cut the tomatoes in two and scoop out the seed sections, which
are put into a well-greased casserole. Mix the meat with the
onions, olive oil, breadcrumbs, parsley, water, eggs, coriander,
salt, and pepper. Put the meat mixture into the tomato shells.
Dip the stuffed tomatoes in the beaten egg, then in the flour. Fry
the open side (meat down) for a moment, then put into the
casserole, meat side up. Pour a little water into the casserole and
bake in a 400° oven for about 30 minutes. (Serves 6.)

NOTE: Some North African immigrants use cinnamon instead
of coriander. Others make this dish of young squashes (prepare
as for Squash Cheese Medyas, for which *see* Index).

EGGPLANT MOCK LIVER *Ju Besh'vat*

The number of vegetarians in Israel is astonishingly great. It is not because they do not like the taste of meat, but because they always were ideologists or simply because their macabre experiences in Europe have given them an overwhelming feeling for life of man or beast. They—and the many thrifty housewives who avoid the costly liver in their budgets—developed this tasty, liver-like dish.

1 large eggplant	2 tablespoons powdered
1 medium onion, chopped	chicken soup
2½ tablespoons cooking oil	salt and pepper
2 eggs	

Cook the eggplant whole, with the skin, in salted water (30–45 minutes). Cool, remove the skin, and cut up. Fry the onion in oil 5 minutes. Add eggplant and fry. Beat the eggs, powdered chicken soup, salt, and pepper and pour on top. Mix all together well. Remove from heat and with a pastry cutter chop all the ingredients well. Cool. Serve on lettuce garnished with tomato, as an hors d'oeuvre. (Serves 6–8.)

COCKTAIL MONICA *Ju Besh'vat*

The only thing I object to in this delightful cocktail is its un-Israeli name, for it was conceived here and is a regular feature at the chain of King David, Dan, Dan-Carmel, and Accadia Hotels. I really think it should have been called "Cocktail Malka" (Hebrew for "queen").

The Cocktail

cooked chicken breasts
3 slices pineapple, diced
2 oranges, diced
1 grapefruit, diced
1 cup cooked cherries

The Sauce

1 cup mayonnaise
½ cup ketchup
1 tablespoon tomato purée
1 teaspoon grated horse-
    radish
1 teaspoon brandy

Dice the chicken breasts and mix with the diced fruit. Mix ingredients for the sauce and dress the chicken-fruit mixture with it. Serve chilled. (Serves 6.)

BREADS

SAVORY ONION BISCUITS

Shavuot

The ancient Egyptians "swore by onions," not only loving them loyally as food, but actually taking a sacred vow with their right hand on an onion! For the onion was symbolic of eternity, with one enclosure over another to infinity. The onion was a protector from the evil eye, its odor frightening off demons and its health-giving properties fighting off illness.

1 package dehydrated onion soup or 3 large onions, grated, and 1 teaspoon salt
5 cups flour
3 eggs

5 teaspoons baking powder
½ cup sesame seed
½ cup grated yellow cheese (optional)
water as needed (approximately 1 cup)

Mix all the ingredients together and roll out rather thin. Cut into rectangles and bake in a 350° oven about 25 minutes.

Independence Day

PITA—MIDDLE EAST PANCAKE BREAD

Bread in the ancient days of the Bible was baked as it is today by the Bedouins in Israel. They use only flour, water, and salt (no yeast). A concave earthen plate, set over hot coals, is used for an oven. Pita is much loved in Israel, and is today made thus:

1 oz. fresh yeast (or 2 packages dry)
1 teaspoon sugar

1¼ cups lukewarm water
4 cups flour
1 teaspoon salt

Dissolve the yeast and sugar in the water. Sift flour and salt and dissolved sugar and yeast. Mix and knead. Divide the dough into 20 balls and roll each one out, as thin as possible, on a floured board. Cover and set to rise in a warm place for about half an hour. Roll out once more, again as thin as possible, and let rise for another half hour. Pitas should be baked in a 500° oven for only a very few minutes, until they puff up. When cut open, the pita, being hollow, can be filled with felafel and salad or used for dipping into homos and tahina.

KHUBS—YEMENITE PITA AND LAKHOACH—
YEMENITE FLAPJACK BREAD *Shavuot*

Lakhoach, Yemenite bread, looks like an American flapjack before it is turned over (brown on one side and doughy-dry and bubbly on the other). The same ingredients (but double the amount of flour) make the khubs pita. The lakhoach is made on a heavy pan or griddle (the Yemenites bake it just as the Bedouins do—on a rounded iron over embers): the khubs is baked as it was in Biblical times, on the wall of a "tannour," a primitive oven heated with embers and the fire put out before the baking. The khubs stick to the wall of the stove and when ready are lifted off with a kind of spatula. These breads are eaten rolled up and dipped into hilbeh and schoog (see Index) or into the gravy of the Yemenites' very soupy stews.

3 cups flour for lakhoach,   *3 cups water*
     6 cups flour for khubs   *1 package dry yeast*
1 teaspoon salt

Mix all the ingredients and set aside to leaven for 2 hours or more. For lakhoach, ladle out ½ cup of batter at a time onto a thick pan or griddle and cook until the bubbles on the top are set and the surrounding area cooked. Remove from the griddle and serve hot or cold.

For khubs, roll out the dough as thin as possible and bake for about five minutes in a hot oven.

FESTIVE POTATO BREAD *Hanuka*

1 ounce fresh yeast   *½ cup sugar*
     (or 2 packages dry)   *1½ cups cooked, riced*
½ cup lukewarm milk   *potatoes*
½ cup butter   *raisins, if desired*
5 to 6 cups flour, sifted   *walnuts, if desired*
3 eggs, beaten   *egg yolk, diluted*
*½ cup cinnamon water ***

Dissolve the yeast in the lukewarm milk. Cut the butter into the flour, then add the dissolved yeast, eggs, cinnamon water, sugar, potatoes, raisins, and nuts. Knead the dough until elastic. Cover and allow to rise for half an hour. Knead again and place in loaf pans. Let stand in a warm place until doubled in bulk. Brush with diluted egg yolk and bake in a 350° oven for about an hour.

---

* This is made by boiling a cinnamon stick in water for 5 minutes.

CHALLAH—SABBATH AND FESTIVAL BREAD   *Shabbat*

The festive loaves on the Sabbath board are symbolic of the shew-bread put upon the altar of the Temple. The poorest Jewish home has this special bread on festivals. In his story Poverty, *Mordecai Spector tells of his visit to pick up a book from Sein-well, the bookbinder, who lived with his large family in one room. It was Friday afternoon, and the book had still to be lettered in gold. On the large bed, spread out on a clean white cloth, were the Sabbath challah loaves waiting to be put into the oven. In the corner a hen sat on a nest. Spector kept waiting and waiting, like the loaves, and the bookbinder kept saying, "Just a few minutes more. I'm waiting for the hen to lay an egg: the yolk is needed to glaze the challah and I need the whites to glue on the gold lettering." They waited. They looked at the hen. But not even a cackle. Poor Seinwell did not have the kopek to buy an egg and refused to borrow. Finally, with Sabbath approaching and the bread turning cold, the bookbinder agreed to borrow the price of an egg. No sooner was it brought and the loaves gilded for their Sabbath glow and the gold lettering affixed, when the hen produced its egg! "Well, now," said Seinwell, "she could always be relied on to do so in time for the Sabbath!"*

Though the challah loaves are braided for Sabbaths and festi-vals, on Rosh Hashana they are round—for a good year "all year round." Figures of birds and ladders are often used in decorating these loaves—so that pleas and prayers can more easily rise to heaven.

3 tablespoons sugar	*3 eggs*
1 ounce (4 packages)	*4 tablespoons oil*
dry yeast	*egg yolk diluted in*
2½ cups warm water	*water*
9 cups flour, sifted	*poppy or sesame seed*
4 teaspoons salt	

Mix the sugar, yeast and ½ cup of the water and set aside. Sift the dry ingredients into a warm bowl. Add the eggs, oil, yeast mixture, and the remaining water and stir. Knead on a floured board until smooth and springy. Set aside in a bowl covered with a towel, in a warm place, for 1 hour. Knead again and return to rise until doubled in bulk. Divide the dough in half and cut each half into three equal parts. Roll these into ropes on a floured board. Fasten three ropes at one end and braid together, fasten-ing the ends when finished. Place in greased loaf pans or on a baking sheet, cover once more, and set aside to double again in bulk. Brush the loaves with diluted egg yolk and sprinkle with the poppy or sesame seed. Bake in a 375° oven until done (about 50 minutes).

QUICK CINNAMON ROLLS   *Yom Kippur*

Most good wives leave the synagogue on Yom Kippur before the end of the service so they can have a hot pot of coffee ready for their husbands when they arrive home to break the fast. Some will prepare a pan of quick, hot cinnamon rolls like these.

2 cups self-rising flour, sifted	*raisins*
pinch of salt	*candied peel*
⅔ cup milk	*chopped nuts*
3 tablespoons melted margarine	*4 tablespoons sugar*
	1 teaspoon cinnamon

Mix the flour, salt, milk, and melted margarine. Roll the dough out to a thickness of about an inch. Brush with more melted margarine and sprinkle with the fruits, nuts, sugar, and cinnamon. Roll up like a jelly roll. Cut into one-inch pieces. Place, close together, on buttered baking tins and bake for 10 to 15 minutes in a 400° oven. Serve hot, preferably.

KAYEK—SALT SESAME BISCUITS   *Yom Kippur*

Jews from Syria often break the Yom Kippur fast with a very light meal of soft-cooked eggs (as a symbol that this year of life has just begun) and kayek biscuits instead of bread.

3 cups flour	*2 tablespoons cooking oil*
1 teaspoon baking powder	*1 tablespoon salt*
½ cup water	*½ cup sesame seeds*
1 egg, beaten	

Mix all the ingredients together. Roll the resulting dough out thin, cut into rounds and bake in a 375° oven until the cookies are light gold and crisp. These can also be made of a yeast dough, but with far less than the usual amount of yeast, to insure a hard biscuit.

MAMA'S WHITE BREAD *Succot*

My mother baked her own bread. Once when she was sick she got me to do it. Since I was only twelve at the time, I had to stand on a chair to knead the dough, but I followed her instructions carefully. When finished, the bread was so beautiful that Mama suggested I take it to the Country Fair, which was opening that day in Prince Albert. As I was hurrying with it down the hill, I fell and broke the golden crust.

When I reached the bread booth, there was our neighbor, Mrs. B., who had won the first prize for years. Her bread looked lovely. She noticed my damaged loaf and laughed. "D'ye think that banged-up Jew bread has a chance?"

But this time my loaf won the prize—and started me on the career I have followed ever since.

2 cups water	*1 ounce (4 packages) dry*
1 tablespoon salt	*yeast in 2 tablespoons*
2 tablespoons sugar	*lukewarm water*
2 tablespoons cooking oil	*6 cups flour, sifted*
	1 egg, beaten

Heat the water and add the salt, sugar, and oil, then cool until lukewarm. Add the dissolved yeast. Add the flour gradually, sifting and mixing. Knead the dough until smooth and elastic. Cover and set in a warm place (about 80°) overnight. Knead the dough again in the morning on a floured board. Shape into loaves and put in greased pans. Put in a warm place to double in bulk (about 35–40 minutes). Brush the top of the loaves with the beaten egg. Bake in a 350° oven for about 45 minutes, or until the bread stands away from the pan.

ANBEISSEN STUTEN—YOM KIPPUR LOAVES *Purim*

This, in effect, is a bread recipe, but a loaf so much lighter than the usual that it was used to break the fast (Anbeissen means breakfast) on Yom Kippur in parts of Germany. This food, dipped in salt, was chosen so that the first blessing could be "Blessed are Thou Our God, King of the Universe, who draws bread from the earth."

6 cups sifted flour	*1 tablespoon sugar*
1 ounce fresh yeast	*½ cup milk (about)*
(2 packages dry)	*oil or egg yolk diluted*
½ cup margarine	*in water*
pinch of salt	

Mix all the ingredients (except the oil or egg yolk) together and knead to make an elastic dough (add more or less milk, as required). Cover and put aside in a warm place to double in bulk (1–1½ hours). Form into 2 loaves and put into loaf tins. Set aside to rise again for 1–1½ hours. Brush the top of the bread with a little oil or diluted egg yolk. Bake in a 350° oven for about an hour. Serve with butter and jam.

GIANT KEYLITCH   *Purim*

Sometimes these braided loaves are two yards long! But that is on the occasion of a huge feast—this one is normal size for a family-and-friends "seudah gedola" (great feast) of Purim.

2 cakes compressed yeast	*1 cup sugar*
½ cup lukewarm water	*3 eggs, beaten*
2 cups hot water	*8 cups flour, sifted*
4 tablespoons cooking oil	*poppy-seed or confetti*
1 cup raisins	*candy*
1 tablespoon salt	

Soften the yeast in the lukewarm water. To the hot water add the oil, raisins, salt, and sugar and stir. When this has cooled, add it to the yeast mixture. Reserving a little of the egg for brushing the top of the keylitch, add the remainder to the liquid. Add half the flour and beat well, and then add the remaining flour a little at a time, mixing well.

Knead on a floured board until smooth and springy. Cover and put in a warm place to rise for two or three hours. Knead again. Cut into 3 equal parts and roll the dough into long ropes. Fasten the ends together and braid into a loaf. (You can use 6 strands instead of 3.) Place on a well-greased baking sheet.

Dilute the remaining egg with water and brush the top of the dough. Sprinkle with poppy seed or candy confetti. Put to rise until doubled in bulk and bake in a 400° oven for 15 minutes. Then reduce heat to 350° and bake until done. Cover keylitch with a sheet of aluminum or wrapping paper during the last 15 minutes of baking so it will not brown too much.

NOTE: Instead of one giant keylitch you can make about 20 barches of this. (Not the "buttered barches" of Yom Kippur: these are soft and sweet, but plain.)

CROISSANTS—CRESCENTS *Shavuot*

In the austerity food-rationing years following the birth of the State of Israel, we were grateful for our round, crusty, heavy loaves of rye bread. Never did I dream in 1952 that within ten years every kiosk in Israel would be piled high with French croissants.

1 tablespoon margarine	1 egg, beaten
2 tablespoons sugar	2½ cups flour, sifted
pinch of salt	½ cup butter
½ cup warm milk	4 tablespoons lukewarm
½ ounce yeast	water

Melt the margarine and add the sugar, salt, and warm milk. Dissolve the yeast in this mixture, and add the egg. Add the flour and knead lightly on floured board. Cover and allow to rise until doubled in bulk, then knead and refrigerate for two hours. Knead again and roll out into a square, ¼ inch thick. Divide the butter into three parts. Spread on a third of it, fold up the dough and roll again, then refrigerate for another hour. Repeat this process twice more. (The dough may be refrigerated overnight.) Cut the dough into small triangles and roll each one up, beginning with the long side. Curve into a crescent. Bake in a 400° oven for 15 minutes, then reduce heat to 350° and bake 10 minutes longer, until golden and crunchy.

BUTTER BARCHES OR BILKES *Yom Kippur*

The word "Barches" in German sounds like "brachot"—that is, "blessings"—in Hebrew. For that reason the much beloved bun of Sabbath is eaten at the close of the Sabbath of Sabbaths, Yom Kippur, in Austria and surrounding lands. It is usually made with a bit of the challah dough, or, somewhat richer, thus:

1 ounce fresh yeast	½ cup sugar
(2 packages dry)	½ teaspoon salt
2 cups lukewarm water	1 egg, beaten
or milk	raisins and almonds
½ cup of butter or	8 cups flour, sifted
margarine	1 egg yolk, diluted in
dash of cinnamon	water

Dissolve the yeast in a little of the lukewarm milk or water. Pour the remaining milk over the sugar, butter, cinnamon, and salt, and when it cools just a little add the dissolved yeast and the beaten egg. Add the remaining ingredients. Knead well, on a floured board, until elastic. Put aside in a warm place to double in bulk (1–2 hours). Form into small buns or roll into ropes and braid as for Sabbath challah. Brush with diluted egg yolk and put aside to double again in bulk (1–2 hours). Bake in a 375° oven for about one hour, or until browned. Serve these buns fresh.

Yom Kippur
CARAMELIZED SCHNECKEN—CINNAMON ROLLS

Many Israelis from Central Europe and America will break the Yom Kippur fast with these aromatic and nourishing buns.

½ ounce dry yeast	5 tablespoons melted
(2 packages)	margarine
1 cup lukewarm milk	lemon rind, grated
4 cups flour, sifted	sugar
½ cup sugar	cinnamon
½ cup margarine	raisins
2 eggs	chopped nuts
½ teaspoon salt	brown sugar
	2 tablespoons water

Mix the yeast with the milk. Add 1 cup of flour and set aside to rise in a warm spot, covered. Cream the sugar, margarine, and eggs together, then add the remaining flour, salt, and the yeast mixture and mix well. Knead until the dough is elastic, adding flour if necessary. Set aside again to double in bulk (45–60 minutes). Roll out, to a thickness of ¼ inch, into a sheet about 9 inches wide. Brush well with 1 tablespoon of the melted margarine and sprinkle with the lemon rind, sugar, cinnamon, raisins, and nuts. Roll up and slice into one-inch pieces. Brush the sides with 1 tablespoon of melted margarine. Place the remaining melted margarine in a heavy pan and cover with a thick layer of brown sugar and 2 tablespoons of water. Cook one minute and sprinkle with chopped nuts. Place the buttered rolls close together in the pan with the flat side down. Set aside again, in a warm place, to double in size. Then bake in a 350° oven for about 30 minutes. Invert the pan and remove the rolls while still hot. Put on a serving plate with the caramel side up.

RYE BREAD   *Tu Besh'vat*

*Nathan Ausubel, wit and scholar who has collected a wealth of
Jewish folklore and humor in a book that every Jewish home
should possess,* wrote of the faithful to "Culinary Judaism"
who nostalgically hanker for a juicy corned beef sandwich on
Jewish rye bread. Though rye bread is daily fare in Israel,
Jerusalemites revere it from days of the siege of Jerusalem,
when it was the only food available. To get the rye bread ration,
women in each apartment building would take turns braving the
gunfire that sputtered through the streets, so that her family and
her neighbors' families could have the few slices available to
each.*

2 cups lukewarm water	*2 tablespoons caraway*
or part potato water	*seed (optional)*
2 tablespoons sugar	*1½ ounces fresh yeast*
1 tablespoon coarse salt	*(3 packages dry)*
2 tablespoons cooking oil	*4 cups white flour, sifted*
	2 cups rye flour, sifted

Mix ½ cup of the lukewarm water with the sugar, salt, oil, and
caraway seed. Dissolve the yeast in 1½ cups of lukewarm water
or potato water and add to the first mixture. Sift the two flours
together and gradually add to the liquid. Knead the dough on a
floured board and then set in a warm bowl, covered with a cloth,
until doubled in bulk. Knead the dough again, form it into oblong
loaves, and place on a floured baking sheet. Cover and set to rise
again for two hours. Bake in a 375° oven 45 minutes.

Hanuka
ONION ZEMMEL OR ONION PAMPALIK OR ONION FLAT BREAD

*Onion zemmel or just plain zemmel or pampalik, as Jews from
Russia called it, was usually served hot at breakfast, before all
the bread was baked. I can stll smell Mama's, which we eagerly
ate after splitting the flat bread and filling it with butter and jam.*

1 *recipe bread dough*	*coarse salt*
(*see* Index)	*chopped onion*
egg diluted with water	
or milk	

Cut pieces off the bread dough and roll into balls large enough
to hold in your palm. Roll out each ball of dough and brush with

----
* *A Treasury of Jewish Folklore* (Crown Publishers).

egg diluted with water or milk. Sprinkle on coarse salt and chopped onion, and then let the pancakes rise for about an hour. Pierce all but the border rims with a fork. Bake on a floured sheet in a 350° oven about 20 minutes. The onions become brown, the crusts crisp and golden. (Each palmful of dough makes 1 onion zemmel. Serves 4.)

Rosh Hashana   Yom Kippur
BOLLO E COTOGNATA—FRUITED CHALLAH BREAD

Bread is the staff and symbol of the nourishment of life in the Jewish tradition. If a slice falls upon the floor it is not carelessly picked up and thrown away. The bread is picked up, kissed, and then, if it is not to be fed to man, fowl, or beast, it is burned in memory of the offerings in the Temple.

In Italy the quince is included among the first fruits on which the blessing is made on Rosh Hashana.

Quinces are peeled and cut into cubes. They are then stewed in a syrup of water and sugar, and when done, are cooled. These are mixed into the batter for sweet Sabbath bread, the challah (*see* Index), and the baking proceeds as usual. Apples may be used instead of quince.

HONEY BREAD   *Succot*

An ancient custom in Jewish homes is to tear off a piece of leavened dough (just before shaping into loaves) and cast it into the fire. This is to symbolize the first portion, which the Israelites were "taxed" to give to the High Priests.

1 ounce fresh yeast	*3 cups rich milk (part*
(2 packages dry)	*cream or evaporated*
6 tablespoons honey	*milk)*
6 tablespoons lukewarm	*1 tablespoon salt*
water	*10 cups flour, sifted*

Dissolve the yeast and honey in the lukewarm water. Add the milk. Mix the salt with the flour and add half the mixture to the liquid. Mix well. Set aside in a warm place to "prove." Add the remaining flour and mix well and allow to rise until double in bulk (about 1½ hours). Turn onto a floured board and knead. Shape into loaves (this makes two for loaf pans), and set to rise for another hour. Bake in a 375° oven for about 1 hour.

BOBKE—BUTTER BUNS $\mathcal{S}havuot$

"Bobke" means "granny" in Polish. No wonder it has such warm connotations.

The great Yiddish author Peretz tells a heartwarming story about a saintly man, Bontshe the Silent, who has suffered all his life in poverty and finally dies and goes to heaven. There, all the angels honor him for his noble life and goodness and raise him among the great. He is allowed to choose anything he wishes, in heaven and on earth. With joy and gratefulness and trembling he expresses his greatest desire: "A bobke, still warm, yes—and even with butter on it!"

1 cake yeast	4 cups flour, sifted
2 tablespoons warm water	½ cup butter
1 cup warm milk	3 eggs
¾ cup sugar	raisins as desired
pinch of salt	butter for spreading

Dissolve the yeast in the warm water and add to the milk along with a little of the sugar, the salt, and one cup of the flour. Beat well and set aside in a warm place to rise. Cream the ½ cup butter and remaining sugar, mix in the eggs, one at a time, and add to the first mixture. Mix the raisins into the remaining flour and add, beating well to make a thick batter. Cover and let rise until double in bulk. Shape into balls and fit them in next to one another in a large pan, spreading butter on top of and between each bobke. Put to rise again for two hours and bake in a 375° oven for 45 minutes. Serve warm, if possible.

BAGELS $\mathcal{J}u$ $\mathcal{B}esh'vat$

A bagel is a boiled and then baked doughnut, adapted from the Russian bablitcki. "Bagel" comes from the German word "Buegel," for stirrups. The shape changed from a horseshoe to a ring, and the name was Judaized as its most devout consumers moved from Austria to Poland and then to the United States. Today it flies all over the world on El Al planes.

4 tablespoons oil	½ ounce dry yeast
2 tablespoons sugar	(2 packages)
½ teaspoon salt	1 egg
1 cup hot water	3¾ cups flour, sifted

Mix the oil, sugar, and salt with the hot water, and when it cools to lukewarm, add the yeast to dissolve. Beat the egg until frothy,

add it to the liquid, and then mix in the flour. Knead the dough
and shape into doughnuts. Cover and set to rise on a floured
board. When the bagels begin to swell, drop them, one at a time,
into briskly boiling water and cook until they rise to the top
and are light. Place on baking tins and bake in a 400° oven until
crisp and golden (about 15 minutes). (Makes about 30.)

STOLLEN—HOLIDAY BREAD   *Yom Kippur*

*Stollen is as much a Gentile holiday bread as a Jewish one,
being enjoyed by all peoples of Germanic countries and those
bordering on them. Jews coming from such countries often serve
stollen to break the fast on Yom Kippur night.*

1 cup warm milk	*½ cup margarine, melted*
½ cup sugar	*¼ cup chopped almonds*
1 teaspoon salt	*⅓ cup chipped candied*
1 ounce fresh yeast	*peels*
(2 packages dry)	*⅓ cup candied cherries*
2 eggs, beaten	*⅓ cup raisins*
4 cups flour, sifted	*lemon rind, grated*

Mix the milk, sugar, salt, and yeast. Stir in the beaten eggs,
flour, and melted margarine. Knead and put to rise in a warm
place. Knead again and put to rise once more until doubled in
bulk (40–50 minutes). Roll out into two rectangles (this recipe
is enough for two stollen). Sprinkle each with the nuts and fruit
and work in the fruit with a rolling pin. Fold the dough over,
brush with soft margarine and fold again. Seal the edges, brush
the top with margarine and bake in a 375° oven 30–45 minutes,
or until golden brown. When almost cold, cover with glazed
frosting (*see* Index).

UNLEAVENED SANDWICH BUNS   *Passover*

1 cup boiling water	*3 eggs*
2 cups matzo meal	*½ teaspoon salt*
½ cup margarine	

Pour the boiling water over the matzo meal and the margarine
and mix well. When cool, add the eggs and the salt. Form into
bar-shaped buns, place on a buttered pan and bake in a 375°
oven about 20 minutes, or until crusted on top. Split open and
spread with a sandwich filling.

Independence Day
KRENTENKRANZENBROOD—CURRANT CROWN BREAD

This Dutch braided crown of currant bread is served with wine at the kiddush *benediction of all ritual festivities such as circumcisions and weddings. In Israel other fruits are added for special celebrations. The round shape is symbolic of the wheel of fate, the crown of merit.*

1 cup butter or margarine	1 tablespoon candied ginger
½ cup sugar	or 1 teaspoon ginger
4 large eggs	powder and 1 table-
1 ounce yeast	spoon orange marma-
1⅓ cups warm milk	lade
5 cups flour	2 tablespoons candied peels
1 teaspoon salt	3 tablespoons candied
½ cup currants or raisins	cherries
	¼ cup chopped almonds

Cream the fat and sugar and add three eggs, beating well. Dissolve the yeast in the warm milk. Mix the flour with the chopped fruits and nuts. Add the dissolved yeast alternately with the flour mixture to the eggs. Knead well and put to rise in a warm place until doubled in bulk. Divide the dough into three equal parts, roll each into a long rope, and then braid together. Place this loaf in a buttered circular pan, in the shape of a crown, and set to rise again for two hours. Brush the top with diluted egg yolk. Bake in a 375° oven until done (35–45 minutes). When cool, swirl icing over the top.

NOTE: Any simple white icing will do, such as 1 cup confectioner's sugar mixed with 1½ tablespoon cream (or more if desired), and flavored with 1 teaspoon vanilla.

CHELSEA BUNS   *Succot*

On Good Friday in the year 1839, almost a quarter of a million Chelsea buns—every one of them made by hand—were sold on a single day in Jew's Row in Chelsea, London. This sales boom has left me wondering: could it be that on that year Good Friday fell upon the last day of Passover, and that the bread-hungry and matzo-weary Jews simply bought up so many buns after the festival's end? They smell divine, and when they are hot and opened they are maddeningly tantalizing.

2 cups flour, sifted
1/4 teaspoon salt
2 tablespoons butter or
    margarine
1/2 ounce fresh yeast
    (1 package dry)
1/2 cup warm milk
3 tablespoons raisins
3 tablespoons chopped
    candied peel

2 tablespoons sugar
1 egg yolk, diluted with
    water
syrup of 1 tablespoon
    water and 2 teaspoons
    sugar
powdered sugar for
    dusting

Mix flour and salt, rub in the margarine. Add the yeast to the milk. Mix with the flour and margarine. Beat well and set aside in a warm place to double in bulk (about 45 minutes). Knead lightly and roll out to about 10 inches square. Sprinkle the fruit and sugar on and roll up like a jelly roll. Cut into seven pieces and place, cut side up, in a greased cake tin, close enough so the buns will join together in the baking and their sides will remain soft. Brush with diluted egg and bake in a 425° oven about 20 minutes. When the buns are well cooked at the bottom, remove from the oven. Brush at once with syrup and then dust with powdered sugar. Break the buns apart when serving.

EGGS AND EGG DISHES

Independence Day

HAMINDAS (BROWNED HARD EGGS)

Sephardic Jews, whether they be in Spain, Holland, Greece, Italy, Turkey, Egypt, Syria, or Israel, have retained the ancient tradition of serving baked brown eggs on every festival, as the symbol of the mystery of life (eggs being round or oval, there is no gateway to them).

6 eggs
½ cup cold water

1 tablespoon oil
dash of pepper

Cover eggs with water, add oil and pepper, and cook 24 hours over low heat, or put the eggs in the salt–pepper–oil–water mixture and bake them in a 200° oven overnight, the dish being covered with brown paper. The eggs come out brown in color and very delicate within. (Serves 6.)

CHATCHOUKA AND TETCHOUKA EGGS *Yom Kippur*

"You cannot make omelets without breaking eggs" is a Spanish proverb. Well, bless the Spaniards for keeping us from breaking our teeth in trying to pronounce Chatchouka and Tetchouka correctly: they took the omelet from their North African neighbors, tempered its hot flavor and simplified its cooking and renamed Tetchouka "Spanish omelet." Chatchouka is a whole egg poached in the flaming sauce, and Tetchouka uses the same ingredients but as an omelet. Both are loved in Israel.

2 green peppers, slivered
1 small hot chili pepper,
    chopped
2 onions, diced

2 cloves garlic, crushed
    olive oil
8 tomatoes
    salt and pepper
8 eggs

Lightly fry the peppers, onion, and garlic in the oil. Transfer to 8 individual casseroles, cover each with a whole tomato, season, and cook in a 350° oven until tomatoes are soft (20–25 minutes). Break a whole egg into each casserole, return to the oven and cook 15 minutes longer.

To make Tetchouka, dice the tomatoes and fry them with the
other vegetables, then add the eggs, beaten, and cook until set.
(Each recipe serves 8.)

UOVA DI GAZA—GAZA EGGS   *Yom Kippur*

*Eggs represent both the hope of life and the grief of death in
Jewish folklore. They are the symbol of mourning in memory
of the Temple's destruction.*
  *Many families avoid a heavy meal after the fast, and serve an
egg dish instead. This one, being savory, is particularly popular
due to the loss of body salt from the fast. It also is a popular
hors d'oeuvre on other occasions.*

anchovy paste to taste	6 egg yolks
6 tablespoons butter	1 cup milk
12 slices of toast	

Mix anchovy paste with 4 tablespoons of the butter and spread
on the warm toast. Put on a dish and keep warm while preparing the sauce. Mix the egg yolks, milk, and remaining butter in
a small pot and cook on low heat until thick, stirring constantly.
Pour this on the anchovy toast and serve hot. (Serves 12.)

MUSHROOM OMELET   *Succot*

*When the first rains—called the "yoreh" as in the Bible—fall
in Israel, the mushrooms pop up like popcorn in the hand-
planted forests surrounding the kibbutzim settlements. Although
a common kitchen and central dining hall cater to the needs of
the farmers, everyone has a kitchenette-corner attached to his or
her room. The aroma of mushrooms and eggs frying wafts all
over the area, tantalizing every palate.*

2 tablespoons butter or	4 eggs
margarine	4 tablespoons milk
2 cups sliced mushrooms	salt and pepper to taste
1 teaspoon fat	

Heat the butter, put in the sliced mushrooms, and fry until done
(about 5 minutes). In another skillet, melt the fat. Beat the eggs
lightly with the milk, season to taste, and pour into the pan.
When the eggs begin to set, put on the mushrooms and fold the
egg over. Serve at once. (Serves 3–4.)

SEPHARDIC (SPANISH) OMELET *Hanuka*

A superstition listed in the Talmud in "Ways of the Amorites" relates that when a woman wanted a hen to lay an egg she would approach it and say either "I will allow only a virgin to set the hen on the eggs" or "I will only set the hen when I am naked." This frightened the chicken into laying an egg.

The Sauce

2 tablespoons butter
2 tablespoons chopped
   onion
1 green pepper, chopped
   fine
1½ cups chopped tomatoes
1 teaspoon chopped parsley
   pinch of cayenne
   salt and pepper

The Omelet

4 eggs, separated
   salt and pepper to taste
4 tablespoons warm water
2 teaspoons margarine

For the sauce, melt the butter and cook the onions and green pepper for a few minutes, then add the tomatoes and cook a few minutes more. Add the parsley, cayenne, salt, and pepper to taste. Keep this filling hot while you prepare the omelet.

Beat the egg yolks until light yellow, then add the salt, pepper, and warm water. Beat the egg whites until stiff and fold in. Melt the margarine in a pan, and when hot, put in the omelet. When it is set and brown underneath and beginning to solidify on top, put on some of the sauce and fold over. Pour the remaining sauce over and serve at once. (Serves 2–3.)

LEFTOVERS OMELET *Succot*

2 cups leftover meat or
   chicken or fish
1 onion, chopped fine
1 tablespoon chopped
   parsley

   salt and pepper
8 eggs
   cooking oil

Put the meat through the grinder, add the onion, parsley, salt, and pepper. Beat in the eggs. Fry the mixture in hot oil, turn when brown on the bottom. Serve with any desired sauce (*see* Index), or plain. (Serves 4–6.)

SALAMI EGGS   *Succot*

2 eggs
2 tablespoons water
salt and pepper to taste

1 teaspoon cooking oil
6 slices salami

Beat the eggs lightly and add the water, salt, and pepper. Heat
the oil in a pan and put in the salami slices. Turn when they
begin to brown and pour the egg mixture over. Cook until set,
then flip the omelet over. Serve hot. (Serves 2.)

KOSHER "BACON" OMELET   *Succot*

3 strips beefettes (kosher
   "bacon")
1 teaspoon chopped onion
2 eggs

salt and pepper
toast and margarine
1 tomato, sliced
parsley

Fry the beefettes and onion, without any added fat, until they
begin to crisp. Beat the eggs, add seasoning to taste, and pour
over. When the egg has crusted on the bottom, fold it over. Serve
on toast with margarine, garnished with tomato and parsley.
(Serves 2.)

CURRIED EGGS   *Shavuot*

*Many of the spices used in making up curry powder were al-
ready well known in Biblical days, particularly the coriander
seed, cumin, and cassia. These have now come back to Israel with
the Asian immigrants, who have also introduced the fenugreek
seed and hot peppers that go into making the many different
kinds of curry sauces.*

3 tablespoons butter
2 teaspoons curry powder
3 tablespoons flour
2 cups milk

1 onion, chopped
salt to taste
6 hard-cooked eggs, sliced

Melt the butter, and to it add the curry powder and flour. When
the mixture begins to bubble, add the milk and onion. Stir until
the mixture begins to boil. Add salt to taste. Cook until thick.
Pour the sauce over the eggs. (Serves 4–6.)

M'LAVEH MALKA EGGS   *Shabbat*

*Our family, like many Israeli families, has added a bit of its own
tradition to the Sabbath. After the sun has set and three stars
have appeared in the sky, we gather around my husband for the
Havdala service, the ceremony that marks the closing of the
Sabbath. In the unlit room the long braided candle is lit, held
high by our little girl Sharon, as Jaapi sings the blessings over
the wine. The spice box is passed around for all to sniff symbolically the sweet pungency of life. After the candle is snuffed
out with the full goblet for the full week, we all hold hands and
dance in a chain around the house singing "A good week, a
worthy week. . . ." By this time the children have worked up such
an appetite that I am obliged to make what we now call our
"M'laveh Malka" eggs—the meal that is meant to see the Sabbath Queen out.*

1 12-ounce can corn niblets	1 cup milk
1½ tablespoons butter	1 teaspoon salt
12 eggs	pepper to taste
	1 cup grated yellow cheese

Drain the corn, add the butter, and heat through in a large heavy
skillet. Beat the eggs slightly, add the milk, salt, and pepper and
pour over the corn. When the eggs begin to set, sprinkle on the
cheese. Pull the egg from the edges with a spatula, so that the
liquid will go down and cook. Remove from heat while the eggs
are still moist but not raw. Serve with sliced tomatoes and buttered toast. (Serves 6.)

GENOVAS PER HANUCA—SOUFFLÉ   *Hanuka*

*Every type of pancake is served on Hanuka in Israel, for every
immigrant community has brought its own culinary tradition.
This soufflé is certainly not a pancake, though it is sometimes
referred to as such in Israel, by the native-born offspring of
Italian Jews.*

6 whole eggs	1¼ cups cornstarch (or
8 egg yolks	potato flour if made
1¼ cups sugar	on Passover)
¾ cup butter, melted	

Whip the eggs, egg yolks, and sugar together very well, and
when almost white, add the butter and mix again. Add the corn-

starch slowly, mixing all the time. Heat a pan without greasing
it. Pour in the mixture to about half full. Bake in a 350° oven
until done (35–40 minutes). (Serves 6.)

DEVILED EGGS   Shavuot

*Although the Old Testament makes mention of numerous herbs
and spices, mustard is first recorded in the New Testament. It is
believed that the patricians used "must"—unfermented grape
wine—with a hot herb as a condiment; and the name was finally
transferred to the herb—the mustard plant—itself. Recipes fired
with mustard are often called "deviled." In South Africa, for
instance, Britisher, Boer and native alike devil their dishes.
In Israel, deviled eggs take on the fire of the community which
is serving them: mustard for Balkan folk, cayenne for Orientals;
paprika for Hungarians.*

8 hard-cooked eggs	*chopped chives*
2 tablespoons mayonnaise	*pinch of paprika*
1 tablespoon prepared	*8 black olives*
* mustard*	*lettuce*
½ teaspoon salt	

Shell the eggs and cut in two, lengthwise. Remove the yolks and
mash with the mayonnaise, mustard, salt and chives. Refill the
egg whites, sprinkle with paprika, top with a black olive and
serve on lettuce. (Serves 8.)

CLATITE—SPINACH-CREPES SOUFFLÉ   Shavuot

*This dish, developed from a Balkan blintze, is now served at
gourmet tables on Shavuot.*

12 blintzes (see Index)	*1 cup grated Caccio-*
2 cups chopped cooked	* Cavello (Katzkaval)*
* spinach*	* cheese*
3 egg whites, stiffly beaten	*3 whole eggs*

In a buttered casserole alternate layers of blintzes with those of
spinach and of egg white, and a sprinkling of cheese, until all
the blintzes and ½ cup of the cheese have been used up. Top
with a good coating of egg white sprinkled with cheese. Bake in
350° oven 35–40 minutes or until well puffed. Beat the 3 whole
eggs until light and add the remaining cheese. Top the dish with
this, raise the oven heat to 375°, and bake 15 minutes longer, or
until set. Serve at once. (Serves 6.)

CHEESE AND CHEESE DISHES

Independence Day
TEN COTTAGE CHEESE SPREADS

Cottage cheese is Israel's favorite dairy food. It is used in endless dishes and at every breakfast.

1 cup cottage cheese   salt to taste
½ cup sour cream

Mix together to make a smooth spread and then add any one of the following (quantity according to desired taste and color) for varied flavors and colors; put through the blender:

Green—Parsley, celery tops, onion tops, green peppers, or raw spinach
Peach—smoked salmon or lox
Yellow—curry powder
Pink—paprika or pimiento peppers
Mustard—mustard
Brown—black olives, or anchovies
White—celery root
Red—beetroot (raw or cooked)
Almond Green—avocado
Rainbow—shreds of pimiento, green pepper, caraway seed, chopped onion. (Do not put this mixture through the blender, as it should be flecked.)

MANNA CHEESE   *Shavuot*

The Bible-learned Yemenites put coriander into almost every dish. One Yemenite housewife concocted this from Exodus 16:3 which she quoted to me: "And the house of Israel called the name thereof manna; and it was like coriander seed, white; and the taste of it was like wafers made with honey." The native tamarisks of the Middle East shed little tasty whitish balls which the Bedouins call muhn *and which they gather before dawn, as it disappears in the heat of the sun. This is probably the manna of the Bible, for it does taste like honey when eaten on bread.*

1 cup cream cheese   ½ teaspoon coriander seed
½ cup cream   honey to taste

Mix all the ingredients together and serve on crackers. (I like it on apple wedges, too.)

THE PRESIDENT'S PORRIDGE   *Shavuot*

This recipe was given to me by Mrs. Rachel Yanait Ben-Zwi, who created this dish for her husband's breakfast.

1 carrot   *1 teaspoon butter*
½ cup cottage cheese   *1 cup hot milk*
1 tablespoon honey

Grate the carrot fine and mix with the cottage cheese. Place in a breakfast bowl and top with the honey and butter. Pour the hot milk over. (Serves 1.)

BLINTZES   *Shavuot*

One of the theories advanced by modern sages on why we eat dairy dishes on Shavuot is that the Jews had to wait so long at the foot of Mount Sinai that by the time they returned to their tents all the milk had soured and had to be made into cheese. Thus cheese became the traditional dish of the festival. Blintzes— the best loved of all Shavuot fare—was undoubtedly inspired by the Russian blini, which the first Zionist pioneers brought to Israel.

The Batter   *The Filling*

2 medium eggs   *4 cups creamed cottage*
¾ cup milk   *cheese*
½ cup flour, sifted   *4 tablespoons sour cream*
  pinch of salt   *2 egg yolks*
2 tablespoons melted   *3 tablespoons sugar*
  margarine   *1 teaspoon vanilla*
                               ½ teaspoon salt

For the batter, mix the eggs and milk, then add the flour, salt, and melted margarine and beat until smooth. Lightly butter a small pan. Pour some batter from the end of a spoon into the pan and tilt to ensure that the batter is thinly and evenly spread over the bottom. Cook over medium heat until the batter is just set on top and light gold on the bottom. Turn, bottom side up, on a cloth. Mix all the filling ingredients and spread over the pancakes. Fold up into fan shapes. Brown the blintzes in butter just before serving with sour cream, berries, or honey. (Serves 4.)

SHOSH—TOASTED CHEESE   *Shavuot*

After the birth of Israel, the overwhelming immigration (our population doubled and tripled within ten years) of penniless people so drained our resources that the established population was hungry. The American government came to our aid with cheddar cheese and other foods, and we soon learned to make macaroni and cheese, cheese dreams, and our own "shosh"—an abbreviation for "shoshana" or "rose," for we tint the dish with rosy-red paprika.

Israel now makes an abundance and great variety of its own fine cured and soft cheeses for local use and export too.

chopped onion and margarine (optional)	*6 slices bread*
	paprika
6 slices sharp yellow cheese	

If you wish to use onion, mix it with a very little melted margarine. Put the yellow cheese on the bread, sprinkle generously with sweet paprika, and top with a little of the chopped onion. Put under the broiler only long enough for the cheese to melt. Serve hot. (Serves 6.)

CHEESE KNISHES   *Shavuot*

This dish is also called "Shavuot beiglach" by some Jewish communities, and in Vienna it is known as "kaese strudel." There are many kinds of Shavuot knishes. You can use a yeast rolled dough, fill it with cheese, and seal the pastry or slit it to form fancy figured tops. This recipe requires a thin strudel dough and the following filling:

4 cups cottage cheese	*raisins, if desired*
1 tablespoon semolina	*honey and sour cream*
1 egg	*for topping*
2 tablespoons sugar	*4 tablespoons melted butter*
dash of salt	*1 recipe strudel dough*
dash of cinnamon or	*(see Index)*
vanilla	

Mix all the ingredients except the butter, raisins, honey, and sour cream, to a smooth consistency. Sprinkle the butter on strudel sheets, then sprinkle on the raisins. Place the cheese in a roll along one edge and roll up. Put in a pan and then cut through

into serving pieces with a sharp knife. Bake in a 350° oven until
the knishes are golden (about 20 minutes). Serve hot with a topping of sour cream and honey. These knishes are also good cold.
(Serves 6–8.)

MATZO CHEESE DREAMS   *Passover*

1 cup cottage cheese	*4 matzos*
¾ cup grated yellow cheese	*2 eggs*
salt and paprika	*oil for frying*

Mix the cottage cheese with the grated yellow cheese and add the
seasoning. Cut the matzos into quarters. Sandwich the filling
between the pieces. Dip in beaten eggs and fry until golden in
hot fat. (Serves 4.)

NAHARIYA TOMATO-CHEESE PIE   *Shavuot*

The Pastry

½ cup margarine
2 cups sifted flour
½ cup grated yellow cheese
1 egg yolk
2 tablespoons ice water
pinch of salt
dash of cayenne

The Filling

4 large tomatoes, thinly
   sliced
2 large onions, thinly
   sliced
5 tablespoons margarine
2 eggs
1½ cups milk
¾ cup grated yellow cheese
   salt, cayenne and pepper
   to taste

For the pastry, cut the margarine into the flour. Add the cheese
and rub gently until crumbly. Mix the egg yolk with the ice
water, salt, and cayenne, then add gradually to the first mixture.
Roll out the dough. Line a spring pan with this pastry and press
the edges down with a fork.

Cover the dough with tomato slices. Fry two-thirds of the
onion in the margarine. Mix with the raw onion and sprinkle on
the tomatoes. Mix the eggs, milk, ½ cup of the cheese, and the
seasonings. Pour over the onions. Bake in a 375° oven 35 minutes. Sprinkle on the remaining cheese and bake for 5 minutes
more. Serve warm, preferably.

PASSOVER PALATCHINKIN OR BLINTZES *Passover*

5 eggs	3 tablespoons sour cream
1⅓ Cups water	sugar to taste
¼ teaspoon salt	rind of 1 lemon or
¾ cup matzo meal	1 teaspoon vanilla
2 cups cottage cheese	

Beat 4 of the eggs slightly, then add the water, salt, and matzo meal. On a lightly greased heavy frying pan, pour in a little batter and tilt to spread it smoothly over the whole surface. Brown only one side of the pancake and turn out on a towel. Repeat. When all the batter has been used up, mix the cottage cheese, sour cream, sugar, 1 beaten egg, and flavoring. Cover half of each pancake with cheese mixture, fold over and then fold once more to make a triangle. Fry in butter just before serving. Top with sugared sour cream. (Makes 8–10 blintzes.)

CHEESE SHNITZEL *Shavuot*

6 ¼-inch-thick slices firm	1 egg, slightly beaten
cottage cheese (see	2 tablespoons breadcrumbs
Note *below*)	salt and pepper

Dip the cheese slices in egg and cover with the breadcrumbs mixed with the seasoning. Fry quickly and serve at once. (Serves 6.)

NOTE: In Israel cottage cheese can be bought pressed. Any firm white cheese or a mild yellow like Edam can be used for this dish.

EDAM CHEESE OMELET *Shavuot*

This edam dish is a vegetarian favorite.

6 eggs	2 tablespoons butter
1 tablespoon flour	6 thin slices Edam cheese
1 teaspoon salt	1 teaspoon paprika

Beat the eggs and whip in the flour and salt. Heat the butter and pour in the egg mixture. Turn the heat down at once. When the eggs begin to set, put on the cheese and sprinkle with the paprika. Cook over low heat until the cheese begins to melt. Serve hot. (Serves 4.)

CHEESE-ONION TART   *Shavuot*

Jews of Alsace-Lorraine have brought this dish to Israel, and serve it on Shavuot as their grandmothers did. White cottage cheese is less used than the cured Swiss types in France. The savory onion has a long and glorious history. Though scorned in genteel circles for its high odor, the vegetable was prized in Biblical days as a delicacy. Its strong, sweet, pungent flavor made it symbolic of many noble qualities: Egyptian soldiers ate onions for courage and strength.

The Pastry

1½ cups flour
      pinch of salt
½ teaspoon baking
      powder
⅓ cup margarine
⅓ cup cold water

The Filling

1 tablespoon flour
2 cups shredded cheese
      (Swiss types are best,
      mixed)
1 cup finely sliced onions
3 eggs
1 cup rich milk (part cream)
      salt and pepper to taste

For the pastry, mix the flour and salt with the baking powder. Cut in the margarine. Add the water and mix. Roll out on a floured board and pat into a pie dish.

For the filling, mix the flour and cheese and sprinkle over the pastry shell. Cover with the onions (separate the rings). Mix the eggs and milk, add salt and pepper, and pour over the filling. Bake in a 400° oven for about 15 minutes. Reduce heat to 325° and bake for about another 30 minutes. Test by inserting a silver knife into the custard: if it comes out clean, the tart is done. (Serves 4.)

KALSOHNEHS—CHEESE TURNOVERS   *Shavuot*

The Dough

1 egg
⅔ cup flour
      dash of salt

The Filling

1½ cups salt white goat
      cheese
4 tablespoons sour cream
2 eggs

For the dough, mix all the ingredients together and roll out thin. Cut into 2-inch squares. For the filling, mash the salt cheese with a fork, then beat in the sour cream and eggs. Put some of the filling on each square, then fold into triangles and press the edges together. Boil in salted water and then fry. Serve with yoghurt. (Serves 6.)

SAMBOUSEK—FLAKY FRIED TURNOVERS _Shavuot_

This Shavuot dish was brought to Israel by immigrants from Syria. It is a dairy dish, like most fare on this festival.

strudel dough (see	½ _cup goat cheese_
Index)	_1 egg_
melted margarine	_salt to taste_
1½ cups cottage cheese	

Roll out the strudel dough, sprinkle with melted margarine and fold over. Sprinkle with more melted margarine. Cut the dough into rounds. Mix the remaining ingredients and put a spoonful on each round. Fold over and pinch the edges together. Fry the turnover in hot fat. (Borekas made like this are baked.) (Serves 4–6.)

GRAIN DISHES

RICE WITH SWEET APPLES   *Rosh Hashana*

Although it might well go into the dessert family, this is served with the main meat or fowl course on Rosh Hashana in Holland— and today by Dutch Jews in Israel.

2 cups rice	2 cups water
3 apples	ginger, saffron, or
½ cup sugar	lemon rind

Cook the rice 12 minutes in boiling, salted water. Peel the apples, core and cut into sections, then cook with the water and sugar for 10 minutes. Just before the rice is ready, add the apples and their sauce to it, with a little lemon rind or ginger or saffron, and cook 2–3 minutes longer. (Serves 4–6.)

PRUNE AND RICE TZIMMES   *Rosh Hashana*

Although rice is not mentioned in the Bible, the grain was the staff of life in the Far East long before the Book was compiled. Rice has been gastronomically elevated from the bulk food of the Asian masses to elegant dessert and festive main courses, with such dishes as rice à l'impératrice and rice tzimmes high among them.

2 cups prunes	juice and rind of
2½ pounds brisket of beef	½ lemon
3 tablespoons cooking oil	dash of cinnamon
2 teaspoons salt	dash of nutmeg
1 cup rice	2 tablespoons sugar
	water to cover

Soak prunes in hot water 1 hour. Sear the brisket in the oil. Add a little water and the salt and pot roast the meat until almost tender. Add the rice, the prunes, and all the seasonings and flavorings. Cover with boiling water and cook gently 20–30 minutes or until the rice is done. (Serves 6–8.)

RICE WITH TOMATOES *Succot*

Miriam de Leeuw has done so much in Israel for the welfare of Dutch immigrants that Queen Juliana recently decorated her. Some forty years ago, when kibbutz *Zargonia was established by immigrants from Holland, Miriam went there to help set up their dining and kitchen facilities, being an expert in the field. The* halutzim *(pioneers) repeatedly shunned the abundant and healthful tomato, despite its budgetary and culinary attractions. Miriam decided one day to substitute tomatoes for apples in a rice dish with the familiar Dutch flavor. The settlers ate the rice combination with gusto, then asked Miriam where she could have got the apples from. After that, they no longer scorned the plebeian tomato!*

½ *pound firm tomatoes, sliced or quartered*
⅔ *cup sugar*
½ *teaspoon powdered ginger*

½ *lemon, grated rind and juice*
4 *cups boiled rice*

Pour boiling water over the tomatoes and peel off the skins. Cover with the sugar and let stand a few hours, or even overnight. Drain off the liquid and boil until it begins to thicken. Add the ginger, grated lemon rind, lemon juice, and the tomatoes. Cook until the fruit is clear. Stir into the rice and serve either warmed up or cold. It is very good with cream, if desired. (Serves 6–8.)

RICE DISHES FOR SHAVUOT

Rice, being white, is the symbol of purity, and is therefore a Shavuot dish along with dairy products in Middle Eastern countries (and other lands where Sephardic Jews live). In Holland rice with milk and sugar is the Shavuot symbolic dish. In Syria rice with yoghurt and even a little lemon juice, but no sugar, is the fare. In Afghanistan the rice is cooked with butter and dried roses (no sugar) and served with yoghurt.

1 *cup rice*
3 *cups boiling water*

2 *teaspoons salt*

Add the rice and salt to the boiling water. Reduce the heat and cook for about 20 minutes. Drain. The rice will be dry and fluffy.

It can now be served with yoghurt, or milk and sugar, and flavored with rose or vanilla or cinnamon. (Serves 4.)

BUNUELOS—RICE FRITTERS *Hanuka*

"As fit as a fritter for a friar's mouth" is a tongue-twister describing a dish that is tangy-tasting on the tongue.

2 cups boiled rice	*dash of salt and pepper*
½ cup grated yellow cheese	*½ cup milk*
3 tablespoons flour	*3 egg whites, stiffly beaten*
3 egg yolks, beaten	

Mix the rice, cheese, flour, egg yolks, salt, pepper, and milk together. Fold in the egg whites. Drop spoonfuls of the batter onto a hot oiled skillet. Fry until puffed and golden on both sides. Drain and serve hot. (Serves 4–6.)

RISOTTO (RIZI-BIZI)

1 onion, chopped	*pinch of saffron*
¼ pound sliced mushrooms	*(optional)*
2 tablespoons olive oil	*2 teaspoons salt*
2 cups rice	*2 cups drained canned*
3 cups hot chicken soup	*peas*

Fry the onion and mushrooms lightly in the oil. Add the rice and let it roast a little in the mixture. Add the soup, saffron, if desired, and salt and cook until the rice is tender (about 15 minutes). Add the peas, heat through, and serve hot. (Serves 6–8.)

BURGHUL *Succot*

Burghul is cracked wheat and in Bible times it was undoubtedly cooked much in the way it is still prepared in the Middle East. It is a very tasty side dish, eaten like rice.

1 cup burghul	*2 cups soup stock*
4 tablespoons cooking oil	*(lamb, beef, or fowl)*
	salt and pepper to taste

Sauté the burghul in the oil, add the rich soup stock, and simmer until the burghul is soft and the liquid absorbed (1½ to 2 hours). Add salt and pepper as desired. (Serves 4.)

RICE PILAF GREEK STYLE   *Rosh Hashana*

Although the Jews of Palestine were subjected by Alexander of Macedonia in the pre-Maccabean period, he was such a generous ruler that to this day the name of Alexander is very popular in Israel. As a pupil of Aristotle's he was held in high respect among the learned people of the Book. Hellenic culture, on every level except the religious, was embraced—including Greek dishes, some of which have remained.

There are pilaus and pilafs and rice dishes for the main course that run into endless varieties. This one, of Greek origin, is often served on Rosh Hashana night.

½ cup margarine
2 cups rice
4 cups hot beef or chicken
  stock

3 tablespoons tomato juice
salt and pepper to taste

Melt the margarine in a heavy pan and brown the rice in it. Gradually add the stock and simmer for 10 minutes, covered. Add the tomato juice, salt, and pepper and cook, uncovered, 4–5 minutes longer, or until all liquid is absorbed. (Serves 4–6.)

INDIAN PILAU   *Hanuka*

In our wanderings around the world, God gave us Jews a chameleon (or is it a "protective coloration") quality by changing the color of our skin to match that of the people among whom we dwelt. In Germany we became blue-eyed, golden-haired, and fair-skinned. In China our eyes slanted and our hair turned jet black and our skins brown. In India we became dark-skinned and taper-fingered, and all this without intermarriage or losing our identity. Can it be the food and the climate that did it? For in every land we soon learned to eat the foods of the men among whom we dwelt, though we retained the kosher regulations. . . .

3 onions, chopped
2 green peppers, chopped
½ cup cooking oil
2 young chickens, cut up
½ cup flour
1 teaspoon salt
1 teaspoon pepper

water to cover
2 cups rice
4 cups boiling salted water
3 teaspoons curry powder
1 cup raisins
1 cup nuts

In a heavy pot, fry the onions and peppers in the oil. Remove the vegetables. Dust the pieces of chicken with flour, salt, and pepper and fry to golden brown. Add water to cover and simmer until the chicken is tender enough to be boned (about 30 minutes). Cook the rice in the boiling salted water with the curry powder 14 minutes. Meanwhile, remove the bones from the chicken and cut up coarsely. Drain rice and add to the chicken with the raisins and nuts. Serve in a mound with any chutney or fried onions for garnish. (Serves 8–10.)

MEJEDRAH—LENTIL-RICE PILAU   *Hanuka*

Mejedrah appears on the tables of all Near Eastern Jews in Israel on every festive occasion. The lentils must be whole (not split) and brown.

2 *large onions, sliced*
¼ *cup olive oil*
½ *pound lentils*

stock or water as
required
½ *pound rice*
salt to taste

Fry the onion slices in the oil until crisp. Remove. Put the lentils in the oil and add stock or water to more than cover. Cook the lentils until almost done (2–3 hours). Add the rice and more stock or water. Salt to taste. Bring to a quick boil and reduce the heat to low. Cook until the rice is done (30–35 minutes). Serve the rice and lentil mixture, garnished with the fried onions. (Serves 6–8.)

BOKHARIAN PILAFF   *Shabbat*

6 *chicken livers*
½ *cup chicken suet, cut up*
3 *cups, plus 1 tablespoon,*
   water
1 *cup coarsely grated*
   carrots

1 *large onion, chopped*
½ *cup chopped parsley*
1 *cup rice*
1 *teaspoon turmeric*
   salt and pepper to taste

Grill and dice the livers. Sauté the suet (add the 1 teaspoon of water at the start) and when the fat is melted, add the carrots, onion, and parsley and fry lightly for a few minutes. Mix all the ingredients and put into a heavy covered pot on top of the stove or in a casserole in the oven. Cook, without stirring, until the rice is done (about 30 minutes). Begin the cooking at a high heat, until the dish boils, and then reduce heat to very low. (Serves 4.)

COUSCOUS *Hanuka*

Couscous is a North African dish made of semolina, so popular that special utensils have been created to prepare it easily. The dish is eaten in as many ways as rice: in soup, as a side dish to meat or fish, as a main dish like a pilau, or sweetened and as a dessert.

2 cups water	*½ pound semolina*
1 teaspoon salt	*(cream of wheat)*

Pour the hot water and salt over the semolina and stir in the same direction until the grains swell up and cluster together. Put the semolina in a steamer or sieve, cover the pot, and steam for half an hour over rapidly boiling water. Remove from heat and stir the couscous very well. Steam for another half hour. The couscous can be served plain (with margarine added if you like) with meat, fish, or vegetables or with fruits as a dessert. (Serves 4–6.)

NOTE: For the Sabbath, the couscous is usually steamed over the chicken soup.

MAMALIGI AND MALAI (CORNMEAL MUSH) *Hanuka*

Ask a Romanian in Israel about mamaligi and his eyes light up and a long, mouth-watering conversation begins. "But never," they warn you, "should it be served on a holiday, as Israelis sometimes do. It's too vulgar a dish—but also too wonderful." Then they proceed: "Never cook it in a shiny pot but always in a black iron cauldron; serve it on wood always; cut it with a knife never, only with a string; eat it like an ox and don't leave a grain for a fly."

Mamaligi is served in many ways. The choice way is to eat it with sheep's cheese. "Bear mamaligi" is to tuck a piece of this cheese into a dumpling of mamaligi and grill it on the coals; when you open it, the cheese is melted and the world is perfect.

"Malai" is cornmeal to which a little yeast, flour, egg, and sugar has been added and which is baked just after the bread is removed from the oven on Friday morning. It is served at lunch, piping hot and split, with a piece of frozen goose fat in it, and eaten with garlic-flavored lamb. Malais are sometimes made with milk and eaten with butter.

4 cups water	*2 cups cornmeal*
1 teaspoon salt	*3 tablespoons margarine*

Boil the water, add the salt, and slowly add the cornmeal, stirring constantly with a wooden spoon. Continue to stir until the cornmeal mixture is thick. Add the margarine. Reduce heat and simmer about 30 minutes. When the mamaligi no longer sticks to the side of the pan, turn it out on a wooden board. Cool slightly and cut with a string. Serve warm as is or with butter, chicken fat, or grated cheese. Mamaligi may also be served with gravy, meat, mushrooms or whatever you want most as a partner to the dish. (Serves 4–6.)

KASHA WITH MUSHROOMS   *Hanuka*

Kasha—that is, buckwheat groats—was the cheapest fare and so the most used among the poor Jews in Russia. Peretz, in his sad story "The Cabalists," tells of a Biblical student's devout fasting . . . and watching his teacher eating:

As he raised the bowl with trembling hands, the warm vapour of the kasha covered his bony face. He put it on the table, took up the spoon in his hand, warming the other against the bowl. All this time the pupil regarded him intently, and as the master's trembling lips took the first spoonful of kasha, the pupil's heart tensed. . . .

The following dish can be made with wild or cultivated mushrooms.

1 egg	*water (about 3 cups)*
salt and pepper	*4 large onions, chopped*
1 cup buckwheat groats	*1 pound mushrooms, sliced*
(kasha)	*½ cup chicken or other fat*

Beat the egg lightly, add salt and pepper, and stir into the kasha. Place in a 350° oven for about 20 minutes to toast. Stir once or twice. Pour on as much water (about 3 cups) as the groats will absorb. Fry the onions and mushrooms in the fat. Add to the kasha and continue baking until the groats are done (about 20 minutes). (Serves 6.)

FISH

WHITE BREAM IN GOLDEN CURRY

2 pounds white bream
or other fish
salt to taste
½ cup pine nuts
oil for browning
1 cup water

juice of 1 large lemon
1 tablespoon chopped
parsley
1 teaspoon curry powder
dash of cayenne
dash of black pepper

Wash the fish, sprinkle with salt, and let stand for half an hour. Lightly brown the pine nuts in oil. Wash the fish, dry, and put into a pan with hot oil, to brown quickly on both sides. Mix all the remaining ingredients and pour over the fish. Bake in a 350° oven until fish is tender and the sauce pretty well soaked up (about 30 minutes). (Serves 4–6.)

NOTE: Slivered almonds may be substituted for the pine nuts.

BOILED ISRAELI POND CARP   *Independence Day*

". . . make sluices and ponds for fish"
Isaiah 19:10

In Israel, pond carp is bought live, and brought home to swim in a pail until its doomsday, or else killed at the fishmonger's and cooked as soon thereafter as possible. The many natural-looking fish ponds built in the kibbutzim since the creation of the state have altered the Israel landscape in many areas.

2 pounds fresh carp
2 large onions, sliced
2 carrots, sliced
1 pound celery root, sliced

1 parsnip, sliced
1 tablespoon coarse salt
¼ teaspoon whole pepper
1 tablespoon sugar

Clean and salt the freshly killed carp and set aside for half an hour. Wash well. Place the sliced vegetables in a fish kettle or stewing pan, and put the fish on top. Cover with water and add the salt, pepper, and sugar. Cook until the fish is tender (25 minutes, or until it flakes easily with a fork). Remove to a platter. Strain the sauce and pour it over the fish. This dish is generally served cold with its jelly, the vegetable mixture on the side. (Serves 4–6.)

SWEET CARP—SWISS STYLE   *Rosh Hashana*

3 pounds carp (or other fresh fish)	*¼ cup white wine*
2 cups chopped onions	*½ cup brown sugar*
2 teaspoons salt	*4 tablespoons raisins*
½ cup lebkuchen (or ginger-snap) crumbs	*juice of 1 lemon*
	1 lemon, sliced

Simmer the carp on a bed of onions in water to cover, with the salt, for 30 minutes. When the fish flakes easily with a fork, remove to a hot plate. Reserve the stock. Add the remaining ingredients to one cup of the stock and cook until thick and smooth. Pour this sauce over the fish. This dish is usually served cold, but is also very good hot. (Serves 6–8.)

Rosh Hashana
CARP IN POLISH SAUCE, JEWISH STYLE

Swiss Jews and Lithuanian Jews, and Jews from France or the United States, as well as Jews from Poland, serve carp in Polish sauce on Rosh Hashana.

4 pounds carp	*1 bay leaf*
salt to taste	*celery leaves*
½ cup sliced carrots	*5 peppercorns*
½ pound celery root, sliced	*2 cloves (optional)*
1 parsley root, sliced	*½ teaspoon pepper*
1 kohlrabi, sliced	*2 teaspoons sugar*
6 onions, sliced	*water to cover*

Clean and salt the carp. Make a bed of all the vegetables and seasonings. If you cover this with water, bring it to a boil and then add the fish, simmering it gently until done (about 40 minutes), you will get the real Polish-Jewish dish. If you add other ingredients (as so many women do) you'll get a variation. (Serves 8–10.)

CARP IN PAPRIKA SAUCE   *Rosh Hashana*

*This is how the Jews from Hungary serve carp on Rosh Hashana.
It is a dish that the Austrian Jews also serve on this occasion.*

4 pounds fresh carp	*1½ teaspoons paprika*
2 teaspoons salt	*water*
1 cup finely chopped	*½ pound green peppers,*
onions	*chopped*
½ cup margarine	*2 cups chopped fresh*
	tomatoes

Cut the carp into serving pieces and sprinkle with salt. Fry the finely chopped onions in the margarine, sprinkle with paprika, and dilute with a little water. Add the green peppers and tomatoes and bring to the boil. Place the carp pieces in a baking dish and pour the sauce over them. Bake in a 350° oven for 45 minutes, basting occasionally. (Serves 8–10.)

FISH WITH VEGETABLES   *Passover*

The Talmud advises: "He who possesses a mana [100 shekels] should buy a measure of vegetables for his pot; if he possesses ten mana, he should buy a quantity of fish for his pot; if he possesses 50 mana he may have meat cooked for him every day. As for those who possess less than 100 shekels, when may they have their dish of vegetables or fish? Every Friday night for the Sabbath."

3 potatoes, sliced	*3 tomatoes, sliced*
3 carrots, sliced	*1 tablespoon salt*
3 onions, diced fine	*sprinkling of white*
1 clove garlic, crushed	*pepper*
1 celery root, sliced	*6 tablespoons cooking oil*
3 summer squash, sliced	*¼ cup water*
1 3-pound grouper or	
other fish	

Put layers of the potatoes and all the vegetables except the tomatoes into a baking pan. Place the fish on top, covered with the tomato slices. Add the salt and pepper to the oil and pour over everything in the pan. Bake in a 350° oven for about an hour. When the dish has been in the oven about 30 minutes add the water. Good hot or cold. (Serves 4–6.)

CARP "JEZREEL VALLEY"

Israel Singer, in his Hasidic story "Repentance," describes Rabbi Ezekiel's delight in tasting his wife's fish before the Sabbath: "She is a valiant woman, a pearl of price, and her stuffed fish have in them not less than one-sixtieth of the virtue and taste of Leviathan himself." Had the Kozmir rabbi tasted this first-prize-winning fish of chef Cymbalista, as I did at the Tourist Department's Wizard-Chef Contest, his praise would have been heard in our chorus of applause. Carp is raised in abundance in the fish ponds of the Jezreel Valley in Israel.

5 small carp, about ½ pound each	1 large onion, chopped
⅓ cup, plus 1½ tablespoons flour	1 cup dry white wine
2 teaspoons salt	1 cup sweet cream
1 teaspoon dry mustard	1 medium green pepper, diced
2 teaspoons paprika	1 medium red pepper or pimento, diced
¼ pound butter	juice of 1 lemon
3 tablespoons cooking oil	1 ounce cornstarch

Clean the carp, remove the heads, and cut 2 or 3 gashes into each fish. Mix the ⅓ cup flour with the salt, mustard, and ½ teaspoon of the paprika, and roll each fish in the mixture. Heat the butter and oil in a pan and fry the fish over high heat until golden. Put the fish into a baking dish and cover with the following sauce:

Lightly fry the chopped onion in the fat left from frying the fish, add the remaining paprika and flour, and fry 1 minute more. Add the wine and cream and cook until thick. Add the remaining ingredients and pour over the fish. Bake in a slow oven for 45 minutes, basting from time to time with the sauce. (Serves 6.)

COD IN CREAM SAUCE   *Shavuot*

1 cup top milk	2 tablespoons flour
1 onion, sliced	salt and pepper to taste
2 tablespoons butter	2 pounds frozen cod fillets, thawed

Heat the milk and add the onion. Melt the butter, add the flour, and when it begins to bubble add the hot milk, onion, salt and pepper. Stir until thick and smooth. Put in the cod fillets and simmer until the fish is done (about 15 minutes). (Serves 4.)

ROMANIAN FISH GUIVETCH

Succot

sliced potatoes
green beans
peas
squash
tomatoes
eggplant

onions
salt and pepper to taste
1 *2-pound carp*
1 *cup white wine*
1 *cup cooking oil*

The amount and variety of vegetables is a matter of personal choice. Slice or dice all the vegetables as uniformly as possible and make a bed of them in a long casserole. Salt and pepper the fish, then spread it with oil inside and out. Lay it on the bed of vegetables. Pour the wine and the oil over and bake in a 350° oven until the fish is done (30–35 minutes). The liquid (add water if you wish) should cover the vegetables and be basted over the fish during cooking. (Serves 4.)

CARP SHARON

Shavuot

No wonder that Mrs. Liora Zuckerman won a top place in the Israel Culinary Contest. She hails from Poland, where carp is the favorite fish and, in Polish folklore, symbolizes strength. Her fish was the finest carp I ever tasted.

1 *5-pound carp*
  salt and pepper
5 *ounces button mush-*
  rooms
1 *medium onion, grated*
  butter for frying
2 *slices white bread,*
  soaked in milk

3 *ounces mild yellow*
  cheese
½ *pound tomatoes*
4 *tablespoons water*
3 *teaspoons breadcrumbs*
1 *cup sour cream*
1 *teaspoon flour*

Clean and salt the fish. Wash the mushrooms, cut into small pieces, and fry, with the onion, in butter. Squeeze the bread dry and crumble. Grate the cheese and tomatoes. Mix all of the preceding together and add salt and pepper.

Fill the cavity of the fish with this mixture and fasten the flaps well. Put 2 tablespoons of butter or margarine in a pan and add 2 tablespoons of the water and then the fish. Sprinkle the breadcrumbs over the fish. Put in a 400° oven and bake until the fish is golden (about 20 minutes).

Mix the sour cream with the flour and the remaining water. Pour over the fish and bake until golden again (about 20 minutes). Sprinkle on more grated cheese and bake for a further 20 minutes in a 350° oven. (Serves 8–10.)

FRIED FISH IN SOUR CREAM   *Shavuot*

A very ancient legend based on Exodus 35:22 is that the women not only provided the "bracelets and earrings and rings" (for which the men are also credited in the giving), they also provided their men with fish for food—a very rare thing in the desert! This came about in a miraculous way. When the women let their pitchers down into the well to draw water, lo and behold, they brought up fish!

2 pounds halibut fillets	butter for frying and
salt and pepper	for dotting
1 cup flour	2 cups (or less) sour cream
2 eggs, beaten	

Wipe the fillets. Sprinkle with salt and pepper. Dip in flour, then in the beaten egg, and fry lightly in hot butter. Put the fish in a casserole, dot with more butter, and pour over enough sour cream to cover. Bake in a 350° oven for about 15 minutes and serve hot. (Serves 4–6.)

SPANISH RICE WITH TUNA FISH OR SUB-PAELLA   *Succot*

In Israel Spanish rice is often combined with fish (something like paella, but not so fiery, and not including shellfish and chicken), and can be served on fried eggplant, which is so popular here.

1 onion, chopped	1 teaspoon salt
1 green pepper, chopped	pepper to taste
1 sweet red pepper,	1 clove garlic, crushed
chopped	(optional)
1½ cups rice	8 ripe olives, sliced
4 tablespoons cooking oil	(optional)
3 cups hot water	1 pound cooked tuna fish
1 cup tomato purée	or other fish

Lightly fry the onion, green and red pepper, and rice in the oil until golden. Add the water, tomato purée, salt, pepper, and garlic. Bring to the boil and simmer until the rice is done (15–18 minutes). Add black olives if you wish. Flake the tuna or other fish, and stir in. As a variant, dip slices of eggplant in egg and crumbs and fry. Serve the rice mixture on this. (Serves 4.)

HERRING AND HERRING SALADS   *Yom Kippur*

In Israel one is apt to dehydrate if Yom Kippur falls on a hot day. As the fast forbids drinking, it is essential that after the fast the body be replenished with salt. Herring and herring salads have therefore become the health-wise tradition for breaking the fast after one has had a cup of coffee and spiced cake or bun. Each community has its favorite combination.

A French way: Soak the herrings overnight. Clean and fillet the fishes, and cut into small pieces. Cover with French dressing and garnish with parsley and tomato slices.

A Russian way: The great lexicographer and father of modern spoken Hebrew, Eliezer Ben Yehuda, was wont to say, when he had eaten of the gourmet dishes of Paris and longed for his home in Russia, "Give me a piece of Jewish herring, peppered, and with onions, black olives and oil: for this is the soul and savour of food."

A Lithuanian way: A Yiddish folk saying: "Many women look like angels until you see them crunching bread and herring." To avoid such discovery, fillet the herring after soaking, and marinate it in white wine with the addition of a little sugar and vinegar.

To pickle schmaltz or plain herring, soak the fishes overnight. Clean and cut into serving pieces. Make a marinade of vinegar, sliced onions, bay leaves, whole peppers, and celery seed, with a little sugar to taste. Bring the marinade to a boil, and when cool, pour over the herring. It will be ready to eat in a day.

An Israeli way: To prepare this dish, soak the herrings overnight. Put the herrings to pickle (as in preceding) and then put in sour cream mixed with mashed milt roes, for further seasoning.

An Italian way: Archaeology and the records of history provide us with much evidence that in Israel fish was preserved in salt, the herring among others; they are probably eaten today as they were under the influence of the Roman culture of yore—except that today both Italians and Israelis like to dress the pickled or plain soaked herring with mayonnaise!

A Greek way: In 1546, a lavish dinner in Venice served "small

plates of fillets of herring with orange juice." Today in Greece
a Jewish housewife will serve it to you with lemon juice, for
they like lemon on everything.

A Dutch way: Herring somehow strikes the palate of all peoples
who have tasted it. In Holland you buy small herrings from
street vendors, hold them up, and drop them whole in the mouth.
The Dutch also serve this herring salad:

3 pickled herrings	*2 hard-cooked eggs, chopped*
1 dill pickle, chopped	*1 tomato, chopped*
3 sweet-sour pickled onions,	*1 rusk, crushed*
chopped	*7 tablespoons mild vinegar*
1 raw onion, chopped	*4 tablespoons oil*
1 apple, chopped	*1 teaspoon sugar*

Cut the herring fillets into small pieces and mix with the chopped
pickles, onions, apple, eggs, and tomato. Sprinkle on the crushed
rusk. Dress with the oil, vinegar, and sugar mixed.

A German way: A Jewish philosophical aside reads: "If you
cannot afford chicken, herring will do." The thrifty German
Jews have long followed this precept.

4 herrings	*1 teaspoon sugar*
½ pound potatoes, cooked	*1 cup sour cream*
and diced	*4 tablespoons vinegar*
½ pound apples, diced	*parsley, dill, and green*
1 dill pickle, diced	*onion tops, chopped*
2 sweet-sour pickled	*salt (a little)*
onions, diced	*pepper (a lot, to taste)*

Soak the herrings overnight, clean, and fillet. Cut into small
pieces. Mix with the diced potatoes, apples, pickles, and onions.
Mix together the sugar, cream, vinegar, herbs, and seasonings
and gently mix into the salad.

An English way: Although the smoked herring—the kipper—is
Britain's way of tackling this fish, nonetheless the salt herring
is an indispensable snack at all personal religious festivities,
from the Brit Milah, when a baby is circumcised, up to the

golden wedding celebration. This salad is very popular among the English Jews:

3 herrings
1 cup diced celery
3 cups diced boiled
   potatoes
1 onion, chopped
   parsley, chopped

½ cup mayonnaise
½ cup sour cream
   black olives, tomatoes,
   sliced
   green peppers, chopped

Cut up the soaked and filleted herrings and mix with the celery, potatoes, onions, and parsley. Mix the mayonnaise and sour cream and fold into the salad. Garnish with black olives, sliced tomatoes, and chopped green peppers.

A Scandinavian way: Leif Ericson, man of the sea, must have known the herring and was very likely also familiar with most of the other ingredients in this dish. Today it is one of the *pièces de résistance* of the Scandinavian smörgåsbord.

3 herrings
½ cup sugar
1½ teaspoons oil
½ apple, chopped
½ cup wine vinegar

½ teaspoon prepared
   mustard
½ cup tomato sauce or
   ketchup

Soak the herrings overnight. Cut them up. Mix with the remaining ingredients and allow the flavors to blend together for a few hours.

An American way:

3 herrings, soaked, filleted,
   and cut up
1 cup diced celery
1 cup shredded cabbage
1 onion, chopped
4 red radishes, sliced
1 sweet green pepper, sliced

1 sweet red pepper, sliced
2 tomatoes, sliced
2 apples, diced
1 cucumber, sliced
   French dressing
   garlic croutons

Toss all together in a wooden bowl and surround with lettuce.

A Russian-Polish way:

4 herrings	*1 onion*
2 potatoes, cooked	*2 tablespoons vinegar*
4 beetroots, cooked and	*2 teaspoons sugar*
peeled	*dash of pepper*
1 dill pickle	*1 cup sour cream*

Cut up the herrings and dice the vegetables. Mix with the remaining ingredients. Chill.

Chopped Herring—Everybody's way: As long ago as the Second Century the epicure Coelius Apicius described a "dish of minced fish with herbs, vinegar, oil, spices, and white of citron peel crushed fine." As fish in those days was invariably salted for transport, the dish sounds very much like the chopped Jewish herring of today.

3 salt herrings	*½ teaspoon cinnamon*
1 slice white bread	*(optional)*
1 large onion	*¼ teaspoon black pepper*
1 carrot (optional)	*3 tablespoons oil*
3 hard-cooked eggs	*4 tablespoons wine vinegar*
1 large apple	*black olives*
1 teaspoon sugar	*green onions*

Soak the herring overnight and then fillet it. Soak the bread for a few minutes, then squeeze out the moisture. Put the herring, bread, vegetables, eggs, and apple through the meat chopper. Add the remaining ingredients and mix well. Serve garnished with black olives and green onions.

Independence Day
HERRING IN WINE AND SOUR CREAM

Central European Jews (particularly those from Lithuania) have introduced dozens of salt herring dishes to Israel.

6 milt herring	½ cup dry white wine
3 large onions, sliced thin	juice of 2 lemons
3 bay leaves	1 cup sour cream
1 teaspoon peppercorns	

Soak herring in water to cover overnight, and the milt roes about 18 hours. Boil the onions, bay leaves, and peppercorns for two minutes, add the wine, and keep on heat only up to the boiling point. Cool and add lemon juice. Mash the milt roes, mix with the sour cream, and add to the onion mixture. Fillet the herring and cut it into pieces. Layer with the sauce in a jar and allow to marinate for a day. Keep in refrigerator. (Serves 6.)

Rosh Hashana
LEMONED MACKEREL, TUNISIAN STYLE

Lemon is as natural to fish as garlic is to beef, and this has been realized as long as lemons have been used as a condiment. Fourteenth-century banquets, in which hundreds of dishes were sometimes served, inevitably put fish—usually trout—cooked as well as garnished with lemons (and oranges) on the menus as a choice dish.

3 pounds mackerel, red	juice of 1 lemon
snapper, or similar fish	6–10 small potatoes, new if
⅓ cup oil	possible
1 teaspoon salt	6 small onions
pepper to taste	1 lemon, sliced
dash of saffron *	water to cover

Rub the fish with a little salt, sprinkle with pepper, and brown in the hot oil. Put the fish in a baking dish. Sprinkle it with the saffron (*see footnote below*) and lemon juice. Surround with small new potatoes and onions. (If old potatoes are used, cook in jackets first and then cut up and put with the fish, since fish cooks faster than old potatoes.) Cover the fish with the lemon slices. Add the oil and just enough water to half cover the layer of potatoes. Bake in a 400° oven until the fish and vegetables are

---

* Soak threads of saffron in hot water 5–10 minutes, then sprinkle the liquid over the fish, discarding threads.

done (about 35 minutes). Baste the fish from time to time with
the lemon sauce. (Serves 6.)

KEFAL—TURKISH FISH   *Rosh Hashana*

*This is a piquant fish dish, which Jews from Turkey serve on
Rosh Hashana. The fish is cooked whole and the head served to
the master of the house as a symbol of his leadership and wisdom
in the family.*

1 bunch parsley	1 teaspoon salt
2 tomatoes	1 teaspoon sugar
2½ pounds fresh mullet,	juice of 1½ lemons
whole	⅓ cup olive oil

Chop the parsley and tomatoes and put them in the bottom of a
pot. Sprinkle the fish with the salt and sugar and put in the pot.
Add the lemon juice and oil. Cook on low heat so that the fish will
stew and not fry. Turn over after 5 minutes and cook 5 minutes
longer, or until the fish flakes easily with a fork. (Serves 6–8.)

ST. PETER'S FISH (BARBECUED)   *Purim*

*A silver and blue fish, weighing up to two pounds and measuring
a bit more than a foot in length at maturity, lives in the Sea of
Galilee. It is the* Tilapia galilaea, *commonly known as "St. Peter's
Fish," reminiscent of (perhaps even the same as) the fish that
Peter drew out in such a multitude from the right side of the
ship. When I was honeymooning with my husband in Tiberias
many long years ago, some Arab fishermen grilled us St. Peter's
fish on a wood-coal fire, on the seashore, and served it to us with
bread, much as the disciples did in John 21:9. At Kibbutz Ein
Gev, on the Sea of Galilee, the fish is thus prepared for tourists
making the boat trip over the lake.*

8 small St. Peter's fish or	sprig of parsley
trout (cleaned)	salt and pepper
cooking oil	lemon juice
4 onions, cut in thick slices	

Oil the rack over your wood-coal embers. Brush the fish, inside
and out, with oil. Put a couple of onion slices in the cavity of the
fish, along with a sprig of parsley. Salt and pepper the fish. Broil
the fish on the coals, browning it well before turning. Drizzle
with lemon juice and a little more oil during grilling. The fish
should be done in 15 minutes. Serve with lemon wedges. (Serves
4.)

SARDINES VIVANDIÈRE   *Purim*

I was first served this dish in a Moroccan household, and it is possible that the influence of French cuisine in North Africa brought the recipe there, though it is in many ways typical of Middle Eastern cookery. But by the wildest dreams my unlettered hostess could not have known that the dish was named for a camp follower in the days when soldiers had to get their own food, and were assisted in this by the prostitutes, who went with them—for a fee.

3 summer squashes	*salt and pepper to taste*
(6 inches long)	*4 tablespoons hot olive oil*
6 sardines (4 to 5 inches	*1 onion, grated*
long)	*4 tablespoons tomato sauce*
1 tablespoon flour	*1 tablespoon chopped parsley*

Cut the squashes in half, lengthwise. Scoop out the pith and seeds, shaping the squashes like boats. Roll the cleaned and (preferably) boned sardines in the flour, mixed with salt and pepper, and fry in the hot oil. Put each fish into a squash boat. Put the onions into a casserole, and then the filled squashes. Cover each fish with tomato sauce and top with parsley. Add just enough water to steam the squashes. Cook until tender (about 20 minutes).

SARDINES—A WHALE OF A DIFFERENCE   *Shavuot*

½ *teaspoon salt*	*1 small clove garlic,*
2 pounds sardines or	*crushed*
other small fish	*pinch of turmeric*
⅓ *cup lemon juice*	*pinch of cardamom*
1¼ *cups water*	*sliver of bay leaf*
½ *teaspoon pepper*	*1 tablespoon olive oil*
	1 tablespoon flour

Clean and salt the fish and set aside for an hour. Then rinse and put into a baking dish. Cook together the lemon juice, water, salt, pepper, garlic, turmeric, cardamom, and bay leaf. When the mixture has just reached boiling point, mix the oil and flour and add, to thicken the sauce slightly. Pour this hot mixture over the sardines and bake in a 350° oven until sardines are just done

(20–25 minutes). Serve chilled the following day (fish improves with marinating a day or two). (Serves 4–6.)

SOLE IN WINE MARINADE   *Rosh Hashana*

⅓ *cup flour*
  salt and pepper to taste
2½ *pounds whole sole or*
  flounder
4 *onions, chopped*
½ *cup olive oil*

3 *tablespoons raisins*
2 *tablespoons pine or*
  other nuts
¼ *cup wine vinegar*
½ *cup white wine*

Mix the flour with the salt and pepper and roll the fish in this. Fry the onions in the olive oil, then remove. Put the fish in the oil and fry until golden. Remove. Add the raisins, nuts, onions, vinegar, and wine and bring just to the boil. Pour this sauce over the fish and marinate for half a day. (Serves 4–5.)

SOLE DUMAS   *Shavuot*

8 *fillets of sole*
6 *tablespoons butter or*
  margarine
1 *onion, chopped*

½ *pound ripe tomatoes,*
  chopped
  salt and pepper to taste
1 *clove garlic*
½ *cup white wine*

Put the fillets in a pan with the butter or margarine. Do not fry, but just stew the fish in the butter for 5–6 minutes. Remove the fish and keep warm. Add the onion and tomatoes to the butter and cook, but do not brown. Add the remaining ingredients and cook to a rather thick paste. Dress the sole in this sauce and place in a 400° oven for 10 minutes. (Serves 4–6.)

PAN FRIED FISH FILLETS   *Succot*

2 *pounds fish fillets*
  salt and pepper
  celery salt

cornmeal
cooking oil for frying

Thaw out the fillets, if frozen. Sprinkle with the seasoning. Roll in the cornmeal and fry until golden in hot oil (3–5 minutes). (Serves 4–6.)

Hanuka
SEPHARDIC BAKED PALAMIDA (LITTLE TUNA) FISH

The site of Ashdod, the new port-city that is now being built near Ashkelon on the Mediterranean, was in ancient times so famous for its palamida fish catch that the town was nicknamed "Palmia." Fish was smoked, salted and cured there, and even today smoked palamida is a favorite fish for snacks. It is used in as many dishes as tuna fish is in the United States, but palamida baked in the Sephardic fashion wins the day.

5 pounds palamida fish	*6 tomatoes, chopped*
(or 8-pound tuna)	*lemon juice*
salt and pepper	*dash of curry powder*
6 onions, finely chopped	*(optional)*
2 cloves garlic, chopped	*water as required*
½ cup olive oil	*pine nuts*
4 tablespoons chopped	*white wine (optional)*
parsley	

Put the fish on a well-buttered baking pan and sprinkle with salt and pepper. Fry the onions and garlic in the oil and sprinkle over the fish with the parsley. Fry the tomatoes briefly, and place over the fish. Mix the lemon juice and curry powder with enough water to reach about halfway up the fish. Bake in a 350° oven, basting frequently with the sauce, until the fish is quite tender (about 45 minutes). Fry the pine nuts briefly and sprinkle over the fish. Bake a few minutes more. If you like, a little white wine may be added toward the last, when the sauce has simmered down. Serve hot or cold. (Serves 8 if palamida, 14 if tuna.)

NOTE: If you make this dish with a whole tuna the smallest you can get will probably weigh 8 pounds. The other ingredients will be adequate for a fish of that weight.

PETITE PANDORA FISH—DEEP FRIED   *Purim*

The Talmud says that he who makes it a habit to eat small fish will not suffer from indigestion; more than that, small fish make a man's whole body fruitful and virile.

12 pandoras or other small	*flour*
fish, such as sardines,	*2 eggs, beaten*
bleak, herrings	*dry breadcrumbs*
(cleaned)	*oil for frying*
salt and pepper to taste	

Wipe the cleaned fish with a towel and sprinkle with salt and pepper. Dip the fish in flour and then in beaten egg. Roll in the breadcrumbs, and set aside while the oil heats. Use a deep frying pan with an inch of oil in it. When a piece of white bread browns in 45 seconds, the fat is ready. Fry the fish until golden and crisp on the outside. Drain on brown paper and serve with lemon wedges. (Serves 4.)

PALAMIDA (LITTLE TUNA) ROASTED   *Passover*

Tuna fish is often called "chicken of the sea," for the white flesh is so popular. But the dark meat of the tuna is very much like young beef in appearance and taste; I once served it at Passover Seder, during the meat rationing period, and my guests must surely have thought I had bought a roast of beef on the black market.

3 *pounds dark tuna*	*salt and pepper*
(skinned)	1 *teaspoon monosodium*
cooking oil	*glutamate (MSG)*
3 *carrots, sliced*	½ *cup water*
3 *onions, sliced*	20 *button mushrooms*
3 *cloves garlic*	

Sear the tuna in hot oil. Put it on a bed of sliced vegetables, add the seasoning and water, and simmer as for a pot roast for 1 hour, or until the fish flakes easily with a fork. Turn the tuna once during the cooking. Add the mushrooms toward the end of the cooking. (Serves 6.)

JELLIED EGYPTIAN FISH WITH LEMON   *Shabbat*

5 *tablespoons olive oil*	1 *teaspoon curry powder*
2 *cloves garlic, chopped*	*(optional)*
4 *cups water*	5 *tablespoons chopped*
juice of 4 lemons	*parsley*
2 *teaspoons salt*	2½ *pounds sliced fish steaks*
dash of pepper	

Heat the oil and fry the garlic in it. Add the water, lemon juice, seasonings, and parsley. Add the fish steaks. Simmer slowly for 30 minutes. Remove to a serving dish with the liquid. This dish is usually served cold in its jelly. (Serves 6–8.)

BROILED ELATH FISH   *Hanuka*

In a little fish restaurant on the shore of the Red Sea in Elath, you sit among the nets, next to seamen and desert pioneers, scientists and frontier toughs, and smell the ocean and the grilling fish. Every hour a brown and brawny fisherman in a bathing suit brings in a fresh catch. You choose your fish: pandora or lizard fish, red mullet or gray mullet, sea bream or white bream, grouper or red snapper, mackerel or drum fish, little tuna or hake, sole or sardine, barbel or the dentex filosus, which still hasn't got a common name. You can have a big one or a small one, fried or broiled. It comes back to you in half an hour, all decked out in parsley and lemon wedges, with a savory salad and chips on the side. Never, but never, have I had such fish!

fish—any of above varieties	*pepper*
salt	*cooking oil*

Clean and bone the fish. Sprinkle with salt and pepper after washing and brush with oil or butter. Place it on a rack under the broiler, and turn the heat high. Once it is browned on both sides, turn down the heat and cook until the flesh is white when flaked. Dab generously with more butter before bringing it to the table. Say good-bye to your table partner until you've devoured the dish!

SWEET FISH (ITALIAN)   *Rosh Hashana*

Catherine de' Medici, of the great Florentine family, was the one who introduced good cooking to France from Italy. She loved fish and had it transported from her native land packed in kegs of honey. This, a great luxury due to problems of preservation, has left an impression, as seen in this festive fish for Rosh Hashana. This fish is served with the head.

6 whole fish (trout or other)	*⅔ cup water*
salt and pepper to taste	*3 or more tablespoons honey or sugar*
⅓ cup flour	*juice of 2 lemons*
½ cup oil	*3 tablespoons raisins*
1 tablespoon rosemary or mint	*2 tablespoons pine nuts*
	1 clove garlic, mashed

Salt and pepper each fish. Roll in the flour and fry in hot oil, to which the rosemary has been added. Remove the fish and put into a fireproof dish. Bring the remaining ingredients to the boil, pour over the fish and simmer gently for five minutes. Mint may be substituted for rosemary, in which case it is not put in the oil but in the sauce. (Serves 6.)

MUSTARD-EGGED FISH FILLETS   *Hanuka*

Among all the favored herbs and spices mentioned in the Old Testament, mustard does not appear. Yet it is known that this condiment became popular even before it was mentioned in the New Testament. It seems very likely that the Maccabees made a dish not unlike this one, which Yugoslav immigrants have reintroduced to Israel, for egg yolks and mustard are known to have been mixed together as a condiment even in those days.

  salt to taste
2 pounds fish fillets (cod,
      hake, or halibut)
2 tablespoons lemon juice
2 tablespoons prepared
      mustard

2 eggs
2 tablespoons water
  breadcrumbs or cornmeal
  oil for frying

Salt the fillets lightly. Mix the lemon juice and mustard and spread very thinly on the fillets. Set aside to marinate for about half an hour. Dilute the eggs with the water. Dip the fillets into the mixture and then roll in breadcrumbs or cornmeal. Fry in hot oil. (Serves 6.)

BOKHARIAN FISH   *Shabbat*

2 pounds fish fillets
      (any kind)
½ teaspoon salt
  oil for frying
3 large onions, chopped
1 cup water
1 cup mild wine vinegar

2 tablespoons sugar
1 tablespoon flour
1 tablespoon curry powder
4 tablespoons raisins
1 tablespoon apricot
      confiture

Cut the fish fillets into serving pieces, sprinkle with salt, and fry in hot oil. Boil the onions in the water for 3 minutes and mix with the remaining ingredients (except the fish), adding a little more water if necessary. Dress the fish with this hot sauce and allow it to marinate. Serve cold. (Serves 4–6.)

WHOLE BAKED FISH
Tu Besh'vat

The Stuffing

1 cup chopped onion
1 cup chopped celery
  stalk or grated root
6 tablespoons butter
4 cups bread cubes
1 teaspoon salt
½ teaspoon pepper
1 tablespoon chopped
  parsley
  dash of rosemary

The Fish

1 whole 5-pound fish
  (grouper, red snapper,
  little tuna or other fish)
½ cup melted butter or
  margarine
  salt and pepper to taste

For the stuffing, lightly fry the onions and celery root (stalks need not be fried) in the butter and then mix with the remaining stuffing ingredients. Leave the head and tail on the fish. Put the stuffing into the cavity of the fish and secure firmly with toothpicks. Put the fish on a greased pan and pour the melted butter over it, then sprinkle with salt and pepper. Bake in a 500° oven for 15 minutes. Reduce the heat to 350° and bake for an hour longer. Serve hot, with lemon slices. (Serves 8.)

PICKLED FISH
Yom Kippur

After the Yom Kippur fast, one enjoys a spicy dish. The need for something hearty but not heavy has brought pickled fish into favor as post-fast fare. This dish keeps for about a month in the refrigerator.

1 cup vinegar
1 cup water
1 tablespoon salt
3 bay leaves
10 peppercorns

3 cloves
½ teaspoon celery seed
3 onions, sliced
5 pounds fish, cut into
  serving pieces

Boil the vinegar, water, spices, and onion. Simmer the fish in this stock for 25–35 minutes. Remove from heat and cool. Carefully remove the fish and put it into a deep container. Strain the hot liquid over, and add a few more slices of raw onion if you wish. Cool and refrigerate. The fish jells and is very piquant. (Serves 10.)

PICKLED FRIED FISH   *Shabbat*

*Pickled fish keeps very well, and it was often used for that reason
for the Sabbath before the days of refrigeration.*

4 pounds fresh fish,
   sliced ½ inch thick
oil for frying
1 lemon, sliced thin
1½ cups vinegar
3 cloves garlic

1 tablespoon salt
½ cup water
4 or 5 bay leaves
1 teaspoon black pepper-
   corns
4 tablespoons sugar

Fry the fish (without batter) in very hot oil until done. Cool
thoroughly and arrange in a glass jar, with lemon slices in between. Mix the remaining ingredients and bring to the boil. Cool.
Pour over the fish. The dish will be ready within 3 days. (Serves
8–10.)

JANE'S CURRIED FISH   *Shabbat*

*My neighbor Jane Slone has a theory about South African curried
fish. The pickled part of it is definitely Lithuanian (whence the
Jews of South Africa came). The curry is Indian influence in
that land. And in Israel the dish has been enhanced with the
popular pine nuts and the new-grown pecans. Well, whatever its
background, its future as a Sabbath summer brunch dish is prom-
ising in Israel.*

2½ pounds fish fillets
1 teaspoon salt
¼ teaspoon white pepper
1 tablespoon flour
1 egg, beaten
   safflower oil for frying
¾ cup citrus vinegar
1 cup water

1 large onion, sliced
2 bay leaves
6 allspice seeds
2 tablespoons curry powder
2 tablespoons sugar
2 tablespoons pine nuts or
   slivered pecans

Cut the fish into 12 pieces and sprinkle with half the salt and
pepper. Dip in the flour and beaten egg and fry in safflower oil
until golden. Meanwhile, boil the vinegar and ½ cup of the water
with the onion, bay leaves, the remaining salt, pepper, and allspice, until the onion is soft. Mix the curry powder, sugar, and
nuts with the second ½ cup of water and add to the sauce. Boil
for 10 minutes. Put the fish into a serving dish and pour the hot
sauce over. Cool and then refrigerate. This dish improves after
a day or two and keeps very well for over a week. (Serves 6–8.)

THE GOLDEN FISH *Purim*

This glamorous recipe comes from the Tel Aviv–Sheraton Hotel and was created by the chef Robert Steiner.

1 large fresh fish	6 carrots
(6 pounds)	1 sweet red pepper
salt	1 green pepper
water to cover	1 tablespoon gelatin
4 tablespoons vinegar	½ cup hot water
peppercorns	
onions, celery root,	
parsnip, chopped	

Clean the fish, salt it, and put it aside for two hours. Bring the water to the boil with the vinegar, peppercorns, onions, celery root, and parsnip in a fish pot. Immerse the whole fish and simmer gently until the flesh is firm (35–45 minutes). If necessary, add more water to cover the fish. Pour off the liquid and carefully put the fish on a platter on its belly. Chill thoroughly. Parboil the carrots and slice very thin. Slice the peppers into thin rings. Dilute the gelatin in the hot water and dip the carrot slices, one at a time, in the gelatine mixture. Beginning at the tail end of the fish, affix each slice like a fish scale. Keep increasing the size of the slices toward the center of the fish and then reduce them again toward the head. The carrots will stick to the cold fish. Trim the eyes, and the gills along the full length of the fish, with red and green pepper rings. Carefully spoon on the remaining gelatin and chill thoroughly. (Serves 10–12.)

FISH PLAKI *Tu Besh'vat*

1 whole 5-pound fish	a little water
salt and pepper to taste	white wine
lemon juice for sprinkling	lemon slices
onions as desired	—and still more wine in
garlic as loved	a glass to drink it
plenty of parsley	down with! (chilled
olive oil as needed	white)
3 tomatoes, peeled and	
chopped	

Sprinkle the fish with salt and pepper and drizzle inside and out with lemon juice. Put into a baking pan. Fry the onions, garlic, and parsley in the olive oil, add the tomatoes, and fry a few minutes more. Put in a little water to thin the paste and a bit of wine for the flavoring. Pour this over the fish and garnish with very thin lemon slices. Bake for about an hour. Serve with a glass of chilled white wine. (Serves 8.)

TAHINA-FISH "SIN'AYA"   *Shavuot*

Fish is grilled on open fires today at Kibbutz Ein Gev, on the shore of the Sea of Galilee, just as it was in Biblical days. Housewives of Tiberias have gone a step farther and created tahinafish "sinaya," now a favorite all over Israel. This recipe is Shomrona Bigger's, native of Tiberias.

5 fish (weighing ½ pound each), grouper, hake, carp, drum fish, mullet, etc. *salt and pepper* *oil for frying*	*2 large onions* *1 cup tahina paste (see Tahina Paste, introductory note)* *2 tablespoons chopped parsley*

Make 2 or 3 slashes in each fish. Sprinkle with salt and pepper. Fry in the oil and then place the fish in a shallow baking dish. Fry the onion in the same oil and spread over the fish. Pour the prepared tahina over and sprinkle with the chopped parsley. Bake in a 375° oven until the tahina is golden (about 20 minutes). (Serves 5.)

OVEN-FRIED GEFILTE FISH   *Shabbat*

2 slices white bread *1 teaspoon sugar* *1 pound carp, chopped* *1 pound fish of some other kind, chopped* *2 teaspoons salt*	*2 eggs, beaten* *¼ teaspoon pepper* *2 onions, chopped* *1 celery root, grated* *oil for frying*

Soak the bread in water and squeeze dry. Mix all the ingredients except the oil and form into patties. Place the patties in a baking pan with hot oil and bake in a 400° oven until the fish is nicely browned (about 45 minutes), turning once. Serve hot or cold.

NOTE: This dish is often served for the second or third Sabbath meal.

GEFILTE FISH—SWEET SEASONED *Passover*

"Reb Ezriel the fishmonger would call 'Fish, fish, fresh and jumping fish! Fish for Shabbat.' But when the women, be they the great ladies or the servant girls or the poor, came to peer under the gills of the fish, poke at their eyes or prod their bellies to see how fresh they were, Reb Ezriel would offensively shoo them off. But the women had to put up with him for there was no other fishmonger in the village, so what could they do? Lie down and die? Or live through the Shabbat without fish? That is worse than dying, for if she had died it is done with. But if she comes home without fish for Shabbat, then she has to face her husband's anger. And that is worse than death!"

—SHOLOM ALEICHEM

4 pounds fish, of at least two varieties	2 eggs
1 cup water	1 tablespoon sugar
6 large onions	salt and pepper to taste
1 tablespoon matzo meal	3 carrots

Skin and bone the fish and put the skin and bones, with the head, into a pot with the water. Put the fish fillets through the food chopper, then into a chopping bowl. Add 3 of the onions, grated, and chop. Add the matzo meal and eggs, chopping all the time, adding a bit of water as you go along. Add the sugar, salt, and pepper. Slice the other 3 onions and the carrots and place in the bottom of the pot. Cover with a fish rack. Add more water if necessary and bring to a boil. Form the fish into balls and put into the boiling liquid. Cover and cook rapidly for half an hour, then reduce the heat and continue to cook the fish for two hours more. (Serves 10.)

GEFILTE FISH (PEPPERY) *Shabbat*

3 pounds fish, two or three varieties such as carp, snapper, mullet, bream, etc.	¾ teaspoon (or more, if you wish) pepper
	3 onions
	2 slices dry white bread
4⅓ cups water	½ pound celery root
2 teaspoons salt	2 eggs
	1 carrot, sliced

Remove the flesh from the fish. Put the head, bones, and skin in the bottom of a fish pot with half the water, half the salt and half the pepper, and let it cook while you grind the fish with the onion, bread, and celery root. The fish is best if ground two or even three times. (Once upon a time gefilte fish was chopped by hand in a wooden bowl.) Add the eggs, remaining water, and the remaining salt and pepper.

Shape the fish into balls or thick pancakes. Garnish each piece with a slice of carrot. Place a fish rack in the pot (or use a layer of onions) and put the fish into the stock. Cover. Bring to a quick boil and then reduce the heat and cook the fish slowly for at least 1 hour. (Some cook it for 3 hours on very low heat.) Remove the fish from the pot when cool, strain the fish stock over it. Serve chilled, with horse-radish and dill pickles. (Serves 8.)

THE DAN'S GRAND GEFILTE FISH

Culinary historians date gefilte fish back to the Middle Ages. Jewish tastes haven't changed in five hundred years!

The dandiest gefilte fish I've ever had was at the Dan Hotel. My hat off to Chef Sander Goldstein who prepares it in his wonderful way.

1 2¼-pound fresh-water carp, whole	2 hard-cooked eggs
½ pound carrots	2 raw eggs
½ pound onions	1½ teaspoons (or less if you wish) white pepper
6 cups water	⅓ cup sugar
1⅔ teaspoons salt	4 tablespoons cooking oil

Remove the skin whole from the fish by bending its head backward, and beginning at the base of the head, separate the flesh from skin, working toward the tail. Remove the head and skin with care, and in one piece, so that when the skin is filled it will look like an uncut fish. Remove the meat from the bones. Cook the bones with the carrots, onions, water, and 1 tablespoon of the salt and simmer for 1 hour. Strain the juice.

Put the carp and hard-cooked eggs through the meat chopper, add the raw eggs, white pepper, sugar, remaining salt, and oil. Pack the filling into the skin of the fish and cook it gently in the strained sauce for about one hour. Serve cold, surrounded by the fish jelly. (Serves 6–8.)

FISH MOUSSAKA

Shavuot

Nehemiah (13:16) speaks angrily of the men from Tyre who profaned the Sabbath by bringing in fish for sale on that day. Fish was so much in demand that the gates of the city wall had to be closed on Sabbath to keep out the fishmongers.

3 medium eggplant	*½ cup breadcrumbs*
4 tablespoons oil for frying	*2 eggs, separated*
2 onions, diced	*3 cups flaked cooked fish*
1 tablespoon chopped	*4 tablespoons margarine*
parsley or dill	*4 tablespoons flour*
1 tablespoon tomato paste	*2 cups milk*
1 cup water	*1 cup grated yellow cheese*
salt and pepper to taste	

Slice the eggplant (skin left on) and fry lightly in the oil. Drain on paper. Add the onions to the oil, brown lightly, then add the parsley, tomato paste, water, salt, and pepper. Bring to a boil, then remove from heat. Add the breadcrumbs and beaten egg whites. Alternate layers of eggplant with layers of fish and of the crumb mixture, ending with eggplant on top.

Melt the margarine and add the flour, and when the mixture bubbles, pour in the milk and cook until thick, stirring constantly. Remove the sauce from heat and add the grated cheese and then the beaten egg yolks. Pour this over the casserole and bake in a 350° oven until the crust is golden (about 30 minutes). (Serves 6–8.)

FISH CAKES

Shabbat

This dish is traditional in Dutch homes for the Sabbath brunch after morning service.

2 cups cooked fish	*pinch of mace*
1 cup cold mashed potatoes	*salt and pepper to taste*
1 tablespoon chopped parsley	*2 eggs, beaten*

Mix all the ingredients together. Form into small cakes and fry in butter or margarine until golden on both sides. (Serves 4).

SOUP GARNISHES

Yom Kippur

MINESTRA DI CALZONICCHI—ITALIAN KREPLACH FOR SOUP

The history of kreplach is shrouded in mystery. There is no doubt that won ton is a cousin of kreplach, and that ravioli is a relative, too. But whatever the source, Italian kreplach are special in the land of the specialists with pasta.

1 pound brains	3 eggs
2 teaspoons salt	6 cups flour, sifted

Soak the brains in cold water, with the salt, for an hour, then remove membrane. Scald with hot water and cut into pieces. Make a dough of the eggs and flour and roll out. Cut the dough into squares, fill each square with 2 pieces of scalded brain, fold over and pinch into triangles. Cook in chicken soup (*see* Index) for about 20 minutes.

Passover

PASSOVER CLOUD KNAIDLACH (MATZO MEAL DUMPLINGS)

On Passover night at the Seder the youngest child asks the four questions about all the symbolism at the table on this "night different from all other nights." But a fifth question was suggested by a child in Vienna: "Why on this night do we eat knaidlach of matzo meal?" The rabbi replied: "The Jews in Egypt were enclosed within a walled area. Moses threw a round stone—shaped like the knaidlach—to burst the wall and free the Jews." Moral: Eat knaidlach until you burst! (But these cloud knaidlach are so light they'd never crush a feather.)

1 cup matzo meal	¼ teaspoon ground ginger
½ cup water or soup	2 eggs, well beaten
1 teaspoon salt	4 tablespoons oil

Mix all the ingredients together and refrigerate. It is essential that the batter is made at least four hours before cooking to absorb all the moisture. Roll balls out of the batter with wet hands. Drop the knaidlach into boiling water or soup, a few at a time, about 30 minutes before serving.

71

Rosh Hashana
YOICH MANDLEN—ALMONDS FOR CHICKEN SOUP

2 eggs, lightly beaten   ½ teaspoon salt
2 teaspoons oil   ½ teaspoon baking powder
1 cup flour, sifted

Mix eggs and oil and add the dry ingredients. Roll the dough out into ropes about ¼ inch thick and cut into cubes with floured knife. Fry until golden in deep hot fat. Serve in soup.

Rosh Hashana
MERGBALLETJES—MARROW DUMPLINGS

Balletjes are tiny dumplings, usually of meat, that go into festive soups in Holland. In German-speaking countries the dumplings are far larger and are called "Kloesse." Because the finest fats are part of the Rosh Hashana food tradition, marrow dumplings are the garnish for soup on this day.

4 ounces raw marrow   2 thick slices white bread
2 eggs   breadcrumbs
1 tablespoon flour   salt
                                 dash of nutmeg

Melt the marrow and beat with the eggs. Add the flour. Dip the bread in water and squeeze out the moisture, then break it up and add to the first mixture. Add enough breadcrumbs to make a rather firm mass. Season. Roll into small balls and cook in soup.

TRIFLACH—EINLAUF—EGG DROPS FOR SOUP   *Succot*

1 egg   4 tablespoons water
3 tablespoons flour   pinch of salt

Beat the egg. Add the remaining ingredients and mix well. Drop slowly from the end of a spoon into boiling soup. Cook for 4 or 5 minutes, or until the egg drops float to the top of the pot.

FILLED KNAIDLACH

Passover Seder on a kibbutz is one of the greatest occasions of the year. Part of the traditional service is followed, the beloved tunes sung. But most of the evening is used to carry the theme of freedom for our people to our own day. The story of reborn Israel and the history of the settlement itself are wound into the ceremony of the night. Children's choirs and orchestras partici-

pate. Hundreds of guests come to their kibbutz friends on this night to witness the telling of the old and the new from the ancient Haggadah and the new history lived by the pioneers.

1 onion, chopped	¾ cup boiling water
3 tablespoons chicken fat	1½ cups matzo meal
½ cup ground meat or	2 eggs, beaten
grilled liver	salt and pepper to taste

Fry the onion in the chicken fat and mix with the meat. The mixture must be dry. Pour the boiling water over the matzo meal. Beat the eggs and stir into the meal. Season. Let the batter refrigerate for a few hours, then roll into balls. Make a depression in each ball with your finger and stuff in some of the meat mixture. Seal up. Half an hour before serving, drop the dumplings into boiling salted water or soup. (If you prefer, you may mix the meat into the knaidle batter.)

MATZO KNAIDLACH   *Passover*

Old grey bearded Hanoch, the kneader, kneaded his thoughts into the dough. . . . The dough stiffens, the horny old hands work it with difficulty. . . . It is kneaded, cut up in pieces, rolled and riddled—the round matzos, which must wander on a shovel into the heated oven . . . till another shovel throws them out into a new world. . . . There they are arranged in columns, like Pithom and Rameses. Kik-ruk-kuk-ruk, ruk-rush, whisper the still warm matzos to one another; they also are remembering, and they tell the tale of Exodus after their fashion, the tale of the flight out of Egypt. . . . Thus are the matzos kneaded and baked by the Jews, with thoughts.

                                   —from AT THE MATZOS *by* JUDAH STEINBERG

2 matzos	1 teaspoon chopped parsley
2 small onions, chopped	2 eggs, beaten
3 tablespoons fat	matzo meal
salt, pepper, nutmeg	

Soak the matzos in cold water until soft, then squeeze very dry. Beat with a fork. Fry the onion in the fat and add with the fat to the matzos. Add the seasoning, parsley, and egg. Add just enough matzo meal to bind the mixture. Roll into small balls and set aside for half an hour. Drop into boiling soup and cook for half an hour.

HEAVYWEIGHT MATZO KNAIDLACH   *Passover*

These matzo knaidlach were recorded in 1846 in the first Jewish cook book ever published (by T. W. Boone, London). The author (Mrs. Rundell) chose to be anonymous, and called the book Valuable Recipes and Hints Relating to the Toilette.

2 eggs, separated	1 tablespoon marrow fat
1/2 cup matzo meal	1 teaspoon chopped parsley
pinch of ginger	20 almonds
1/2 teaspoon salt	

Beat the yolks and whites separately (but not beyond a light froth). Add all the ingredients except the almonds and mix well. Roll into balls and tuck an almond into each ball. Set aside for 30 minutes and then drop into boiling soup. These knaidlach are not as light as the previous recipe, but they are just as good. (Makes 20.)

MATZO MEAL NOODLES   *Passover*

"Forbidden fruit is the sweetest." Come Passover, and all of a sudden there's a hankering for the forbidden noodles. So what does the Jewish woman of valor do? She makes matzo meal noodles. They aren't really noodles, but they are very tasty.

2 eggs	2 tablespoons sifted matzo
2 tablespoons water	meal
1/2 teaspoon salt	oil for frying

Beat the eggs, water, and salt lightly. Add the matzo meal. Heat the oil in a frying pan and pour in the egg-meal mixture. When brown on one side, flip the pancake over and brown the other. Roll up the pancake and cut it across like noodles. Drop into the boiling soup and cook for a couple of minutes.

Passover
BRODETTO DI PASQUA—PASSOVER SOUP GARNISH

To attend services in the Italian synagogue is a mixture of experiences. The synagogue was brought from Italy and reconstructed in Jerusalem with its ancient treasures. The service is held in the Sephardic manner, with old melodies new to Western ears. The congregation draws not only its own community, but a spellbound large number from other groups. After service on

*Passover eve, worshipers will go home to the Seder, and later on,
at dinner, be served the soup either with this garnish or with
knaidlach.*

4 matzos	*salt to taste*
8 eggs	*dash of cinnamon*
juice of 2 lemons	

Crush the matzos. Add the remaining ingredients. Let the mixture stand for at least an hour. Drop by spoonfuls into boiling
broth.

ALMOND BALLS FOR SOUP   *Passover*

*When we were children in Canada, no sweets kosher for Pass-
over were available in the shops. So it was the custom to provide
nuts for the festival, in abundance. We used to play a game
called "Nuts" in which we might gain or lose our prize. But even
if we lost, there were still almonds in the chremslach and in the
cakes and even in this soup garnish.*

1 egg, separated	*rind of 1 lemon, grated*
salt	*fat for frying*
½ cup ground almonds	

Beat up the egg yolk with the salt and mix in the ground
almonds. Whip the white to a stiff froth, and add. Add the lemon
rind. Mix well and drop, a teaspoonful at a time, into deep hot
fat until puffed and brown. Drain and serve with soup.

SOUPS

IRAQI SOUP WITH KUBEH DUMPLINGS *Shabbat*

Brillat-Savarin scorned those who ate bouillon, for such a soup was mere meat without gravy. To him a soup only began with the bouillon, and after that the vegetables and roots had to be added, with the bread or pastes or other garnishes coming later to render it more nourishing. Such a soup, he said, was a comfort to the stomach. And he came to the conclusion that there was no soup like the soups made in France. However, he had never been to Iraq to try this one, now widely served in Israel.

The Soup

 2 pounds meat, cubed
12 cups water
 3 large onions
 1 clove garlic
 4 stalks celery
 2 tablespoons oil
 2 tablespoons lemon juice
    pinch of basil

The Dumplings

½ cup fine cracked wheat
      (burghul) or semolina
   flour, if necessary
 1 onion, chopped
 4 tablespoons oil
½ pound minced or chopped
      beef or lamb
 2 tablespoons pine nuts
   dash of allspice
   salt and pepper to taste

For the soup, put the meat into the water and simmer about 1 hour. Pound the remaining soup ingredients in a mortar (or put through a mincer or blender) and add to the soup when the meat is done.

For the dumplings, soak the cracked wheat in water long enough to make it paste-like (about 1 hour). It is traditionally then pounded in a mortar with salt (but you can omit this process). Make small balls of the wheat, insert a finger, and work the wheat around and around to make jackets. (If you cannot get fine enough burghul, add a bit of flour to help hold it together.) Fry the chopped onion in the oil, add the chopped meat, and fry until it loses its red color. Add the pine nuts, allspice, salt, and pepper and mix well. Put the filling into the kubeh and smooth the coating over to close them. Flatten them somewhat and cook in the boiling soup for 20 minutes. (Serves 10.)

NOTE: Finely chopped celery and garlic may be substituted for the onion.

NOODLE SOUP MET BALLETJES—NOODLE SOUP
WITH LITTLE MEAT DUMPLINGS *Rosh Hashana*

Soup

1 *pound beef without fat*
1 *pound marrow bones*
12 *cups water*
½ *pound celery root, cut up*
2 *onions, cut up*
2 *carrots, cut up*
1 *kohlrabi, cut up*
  salt and pepper to taste
  dash of saffron, nutmeg

Balletjes

¼ *pound chopped beef*
1 *egg yolk*
1 *tablespoon water*
  dash of nutmeg
  salt and pepper to taste

Noodles

8 *ounces vermicelli*
1 *teaspoon salt*
  water for cooking

To make the soup, cook the beef and bones in the water for 1 hour. Add the remaining ingredients and cook until the vegetables are tender (about 20–25 minutes). Strain the soup and return to the heat. Add more water or seasoning to taste.

Mix all the ingredients for the balletjes and roll into balls the size of marbles. Drop them into the boiling soup. Cook the noodles separately with salt in boiling water for 9 minutes. Drain and add to the soup.

Serve at any festive meal. (Serves 8–10.)

GULYAS SOUP *Succot*

1 *pound soup meat, cubed*
¼ *cup vinegar*
3 *onions, chopped*
2 *tablespoons margarine*
1 *tablespoon paprika*
  dash of marjoram
    (*optional*)

  dash of caraway seed
1 *clove garlic, crushed*
1 *teaspoon salt*
6 *cups water*
2 *potatoes, cubed*

Cube the meat and let it marinate in the vinegar. Fry the onions in the margarine until golden but not crisp. Add the beef and brown it lightly. Add all the spices and seasonings. Simmer in the water for about two hours. Add the potatoes and cook until done (about 20 minutes). (Serves 6.)

OX TAIL SOUP   *Succot*

2 ox tails	1 parsnip, diced
3 quarts water	½ pound celery root, diced
1 bay leaf	2 carrots, diced
2 teaspoons salt	1 tablespoon flour
1 onion, diced	1 tablespoon cooking oil

Cup up the tails, cover with the water, add the bay leaf and salt and simmer until the meat is tender (2–3 hours). Add more water to keep the amount to about 10 cups. Add the vegetables, uniformly diced. When the vegetables are soft, brown the flour, add the fat, and then stir in a little soup to make a smooth paste. Add the paste to the soup and cook five minutes more. Serve the soup with pieces of meat on the bone and the vegetables. (Serves 8–10.)

YEMENITE ROSH HASHANA SOUP   *Rosh Hashana*

The Yemenites in Israel make a very hearty dish of soup. On layers of pita (pancake bread), they pour hot soup and then hilbeh. They make pita somewhat differently from other Middle Eastern peoples, so that it is very thin and leather-like.

The Pita (Salouf-Khubs)
- 6 cups flour
- 1 teaspoon salt
- 3 cups water
- ⅓ ounce yeast

The Soup
- 2 pounds meat or chicken
- 2 onions
- 4 leeks
- 10 cups water
- 1 teaspoon curry
- ¼ teaspoon pepper
- 2 teaspoons salt
- pinch of ground cardamom

The Hilbeh

2 tablespoons fenugreek flour (see Index)	garlic
	coriander
2 cups water	cumin
dash of chili pepper	tomato paste (if desired)

For the Yemenite pita: Mix all the ingredients together and set aside to rise in a warm place overnight. Roll out very very thin and bake in a very hot oven (500°) for a few minutes only. The pita is then folded up like an envelope and put into a deep soup bowl.

The soup is made thus: Cook the meat or chicken with the water and vegetables for 1½ hours. Just before removing the flesh food, add the spices and seasonings and cook a few minutes more. The soup is poured over the pita and the hilbeh over that.

For the hilbeh: Pour the water over the fenugreek flour, and after two hours pour off the liquid, leaving only the moist paste. Whip the paste and add the spices, and if desired, also tomato paste. This soup would be very hot even if it were to be served cold (as it never is)! (Serves 8–10.)

ANTIOCHUS CABBAGE SOUP   *Hanuka*

Motele Tennenbaum is the son of a leading Israeli folklorist, and it was this quip of the little boy's that gave the name to his mama's soup, or "yoich," as it is called in Yiddish. Motele simply loathed soup of any kind, and when, on Hanuka, his mother tried to coax him to eat some, he stamped his foot and said, "no, no— I'm Anti-yoich-us" (Antiochus)!

3 tablespoons oil	10 cups water
2 pounds beef	3 teaspoons salt
2 onions, shredded	dash of paprika
1 pound white cabbage, shredded	5 tablespoons sugar juice of 2 lemons

Heat the oil and brown the meat. Add the onion and cabbage and brown. Add the water, salt, and paprika and simmer until the meat is tender (2–2½ hours), adding more water if needed. Remove the meat. Mix the sugar with the lemon juice and add to the soup. (Serves 6–8.)

NOTE: Serve meat separately.

CHERVAH—BEDOUIN SOUP   *Hanuka*

6 onions, chopped	1 clove garlic, crushed
3 tablespoons cooking oil	1 cup mint sprigs
6 tomatoes, chopped	salt, pepper, cayenne
12 cups water	rice, as garnish
2 pounds mutton (tough parts)	

Fry the onions in the oil, add the tomatoes, and stew together. Put all the ingredients except the rice into a pot and simmer for 3–4 hours. Add the rice for the last ½ hour for a soup garnish. Serve pieces of the meat, cut up, in the soup. (Serves 8–10.)

CARAWAY SOUP

Succot

1½ pounds soup bone or
    meat
  1 ounce caraway seeds
 12 cups water
  1 tomato, chopped
  1 parsley root, cut up

2 carrots, chopped
1 onion, chopped
2 tablespoons flour
2 tablespoons fat
  salt to taste
  cold water

Put the meat and caraway seeds in salted water. Cook until the meat is tender (about 2 hours). Remove the meat and add the vegetables. When the vegetables are done (about 20 minutes), strain the soup. Brown the flour lightly, add the fat, and mix with a little cold water. Add to the soup. Salt to taste. Cook for five minutes more. (Serves 8–10.)

CABBAGE BORSHT

Succot

The Talmud says that "cabbage is good as a nourishing food, and beets as a remedy." It also says that "the broth of beet is pleasant to the heart and good for the eyes, and how much more so for the bowels. This is, however, only so when it remains on the stove and makes the sound of 'tuk tuk.' "

   beef bones or meat
 10 cups water
  2 pounds cabbage,
    shredded
  3 beets, grated
  3 onions, grated
  6 tomatoes, diced

1 tablespoon salt
  dash of pepper
  dash of celery salt
  juice of 1 lemon
2 tablespoons sugar
  raisins, if desired

Boil the bones in the water. After an hour add the vegetables and seasonings and cook until the cabbage is very soft (about 25 minutes). Add the lemon juice and sugar, and, if you wish, the raisins, and cook 5 minutes longer. Remove the bones and serve hot. (Serves 8.)

SNERT—DUTCH PEA SOUP

Hanuka

When the "snert," the least snooty of all soups, is on the stove, my Dutch husband turns nostalgic for his childhood, when, in his wooden shoes, he hurried to the kitchen door for a whiff of the dish. The Dutch appreciate the art of cookery not only on their table but in their painting, too, with many kitchen scenes and still-life studies of victuals. "Souper"—or supper—featured "soup," particularly the savory snert.

1 *pound split peas*	1 *pound celery root, peeled*
1 *pound head meat*	*and cut up*
½ *pound sausage*	2 *onions, peeled and cut up*
12 *cups water*	1 *slice white bread*

Cook all the ingredients together. The bread will disintegrate
and thicken the soup. Stir occasionally. Let the soup simmer
slowly for three or four hours, until the peas have dissolved.
Remove the meat and serve separately. Strain the soup and
serve with fried croutons.

SCOTCH BROTH (ISRAEL STYLE)   *Succot*

1 *cup split peas*	10 *cups cold water*
1 *pound leeks*	½ *cup pearl barley*
1 *carrot*	*salt and pepper to taste*
1 *turnip*	1 *tablespoon chopped*
2 *pounds mutton* (*lean*)	*parsley*

Soak the peas overnight and put into a large pot. Cut up all the
vegetables into small cubes or slices. Put the mutton in the pot
and add the cold water. Bring to the boil and simmer for an
hour. Add the vegetables, barley, salt and pepper and cook another half hour, or until meat is done. Remove the meat. The
soup is very hearty and thick. Add more water if you like it
thinner. Sprinkle on parsley. A good hot dish to eat in the
succah! (Serves 8.)

ZUPPA PASQUALE "DAYENU"—PASSOVER SOUP   *Passover*

Dayenu *is a beautiful hymn of thanksgiving in the Passover
Seder in which we bless God for all the good things he gave our
people, saying "If He had given us only this—*Dayenu, *it would
have been enough," "and this—*Dayenu," *recounting, one after
the other, the bountiful blessings with which He has enriched
us. When the* Dayenu *hymn is sung every housewife knows it is
time to put either the knaidlach or this garnish into the soup, for
supper is about to follow.*

3 *quarts meat or chicken*	4 *matzos*
broth	4 *egg yolks*

Break the matzos into the soup and let simmer. Beat the egg
yolks in a tureen. Pour the soup over the eggs very slowly, stirring all the time. Serve at once. (Serves 12.)

BEAN SOUP WITH TEYGLACH   *Succot*

Though far from being a festive food in Romania, where it orig-inated, this dish is so ideal for serving in the succah if the night is cold that it has won a place on the Succot menu.

The Soup

1½ cups navy or broad
        beans
  1 onion
½ pound celery root
  1 marrow bone
  5 cups water
  1 teaspoon salt
    pepper to taste

The Teyglach Garnish

3 tablespoons flour
1 egg
  salt to taste

Soak the beans overnight. Bring to the boil, with the vegetables and bone, in fresh water. Reduce heat and cook gently until the beans are soft (2–3 hours). Add salt and pepper. Put the beans and vegetables through a sieve, add water if necessary, and return to the heat. To make the teyglach, mix the flour, egg, and salt, and when the soup is boiling, drop small bits of the mixture from the end of a spoon into the soup. Reduce heat and simmer for 10 minutes. (Serves 4–6.)

BARLEY-MUSHROOM SOUP (KRUPNICK)   *Succot*

The poor Jews of Poland and Russia ate krupnick (without meat but with potatoes, beans, and groats added) even for breakfast, for they could afford nothing better except on the Sabbath.

½ cup pearl barley
½ pound celery root
  2 carrots
  2 onions
  8 dried mushrooms
  1 calf's foot

1 pound beef or 1 ox tail
12 cups water
  1 tablespoon salt
  1 bay leaf (optional)
    dash of pepper
  1 tablespoon cooking oil

Wash the barley in cold water. Dice all the vegetables. Simmer the barley, calf's foot, and beef in the water (1½–2 hours). When beef is almost tender, add the remaining ingredients (except onions) and cook until barley, vegetables, and meat are tender. Add a cup or two of water if soup evaporates too much. Fry the onions in the oil until golden and add. Cook a few min-utes more. (Serves 8–10.)

NORTH AFRICAN PASSOVER SOUP   *Passover*

Try as I might, no North African immigrant woman could give me a precise recipe for their much beloved Passover soup. This is the best I could get, and actually that is good enough, for the soup always seems to taste just right!

cabbage	salt	cooking oil
artichoke hearts	pepper	water
green beans	cinnamon	bones
leeks	cloves	pieces of lamb
onions	rose petals	broken matzo

Choose vegetables in season. Cut them up. Add all the other ingredients, using enough water to make the soup thick or thin as you desire. Simmer until the vegetables are done (30–45 minutes). Remove the bones. Add the broken matzo for garnish at table.

AVGOLEMONO (LEMON) CHICKEN SOUP   *Yom Kippur*

The Jewish community in Greece dates from the time of the first dispersion from Israel up to the creation of the Jewish state of Israel, to which most of Hitler's remnant made their way. During this long period of residence, good Greek food, like all Greek culture, was adopted by the Jews. They have introduced this lemon soup to Israel, and with growing success, for it is refreshing and stimulating in the climate. The dish is served at the post-fast Yom Kippur meal.

1	3-pound stewing chicken	
	parsley, celery, as desired	12 cups water
2	carrots, cut up	½ cup rice
2	onions, peeled	4 eggs
	salt and pepper	3 tablespoons water
		juice of 2 lemons

Cook the chicken, herbs, vegetables, and seasonings in the 12 cups of water until the chicken is done (about 2 hours). Strain the soup, add the rice, and boil 14 minutes. Remove from heat and prepare the lemon sauce as follows:

Beat the eggs and the 3 tablespoons of water until light and fluffy. Add a little hot soup gradually, continuing to beat. Then slowly pour in the lemon juice, beating all the time. Add the sauce to the remaining soup and mix well. It should be served hot but not boiled again. (Serves 8.)

NOTE: The chicken is eaten separately.

MINESTRONE   *Succot*

This Italian soup—or stew-soup, for it is so thick—dates back to the days before Paltina (mid-fifteenth century) who wrote the first cook book ever printed. In Israel it is served without cheese if meat is used in the dish, or with cheese when no meat is used.

½ cup chick-peas	½ cup shredded beets
soup bones	½ cup diced carrots
9 cups cold water	½ pound celery root, diced
2 cloves garlic, crushed	1 cup diced potatoes
1 onion, chopped	1 small squash, diced
2 tablespoons minced	2 ounces sausage, diced
parsley	1 small tin tomato purée
3 tablespoons fat	salt and pepper to taste
½ cup shredded cabbage	4 tablespoons rice
1 cup chopped spinach	

Soak the chick-peas overnight. Cook in a covered pot with the meat bones and water. Fry the garlic, onion, and parsley in the fat. Put all the ingredients except the rice into the pot and simmer slowly, well covered, until all the ingredients are soft (2–3 hours). Add the rice and simmer until done (about 20 minutes). The liquid should be reduced considerably to make a very thick soup. Noodles may be used instead of rice. (Serves 8–10.)

KAPPARAH CHICKEN SOUP   *Yom Kippur*

Orthodox Jews make an atonement sacrifice on the eve of Yom Kippur, known as the "kapparah." A cock or a hen (depending on whether the person is a man or woman) is swung thrice over the head of the penitent, with a prayer that the bird assume the role of the scapegoat, then is killed as a sin offering. These fowl are always white as a symbol of purity; one (as in Leviticus) is kept and one is given away. Soup is made of this fowl for the pre-fast meal.

1 stewing chicken	1 parsnip, cut up
salt and pepper to taste	1 summer squash, cut up
12 cups water (or more)	1 kohlrabi, cut up
2 carrots, cut up	1 sweet potato, cut up
2 onions, chopped	1 leek
½ pound celery root, cut up	

Cut up the chicken, sprinkle with salt and pepper. Simmer gently with the water and all the vegetables and seasonings. Add more water from time to time if required. Cook for 2 hours. When the chicken is done, strain the soup and serve with kreplach (*see* Index). Do not skim off the fat. (Serves 8.)

NOTE: The chicken is eaten separately, bland and plain, before the fast.

LENTIL SOUP   *Independence Day*

Lentil pottage is the world's oldest known soup; it is no longer the "mess of pottage" it once was, but a dish that varies from the plainest fare to a gourmet speciality.

1 cup red lentils	½ pound celery root,
½ pound hard smoked	chopped
sausage	1 onion, chopped
6 cups cold water	1 slice rye bread
1 bay leaf	salt and pepper
2 tomatoes, chopped	½ cup dry red wine,
1 carrot, chopped	if desired

Put all the ingredients together and simmer until the lentils are mushy. Remove the sausage and cut into cubes. Put the soup, including the vegetables, through a sieve. Reheat. Serve with croutons and the diced sausage. Gourmet housewives add a little dry red wine before serving, on a cold rainy day. (Serves 4–6.)

AVOCADO SOUP   *Passover*

This soup is a Chilean favorite becoming increasingly popular in Israel as avocado crops grow greater. Mrs. Pnina Swartz's soup (without the wine) was one of the twenty-seven regional finalists in Israel's national culinary contest.

6 cups chicken broth,	1 cup dry white wine
strained	juice of ½ lemon
3 avocados, cut up	lemon slices for garnish
salt and pepper to taste	

Heat the broth and put into a blender, together with the avocados, salt, and pepper. Blend for 3 minutes. Add the heated (but not boiled) wine and lemon juice and blend 1 minute more. Serve with lemon slices for garnish. (Serves 6–8.)

PURIM LEEK SOUP   *Purim*

*My father's family was the only Jewish one in the Carrot River
Valley in Saskatchewan, a district largely settled by Scotch immigrants. Papa was the only non-Scot invited annually to the
Bobbie Burns Banquet, because the affinity (thrift, jokes, kind-
ness) between the two peoples was so great. "Ethel," he would
say to my mother, "that cockaleekie smells like your Purim
soup."*

*And indeed, the ingredients are very similar. The Scotch ver-
sion has its origin in olden times, when the defeated cock in a
cockfight was cooked up with leeks for the feast of cockaleekie.
The Jewish origin is unknown; it is sometimes called "sour
soup."*

2 pounds chicken	2 tablespoons sugar
12 cups water	few grains citric salt or
2 leeks, slivered like	2 tablespoons vinegar
vermicelli	salt and pepper to taste
¼ cup tomato purée	2 egg yolks, beaten lightly

Cut up the chicken. Cook with all the remaining ingredients except the egg yolks. In about 2 hours, or when the chicken
literally falls apart (you can leave it in when you serve the soup,
if you wish), remove the soup from heat. Beat a little hot soup
into the egg yolks, and then pour back into the soup, mixing well.
(Serves 8–10.)

SCHORBAH—MINT SOUP   *Purim*

*In the eighteenth century a soup vendor advertised the restora-
tive powers of his wares by putting up a notice over the door of
his shop reading "Restaurant." Thus, from soup the word "Restaurant" came to be known as a place where healthful foods are
served. You will even see it in Tunis, where Schorbah mint soup
is a favorite dish.*

1 clove garlic, crushed	½ cup cold water
½ cup fresh mint leaves	salt and pepper to taste
(or 2 tablespoons	dash of cayenne
dried mint)	4 cups chicken soup
1 tablespoon olive oil	3 egg yolks
2 tablespoons cornstarch	

Fry the garlic and mint, on very low heat, in the oil about 8–10
minutes. Put through a sieve. Add the cornstarch dissolved in the

water, and the seasonings. Bring the chicken soup to the boil.
Stir in the mint mixture and cook for 5 minutes. Beat the egg
yolks and slowly add some of the soup mixture, stirring constantly. Add the yolk mixture to the soup, mix well, and serve at
once. (Serves 4.)

MALLOW (MELOKHIA) SABBATH SOUP   *Shabbat*

*The Egyptian melokhia herb is similar to the "khubeisa"—both
of the Mallow family—which kept us from starvation during the
Jerusalem siege. It makes one of the most loved soups in Middle
Eastern countries (perhaps because it grows wild in the spring-
time and is therefore available for the hungry multitudes.) You
can make the dish of spinach or chard, adding parsley generously.*

giblets of 2 chickens	*3 cloves garlic*
6 cups water	*1 small chili pepper*
1 pound mallow, spinach,	*dash of coriander*
chard, or beet greens,	*salt to taste*
with chopped parsley	

Boil the giblets in the water for 1 hour. Chop the greens and
crush the garlic. Add these to the giblets. Simmer until tender
(10–20 minutes) and remove from heat. Add the chili, salt, and
coriander. The spice will penetrate the soup even without cooking further. Heat up before serving. (Serves 6.)

LEBEN SOUP   *Shavuot*

*A most refreshing summer drink, made of leben—Israeli yoghurt.
In the settlements of Israel milk is treated to make it sour without breaking up into curds and whey. Farmers down it lustily,
ladling it up from porridge bowls at breakfast.*

4 medium cucumbers	*1 tablespoon chopped dill*
1 teaspoon salt	*4 cups leben (yoghurt)*
2 cloves garlic	*1 tablespoon chopped mint*
juice of ½ lemon	

Draw a fork down the length of the fresh cucumbers so that
when they are sliced (unpeeled) their skin is scalloped. Slice the
cucumbers thin and sprinkle with salt. Crush the garlic and add
the lemon juice, dill, and leben. Add most of the cucumbers. Put
into the blender if you wish to have an unusual texture: it should
not be too smooth. Chill and serve with the chopped mint and
remaining sliced cucumbers as garnish. (Serves 4–6.)

ISRAEL'S ONION SOUP

Hanuka

*Israel's poet laureate Israel Efrat recalls an icy day in Quebec
when half sleet and half rain chilled his bones. His wife Mildred
coaxed him into a little restaurant, where, for the first time, he
tasted the famous French onion soup. "Make it at home, Milly,"
he said, "but without croutons!"*

*Whenever it rains in Tel Aviv on a cold day, this soup goes
into the Efrats' pot, and to his acknowledgments of delight Israel
also adds, "Onion soup in the Holy Land—see how international
we are!" (And indeed, this soup has become so popular that it
comes dehydrated in packages, made in Israel.) If the day is
very, very cold, Mildred pours the soup over beaten egg yolks to
thicken and enrich it. And if the day is very, very, very cold, she
also adds a hint of brandy. I'd love to visit her when it's freezing
outdoors!*

6 large onions	6 tablespoons grated yellow
3 tablespoons butter	cheese
5 cups soup stock	2 egg yolks (optional)
	1 teaspoon brandy (optional)

Slice the onions and fry in the butter until just golden. Add the
soup stock and cook 5 minutes. Beat in the egg yolks and brandy,
if desired. Serve hot with grated yellow cheese sprinkled on top.
(Serves 4–5.) (The French float cheese on crusts of fried toast.)

SCHAV—COLD SORREL SOUP

Shavuot

1 pound sorrel leaves	salt and pepper to taste
8 cups soup stock	1 cup sour cream
1 tablespoon lemon juice	sliced hard-cooked eggs,
3 tablespoons sugar	for garnish

Chop the sorrel leaves and cook in the soup stock over low heat
for about 1 hour. Add the lemon juice, sugar, salt, and pepper.
Serve cold with sour cream, and if you wish, slices of hard-
cooked eggs for garnish. (Serves 6.)

POTATO SOUP

Succot

1 tablespoon chopped	pinch of pepper
onion	1 tablespoon chopped
2 tablespoons margarine	parsley
4 large potatoes, peeled	powdered chicken stock
and diced	(optional)

1 teaspoon salt	½ teaspoon paprika
5 cups boiling water	1 tablespoon flour

Fry the onion in half the margarine, then add to the potatoes, salt, water, pepper, and parsley. Cook until the potatoes are soft (about 20 minutes). Add the chicken stock, if desired, and the paprika. Cook ten minutes more. Make a paste of the remaining margarine and flour, and add to thicken the soup. (Serves 4–6.)

CARMEN TOMATO SOUP   *Succot*

½ cup rice	1 teaspoon sugar
4 cups water	salt and pepper to taste
4 cups soup stock	1 cup sour cream or
½ cup tomato purée	sweet cream
1 pimento, shredded	2 egg yolks
1 onion, chopped	

Cook the rice in the water for 10 minutes. Add the soup stock, tomato purée, pimento, and onion and cook until rice is soft (4–5 minutes). Add the sugar, salt, and pepper. Heat the cream and beat in the egg yolks. Stir this into the soup just after removing from the heat. Serve hot. Do not reheat: it can also be served cold. (Serves 6–8.)

SOUR CREAM BORSHT   *Shavuot*

8 medium beets	2 or more tablespoons
1 clove garlic	sugar
½ pound celery root	3 tablespoons lemon juice
1 onion	3 egg yolks
2 tomatoes (optional)	1 cup sour cream
2 teaspoons salt	fresh cucumbers, thinly
1 tablespoon vinegar	sliced, for garnish
10 cups water	

Grate all the vegetables, and cook until tender with the salt, vinegar, and water. Strain the hot soup if you wish, or leave in the vegetables. If you like, the whole can be whirled in the blender. Add the sugar and lemon juice. Beat the egg yolks, add a little of the hot soup, and then return the mixture to the pot, but do not allow it to boil. Cool. Serve chilled, with sour cream in one lump or stirred into the soup. Garnish, if you wish, with thinly sliced fresh cucumbers. (Serves 8.)

DAIRY ROSSEL BORSHT $P_{assover}$

4 cups rossel (beet sour)	*lemon juice and sugar*
(see Index)	*to taste*
2 onions, sliced thin	*sliced cucumbers*
salt and pepper to taste	*6 tablespoons sour cream*
	4 boiled potatoes (hot)

Simmer the rossel with the sliced onion for 15 minutes. Strain.
Add salt, pepper, lemon juice, and sugar to taste. Chill and serve
with a garnish of sliced cucumbers and sour cream. Serve a hot
boiled potato on the side. (Serves 4.)

HOT MEAT BORSHT S_{uccot}

3 onions, chopped	*½ cup vinegar or ⅓ cup*
6 beets, grated	*lemon juice or ¼*
6 tomatoes, diced	*teaspoon citric acid*
1 tablespoon salt	*grains*
2 pounds beef	*¼ cup sugar*
10 cups water	*6 whole potatoes*

Cook all the ingredients except the potatoes together in a large
pot. Simmer gently until the meat is done (about 2 hours). At
the end of the first hour add the potatoes. When done, remove the
meat and serve the borsht with a potato in each bowl. If you
wish to be more exacting, you can add the vinegar at the last
instead of the start of the cooking, but the color of the borsht
is better if you add it at the start. (Serves 8.)

NOTE: Use the meat for another meal.

MEAT ROSSEL BORSHT $P_{assover}$

*"He had to admit it: never before in all his life had he tasted a
borsht like this. Never. He even started to ask how you made the
borsht, what you put into it, and how long you cooked it."*
                                        —SHOLOM ALEICHEM

6 whole potatoes	*1 bay leaf*
3 cups rossel (beet sour)	*salt and pepper*
(see Index)	*lemon juice or vinegar*
2 onions, diced	*to taste*

2 carrots, diced	sugar to taste
2 pounds brisket of beef or	1 clove garlic
other soup meat	4 egg yolks
5 cups cold water	

Cook the potatoes, rossel, vegetables, and meat in the water on medium low heat until the meat is tender (about 1½ hours). Remove the meat. Add the remaining ingredients, except the egg yolks, and cook on low heat for another 10 minutes. Beat the yolks in a soup tureen and slowly add the hot soup, stirring constantly. (Serves 8.)

NOTE: Serve the meat at another time.

DRORIA CUCUMBER-CORN CHOWDER   *Shavuot*

Alexandre Dumas, in his Grand Dictionnaire de Cuisine, *tells of Sardanapalus, who decreed that "Whoever invents a new dish shall be rewarded with a thousand pieces of gold." This prize-winning dish (in the Tourist Department's contest) by Chef Cymbalista of Israel's Zim Shipping Lines, is worthy of such a reward, though it reads as if it were inspired by Dumas's cucumber dish, or Yankee chowder, or Chinese cucumber soup. Is there, indeed, nothing completely new under the sun? But even a degree of difference is noteworthy when it improves a dish.*

1 pound cucumbers	1 cup canned corn kernels
1 tablespoon fresh chopped	½ ounce cornstarch
dill	2 tablespoons water
1 medium leek	2 egg yolks, beaten
1 ounce butter	⅔ cup sour cream
2 cups milk	½ cup whipped sweet cream

Dice the cucumbers into very small cubes. Chop the dill and leek and sauté lightly in butter (do not allow to turn color). Add the cucumbers and cook for 5 minutes more, stirring often. Add the milk and corn kernels and simmer for 20 minutes. Dissolve the cornstarch in the 2 tablespoons water and add, stirring until thick. Remove the soup from heat and add a little of it to a mixture of the beaten egg yolks and the sour cream, then stir the yolk mixture into the soup. Serve at once with a topping of whipped cream. (Serves 6.)

CHLODNIK—COLD CUCUMBER SOUP   *Shavuot*

½ *pound beets*
½ *pound spinach or beet*
  greens
  water to cover
½ *cup liquid from salt dill*
  pickles or rossel (beet
  sour) (see Index)

3 *cups sour cream*
1 *bunch fresh dill, chopped*
2 *green onions, chopped*
3 *hard-cooked eggs, sliced*
2 *fresh cucumbers, sliced*
  salt and pepper to taste,
  if necessary

Cut up the beets, add the spinach, and just cover with water. Cook until tender (about 20 minutes). Whirl the beets and spinach in the blender with ½ cup of the liquid in which they were cooked. Add the liquid from the dill pickles or rossel. When quite cool, stir in the sour cream, dill, onion, eggs, and cucumbers. If necessary, add salt and pepper. Serve very cold. (Serves 4.)

NECTARED FRUIT SOUP   *Tu Besh'vat*

4 *cups diced fruits (any*
  kind)
  honey to taste

1 *cup water*
1 *cup cracked ice*

Put half the water, fruits, and honey into a blender and whirl until it becomes a liquid. Whirl the second half. Add crushed ice and swirl through the mixture. Serve, if you like, with a garnish of sour cream or whipped cream. (Serves 4–6.)

CIDER SUMMER SOUP   *Shavuot*

Cider is a new drink in modern Israel. It first became known through the writings of St. Jerome, who said it was a common drink among the Hebrews. When Mohammed forbade the drinking of alcohol, the Arabs are said to have imitated the ancient Hebrews and made cider from apples and pears. With the spread of Islam the Moors brought it from Africa to Europe. By the Middle Ages it was as popular as ale in England.

3 *cups syrup from apple*
  compote (see Index)

2 *cups apple compote*
  sectors (see Index)
3 *cups apple cider*

Chill the apple compote and then divide it into eight soup bowls. Pour on the chilled bottled cider just before serving. (Serves 8.)

ISRAELI FRUIT SOUP   *Independence Day*

*Suitable Israeli fruits for cooking in fruit soup: apples, quince,
strawberries, apricots, raspberries, mulberries, cherries, feijoa,
figs, grapes, guavas, loquats, mangoes, melons, granadilla,
peaches, pears, persimmons, plums, pomegranates, prickly pears
(sabras), rhubarb, or any dried fruits.*

3 cups of any of the above
   fruits, mixed, chopped
	3 cups orange juice
	   lemon juice to taste

8 cups water	chilled dry white wine,
3 tablespoons cornstarch sugar to taste	if desired

Boil together the fruits, water, and sugar (to taste, depending
on the sweetness of the fruits used), until tender. Press through
a sieve and return to the heat. Add the orange juice and lemon
juice to taste. Dilute the cornstarch in a little water, add to the
mixture, and bring to a boil. Cool, then chill. Serve very cold,
with a sprig of fresh mint or a topping of sour cream, in each
bowl or glass (this soup is often served as a refreshing porch
beverage). Chilled wine can be added, to taste, if desired, at
serving time. (Serves 6.)

SYCAMORE FIG SOUP   *Shavuot*

*The sycamore fig tree is native to Israel and even in Biblical times
its figs were eaten and the trees tended. The prophet Amos was
a "dresser of sycamores." During Israel's austerity days, with
years of drought, this fruit was not disdained. It is good in fruit
soups, along with other figs. The sycamore also grows in Egypt
and is known abroad as Pharaoh's fig.*

3 cups sliced sycamore and/or other figs	dash of ginger sugar to taste
3 cups water	lemon juice to taste
3 tablespoons cornstarch	2 fresh apples, grated
2 cups orange juice	sour cream, if desired

Cook the figs in the water until mushy. Add the cornstarch and
cook until clear. Whirl the mixture in the blender. Add the remaining ingredients and chill thoroughly. Serve with a garnish
of sour cream, if you like. (Serves 4–6.)

CHERRY WINE SOUP

Shavuot

1 pound red cherries
4 whole cloves
1 small stick cinnamon
1 cup sugar
5 cups water

3 tablespoons cornstarch
1 cup red wine
½ teaspoon lemon rind
lemon juice to taste
sour cream for garnish

Cook the cherries, cloves, cinnamon, sugar, and water until the cherries are tender. Remove the spices. Dissolve the cornstarch in the wine, add the lemon rind and juice and stir into the cherry liquid. Cook only until clear. Serve chilled with a topping of sour cream. (Serves 6.)

DRIE IN DE PAN—DUTCH PANCAKES *Hanuka*

2 cups self-rising flour
   pinch of salt
1 egg
1½ cups lukewarm milk

1 cup raisins
   butter for frying
   sugar as desired

Sift the flour with the salt. Make a well in the middle and pour in the egg and 1 cup of the milk. Mix to a smooth batter. Add the remaining milk and raisins. Melt butter in a heavy pan. Drop three pancakes at a time into the hot butter, turning them when they are puffed and bubbly. Fry on both sides until golden brown. Serve hot with a sprinkling of sugar. (Makes about 16 pancakes.)

MAKLA—ARAB PANCAKES *Shabbat*

A pile of makla pancakes are prepared when an Arab baby is born and served to the new mother soon after the delivery. The reason: such a good dish is sure to increase the mother's flow of milk. Now that Israel's Arab mothers have their babies in the hospital, and usually go home on Friday for their Sabbath, the pancakes greet them on arrival that day.

7 cups flour
1 cup soy flour
1 tablespoon table salt
1½ tablespoons baking
   powder
4½ cups water
3 eggs, beaten

1 pound green onions,
   chopped
½ teaspoon coarse salt
¼ teaspoon saffron
¼ teaspoon black pepper
½ teaspoon ground
   coriander seed
   soy oil for frying

Sift together the flour, soy flour, table salt, and baking powder. Gradually, as you mix the dough, add the water mixed with the beaten egg. Sprinkle the onions with coarse salt and mix well. Rinse the onions under the tap and add them to the batter. Add the remaining ingredients and mix well. Heat the soy oil and drop the batter in from a large spoon. Deep fry until golden on all sides. Serve hot.

CORNMEAL PANCAKES   *Hanuka*

*It took angels to create this dish, for when they visited Abraham
in the Negev, he "hastened into the tent unto Sarah, and said,
Make ready quickly three measures of fine meal, knead it, and
make cakes upon the hearth." Who knows—perhaps that was why
quick breads and hearth cakes (later to be called pancakes) grew
increasingly popular, like this one made of fine cornmeal, and
very fitting for Hanuka.*

1 cup flour, sifted	2 eggs
1 cup cornmeal	1 tablespoon honey
1 teaspoon baking soda	2 cups yoghurt (or part
1½ teaspoons salt	sour cream)

Mix the dry ingredients. Beat the eggs, add the honey and
yoghurt, then mix all together. Heat a heavy pan (or griddle
iron) on the stove and grease lightly. Drop the batter for the pancakes from a large spoon. When the pancake is full of bubbles,
flip it over and brown the other side. Grease the pan after each
batch of pancakes has been made. (Makes about 18 pancakes.)

BUCKWHEAT PANCAKES   *Hanuka*

*The buckwheat pancake belongs to Hanuka in Israel! And this,
notwithstanding that Brittany in France lays claim to it, as do
the Polish immigrants, who give you its original name as
"hreczuszki," to which Russian Jews in Israel take exception,
saying it was born of their own "grechnevaia."*

½ ounce fresh yeast	1½ teaspoons salt
(2 packages dry)	2 tablespoons sugar
½ cup lukewarm water	¼ cup melted margarine
2 cups cold water	1 teaspoon soda dissolved
1 cup flour	in ½ cup water
2 cups buckwheat flour	

Dissolve the yeast in the lukewarm water and add the cold water.
Sift together the flour, buckwheat flour, and salt and stir in. Beat
well until smooth. Cover and refrigerate overnight, and in the
morning stir in the sugar, margarine, and dissolved soda. Let
stand at room temperature for half an hour and then drop from
a spoon onto a hot greased griddle or thick pan. As soon as the
pancakes are bubbly and puffed, turn and brown on the other
side. (Makes about 32 pancakes.)

POTATO LATKES *Hanuka*

How did the Hanuka pancake of yore become a raw potato latke in recent years, since the discovery of the spud? Because potatoes are ideal cold-weather food, and so good with greben (cracklings) and applesauce, both at their peak at this season. But in Shannon, at the airport stop, I was told that "boxy on the pan" was the forerunner of all potato pancakes, and that indeed most potato dishes are Irish. In fact, some Irish even claim to be one of the lost tribes of Israel—can evidence of this be the Hanuka potato latke?

6 *medium potatoes*	*dash of ginger or nutmeg*
½ *teaspoon baking soda*	*(optional)*
2 *onions, chopped*	½ *cup flour*
(optional)	*salt and pepper to taste*
2 *eggs*	*fat for deep frying*

Peel the potatoes and grate very fine. Sprinkle with the soda and squeeze out the excess liquid. Mix with all the other ingredients. Drop the batter by spoonfuls into hot fat and fry until pancakes are crisp on the outside. Drain on paper and serve hot with applesauce. Good warmed over, too. (Serves 6–8.)

COOKED POTATO LATKES *Hanuka*

It is said that the reason fried cakes and pancakes are served on Hanuka is because the oil used in the frying is symbolic of the oil in the cruse in the Temple, which was enough for only one day but sufficed, by a miracle, for eight.

1 *large onion, chopped*	2 *cups mashed potatoes*
3 *tablespoons chicken fat*	*salt and pepper to taste*
2 *tablespoons self-rising flour*	2 *eggs, beaten*

Fry the onion in some of the fat until golden. Mix all the ingredients together. Form into pancakes and fry in the remaining hot chicken fat. Drain. Serve with applesauce and meat or fowl. (Serves 4.)

CZECH HANUKA LATKES (PANCAKES) *Hanuka*

3 *large potatoes*	*rind and juice of 1 lemon*
3 *eggs*	*salt*
1 *tablespoon sugar*	*goose fat, if obtainable*

Boil and mash the potatoes. Add the eggs, sugar, salt, lemon juice, and grated rind. Fry in hot goose (or other) fat. (Serves 4.)

APFEL SCHMARREN—APPLE PANCAKES   *Hanuka*

This German pancake is tasty, but is often remembered in Israel with bitter tears.

1 *cup self-rising flour*	*2 tablespoons butter,*
dash of salt	*melted*
3 eggs	*powdered sugar*
1 cup milk	*lemon juice*
2 large apples, sliced	

Mix the flour and salt. Add the eggs and milk and beat until smooth. Stir in the apples. Put the butter into a baking pan and pour in the pancake mixture. Bake in a medium oven for about 15 minutes, or until the pancake puffs up at the sides and is crisp and brown. Tear apart with 2 forks and sprinkle with sugar and lemon juice. (Serves 4–6.)

Hanuka — Passover
LABTAH—POTATO WALNUT PANCAKES

This is a Georgian dish usually served on Passover, but in Israel the treat will turn up also on Hanuka at the family table. It is made into one big pancake.

2 tablespoons suet	*3 eggs*
1 tablespoon cooking oil	*1 cup chopped walnuts*
3 potatoes, boiled	*salt and pepper*

Put the suet in a heavy pan to melt. Add the oil and heat well. Meanwhile mash the potatoes, mix in the eggs and walnuts, and add the salt and pepper. Pour onto the hot fat and fry until the pancake is well crusted and golden. Turn over and fry until the other side is also crusted. Serve hot. (Serves 4.)

ALSATIAN SPONGE DUMPLINGS
Succot

Dumplings cooked in broth and served with a piece of hot corned beef have long been a hearty cottage dish. It was a dish that made Dickens nostalgic for his childhood. Sponge dumplings vary in texture; the Alsatian ones (the real Alsatian ones) are heavier even than those in this recipe.

3 cups flour, sifted	milk
1 teaspoon salt	crumbs
2 large eggs	oil for frying

Mix the flour and salt and add the eggs. Add enough milk to be able to stir—even though with difficulty—with a spoon. When the dough is elastic, set it aside for a couple of hours to rest. Drop from a spoon into boiling water or broth and cook 5 minutes. Drain well. Fry in oil until golden, then roll in bread crumbs.

THE GANEF KNAIDLE
Shabbat

Once upon a time, a century ago, the huge dumpling today known as the knaidle, was called a "ganef"—a thief—when it was cooked in the Sabbath cholent or tzimmes, or next to a kishke or a roasting chicken. It received this title because the coarse lump of dough stole succulent flavors from the fat, the meat, and the vegetables in the pot, to emerge enriched, puffed, and delightful upon the festive board.

¾ cup self-rising flour	3 tablespoons water
¼ cup semolina	½ cup chopped fat
salt and pepper to taste	dash of ginger
1 egg, beaten	

Mix all the ingredients together and put the resulting lump of dough into the cholent or tzimmes or what-you-will in the meat and vegetable pot, after the other ingredients have come to a boil. Let the ganef stew in the juice of its neighbor as long as that cooks.

POTATO DUMPLINGS (KARTOFFEL KLOESSE)   *Succot*

8 medium potatoes, cooked
   and cooled
2 eggs
1 teaspoon salt

4 tablespoons semolina
1 tablespoon oil or chicken
   fat
1 cup flour

Grate the cold cooked potatoes and beat the eggs. Mix all the ingredients. Form into balls. Cook in boiling salted water 10–15 minutes. Serve plain, fried, or rolled in fried crumbs, as a side dish to meat or fowl. (Serves 10–12.)

PAPANUSH—SEMOLINA DUMPLINGS   *Shavuot*

2 cups milk
1 cup semolina
¼ cup margarine
½ teaspoon salt

4 eggs
1 cup cottage cheese
   sour cream
   honey

Heat the milk and slowly stir in the semolina, stirring constantly. Add the margarine and salt and cook until the mixture is thick. Cool to lukewarm. Beat the eggs well and sieve the cottage cheese into them. Stir into the lukewarm mush. Shape into small dumplings and make a dent in each with your thumb. Boil in salted water 20–25 minutes. Serve hot with a pat of butter in each thumb-well, and in a sauce of sour cream and honey, mixed. (Serves 6.)

SCHNITZEL-KLOESE—CUT-UP FRUIT DUMPLINGS   *Shabbat*

Maimonides, who was a doctor, a researcher, a philosopher, and a Biblical scholar, would have been dead-set against this dish containing suet and cooked dough. He traced cooked doughs to Persia, and advised against their use. He also deplored the eating of animal fats. Did he know about cholesterol and calories a thousand years ago?

This is a Sabbath dish that cooks overnight in a hay box or Dutch oven or (in Israel) on a very low oil-burner flame. It was introduced to Israel by Orthodox German Jews. The measurements need not be exact, since taste varies in such a dish.

1 cup flour
½ teaspoon baking powder
½ cup suet, chopped

3 or 4 tablespoons water,
   plus water to cover
   chicken fat

¼ teaspoon salt
   dash of nutmeg
2 tablespoons sugar, plus
   sugar to taste

cut-up dried fruits: prunes,
peaches, pears, apricots

Mix the flour, baking powder, suet, salt, nutmeg, the 2 table-spoons sugar, and the 3 or 4 tablespoons water to make a dough. Divide into three or four large kloese and fry in chicken fat, to brown a bit on all sides. Put into a casserole with the chicken fat and top with the cut-up ("geschnitzeled") dried fruits and sugar to taste. Cover with water. Bring to a boil and then put into a hay box or Dutch oven or in a Shabbat oven over low heat and cook covered, overnight.

ORANGE DUMPLINGS   *Hanuka*

2 cups flour, sifted
   dash of salt
4 teaspoons baking powder

grated peel of 1 orange
2 eggs, beaten
1 cup orange juice

Sift the dry ingredients together and mix in the grated orange peel. Combine the eggs with the orange juice and add. Mix lightly to make a soft dough. Drop by tablespoonfuls into boil-ing water if you wish to eat them as a separate dish, or into a stew of meat and vegetables. Cook for about 8 minutes. (Serves 6.)

BOILED APPLE DUMPLINGS   *Succot*

2 pounds potatoes
6 apples, peeled and
   quartered
   sugar
   margarine for frying

2 eggs
1 teaspoon salt
1 cup flour
   cinnamon
   breadcrumbs, fried

Boil the potatoes in their jackets. While the potatoes are cook-ing, sprinkle the apples with sugar and fry lightly in the mar-garine. Grate or mash the potatoes. Mix in the eggs, salt, and flour. Knead until smooth. Roll out the dough and cut into thick rounds. Put an apple quarter, dash of cinnamon, and sprinkling of sugar on each round. Fold the edges and pinch together firmly to make a ball. Cook in boiling water for ten minutes. Serve with a sprinkling of fried breadcrumbs and sugar. (Serves 6.)

NOTE: A stoned apricot or plum that has been filled with sugar may be substituted for each apple quarter.

BAKED APPLE DUMPLINGS

Purim

The Dough

 2 cups self-rising flour,
   sifted
   pinch of salt
 4 tablespoons sugar
 ½ cup margarine
 ¾ cup water or milk

The Filling and Sauce

 8 small apples, peeled and
   cored
 1 cup water
 1 cup sugar
 1 teaspoon vanilla

Mix the flour, salt, and sugar. Cut in the margarine. Add the water or milk all at once and mix. Roll out on a floured board and cut into squares large enough to hold a small apple. Peel and core apples, then place each one on a square of dough and fill the core with sugar. Bring up the corners of the dough and pinch all the edges together. Place the apples in a greased baking dish. To make the sauce, mix the water with the vanilla and remaining sugar. Pour over the dumplings and bake in a 400° oven until the dumplings are crisp (about ½ hour). Serve hot. (Serves 8.)

BOYRISCHI DAMPFNUDLEN — *Shavuot*

This dish is called "boyrischi" because it is the Yiddish word for "peasants"—who made the dish and taught it to the Jews.

1 ounce fresh yeast (or 2 packages dry)	1 egg, slightly beaten
¾ cup sugar	6 cups flour, sifted
2 cups lukewarm milk	4 tablespoons margarine
4 tablespoons butter	1 cup cold water or milk
1 teaspoon salt	½ pound dried prunes

Crumble the yeast with 1 teaspoon of the sugar and ½ cup of the warm milk and set it aside to swell. Add the butter to the remaining warm milk, stir in remaining sugar, the salt, and the egg. Combine with the yeast mixture. Add the flour gradually and work to make a smooth elastic dough. Cover with a cloth and set to rise until doubled in bulk. Roll out on a floured board and cut into rather broad noodles. Butter a pot with the margarine, put in the noodles, and allow to rise again for a hour. Pour the cold water or milk over, add the dried fruit, cover, and put into a 350° oven. After about 30 minutes, the liquid will evaporate and the noodles will begin to sizzle. Remove the cover and bake until the noodles are browned (about 15 minutes). (Serves 6–8.)

SAVORY LOKSHEN (NOODLE) KUGEL — *Shabbat*

4 cups broad noodles	salt and pepper
boiling water, salted	dash of nutmeg
4 eggs, well beaten	(optional)
¾ cup chicken fat or margarine, melted	

Boil the noodles in salted water for 9 minutes. Drain. Mix with the eggs, melted fat, and seasonings. Bake in a greased casserole in a 375° oven until golden (about 20 minutes). Serve hot, warm, or cold, with the main course. (Serves 6–8.)

HOMEMADE NOODLES *Shabbat*

How nostalgic are the memories of Mama making noodle dough! The whole house was covered with white sheets draped over every table, chair, couch, and bed. On these the round sheets of dough dried before they were folded and cut into broad noodles for kugel and fine ones for soup. For how many generations did this go on? Records dating back to the year 1500 in Poland refer to frimsels *or* farfel *and* lokshen *(noodles) as favorite Jewish dishes! Today in Israel few women (except farmers' wives who have to use up a lot of cracked eggs quickly) make* lokshen, *since a top-quality product is locally manufactured and widely exported.*

4 cups flour	2 tablespoons cold water
4 eggs	

Sift the flour into a heap. Make a well in the center and put in the eggs and water. Work into a dough and knead until elastic. Roll out thinly on a floured board. Put the sheets to dry somewhat for about 30 minutes on a floured cloth. Fold over lightly and cut into noodles with a very sharp knife. Sprinkle the noodles on the floured cloth and let dry until hard.

NOTE: Farfel is made as above, but an additional cup of flour is used in the dough. The dough is formed into a ball, left to dry and harden a little for 30 minutes, coarsely grated or chopped fine in a wooden bowl, and then dried. It is used as a soup garnish or a side dish, like noodles.

MANNA NOODLES *Purim*

Poppy seed is a symbol of manna, and indeed tastes like something very special in this dish.

6 cups water	4 tablespoons poppy seed
1 teaspoon salt	4 tablespoons butter
½ pound noodles	3 tablespoons sugar

Boil the water, add the salt and noodles, and cook for 10 minutes. Drain and toss in the poppy seed and butter and mix well. Serve with a sprinkling of sugar. Ground almonds or walnuts may be substituted for the poppy seed. (Serves 4.)

NOODLES WITH COTTAGE CHEESE   *Shavuot*

½ *pound broad noodles*	½ *pound cottage cheese*
2 *eggs*	½ *cup sugar*
dash of salt	*raisins and chopped*
2 *cups milk*	*almonds, if desired*
2 *tablespoons margarine*	

Cook the noodles until almost done, then drain. Beat the eggs, then add the salt and milk. Mix with the remaining ingredients, adding raisins and chopped almonds, if desired. Pour into a buttered baking dish and bake in a 375° oven until the pudding sets off from the sides of the pan (about 30 minutes). (Serves 6.)

NOTE: Boiled noodles are also very good with cheese and sour cream stirred in just before serving (no baking needed). Sugar is added to taste.

NOODLES AND MUSHROOMS   *Hanuka*

"Love is grand, but love with noodles is even better," goes a Yiddish saying. In the nineteenth century, it was considered that one of the virtues of a bride was her ability to make good noodles for the Sabbath, and indeed the mother-in-law-to-be made it a test to see how the bride-to-be could roll out the noodle dough.

A hoary legend set this theme, for it is related that Isaac took Rebekah to the tent of his mother Sarah, where the bride showed herself worthy to be her successor: the blessing that had hovered over the dough kneaded by Sarah returned with Rebekah, light shone in the tent, and its gates were again widely opened for the needy and weary, to eat and rest.

½ *pound noodles*	4 *tablespoons butter*
salt and pepper to taste	1 *tablespoon flour*
½ *pound mushrooms*	½ *cup top milk*

Boil the noodles in salted water 9 minutes. Drain and add salt and pepper to taste. Meanwhile slice the mushrooms and lightly sauté them in the butter (5 minutes). Add the flour, and when it bubbles gradually pour in the milk, stirring constantly, until thickened. Pour this sauce over the noodles and serve hot. (Serves 4.)

NOTE: The flour and milk may be omitted and the noodles covered with the sautéed mushrooms and butter.

KASHA VARENITCHKES—NOODLES AND GROATS *Hanuka*

Varenitchkes are often confused with varenikis, but the only thing they have in common is that the dough is the same—a good egg-noodle dough. On Hanuka in the Balkan lands and in Russia, varenitchkes are eaten even more than latkes (potato pancakes). Kasha are buckwheat groats, and are more commonly known as "grechnevaia kasha." This dish is often made with goose fat or greben (cracklings) and fried onions, instead of kasha.

The Dough

2 *cups flour*
2 *eggs*
   pinch of salt
1 *tablespoon water*

The Kasha

1 *cup buckwheat groats*
1 *cup chopped onions*
5 *tablespoons chicken fat*
   boiling water
   (about 4 cups)
1 *teaspoon salt*
   dash of pepper

For the noodle dough, sift the flour and make a well in the center. Add the eggs, salt, and water and work into the flour. Knead. Roll out the dough. Cut into squares and allow to dry while you prepare the kasha.

For the kasha, put the groats in a 350° oven to toast to a light brown (about 20 minutes). Meanwhile, fry the onions in the chicken fat. Add to the groats and stir, allowing the mixture to toast a minute. Add the boiling water to the groats, which will swell to double their size, and leave in the oven for a few minutes more. Season with salt and pepper. Cook the dough squares in boiling salted water, and when done, mix with the kasha and serve hot. (Serves 6–8.)

MILINA—TUNISIAN NOODLE-CHICKEN BAKE *Succot*

2 *large onions, chopped*
1 *bunch parsley, chopped*
4 *tablespoons cooking oil*
1 *calf's brain, cooked*
1 *chicken breast, cooked*

8 *ounces noodles, boiled*
3 *hard-cooked eggs, sliced*
5 *raw eggs*
   salt and pepper

Fry the onion and parsley in the oil until golden. Dice the brain and chicken breast fine and add to the first mixture. In a greased casserole put alternate layers of noodles, meat mixture, and hard-cooked egg slices. Finish with a topping of noodles. Beat the raw eggs, add the seasoning, and pour over the mixture. Bake in a 250° oven for about 45 minutes. (Serves 4.)

TIMBALLO DI TAGLIATELLI   *Succot*

This is one of the many pasta dishes from the Italian Jewish kitchen that have been introduced to Israel, where we, too, make very fine noodles.

1 pound very fine noodles	*1 cup mixed pine nuts and*
4 tablespoons (or more)	*raisins*
hot chicken fat	*½ pound salami, sliced*

Cook the noodles for 5 minutes and drain. Pour the hot fat into a shallow baking dish, spread on the noodles, and top with the raisins and nuts, then the sliced salami. Bake in a 375° oven about 15 minutes. When the bottom is crusted, turn the whole over and continue to bake in a 325° oven another 30 minutes. (Serves 8.)

NOTE: Almonds (slivered) may be substituted for pine nuts.

RUOTA DI FARAONE—PHARAOH'S WHEEL   *Ju Besh'vat*

This casserole is symbolic of the wheel of Pharaoh's fate. The sauce is reminiscent of the Red Sea, the black raisins and white nuts swimming in the gravy represent the Egyptians and their steeds. As this dish is eaten on Shabbat Beshalach, when the portion of the Law pertaining to this event is chanted in the Synagogue, it can be kept in a warming oven overnight (in plenty of sauce).

½ pound narrow egg	*6 ounces goose sausage*
noodles (tagliarini)	*(or salami),*
2½ cups meat gravy	*thinly sliced*
½ cup raisins	*½ cup pine nuts*

Boil the noodles 9 minutes. Drain. In a greased casserole put alternate layers of the noodles, meat gravy, and sausage, sprinkled with raisins and pine nuts. The top layer should be of noodles, with a circular border of sausage. Heat in a 400° oven 15–20 minutes. The dish should have plenty of gravy, as it must be succulent. (Serves 4–6.)

ROAST FARFEL   *Hanuka*

3 onions, chopped
4 tablespoons chicken fat
1 cup dry farfel
  (*see* Homemade Noodles
  recipe)

2 cups soup or water
1 teaspoon salt
  pepper if desired

Fry the onions in the chicken fat on very low heat. Add the farfel and fry it lightly. When brown, pour on the soup or water and cook until the farfel swells to double its size (about 20 minutes). Add the salt and pepper and serve with meat. (Serves 4.)

BEN-GURION'S RICE   *Shavuot*

Eastern Jews in Israel felt the scarcity of rice more than any other shortage in the austerity days. Israel's leading macaroni manufacturers thereupon made pasta into the shape of rice, both white and toasted. Israelis soon dubbed it "Orez Ben-Gurion" and the mock-rice has remained as popular as the former Prime Minister.

1 teaspoon salt
6 cups boiling water
¼ pound rice-shaped pasta
1 tablespoon butter
  salt and pepper to taste

1 egg, beaten
1½ cups yoghurt or sour
  cream
  cottage cheese, if desired

Add the salt to the boiling water, and when cooking rapidly, add the rice-shaped pasta. Cook for 5 minutes and drain in a colander. Add the remaining ingredients and bake in a 350° oven for about 30 minutes. Cottage cheese is sometimes added to this recipe, if desired. (Serves 2–3.)

Hanuka
LIVER KNISHES MIT NESHOMES—PÂTÉS WITH SOULS

Jewish women lay claim to the knish, especially the one like the "knaidle (dumpling) with a soul." Alas, I have to destroy that grand illusion, for the knish is the scion of the aristocratic "pâté de foie gras with a soul," first created in 1762 for Contades, Marshal of France, while he was serving in Alsace. The foie gras was surrounded by chopped veal and encased in an "armor" of baked pastry, with a truffle tucked into the pâté for a "soul." But who knows, I may be wrong, for maybe the noble dish was copied from the Jews of Strasbourg? Here's an Israeli version:

The Pastry

1 *cup margarine*
3 *cups flour, sifted*
1 *cup boiling water*
4 *tablespoons melted*
margarine

The Topping

1 *egg yolk*
6 *tablespoons sesame seed*

The Filling

1 *cup chopped goose liver*
and other meat, chicken
or lung
1 *onion, chopped*
salt and pepper
1 *egg*
small cracklings

To make the pastry, mix the margarine with the flour and add the boiling water. Work into a dough and refrigerate for one to three days. Roll very thin, spread with melted margarine, and cut into squares for individual knishes.

For the filling, grind the liver and other meat and onion. Season and mix in the egg. Put a tablespoon of this mixture on each pastry square and tuck a small crackling (greben) in the middle, for the "soul." Bring the corners of the dough together and seal each knish into a ball. Turn over and pat down somewhat. Brush the tops with egg yolk and sprinkle with sesame seed. Bake in a 350° oven about 30 minutes. Serve warm. (Makes 18–20 medium-size knishes.)

SOY MUSHROOM STRUDEL   *Shabbat*

The Dough

½ *pound potatoes*
4 *tablespoons margarine*
1 *tablespoon salt*
4 *tablespoons water*
1 *cup flour*
¾ *cup soy flour*
2 *raw eggs, beaten*

The Filling

1 *cup chopped onion*
1 *cup sliced mushrooms*
¼ *cup melted margarine*
2 *cups ground cooked meat*
2 *hard-cooked eggs, mashed*
salt and pepper

For the dough, peel and boil the potatoes and put them through a sieve. Add the margarine and mix well. Add the remaining ingredients and work into a dough. Roll out on a floured board.

For the filling, fry the onion and mushrooms in the margarine. Add the remaining ingredients and mix well. Cover the pastry with the mushroom filling. Roll up the dough as you would any strudel and bake in a 350° oven until golden. (Serves 6.)

SPINACH BOREKAS (TURNOVERS) *Independence Day*

Borekas are a Spanish Jewish dish very similar to the Turkish burek. They can be made of paper-thin strudel dough, flaky pastry, a rich noodle dough, or the following:

Dough

½ pound margarine
1 teaspoon salt
3 cups self-rising flour
  lukewarm water

Filling

½ cup grated Caccio-Cavello
  (Katzkaval) cheese
1 cup cooked spinach
3 egg yolks

For the pastry, melt the margarine and rub into the flour and salt. Add just enough lukewarm water to make a dough that can be rolled. Roll out on a floured board and cut into rounds. Mix the ingredients for the filling (any yellow cheese or cottage cheese may be used instead of the customary Caccio-Cavello) and put a spoonful in the center of each round of pastry. Fold over each round and pinch to form a half circle. Dilute another egg yolk with water and brush the tops of the borekas with this. Sprinkle with sesame seeds and bake on a buttered pan in a 375° oven, until golden brown (20–25 minutes). The borekas are best eaten hot. Fillings are sometimes made of yellow and cottage cheese only, or of meat, or of meat and spinach.

PUMPKIN PESTELLES (TURNOVERS) *Rosh Hashana*

Israelis from Greece, like those from Turkey, serve patties of green spinach, white leeks, and yellow pumpkin as symbols of the color variety of the first fruits of the season, which are blessed on Rosh Hashana. Sometimes the vegetables are put into pestelles, or turnovers, and are either fried or baked. As these pestelles are eaten hot or cold, at meals or between them, the vegetables are often mixed with cottage or "feta" cheese.

Filling

1 pound pumpkin, cut up
½ cup olive oil
½ cup water
½ cup sugar
1 teaspoon cinnamon

Pastry

⅓ cup olive oil
1 cup water
3 cups self-rising flour
1 tablespoon sugar

    oil and diluted egg yolk for glazing

Cook the pumpkin with the oil, water, sugar, and cinnamon until all the liquid is absorbed and the vegetable mushy. For the pastry: Mix all the ingredients until well blended. Roll out the dough to about 1/4 inch in thickness. Cut into rounds and put a tablespoon of the filling on each round. Fold over and press the edges together. Brush with oil and diluted egg yolk, and bake in 400° oven 20 minutes, or until golden. Or fry in olive oil. (Serves 4–6.)

Rosh Hashana
PESTELLES (TURNOVERS) WITH BRAINS

While in some countries a sheep's or fish's head is served on Rosh Hashana, many families in Greece serve pestelles—baked turnovers—filled with brains for the same symbolic reason.

1 calf's brain	dash of oregano or sweet
juice of 2 lemons	basil
6 hard-cooked eggs, mashed	salt and pepper to taste
2 tablespoons melted	1 recipe pestelle pastry
margarine	(see preceding recipe)
1 teaspoon chopped parsley	

Put the brain in cold water for about an hour, then remove the membrane. Cook, with the lemon juice, over low heat in boiling salted water about 10 minutes, then cool in the water. Drain and cut the brain up into very small pieces. Mix with the eggs, melted margarine, herbs, and seasoning.

Roll out the pastry 1/4 inch thick. Cut into rounds. Place some of the filling on each, fold over and pinch the edges together. Brush the tops of the pestelles with diluted egg yolk if you want a golden glow on them, then bake in a 400° oven about 20 minutes. (Serves 4–6.)

POTATO KNISHES
Succot

1/2 cup chopped onions	1 teaspoon salt
5 tablespoons chicken fat	dash of pepper
2 cups mashed potatoes	dough
2 eggs	(*See* Liver Knishes)

Lightly fry the onions in the fat, and mash into the potatoes. Mix in the eggs, salt, and pepper. Prepare the dough and cut into rounds. Put a tablespoon of the potato filling into each and pinch the edges together. Brush the knishes with oil and bake in a 375° oven 30 minutes, or until golden brown. (Serves 6–8.)

CHICKEN LIVER KNISHES *Rosh Hashana*

Filling

2 *onions, chopped*
   a few mushrooms,
      chopped (*optional*)
6 *tablespoons margarine*
½ *pounds chicken livers*
1 *teaspoon salt*
   dash of pepper
½ *rusk or piece of dry bread*

Pastry

2 *cups flour, sifted*
1 *teaspoon baking powder*
   dash of salt
2 *eggs*
½ *cup oil*
2 *tablespoons water*

diluted egg yolk for glazing

For the filling: Brown the onions and mushrooms in half the margarine. Remove. Brown the lightly grilled livers in the remaining margarine. Add the seasonings. Put the onions, mushrooms, and livers through meat chopper, along with the half rusk or piece of dry bread.

For the dough: Mix the dry ingredients and make a well in the center. Put in the eggs, oil, and water and work into a smooth dough. Roll the dough out thin, brush with oil, and cut into rounds. Place a tablespoon of filling on each round and pinch the edges together in the middle. Brush the tops with diluted egg yolk and bake on an oiled pan, pinched sides down, in a 350° oven 30–35 minutes, or until nicely browned.

KASHA KNISHES *Hanuka*

3 *eggs*
1 *cup buckwheat groats*
   (*kasha*)
7 *large potatoes*
1 *tablespoon margarine*

salt and pepper to taste
1 *teaspoon baking powder*
   flour as needed
6 *medium onions, chopped*

Beat one egg and mix with the buckwheat groats, then put into a 300° oven. When dry, break up the lumps with a spoon and cover with boiling water. Return to the oven to dry once more. Boil and mash the potatoes. Add the two remaining eggs, and the margarine, salt, and pepper. When cooled, add the baking powder and just enough flour to be able to roll the mixture on a board. Fry the onions in oil or margarine, add the groats mixture, mix well, and correct the seasoning. Roll out the potato dough and cut into 2½-inch squares. Place 1 tablespoon of the groats mixture in the center of each square, then pull up the corners and pinch the edges together. Bake, in a greased pan, in a 350° oven until golden (about 20 minutes). (Serves 8.)

MANICOTTI—ITALIAN "BLINTZES" *Shavuot*

The Batter

1 cup flour
1⅓ cups milk
4 eggs, well beaten
2 tablespoons melted butter
1 teaspoon salt

The Filling

1 pound ricotta-type cheese
2 eggs, beaten
½ cup grated Parmesan cheese
½ cup chopped parsley
1 teaspoon salt

3 cups tomato sauce (see Index for tomato sauces)

Mix all the ingredients for the batter. Grease a heavy pan. Pour in a small ladle of batter and tilt the pan to spread the batter. Fry one side and remove to a large platter, piling up the pancakes.

Mix all the ingredients for the filling. Spread a spoonful on each pancake as for blintzes, roll up, and put them into a casserole. Pour sauce over. Bake in a 375° oven 30 minutes. Serve hot. (Serves 4–6.)

SAUERKRAUT KNISHES OR PIROGEN *Succot*

The Crust

1 egg
½ cup sour cream
2 tablespoons margarine, melted
½ teaspoon salt
1½ cups flour, sifted
milk or diluted egg

The Filling

2 cups sauerkraut
1 onion, chopped
3 tablespoons butter
1 tablespoon brown sugar
dash of pepper

To make the crust, beat the egg, and add the sour cream, margarine, salt, and flour. Roll the dough out rather thin on a floured board. Cut into large rounds.

For the filling, rinse and drain the sauerkraut very well. Fry the onion in the butter and then add the sauerkraut. Cook on low heat 20 minutes. Add the sugar and pepper and stew until the kraut is golden. Cool and then put a portion of the filling in the center of each round. Fold over and pinch the edges together to form half moons. Brush the tops of the pirogen with milk or diluted egg and bake on a greased tin in a 375° oven for about 30 minutes. (Serves 4–6.)

PIEROGI, PIROGEN—PASTRY POCKETS   *Shavuot*

An argument is sure to arise if you ask women from Poland, Russia, Lithuania, and America about pierogi, pirogen, piroshki! One will tell you there is no difference except in size; another will say it is a matter of yeast dough or noodle dough; the third will tell you it is a matter of baking or boiling. The fourth will settle the quarrel by suggesting that these pastry pockets no longer be called by their Gentile names but referred to henceforth in Yiddish as either kreplach or knishes, and never mind the shape—it's the taste that counts!

The Dough	The Shavuot Filling
2 cups flour, sifted	2 cups cottage cheese
2 eggs	2 egg yolks
lukewarm water	2 tablespoons margarine
	2 tablespoons sugar
Topping	dash of salt
sugar	raisins, if desired
cinnamon	
sour cream	

To make a stiff dough, mix the flour, eggs, and a few tablespoons of lukewarm water. Roll out thin on a floured board and cut into rounds.

Mix all the filling ingredients together and put a spoonful of filling on each round. Fold over and press the edges together to make half moons. Cook in slightly salted boiling water. When the pierogi rise to the top, remove and serve with sugar, cinnamon, and sour cream. (Serves 6.)

PIROSHKI—BAKED PASTRY POCKETS

The Pastry	The Filling
1 cake yeast	2 pounds potatoes, cooked
(or 2 packages dry)	2 onions
6 tablespoons sugar	3 tablespoons margarine
2 cups lukewarm milk	½ cup grated yellow cheese
4 cups flour	4 tablespoons cottage cheese
4 eggs, beaten	
½ cup margarine	
dash of salt	
1 teaspoon vanilla	
1 egg yolk diluted with	
water (optional)	

To make the pastry, dissolve the yeast with the sugar and a little of the warm milk. Sift the flour. Add the milk and yeast mixture and mix well. Put to rise in a warm place for 30 minutes, then add the remaining pastry ingredients and knead until the dough is elastic. Cover and set in a warm place to rise until double in bulk. Roll out the dough and cut it into rounds.

Mash the potatoes. Fry the onions in the margarine and mix with the potatoes and cheeses. Put a tablespoon of the filling on each pastry round. Fold over the piroshki to make half moons and press the edges together. If you want a good color, brush the tops with diluted egg yolk. Bake in 350° oven about 30 minutes. Serve with sour, plain, or sugared cream, or with any favorite confiture added to the cream. (Makes about 40 piroshki.)

FRUIT PURIM KREPLACH (VARENIKIS)   *Purim*

1 recipe kreplach dough	cherry or apricot jam
(see Index)	(with fruit pieces in it)
	breadcrumbs

If the jam is firm you will need very few crumbs. If it is runny, add more. Cut the noodle dough into squares and place some of the fruit and crumb mixture in the center of each. Fold over into triangles and pinch the edges together. Bring two ends together to make a little purse shape. Drop into salted boiling water and cook until the kreplach rise to the top. Serve hot, with butter or a sprinkling of sugar. (Serves 6–8.)

MEAT-FILLED KREPLACH   *Yom Kippur*

1 egg	1 tablespoon chopped onion
1 cup flour, sifted	2 tablespoons oil
pinch of salt	salt and pepper to taste
1 cup chopped cooked beef	
or chicken	

Make a dough of the egg, flour, and salt. Knead well and roll out thin. Cut into squares of about two inches. Mix the remaining ingredients. Place a spoonful of this mixture on each square. Fold over to make triangles and pinch the cut edges together. Pinch together two corners of the triangles to make heart-shaped purses. Drop into boiling water or soup and cook for 20 minutes.

CHEESE KREPLACH

Purim

"Look, it may not be proper, for after all we're Jews, to talk about milk and dairy things while we're eating meat, but I'd like to have your frank opinion: what do you think of cheese kreplach? With such kreplach my traveller had to admit that it was all true: indeed, he has a wife too, and she makes kreplach too, but how can you compare hers to these? It's like night and day."

—SHOLEM ALEICHEM

The Dough

2 cups flour
1 egg
2 tablespoons cold water
  pinch of salt

The Filling

2 cups cottage cheese
3 tablespoons sour cream
1 egg
  pinch (or more) of salt

To make the dough, sift the flour into a pile and make a well in the middle. Put in the egg, water, and salt. Work into a dough. Roll rather thin and cut into squares of about 2 inches. Mix all the ingredients for the filling and put a spoonful in the middle of each square. Fold over into triangles and pinch the edges together. Bring two points together to form a little purse. Drop the kreplach into boiling water, one at a time. Cook for about 10 minutes in rapidly boiling water. Reduce heat and cook 5 minutes more. Drain the kreplach and serve hot with butter. Kreplach are also good warmed over by frying in butter. (Serves 6–8.)

CHICKEN KREPLACH

Succot

The Pastry

2 cups flour, sifted
2 eggs
3 tablespoons water

The Filling

1½ cups cooked chicken
1 onion, chopped
¼ cup chopped greben
  (cracklings) or 3
  tablespoons chicken fat
1 tablespoon breadcrumbs
1 egg
  dash of nutmeg
  salt and pepper

For the pastry, make a well in the mound of flour and pour in the eggs and water. Mix and knead. When the dough is plastic, roll out thin.

For the filling, grind the chicken, onion, and greben (cracklings) together. Stir in the crumbs, egg, and seasoning. Cut the dough into 2-inch squares and place a ball of this filling on each. Fold over and pinch the edges together, then bring two points of each triangle together to make a little purse. Drop the kreplach into rapidly boiling salted water or soup and cook until the kreplach rise to the top (or a little longer if you wish). (Serves 4–6.)

CAPELLETTI FREDDI ALL'EBRAICA
(COLD MACARONI, HEBREW STYLE)   *Purim*

In a book called Maseket Purim, *the life of the Jews in the Middle Ages is recorded in much detail. Jewish cooking in Italy was full of luxury dishes, but noodles, the most common Italian food, is not listed. This seems to attest to the wealth of the Jewish population of that period in Italy.*

3 tablespoons olive oil	*½ teaspoon salt*
1 onion, chopped	*dash of pepper*
1 bunch parsley, chopped fine	*½ teaspoon basil*
1 clove garlic, crushed	*½ pound macaroni (capelletti)*
6 large tomatoes, chopped	*4 cups water*
1 tablespoon tomato purée	

Heat the oil and brown the onion, parsley, and garlic. Add the tomatoes, tomato purée, salt, and pepper. Simmer for about 1 hour. Add the basil and cook 10 minutes more. Boil the macaroni in 4 cups of water with a little salt. When tender but not too soft (8–9 minutes), drain. Pour the sauce over the noodles, and when the dish has cooled, serve. You can also eat it hot. (Serves 4–6.)

CORN FRITTERS   *Hanuka*

Corn is more American than the Pilgrim Fathers, having preceded their arrival to the United States. The founding father of this vegetable in Israel is the American diplomat James Macfarland, stationed in Tel Aviv. He brought the first Golden Bantam corn to Israel and planted the first crop in 1961. Mr. Macfarland turns all proceeds from his crops into the coffers of the Shatlem Israel Association for Cerebral Palsy Patients. *The corn is getting so popular that this dish is becoming a Hanuka favorite:*

1½ cups cooked corn	*2 tablespoons flour*
2 eggs, separated	*salt and pepper to taste*

Mix the corn, egg yolks, flour, salt, and pepper. Beat the egg whites until stiff and then fold into the corn batter. Drop by spoonfuls onto a greased pan and cook until golden on each side. (Makes about 8 fritters.)

PIZZA   *Hanuka*

*The Italian community was the first to serve their orégano-
flavored pizza in Israel. Today, with Israel's large selection of
cured cheese, almost every housewife not only makes a quickie
pizza on a piece of bread, but takes the time to prepare this
batter and topping (not as elaborate as the original, but very
good). There are cafés in Tel Aviv that make only pizza for
the public.*

The Pastry

1 teaspoon sugar
1 ounce fresh yeast
   (2 packages dry)
1 cup lukewarm milk
4 cups flour, sifted
½ teaspoon salt
4 tablespoons cooking oil
   pat of butter

The Paste

1 onion, grated
1 sweet red pepper, grated
2 tablespoons olive oil
½ pound tomatoes

The Topping

⅓ pound yellow cheese,
   sliced thin
1 pound onions, sliced
   anchovies
   black olives
   orégano
   salt and pepper

For the pastry, mix the sugar and yeast, dissolve in lukewarm
milk, and set aside while you make the paste.

For the paste, fry the onions and sweet red pepper in the olive
oil. Add the tomatoes and cook until a paste is formed. (10–15
minutes).

Add the flour, salt, and oil to the yeast-milk mixture and
knead. Set to rise in a warm place until doubled in bulk. Roll out
to a half-inch thickness and put into a greased pan. Spread with
the softened pat of butter. Cover with the tomato paste. Put the
cheese slices on the top, put the onion slices over the cheese, and
top each onion slice with a piece of anchovy. Garnish with cut
black olives. Sprinkle with oregano, salt, and pepper and drizzle
with a little oil if you wish. Bake in a 350° oven for about 30
minutes. Cut into wedges and serve hot.

RAVIOLI DI SPINACI   *Succot*

*The Italians have their ravioli, the Chinese their won ton, the
Poles their pirogen, we Jews our kreplach. All of which, being
basically the same, is mere proof of the brotherhood of men.*

The Dough

4 cups flour, sifted
3 eggs
3 tablespoons water

The Filling

2 pounds spinach, rinsed
1 onion, grated fine
1 carrot, grated fine
  cooking oil
6 ounces minced meat
2 eggs, beaten
  salt and pepper to taste

For the dough, mix together the ingredients and roll out into 2 very thin sheets. Cook the rinsed spinach without adding extra water, and when it begins to boil, drain off the liquid. Fry the onion and carrot in a little oil. Add the meat, spinach, eggs, and seasonings. Mix. Place the mixture on the dough, a spoonful at a time, each spoonful separated from the next by the width of two fingers. Cover with the second sheet of dough and press together between each lump of meat. Cut with a spiral cutting wheel. Drop the ravioli in boiling water and remove when they rise to the top. Serve with a good tomato sauce (*see* Index). (Serves 6.)

MATZO AND MATZO MEAL DISHES

MATZO MEAL PANCAKES *Passover*

1 cup matzo meal
⅔ cup milk or soup
5 eggs, separated
1 onion, grated

dash of nutmeg
salt and pepper to taste
fat for frying

Mix the matzo meal with the milk or soup and set aside for half an hour. Beat the egg yolks, add the onion and seasoning, and mix into the meal. Fold in the stiffly beaten egg whites. Fry by spoonfuls in hot fat, browning on both sides.

PASSOVER LEVIVOT (PANCAKES) *Passover*

"Levivot" comes from the word "lev" or "heart," and these are indeed hearty and much loved by children. The levivot are sprinkled with "sugar and spice and all things nice."

4 matzos
2 eggs
1 teaspoon salt
fat for frying

sprinkling of sugar
sprinkling of cinnamon
sour cream, honey, or jam,
for garnish

Pour boiling water over the matzos and let stand for 10 minutes. Squeeze them dry and mash to a pulp. Add the eggs and salt and beat well. Drop from a spoon into hot fat and brown on both sides. Serve hot, with a sprinkling of sugar and cinnamon and anything else that's nice, such as sour cream or honey or jam. (Serves 5–6.)

ONION MATZOS *Passover*

"Matzos gently coated in chicken fat over which a good healthy tsibbeleh had been rubbed. This rubbing the half-onion over the matzo became in itself an experience in ecstatic anticipation. I've never sampled marijuana but I can't imagine that it would produce a more glowing sensation than golden chicken fat on hemstitched boards. But this voluptuous experience must have

been a sin, because, just as you were reaching the climax of sense experience, the matzo would snap, and the reality of a dimly lighted slum kitchen would burst in upon this little piece of heaven."

—*from* FOODS *by* SAMMY LEVENSON

3 matzos	*poultry fat*
1 onion	*coarse salt*

Rub the matzos with the cut side of an onion. Brush with poultry fat and strew with coarse salt. Grill or toast in a hot oven. (Serves 3.)

MATZO BRIE   *Passover*

I. *Savory*   **II.** *Sweet*

6 matzos
boiling water

6 eggs
salt and pepper to taste
celery salt or soup season-
   ing (*optional*)
fat for frying

(*Use ingredients as in Matzo Brie I, but omit the pepper and savory seasonings, and use cinnamon instead.*)

Break the matzos and pour boiling water over them. Drain at once. Beat the eggs, add the seasoning, and mix well. Pour into a pan with hot fat. Brown on both sides. Serve hot, and serve the sweet matzo brie with a sprinking of sugar or honey. (Serves 4.)

MAHMOURAS   *Passover*

Matzos were round in the Middle Ages, before the factory stepped in to manufacture them in a more practical shape for storing and shipping. But in some countries in the Middle East, round matzos still prevail; they are made in small quantities by hand, under the strictest supervision. This dish is a typical Turkish one for Passover, now made in Israel, where Katzkaval cheese is also available for Passover.

6 matzos	*3 tablespoons olive oil*
2 cups grated yellow cheese	

Dip the matzos in boiling water for just one minute. Put them in a baking dish, alternating layers of matzo with cheese and a sprinkling of oil. Heat in the oven just long enough for the cheese to begin to melt. Cut up and serve hot. (Serves 4–6.)

FAHTHOOT—YEMENITE MATZO-MIX *Passover*

It was Passover week. We gave a lift to an old Yemenite couple of the Haban tribe, going to visit their family in a border settlement. On arrival the men greeted each other by picking up and kissing the tip of one another's beards with the grace of someone fingering a harp. The women sat on the floor to smoke the narghile hubble-bubble pipe as the bearded but moustache-less men talked Torah in the half-chant of desert melody, pouring blessings upon one and all. Our host was the rabbi, a true scholar, with his nine children and two wives (married in Yemen—Israel law forbids multiple spouses). This is what we were served by the women bejewelled in silver belts and wide bracelets. They had made the matzo themselves, on an open wood fire, of wheat and corn which they had guarded in the fields and ground by hand as their forebears did in Biblical days:

4 matzos	1 chili pepper
4 cups hot soup (lamb	dash of cumin
broth or chicken soup)	pinch of chervil or
1 cup fenugreek sauce	coriander
(hilbeh) (see Index)	juice of ½ lemon
1 clove garlic	

Break the matzos into the soup (lamb broth is usual, but chicken soup may also be used). Stir in the fenugreek sauce mixed with the garlic, spices, and lemon juice. Serve medium warm. (Serves 4.)

Passover
MATZO KNAIDLACH (DUMPLINGS) STEWED IN FRUIT

When Passover comes, the loquat trees are heavy with fruit. They are particularly suited to this dish, but the fruit most commonly used abroad is the dried prune, which is also very fine, as is the preserved cherry, or apple compote, and most other fruits.

3 eggs, separated	2 cups stewed fruit
1 cup matzo meal	2 cups syrup from stewed
salt	fruit
3 tablespoons oil	

Beat the egg yolks well, stir in the matzo meal, salt, and oil. Fold in the egg whites, stiffly beaten, and shape into dumplings. Put the stewed fruit into a casserole, put the dumplings in, top with more of the fruit, enough to cover the knaidlach. If necessary, make the syrup up to 2 cups by adding water. Pour over the fruit and dumplings. Bake in a 350° oven about 30 minutes. (Serves 6.)

MINAS OF MANY KINDS

Passover

The popular Turkish minas can be filled either with various cheeses, potatoes, onions, leeks, leaf greens and herbs, or meat or fowl. The oil is not absorbed if poured off immediately after baking.

Potato Type

1 cup hot oil
4 matzos
3 large boiled potatoes
1 cup grated yellow cheese
4 eggs
   salt and pepper to taste

Leek or Onion Type

1 cup hot oil
4 matzos
2 pounds leeks or onions,
   boiled
2 potatoes, mashed
1 cup grated yellow cheese
4 eggs
   salt and pepper to taste

Spinach or Chard Type

1 cup hot oil
4 matzos
2 pounds spinach, boiled
1 cup cottage cheese
$\frac{1}{4}$ cup grated yellow cheese
4 eggs
   salt and pepper to taste

Meat or Fowl Type

1 cup hot oil
4 matzos
3 cups diced cooked meat
   or fowl
3 green onions, chopped
$\frac{1}{2}$ cup chopped parsley,
   dill, etc.
2 eggs
   salt and pepper to taste

No matter which mina you make, put ½ cup of the hot oil in a casserole. Dip the matzos in water and line the bottom of the casserole with 2 of them. The basic material for the filling is chopped or sliced or cubed and is always precooked, whether it is the leek bulb, spinach or chicken (but the cheese, of course, is not cooked). On the bottom layer of matzos put the basic ingredient and top with the grated cheese (except for the meat mina, which you top with the herbs). Cover with the remaining water-dipped matzos and pour the beaten eggs over. Grate a little yellow cheese on top. Put into a 400° oven, and after 10 minutes pour on the remaining hot oil. Bake until done (about 30 minutes). Pour off the oil. Cut into serving pieces. This can be eaten hot or cold, but it is best hot and fresh. (Serves 4.)

SAVORY MATZO KUGEL

Passover

1 *pound stewing beef, cubed*
3 *tablespoons oil*
2 *onions, chopped*
1 *clove garlic, crushed*
1 *carrot, grated*

4 *matzos*
   broth or hot water
2 *pounds spinach*
   gravy
   salt and pepper

Brown the meat in the oil with the onions, garlic, and carrot. Cover with water and simmer until tender (about 1 hour). Dip the matzos in a little broth or hot water and cover with a cloth. Cook the spinach and drain. In a greased casserole put alternate layers of matzos, meat and the liquid in which it was cooked, and spinach until the casserole is full. The top layer should be of spinach with gravy on it. Add salt and pepper as desired on the various layers. Bake in a 375° oven 30 minutes. (Serves 4–6).

MEATS

ROAST BEEF *Passover*

4 *cloves garlic*   *salt, pepper, paprika*
1 *4-pound rib roast*

Insert slices of garlic under and into the fat of the rib roast. Sprinkle the meat with salt, pepper, and paprika. Place the meat in a greased dripping pan, with the fat side up, in a very hot oven (500° F) for 20 minutes. Reduce the heat to 250° and continue cooking for 1 hour longer if you want the meat rare. Cook for 1 hour and 20 minutes longer if you want the meat well done. Baste the meat occasionally during cooking. (Serves 8.)

NOTE: A rib can be cooked on top of the range in a heavy pan by searing the meat first on all sides, then reducing the heat and cooking it uncovered for 15 minutes on each side for rare, and longer if desired well done.

GLAZED ROAST BEEF WITH ORANGES *Passover*

Dishes have changed but tastes have not, for the palate is still the same in man. In the eighteenth century it is recorded that the Italians liked to season "every kind of roast meat" with the juice of sour oranges, which "they regarded as more palatable even than lemons!"

1½ *cups brown sugar*   1 *teaspoon dry mustard*
  3 *tablespoons lemon juice*   1 *4-pound roast of beef*
  4 *tablespoons orange juice*   *orange slices for garnish*
    dash of ginger

To achieve a fabulous golden glaze on your roast, as well as do wonders for the flavor, make a mixture of the lemon juice, orange juice, ginger, and mustard and rub the uncooked roast with it. Roast the meat at 500° for 20 minutes. Reduce heat to 300° and roast 1½ hours more. Baste the roast with the drippings three or four times during the roasting. Serve the meat surrounded by plain or grilled orange slices. (Serves 8–10.)

STEAK ON THE ROAD   *Succot*

Author Meyer Levin says of his truffle-loving gourmet wife, "She can't cook anything I like, and I don't like anything she cooks," so he was only too happy when a Turkish vendor set up a roadside grill on the highway to Tel Aviv, where he could get a steak in a pita (Arab pancake bread) with the "world's hottest and most delicious relish." But the police kept moving the Turk from place to place, as no license was available for such a stand. Tired of searching him out, Meyer Levin returned to his American habit of grilling steaks in the backyard, and made this concoction— the relish much like the Turk's—which he now calls "Steak on the Road."

½ cup olive oil
1 tablespoon anise liqueur
   (arrack)
4 steaks (1 inch thick)
2 cloves garlic, crushed
1 teaspoon sweet paprika
1 teaspoon salt
1 onion, chopped

1 red chili pepper, minced
½ cup minced sweet red
   peppers
2 cups chopped tomatoes
2 tablespoons chopped
   parsley
4 pitas (see Index)

Mix the olive oil with the anise liqueur and marinate the steaks in this liquid for a few hours. Grill the steaks for 8 or 9 minutes (they should be very rare) over glowing wood coals. Meanwhile mix the marinade with all the remaining ingredients and simmer. If necessary, a very little water may be added. Serve each steak, with this sauce, inside the pocket of a pita that has been warmed up on the grill. (Serves 4.)

THE NOBLE CHATEAUBRIAND   *Purim*

Created originally (with a pocket-slit full of chopped shallots and beef marrow) for a French vicomte, the Chateaubriand has become popular in Israel partly through a Jewish baroness, known here either as "Bathsheba" or plain "Mrs." Bethsabée de Rothschild has taken up residence in the land where her uncle, Baron Edmond de Rothschild, established Israel's earliest agricultural colonies. Her sponsorship of Israel's finest arts—particularly glass, ceramics, and silver—have helped win them their due fame. Israel chefs have responded to her tastes, too: her favorite locally adapted, French-inspired Chateaubriands (which are as varied as the chefs' moods) are served grandly in every worthy restaurant, large or small, in Tel Aviv.

1 *4- to 5-pound filleted rib
   cut into 8 2-inch steaks
   olive oil
   lemon juice
   salt*

   *dash of cayenne
2 medium onions, sliced
8 chicken livers, grilled
   wine, if desired
   mushrooms, if desired*

Rub the fillet steaks with olive oil and sprinkle with lemon juice and set aside for an hour at room temperature. Grill on both sides under high heat, reduce heat and cook until done to your taste. Season with salt and a dash of cayenne. Lightly fry the onions and place on the steaks, with the grilled chicken livers. Wine may be added to the drippings in the pan for a sauce. Serve with sautéed mushrooms if you wish. (Serves 8.)

WIENER SAUERBRATEN—VIENNA MARINATED ROAST

Brillat-Savarin, the great gourmet, wrote that "cooks are made, but roasting experts are born." Man has been roasting meat in many forms since his cave days; this way is particularly succulent, and was introduced to Israel by the large influx of Viennese, who put much love into the preparation of their hearty meat dishes.

1 *4-pound shoulder of beef*
2 *teaspoons salt*
   sprinkling of pepper
   dash of ginger
6 *cloves*
2 *cups vinegar diluted with
   water*
4 *tablespoons cooking oil*

2 *onions, sliced*
3 *tomatoes, diced*
½ *cup white wine
   sugar to taste, if desired*
1 *tablespoon flour, if
   desired*
1 *tablespoon fat, if desired*

Sprinkle the meat with the salt, pepper, and ginger and stick in the cloves. Heat the vinegar (diluted with water to make it pleasantly mild). Put the meat in a casserole, pour the vinegar over, cool, and refrigerate overnight. Heat the oil, dry the meat, and brown it on all sides. Add the vinegar in which it marinated, and the onions, tomatoes, white wine and sugar, if desired. Cover well and stew gently until the meat is tender (2½–3 hours). Turn the meat over from time to time. Strain the sauce, and if you wish, thicken it with a tablespoon each of flour and fat, mixed. (Serves 8–10.)

POLLY'S BOILED BEEF
Yom Kippur

2 pounds lean beef	1 kohlrabi
a few grains saffron	2 teaspoons salt
(optional, but	dash of white pepper
desirable)	1 tomato
½ pound celery root	1 summer squash
1 parsnip	chopped parsley
1 onion	water to cover

Put all the ingredients into a heavy pot and just cover with hot water (otherwise too many juices will escape from the meat into the soup). Bring to a quick boil and simmer for about two hours, or until the meat is tender and most of the liquid evaporated. The meat is served with horse-radish, dill pickles, or other condiments. The vegetables are discarded. (Serves 4–6.)

MANZO IN UMIDO—STEWED BEEF
Passover

Lyla Levkowitz was up to her ears in preparing for the Bar Mitzvah of her son. She asked her father, who had come for the event from Italy, and their guest the Catholic priest who was building the Nazareth Church with architect Moshe Levkowitz, to please help her by cooking the Manzo in Umido (for Italian men are very good in the kitchen). To her dismay, they suddenly stopped in the work. No rosemary! How can you cook without rosemary? Lyla went to a neighbor and got a pinch of rosemary. Again a stoppage. No real olive oil! How can you use any other oil? Lyla rushed to the shop and got some olive oil. A final strike of Papa and priest. No wooden spoon! How can you use any other?

2 cloves garlic, sliced	2 stalks celery, diced
3 pounds chuck beef	1 carrot, diced
salt and pepper	pinch of rosemary
3 tablespoons olive oil	1 tablespoon tomato purée
1 onion, diced	meat stock or water

Insert the garlic under bits of fat or tissue in the beef. Salt and pepper to taste. Heat the olive oil and brown the beef in it. Add the vegetables and brown them slowly. Sprinkle with a little rosemary and add the tomato purée diluted with a few table-spoons of meat stock or water. Cover the pot and simmer on low heat. From time to time add a spoonful or two of water so the meat will stew and not dry out. Cook gently for about 3 hours in all. (Serves 6–8.)

ESSIG FLEISCH—SWEET SOUR ROAST *Succot*

How the Jews of Europe came to this sweet-piquant sauce for meat remains a mystery: the new generation of Israelis scorns the dish, but their parents love it, since it is the only bold sauce for meat in European-Jewish cooking.

5 pounds chuck	1 cup wine vinegar
3 tablespoons cooking oil	1/2 cup brown sugar
4 large onions, chopped	water as needed
salt and pepper to taste	2 tablespoons flour
dash of ginger	
(optional)	

Brown the meat in the oil. Add the onions and simmer for 10 minutes. Mix the seasonings with the vinegar and sugar and add to the meat. Add 1/2 cup water and cook, covered, until the meat is almost tender (2 1/2–3 hours). Add more water if necessary. When the meat is done, brown the flour, dissolve in 1/2 cup water, and add to the sauce to thicken it. Cook for 15 minutes longer. (Serves 10–12.)

ROLLADE (ROLLED ROAST) *Shabbat*

4 pounds chuck, rump or	2 tablespoons drippings
flank	3 onions, chopped
1/2 cup vinegar	1/2 pound celery root
3 bay leaves	2 carrots
salt and pepper	1/2 cup water
dash of cloves	

Have the butcher pound the meat somewhat and then roll it up. Put this in a bowl in the refrigerator with the vinegar and bay leaves for half a day, turning from time to time. Dry the meat and season it. Heat the drippings and brown the meat on all sides. Add the vinegar in which it was soaked and the remaining ingredients. Cover, bring to a quick boil, and then simmer gently, turning from time to time, until meat is tender (about 2 hours). (Serves 8–10.)

BEEF IN WINE AND OLIVES *Purim*

4 onions, diced
1 large celery root, diced
3 parsnip roots, diced
½ pound carrots, diced
4 tablespoons olive oil
1 cup dry red wine
  salt and pepper
4 cloves garlic
2 bay leaves

2 tablespoons chopped
  parsley
1 tablespoon chopped dill
3 pounds beef chuck
½ pound black olives
4 large tomatoes, diced
  smoked sausage, thinly
  sliced (optional)

Fry the onions, celery root, parsnips, and carrots in the oil for a few minutes. Add the wine, salt, pepper, garlic, and herbs. Simmer for a few minutes. Cool and pour over the meat to marinate overnight. Turn the meat two or three times in the marinade. Put the meat, with the marinade, in a casserole, well covered. Bake in a 350° oven 1½ to 2 hours. When the meat is almost done, add the olives, tomatoes, and if you wish, a few thin slices of smoked sausage. Cook until tender. (Serves 6–8.)

BASIC CHOLENT (ALIAS SHALET OR SHOLET) *Shabbat*

Moritz Saphir wrote of the cholent about one hundred fifty years ago: ". . . Börne called the dish 'Schalet,' for he must have heaved a gastronomic 'Ah!' when he tasted it. I call it 'Scholet,' for when I first ate it I exclaimed 'Oh!' " His recipe: "Combine classical barley and romantic peas and crown it with a joint of beef. But before you set it in the village oven on Friday, add suet and a whiff of odeur de garlic. Let it simmer until Sabbath dinnertime, so the classical and romantic mingle with the beef principles to create an original philosophic system known as 'Scholet.' "

½ pound chick-peas or
    dried beans
2 or 3 tablespoons fat for
    browning
2 pounds beef brisket or
    fat meat
3 onions, chopped
1 clove garlic, chopped

4 tablespoons pearl barley
8 medium potatoes,
    peeled and sliced
1 bay leaf (optional)
  salt and pepper to taste
  water as needed
  knaidle (dumpling) if
    desired (see Index)

Soak the chick-peas or dried beans overnight. Heat the fat and brown the meat on all sides. Put into a heavy iron or earthen pot. Surround with the drained chick-peas or dried beans. Sprinkle with the onion, garlic, and pearl barley. Cover with the potatoes. Add the seasoning. Cover with boiling water and bring to the boil. Set into a 225° oven, or over very low heat, and simmer overnight. If the dish is cooked enough before that, put it on an asbestos plate. Water and 2 tablespoons of browned flour may be added if desired. Shake the pot but do not stir up the cholent. (Serves 6.)

BEEF CHOLENT WITH FLOHMENTZIMMES (PRUNES OR APRICOTS) *Shabbat*

This dish may be from the period (eleventh and twelfth centuries) when great Jewish writings as well as cooking were created in Italy. "Cholent," a hot Sabbath dish, may derive its name from the Italian word "caldo" (warm). It became a favorite all through North Africa, the Middle East and Central and Eastern Europe.

It was cooked overnight in the village baker's oven and brought home after synagogue. Since religious Jews would not carry things beyond their household (this being work on Sabbath) a wire (called an "Eruv") was put around the village to make it "one home." If the wire was broken, the cholent was passed from hand to hand so as not to carry it on the Sabbath.

2 pounds fat beef, cut into serving pieces	1 tablespoon salt
2 pounds sweet potatoes or yellow turnips	½ teaspoon pepper
1 pound prunes or dried apricots	5 tablespoons brown sugar or honey
	juice of 1 lemon
	water as needed

In a casserole, alternate layers of meat with layers of sweet potatoes (or turnips) and prunes (or apricots). Repeat until used up. Mix the salt, pepper, sugar (or honey), and lemon juice with enough water to cover the ingredients. Cover the pot and bring to a boil then reduce heat to very low and cook for at least 3 hours. If cooked overnight on the lowest possible heat (or in the oven at 200°) for about 12 hours, the dish is as mellow as butter. Most of the sauce will be absorbed in the cooking. (Serves 6.)

POT ROAST   *Passover*

3 pounds chuck or other
      suitable cut
   cooking oil
1 clove garlic, cut
4 onions, cut up
3 carrots, diced

1 celery root, diced
   salt and pepper
2 cups water
1 bay leaf
12 whole medium potatoes

Brown the meat, with the oil, in a hot pot. Surround with the cut-up vegetables, (but not with the potatoes) and add the seasoning. Add the water. Put the pot in a 300° oven or on top of the range over low heat and simmer until tender (about 2 hours). Add the potatoes and cook next to the meat until done (about 30 minutes). (Serves 6.)

FERIK—GREEN WHEAT HAMIM   *Shabbat*

The desire for hot hearty food on the Sabbath, when cooking is not permitted, gave birth to the cholents and the hamims of many kinds all over the world. This is the Egyptian variety.

2 pounds fat meat (brisket,
      or other)
2 cups green wheat or
      burghul (cracked wheat)
6 eggs, unshelled

1 calf's foot
   salt and pepper to taste
   cayenne as desired
2 cloves garlic
   water as needed

Brown the meat in a heavy pot. Put it on a bed of wheat and surround with the eggs in their shells and the calf's foot, chopped into a few pieces. Put in the seasoning and garlic and cover with water. Bring to the boil slowly. Cover tightly and let stew overnight, until ready to serve after the synagogue service on Shabbat. (Serves 4–6.)

DFINA—ALGERIAN HAMIM (OR CHOLENT)   *Shabbat*

This dish provides a full Sabbath meal, except for dessert. Sometimes a "kouclas," a dumpling similar to a knaidle, is cooked with it. An unusual feature is the use of unshelled eggs; they come out a deep brown outside and inside and are as soft and flavorful as the dumpling.

Like the European cholent, dfina may be left in a baker's oven overnight and brought home right after synagogue.

The Dfina

- 1 cup chick-peas
- 1½ pounds fat beef
- 1 pound calf's foot
- 4 cloves garlic
- 1 large onion
- 6 eggs in their shells
- 1 very small chili pepper
  (*or 1 teaspoon chili sauce*)
- 1 pimento
  salt and pepper to taste
  water to cover

The Kouclas

- 2 eggs
  salt and pepper to taste
- 1 tablespoon chopped parsley
- 1 onion
- ¾ cup breadcrumbs
  (*approximately*)

Soak the chick-peas for a few hours. Drain. In an earthenware casserole put the fat beef, calf's foot, garlic, onion, eggs in their shells, chick-peas, chili pepper or sauce, pimento, and salt and pepper. Cover with water.

For the kouclas, combine the eggs, salt and pepper, parsley, chopped onion, and breadcrumbs. Shape into a ball and add to the casserole. Close the casserole firmly and either simmer overnight on low heat or put into a baker's oven overnight. Serve hot. (Serves 8.)

MOCK HAM   *Purim*

Miriam—who called herself Maria when she was masquerading as a Christian to save her life during the Hitler holocaust—told me that the Germans with whom she lived and worked as a housemaid never doubted her Aryan blood, for they saw how "eagerly" she ate ham. In Israel she keeps a kosher home, but when it comes to Purim she makes kosher mock ham to scorn both Haman and Hitler.

- 14 whole cloves
- 4 pounds pickled brisket, uncooked (*see* Index)

- margarine
- 1 cup pineapple jam

Insert the whole cloves into the flesh of an uncooked pickled brisket with the aid of a fork prong. Rub the meat generously with margarine. Put into a greased casserole and cover with pineapple jam. Roast in a 375° oven for one hour. Serve hot or cold. (Serves 10–12.)

KASHA CHOLENT

Shabbat

Heinrich Heine writes of the schalet or cholent he ate at a friend's home in Frankfurt: "True to Jewish custom," he placed a dish of the traditional schalet before me at the Sabbath noon. I liked the ancient dish enormously: it perhaps dates back to the Jewish sojourn in Egypt and is as old as the Pyramids. . . . With what savour, with what delight and eagerness, with what appetite, I polished off this age-old Jewish dish of schalet!"

1 cup dried beans	1 clove garlic, crushed
4 tablespoons oils	salt and pepper
2 pounds brisket or fat meat	water to cover
2 onions, chopped	1 celery or parsnip root,
1 cup buckwheat groats	grated
(kasha)	

Soak the beans overnight. Heat the oil and brown the meat in it. Remove the meat. Lightly fry the onions and remove. Fry the groats for just a minute or two. In a heavy pot put the drained beans. Place the meat on the beans and surround with the groats, onions, garlic, grated root, and seasoning. Cover with water and bring to a boil. Put on low heat or in a 225° oven and simmer overnight. (Serves 4–6.)

STIFATHO—GREEK SAVORY STEW

Hanuka

One wonders, in reading the culinary history of the Holy Land, whether the Greeks learned this dish from the Jews, or whether the Hellenic influence of the time of the Maccabees brought this dish to Palestine. It no longer bears a Hebrew name, but many Israelis make meat dishes flavored with cinnamon and saffron as they did two thousand years ago.

2 pounds tender beef	dash of saffron
1/2 cup red wine	(optional)
1 cup very small onions	1/2 teaspoon pickling spice
4 tablespoons cooking oil	(without peppers and
1/2 cup margarine	bay leaf)
1/2 cup tomato paste or	2 cups water
ketchup	salt and pepper to taste
1 cinnamon stick	1 tablespoon vinegar

A real gourmet will first marinate the meat in the wine overnight, but this is not essential. Cut the meat into 2-inch cubes. Peel the onions. Brown the meat in the hot oil, then add the margarine and remove the meat into a casserole. Brown the

onions slightly and set aside. Cook the tomato paste in the remaining margarine and pour over the meat with the remaining
ingredients (except the onions). Bring to the boil on high heat,
then reduce heat to just simmering. Close the casserole tightly
and cook gently until the meat is almost tender (about an hour).
Then add the onions and complete cooking (about 20 minutes).
(Serves 4–6.)

MEAT AND CHICK-PEA STEW (PUCHERO)   *Hanuka*

2 cups chick-peas	3 carrots, diced
8 cups water	1 ½-inch thick sausage,
2 pounds beef, diced	diced
1 onion, chopped	salt and pepper to taste

Soak the chick-peas overnight. Drain and add the water. Simmer on low heat for about an hour. Add the remaining ingredients and continue to simmer until the beef is done and the
chick-peas are tender (about two hours on low heat). Other and
more vegetables are sometimes added to this dish, brought to
Israel by South American immigrants. (Serves 6.)

TUNISIAN MAGUINA (BEEF BAKE)   *Shabbat*

Upon what meat doth this our Caesar feed
That he is grown so great?"
                                                    —SHAKESPEARE

Well, one thing is certain; he didn't grow fat on maguina, for
this dish is served only by Jewish families originating in Tunisia
—hot on Friday nights and cold for Sabbath lunch.

1 pound beef, thinly sliced	½ pound potatoes, sliced
4 tablespoons olive oil	salt and paprika to taste
2 onions, chopped	dash of nutmeg or
1 pound tomatoes, diced	cinnamon
1 cup sliced mushrooms	10 eggs

Fry the beef slices in the oil, add the onions and tomatoes and
stew 10 minutes. Add the mushrooms, potatoes, and seasoning.
Simmer until the potatoes are done. Remove from the heat and
cool. Grease a baking dish very well. Beat up the eggs. Add the
remaining ingredients, put into a baking dish, and bake in a
350° oven about 30 minutes. The dish is done when a silver knife
is inserted into the center and comes out clean. (Serves 4–6.)

KOSHER BEEF STROGANOFF P_{urim}

Once when the Hotel Accadia served this dish, normally made in cream, a very Orthodox guest complained. The official kosher supervisor of the hotel was called to assure the diner that there was not one drop of cream in the dish, even if it looked and tasted as if there was!

The Meat	*The Sauce*
1½ *pounds shoulder steak*	4 *cups meat gravy, plus*
flour for coating	*beef stock*
1 *teaspoon salt*	2 *tablespoons flour*
dash of pepper	*dash of paprika*
3 *onions, chopped*	6 *tablespoons ketchup*
mushrooms, sliced	1 *tablespoon Worcestershire*
1 *clove garlic, crushed*	*or Tabasco sauce*
6 *tablespoons margarine*	4 *tablespoons mayonnaise*

Remove the fat from the meat and cut into ¼-inch-thick strips. Dip the meat in flour and season. Fry the onions with the mushrooms and garlic in the margarine for 4–5 minutes. Add the meat and cook 3 minutes more.

To make the sauce, drain off the juice from the meat and vegetables and add enough beef stock to make 4 cups. Blend in the flour smoothly. Add the paprika, ketchup, and Worcestershire or Tabasco sauce. Cook until thick and smooth. Remove the sauce from heat and slowly stir it into the mayonnaise. Keep warm but do not cook again. Serve the sauce over the beef. (Serves 4–6.)

THE SHARON'S SUBSTITUTE SUKIYAKI P_{urim}

Though Israel has no Jewish-Japanese community, it does have cultural and economic ties with the "Land of the Rising Sun." The Japanese ambassador introduced the traditional Sukiyaki "Friendship Dish" to Israel at the Sharon Hotel, and this Israeli version has become a pièce de résistance on the menus. You can prepare it for parties as the Sharon does, substituting local for unavailable Japanese ingredients, in a chafing dish at table, with all the ingredients beautifully laid out on a platter (or cook it in the kitchen in a heavy skillet, in about 20 minutes).

Celery stalks are used to replace the traditional Chinese cabbage, kohlrabi is a substitute for water chestnuts, and sweet potatoes replace the shirataki or bean sprouts (you can use carrots if you wish). These vegetables are not traditional to the dish, but the results are almost as good. This recipe should be made in two batches (unless your skillet is very large).

6 tablespoons peanut oil
2 pounds steak, cut into thin
    strips
1 cup thinly sliced onions
2 cups parboiled sweet pota-
    toes or raw carrots, cut
    into thin 3-inch strips
2 cups coarsely shredded
    white cabbage

2 cups kohlrabi, cut into
    thin strips
1 cup celery, cut into
    3-inch strips
6 ounces mushrooms,
    sliced thin
1 cup hot water
6 tablespoons soy sauce
1 tablespoon dehydrated
    chicken soup

Heat the oil and fry the meat for 3 minutes, then push it to the edge of the pan. Do the same with each vegetable, frying them for 2 minutes each, in the order in which they are listed (longest-cooking are fried first). Mix the water, soy sauce, and soup powder. Sprinkle over each vegetable right after frying. Add any of the remaining liquid after all vegetables have been fried and cook everything for 5 minutes longer, stirring often. The vegetables should be crisp, but not raw. Serve with boiled rice and more soy sauce, if desired. (Serves 6–8.)

PASSOVER CARNATZLACH   *Passover*

How we longed for carnatzlach during the austerity days of Israel! Our meat ration was very small (½ pound a month), and we used to stretch the taste with so much flour or crumbs that a standing joke arose: "Make the bread blessing on hamburgers." Carnatzlach are made without any crumbs and so we serve them during Passover, and buy them on the streets from Romanian kiosks, where they are grilled on charcoal-ember barbecues.

2 pounds very finely ground
    beef
2 cloves garlic
1 large onion
2 stalks celery or fennel
    (optional)

dash of cayenne
1 teaspoon salt
    pinch of pepper
2 eggs

Put the meat and vegetables through the meat chopper twice, then add the remaining ingredients. Shape into little "fingers" and grill the miniature rolls over a hot charcoal fire until the carnatzlach are lightly browned. (Serves 6.)

KLOPS—MEAT-EGG-LOAF *Independence Day*

Many an Israeli housewife—particularly if she hails from some Germanic country—will prepare a cold repast of potato salad and assorted cold cuts of meat and sausages for Independence Day. The choice morsels on the plate will be rare roast beef, pickled tongue, and klops (meat loaf), dishes now common but only a few years ago a rationed rarity.

2 pounds ground beef	dash of nutmeg
3 slices bread, soaked	2 teaspoons salt
2 eggs	dash of pepper
½ pound celery root, grated	1 tablespoon chopped
6 tablespoons stock	parsley
1 carrot, grated	6 hard-cooked eggs, shelled
2 onions, grated	margarine for dotting
2 cloves garlic, crushed	

Mix all the ingredients (except the hard-cooked eggs and margarine) together. Put half the meat mixture into a well-greased loaf pan. Put the hard-cooked eggs along the middle and cover with the remaining meat. Dot with margarine and bake for 15 minutes in a 550° oven and then reduce heat to 350° and cook until the meat is brown on top and shrinks from the sides of pan (about 45 minutes). Serve in thick slices, so that the egg centers each piece. Serve with tomato sauce. (Serves 6–8.)

PICKLED BRISKET OR TONGUE *Purim*

5 pounds brisket or tongue	10 peppercorns
	1 teaspoon celery seed
½ cup coarse salt	½ teaspoon mustard seed
10 bay leaves	water as required
5 cloves garlic	½ teaspoon saltpeter

Rub the meat all over with salt. Put into a crock with all the seasonings and add cold water to cover. Dissolve the saltpeter and add. Cover with a plate to weigh down the meat. (Be sure it remains under the brine all the time.) Keep in a cool place. Turn the meat twice a week and add a tablespoon or two of salt every week. After one month, remove the meat from the brine. Cover with fresh water (leave the spices in), and add a piece or two of **fresh** garlic. Bring to a quick boil and then reduce heat and cook gently for about an hour, or until the meat is tender. Skin the tongue while it is still warm. Serve cold, thinly sliced, or in various dishes (such as corned beef and cabbage). (Serves 15–18.)

TONGUE—ALSATIAN FASHION   *Rosh Hashana*

1 *4-pound beef tongue*
2 *whole cloves*
2 *bay leaves*
2 *onions*
2 *cloves garlic*
2 *peppercorns*
2 *teaspoons salt*
  water to cover
  dash of ginger

2 *lebkuchen (gingersnaps)*
  or 2 slices honey cake
2 *tablespoons sugar*
½ *cup raisins*
2 *tablespoons wine vinegar*
2 *tablespoons cornstarch*
2 *tablespoons water*
  juice of 1 lemon
  (if desired)

Cook the tongue with the cloves, bay leaves, onions, garlic, pepper, salt, and water to cover until just tender (3–4 hours). Skin the tongue and strain the liquid back into the pot. Add the ginger, lebkuchen (or honey cake), sugar, raisins, and vinegar and cook with the skinned tongue 15–20 minutes. Mix the cornstarch and water and add, to thicken the sauce somewhat. If you like the sauce sweeter, add more sugar; if you like it more piquant, add the juice of a lemon. (Serves 8–10.)

UDDER   *Rosh Hashana*

This is the only meat that Jews eat with milk—that is, its own milk, for then it cannot possibly contravene the humane, merciful law of "thou shalt not cook the kid in its mother's milk."

1 *udder, slashed (about 3*
  pounds)
  water to cover
6 *bay leaves*

1 *teaspoon peppercorns*
1 *teaspoon mustard seed*
2 *teaspoons salt*

Slash the udder to release the milk. It must be koshered in a vessel for udder only. Cover the udder with boiling water, then change the water and cook on low heat with the seasonings until tender (about 2 hours). Serve sliced cold (best this way) with plenty of mustard, or serve hot with any favorite mustard sauce. (Serves 6–8.)

KAHKLEHTIN (ROAST HAMBURGERS)   *Purim*

2 pounds ground beef   4 tablespoons oil
1 cup breadcrumbs   1 bay leaf
1 clove garlic, crushed   1 onion, chopped
2 eggs   1 cup tomato juice or stock
   salt and pepper

Mix the ground meat with the breadcrumbs, garlic, eggs, salt, and pepper and form into hamburgers. Fry in the hot oil until just brown on both sides. Add the bay leaf, and tomato juice or stock and simmer for half an hour, on very low heat. (Serves 4–6.)

STUFFED MILTZ (MILT)   *Hanuka*

1 miltz   1 teaspoon salt
4 slices white bread, crust   dash of pepper
      removed   4 large onions, sliced
1 onion, chopped   4 tablespoons cooking oil
3 tablespoons margarine   water to cover

With a long sharp knife, make a pocket in the miltz almost from end to end. Put the bread to soak in water or soup, and then squeeze dry. Fry the chopped onion in the margarine and mix with the bread, salt, and pepper. Stuff into the miltz (not too full or it will split) and sew up. Put the miltz on a bed of sliced onions, pour the oil over, add water to just cover, and simmer gently for about 1½ hours. As the water is absorbed, the miltz will begin to pot roast. Turn and baste. (Serves 4.)

STUFFED STOMACH   *Hanuka*

The phrase to retort to and describe rubbish or nonsense in conversation is "Oh, tripe," and yet tripe is looked upon as a delicacy in West European cuisine, including Jewish festival cooking. One thing is sure, whether dainty or not, when you eat stuffed stomach you'll end up with a stuffed stomach.

1 beef or veal stomach   2 onions, chopped
6 white rolls   salt and lots of pepper
3 boiled potatoes   1 egg
¼ pound suet or margarine,   2 tablespoons flour
      chopped

Clean the stomach thoroughly. Soak the rolls in water and squeeze dry. Mash the potatoes. Mix all the ingredients, stuff into the stomach, and sew up. Cook in a pot with fat and water or next to a cut of meat. Keep under liquid for the first 2 hours of gentle cooking and then allow the stomach to cook until most of the liquid is evaporated (about 1 hour longer). It is still better to bake the stomach for the last hour of cooking, with very little liquid. (Serves 4–6.)

KIRSEH—YEMENITE TRIPE   *Passover*

Go into a Yemenite restaurant in Tel Aviv, and you'll hear one customer after another calling, "Kirseh! Kirseh!" to the waiter —so much so, in fact, that you'll think the word is a greeting. Kirseh is the much-loved tripe of the Yemenites, whose meat foods are chiefly the inner organs of beef or mutton. Yemenites like long, slow cooking (often half a day for a dish like this) but that is not essential.

1 pound tripe	2 cloves garlic, chopped
1 cup water	dash each (to taste) of:
1 teaspoon salt	cardamom, coriander,
1 large onion, chopped	cumin, cayenne, black
3 tablespoons oil for frying	pepper, turmeric or saf-
1 large tomato, chopped	fron

Blanch the tripe before cooking by pouring boiling water over it. Cut into 2-inch squares. Bring to a quick boil with the water and salt. Fry the onion in the oil and add to the meat, with the tomato and garlic. Cook over low heat for about an hour. Add the remaining ingredients and simmer for at least another hour. Serve hot. (Serves 4.)

LUNG OR LIVER STRUDEL   *Shabbat*

2 onions, chopped	3 hard-cooked eggs, chopped
4 tablespoons chicken fat	salt and pepper to taste
2 cups ground cooked lung	1 recipe any strudel or
1 cup ground cooked meat	noodle dough (see Index)
or liver	

Fry the onions in the chicken fat and mix with the remaining ingredients. Sprinkle over the rolled or stretched strudel dough. After rolling up, brush with melted fat and bake in 400° oven until golden (30–35 minutes). (Serves 4–6.)

WIENER SCHNITZEL   *Purim*

"Meat's to be eaten: maid's to be wed," says an old proverb. But a maid who can make meat good pleases the man whom she weds. Wiener schnitzel, to be successful, should be prepared like a fine delicacy.

1 pound veal steak	1 tablespoon water
(2 steaks)	fine breadcrumbs
juice of ½ lemon	salt and pepper to taste
1 egg	margarine for frying

Pound the meat lightly with a wooden mallet (do not pulp or tear the meat). Drizzle with lemon juice and marinate for half an hour. Beat the egg and add the water. Dip the steaks in the egg, then in the breadcrumbs. Sprinkle with salt and pepper. Brown the steaks, in the margarine, over high heat. Turn down the heat and let them cook 10 minutes more on low heat. Garnish with lemon wedges. (Serves 3–4.)

VEAL IN WINE   *Shabbat*

3 pounds veal	1 bay leaf
4 cups dry red wine	4 whole peppercorns
2 onions	2 ounces chicken fat
2 carrots	salt to taste
6 celery stalks	

Marinate the meat in the wine for 24 hours, together with the sliced vegetables, bay leaf, and peppercorns. Turn the meat a few times. Dry the meat and fry it in the fat. Strain the wine. Add salt to the meat. Pour the wine over and simmer about 2 hours, or until tender. (Serves 6–8.)

VITELLO ARROT OLATI—ROLLED VEAL   *Shabbat*

Most Italians have large families and small budgets. So when it comes to the Sabbath and the housewife wishes to serve delectable veal, she knows how to stretch it.

2 pounds veal in one slice	1 pound young squash, sliced
a few chicken livers	salt and pepper
4 eggs	fat as needed
olive oil	water as needed

Pound the meat with the side of a cleaver so that it enlarges in area. Grill the livers and dice. Beat the eggs and scramble them in oil. Put on the meat and cover with squash and pieces of liver. Add salt and pepper to taste. Spread on any oil left from cooking the eggs. Roll up the meat and tie it. Simmer in a little fat and very little water, turning from time to time, for 35–40 minutes. Serve hot or cold in slices. (Serves 4–6.)

SEFRITO—VEAL, EGYPTIAN   Purim

¼ cup margarine   2 pounds boned veal
½ teaspoon salt   1 cup water
  few grains saffron   1 small chili pepper
  juice of 1 lemon

Mix the margarine with the salt and saffron. Drizzle the lemon juice over the meat and then spread with the margarine. Put the meat in a casserole with the water and chili pepper. Bring to a boil and then reduce the heat. Simmer the veal for about 1 hour, or until tender, basting from time to time. (Serves 6.)

THE PASCHAL LAMB   Passover

When the Angel of Death killed the first-born in all Egypt, he entered not one single Jewish home, recognizing them by the blood of the slaughtered lambs that had been brushed on the doorposts. For that reason, and in rememberance of the sacrifices, it has become traditional in many communities to eat lamb on Seder night.

In Israel the hindquarters of cows and sheep are eaten, since they are "treibert"—freed of the main blood vessels—a process requiring special training for which experts are hard to find abroad.

1 large shoulder of lamb   *salt and pepper*
garlic   *rosemary*
margarine

Make incisions through the skin of the roast and insert pieces of garlic. Spread margarine over the surface of the meat if it is lean. Sprinkle with salt and pepper, and if you wish, a few needles of rosemary. Put into a roasting pan and roast in a 450° oven for half an hour. Reduce the heat to 300° and continue roasting as much as desired (30 minutes to a pound for well

done, 18–20 minutes to a pound for rare, including searing time).
Brush with margarine from time to time if the meat is lean.
(Serves 6–8.)

WHOLE ROAST SHEEP   *Independence Day*

On the night of Independence Day, whole sheep are roasted in
some of the city squares at a public kumzits (literally, "come and
sit") or get-together.

Meat	Stuffing
young sheep	4 or 5 cups partly cooked
handful of salt	rice or burghul (cracked
plenty of margarine	wheat)
few handfuls of chopped	raisins
onion	pine nuts
pepper	cinnamon
	salt, pepper, and cayenne
	margarine
	chopped fresh mint
	(if desired)

The coarse fat should be removed from the sheep. After clean-
ing, rub the meat inside and out with coarse salt and plenty of
margarine, then sprinkle with pepper. If you are not going to
stuff the lamb, mix the chopped onion with the margarine when
rubbing the inside of the carcass. If the meat is to be stuffed, add
the onion to all the ingredients for the stuffing, mix well, fill the
sheep, and fasten with skewers. Roast outdoors on spits over a
pit of glowing coals (these have to be prepared hours before-
hand) for a *kumzits*. Or roast in a 325° oven (if you have one
big enough!) 20–35 minutes per pound. Or sear the meat in a
very hot oven, reduce heat to 325°, and roast. Baste during
roasting.

ROAST SHOULDER OF LAMB   *Rosh Hashana*

Lamb is served on Rosh Hashana because it recalls the sacrifice
of the ram instead of Isaac. A sweet fruit sauce is the festival's
accompaniment to this dish.

1 3-pound shoulder of	½ cup diced dried pears
lamb	1 sprig rosemary
2 tablespoons cooking oil	2 tablespoons sugar
3 sprigs mint	salt and pepper

2 cups hot water	1 tablespoon flour
½ cup raisins and currants	

Brown the lamb in hot oil. Steep the mint in the hot water. Discard the mint and pour the liquid, along with the raisins, currants, pears, sugar, and seasonings, over the meat. Cover and simmer until tender (about 2 hours). Mix the flour with the wine and thicken the sauce. Serve with a garnish of fresh mint sprigs. (Serves 6.)

LAMB IN WINE

An ancient legend of the Jews tells about a he-goat who got drunk on wild grapes, whereupon it was said that intoxication is the cause of all sins and the ruin of individuals, as well as nations; therefore Jewish sources condemned it. But moderate enjoyment of the vine is permitted, and even recommended, in Jewish life.

4 onions, chopped	salt and pepper
1 4-pound boned shoulder	1 cup white wine
of lamb	10 black olives
flour	mint leaves

Make a nest of the chopped onion. Rub the meat with the flour, salt, and pepper. Roast in a 450° oven for half an hour. Pour the wine over and add the olives. Roast until desired degree of doneness is achieved (30 minutes to the pound for well done, 18–20 minutes to the pound for rare, including searing time), basting with the wine from time to time. Add mint leaves to the pan juice 15 minutes before removing from the oven. (Serves 4–6.)

VEAL GOULASH   *Succot*

3 onions, chopped	1 teaspoon salt
1 clove garlic (optional)	2 cups plus 2 tablespoons
4 tablespoons cooking oil	water
3 ounces tomato purée	2 pounds veal, cubed
1 tablespoon paprika	1 tablespoon flour

Stew the chopped onions (and garlic, if desired) in the oil over very low heat. Add tomato purée, paprika, salt, and the 2 cups of water. Add the cubed veal and simmer until tender. Add water only if the sauce evaporates too much. Dissolve the flour in the 2 tablespoons water and add to the meat, stirring for a minute. (Serves 6.)

JOO JOOH STUFFED LAMB BREAST *Rosh Hashana*

*Lamb is traditional for Easterners on Rosh Hashana, served in
many ways. The breast is often served with a stuffing, the
variety of which depends also on tribal taste. It may vary from
a sage-spiced bread stuffing to a rice and apple-raisin filling.
A popular one in Israel is the Persian Joo Jooh chicken stuffing.*

1 4-pound breast of lamb	1 cup diced, cooked chicken
1 cup chick-peas	1 tablespoon margarine
8 cups water	2 teaspoons salt
½ cup burghul (cracked wheat) or brown rice	black pepper
	½ cup toasted almonds

Soak the chick-peas overnight and then cook in the water over
low heat until soft (about 2 hours). Meanwhile, cook the burghul
or rice until almost tender (about 30 minutes). Drain the water
from the chick-peas and mix with all the remaining ingredients.
Stuff into the breast of lamb, sew up, and roast in a 450° oven 30
minutes. Reduce heat to 300° and cook 25 minutes per pound of
lamb for medium-done meat, adding water if needed. (Serves
6–8.)

LAMB CHOPS AND SHPRITZ *Purim*

*The great Eliezer Ben Yehuda, for whom many main streets are
named in Israel, was the father of modern Hebrew, giving us
words for "ice cream," "doll," and "soldier"—all new in the
modern life of the Jewish people. But he failed to give us a word
for "shpritz" (which is Yiddish for "splash"), for the wine-and-
soda drink that he always took with lamb chops, his favorite
dish.*

*Eliezer Ben-Yehuda would have this dish served with an Orien-
tal pilau and fried potatoes, followed by a prune compote and
Turkish coffee. His "shpritz" drinks, then as now, were very popular in Israel, made of dry red wine or a dry white wine—red
wine on cold days, chilled white wine shpritz on hot days. Just
add soda water to a glass one-third full of wine.*

6 lamb chops, 1 inch thick	salt and pepper
flour	oil for frying

Mix the salt and pepper into the flour and dip the lamb chops
into the mixture. Have a pan very hot and add a little oil. Brown
the chops quickly on both sides and then reduce heat (pouring
off extra fat) and fry until done to your taste (7–15 minutes).
(Serves 6.)

Independence Day
KEBABS OF LAMB—(GROUND AND GRILLED)

Lamb in Hebrew is "kebes," and the term "kebab" comes from it. This is the favorite meat dish in Israel, as it is in all the Middle East.

1½ pounds lamb, chopped   onion, quartered
  1 onion, chopped fine   tomato, quartered
  1 tablespoon chopped   liver, cubed (optional)
     parsley   oil
    salt and pepper to taste

Put the meat and onion through the meat chopper twice, and the parsley, salt, and pepper. Form into finger-shaped hamburgers and string on skewers alternately with the quartered onions, tomatoes, and if you wish, cubes of liver. Drizzle a little oil over the kebabs and grill over an open fire. Serve on a bed of chopped parsley with rice. (Serves 4–6.)

KIBBE—WHEAT-LAMB LOAF   *Independence Day*

Jewish housewives from Iraq make egg-shaped forms of kibbe. They do this by dividing the burghul mixture into balls, which they hold in the palm of the hand. Then, to make a cavity in the ball, they insert a finger, and work it round and round until the ball is hollow. They then fill the cavity with the meat mixture, close the kibbe, and fry or boil it. It is a long day's work—or play! This recipe is easier.

  1 cup burghul (cracked   ½ cup margarine
     wheat)   4 tablespoons pine nuts
 ½ pound fat lamb, ground   1 teaspoon chopped parsley
1½ pounds lean lamb,   dash of cayenne
     ground   salt and pepper to taste
  6 onions, chopped

Soak the burghul for about an hour and then dry in a collander. Mix with the fat lamb. Lightly fry the ground lean meat and onions in the margarine and then toss in the pine nuts for a light toasting. Add the parsley and seasonings. Pat a base of the burghul mixture into a greased baking dish (as you would for a pie with a cracker-crumb crust). Press down firmly and put in the meat mixture. Cover with the remaining burghul mixture, pat down well, and mark into servings with a sharp knife. Bake in 350° oven, for about an hour. (Serves 6–8.)

Independence Day
MOUSSAKA—EGGPLANT-LAMB CASSEROLE

Moussaka, originally a Greek dish, was introduced into Turkey, and from there it won over the Middle East, which remained captive forever. In some countries this dish is topped with cheese; in others the sauce is made with milk or yoghurt. This is the Israeli version.

2 medium eggplants	2 tablespoons flour
1 teaspoon salt	¼ cup tomato paste, mixed
1 pound ground lamb	with ¼ cup water
2 tablespoons water	1 tablespoon cornstarch
3 onions, chopped	2 cups water or stock
2 cloves garlic, crushed	4 eggs
6 tablespoons oil	

Slice (do not peel) the eggplant. Sprinkle with the salt and put in the sun to evaporate for about an hour, then wash and dry the slices. Mix the meat with the water. In the oil, lightly fry the onions, then the garlic and chopped meat, and remove from the pan. Sprinkle the eggplant with flour and fry it. Into a greased casserole put alternate layers (beginning and ending with the eggplant) of tomato paste, onions, meat, and eggplant, until casserole is filled to within 1 inch of the top. Bake in a 350° oven for about 40 minutes, until the meat is done. Dissolve the cornstarch in the water or stock. Beat the eggs and add. Pour this mixture over the casserole. Return to the oven and bake until the sauce has begun to set (about 20 minutes). Serve hot. (Serves 6.)

LAMB AND SQUASH BAKE   *Passover*

When my sister Becky was nursing with UNRRA at the Yugoslav refugee camp in Egypt, she learned to love this dish, which is a sort of cousin to the Balkan moussaka. It became very popular in Israel with the immigration after the war of the Jewish remnant from Balkan countries.

1 pound ground lamb	6 large tomatoes, sliced
2 cloves garlic, minced	1 pound summer squash,
dash of nutmeg	sliced
salt and pepper to taste	boiling water
3 tablespoons chopped	
parsley	

Mix the meat with the garlic, nutmeg, salt, pepper, and parsley. Form into balls. Grease a casserole and layer alternately with tomatoes and squash. Place the meat balls on top and cover with more tomato and squash slices. Pour in just enough boiling water to half cover the meat. Cover and bake in a 350° oven for an hour. (Serves 4–6.)

SHEEP'S HEAD   *Rosh Hashana*

No Western housewife is likely to cook this symbolic Rosh Hashana dish, which is sure to be on the tables of West Asian Jews from Yemen and Afghanistan. The head is spiced with fenugreek sauce—a red-hot legume mixture known in Hebrew as "rubia" and better known for the Arabic "hilbeh." The vegetables used in this recipe are all a play on words on the blessings of freedom, luck, and plenty. "Rubia," for instance, can be punned for the Hebrew word "harbeh," "plenty."

1 *sheep's head*	*fenugreek sauce (hilbeh)*
beets	*(see* Index*)*
squash (vegetable marrow)	*salt and pepper*
pumpkin	

The sheep's head is put into boiling salt water for a few minutes; then the water is discarded. This is repeated twice more. A bed of beets, vegetable marrow, and pumpkin are put into the pot, and the sheep's head on top of it. This is slowly cooked until all the meat is tender. Fenugreek sauce is served with the sheep's head upon the table (or upon the carpet center, if the family still retains its former custom of eating while sitting on cushions around a rug on the floor).

LAMB IN LEMON (TUNISIAN)   *Passover*

½ *cup cooking oil*	1 *lemon, peeled and sliced*
1 *cup water*	*fine*
dash of saffron	2 *pounds lamb chops*
dash of cinnamon	
salt and pepper	

Into a casserole, put the oil, water, saffron, cinnamon, salt, pepper, and the lemon. Add the lamb chops and simmer over low heat, covered, for 1 hour. (Serves 4.)

MOCK VENISON   *Independence Day*

Deer still roam the Negev in Israel as they did in the days of Esau the hunter, but they are rarely trapped for meat. Though this savory lamb is often made by Israeli housewives, few of them realize that it is the dish Rebecca deceived Isaac into believing was venison.

1 cup water
1 cup wine vinegar
2 teaspoons sugar
½ teaspoon whole pepper-
    corns
1 tablespoon salt
1 teaspoon caraway seed

2 bay leaves
3 pounds boned lamb
1 clove garlic, minced
2 onions, minced
½ cup port wine
    margarine (optional)

Boil the water, vinegar, sugar, peppers, salt, caraway seed, and bay leaves for a minute, then cool. Put the lamb in an earthen or glass bowl with the minced garlic and onions. Pour the liquid over and add the wine. Marinate the meat in this for 24 hours, turning occasionally. Remove the meat from the liquid and dry with a paper towel. If the meat is lean, spread with soft margarine. Roast in a 450° oven for thirty minutes, to brown. Reduce heat to 300°, add the liquid from the marinade, and continue to cook until tender (about 1½ hours), basting or turning the meat from time to time. (Serves 6–8.)

HUTZPA-HUTSPOT   *Succot*

No Dutchman would eat this "poor man's food" on a festival, but those of us who have learned to make it in Israel do take delight in serving it in the succah on Succot. The dish came to Holland in 1573 when the Spanish army was ousted from Leyden, leaving stew simmering in hot pots. Israelis had the hutzpa (nerve) to add cabbage and beans to the traditional version of a Dutch dish.

2 pounds soup meat
¼ pound fat sausage
    water to cover
    salt and pepper to taste
2 cups shredded cabbage

2 cups shredded green beans
2 cups sliced onions
2 cups grated carrots
2 pounds potatoes, diced

Simmer the meat and sausage, covered with water, and with salt and pepper to taste, slowly for an hour. Add the cabbage, beans, onions, and carrots and simmer until tender (about 15 minutes).

Add the potatoes and cook until tender (about 15 minutes). When the dish is ready, almost all the water should be cooked away. Remove the meat. With a wooden spoon, mash the remainder of the stew to a pulp. Serve with the meat. (Serves 8–10.)

IABRAK—TUNISIAN MEAT BALLS   *Rosh Hashana*

1 cup chick-peas	oil for frying
2 tablespoons water	2 onions, chopped
1 pound chopped meat	2 tomatoes, chopped
½ cup breadcrumbs	1 tablespoon chopped
1 tablespoon chopped	parsley
parsley	½ teaspoon salt
dash of nutmeg	dash of saffron
salt and pepper to taste	dash of cinnamon
1 egg, slightly beaten	dash of pepper

Soak the chick-peas overnight and then cook gently until almost soft (about 2 hours). Mix the meat, breadcrumbs, parsley, nutmeg, salt, pepper, egg, and water. Form the mixture into balls and brown in the oil. Remove the meat and fry the chopped onions, then the tomatoes. Put the meat, vegetables, chick-peas, and all the remaining seasonings into a pot. Close tightly and simmer gently for half an hour. (Serves 4–6.)

SWEET-SOUR MEATBALLS   *Succot*

½ cup hot water	1 cup cold water
1 heaping tablespoon	½ cup ketchup
breadcrumbs	rasins, to taste
1 pound chopped meat	3 tablespoons sugar
2 onions, chopped	1 lemon, sliced
2 eggs	1 tablespoon margarine
salt and pepper to taste	1 tablespoon cornstarch
oil for browning	

Pour the hot water over the breadcrumbs and then add to the meat, onions, eggs, salt, and pepper. Form into balls and brown them lightly in oil. Meanwhile, bring the cold water, ketchup, raisins, sugar, and sliced lemon to a boil. Put in the meatballs and simmer gently for about 30 minutes. Mix the margarine with the cornstarch to thicken the sauce. Correct seasoning, if desired, to make the meatballs more sweet or more sour. (Serves 4.)

HENAGHI—MEAT-NUT CASSEROLE *Rosh Hashana*

*This is a Caucasian dish served on Rosh Hashana. A very special
one, it requires long and careful cooking. Perhaps that is why
it is fare for the most important Jewish festival.*

1 cup water	1 pound veal
2 tablespoons oil	6 eggs, well beaten
1 teaspoon salt	2 cups ground nuts

Combine the water, oil, and salt, then cut the veal into very
small pieces and stew gently in the resulting stock. When tender
(about 20 minutes), beat the eggs and mix in the nuts. Pour this
over the hot veal, still in the stock, and cook over very low heat
for 5 hours. Serve hot. (Serves 4.)

Independence Day
SHASHLIK—GRILLED MEAT CUBES

*Meat from the sacrifices was cooked in this way for the priests in
Biblical days.*

1 pound tender meat	4 tablespoons oil
1 clove garlic, crushed	salt and pepper to taste

Cut the meat into 1-inch cubes and put to marinate, with the
garlic, in the oil. After half an hour, string the cubes on skewers,
sprinkle with salt and pepper, and grill, preferably over a bed of
wood coals. (Serve 3.)

SARMIS—FILLED GRAPE LEAVES *Independence Day*
(also called Sarmali, Dolmas and Malfouf)

*In Israel this dish is made both in the Bulgarian fashion, using
cabbage leaves, and the Near Eastern one, using grape leaves.
Unlike the Balkan recipe, this one omits the tomato sauce and
uses water and wine, and sometimes a hint of mint. The grape
leaves are essential, for their aroma.*

2 large onions, chopped	salt and pepper to taste
½ cup olive oil	pine nuts and raisins
¾ cup rice	(if desired)
1½ pounds ground veal or beef	dash of cinnamon or nutmeg (if desired)
1 teaspoon chopped mint	grape leaves (large)
½ cup dry white wine	

Fry the onions in the oil, add the rice and fry until slightly golden. Remove from heat, mix with the meat, mint, salt, and pepper and, if desired, a sprinkling of pine nuts and raisins. In some families a dash of nutmeg or cinnamon is also added. Put the large grape leaves in very hot water for a few minutes, to soften. In the center of each leaf put a spoonful of the meat mixture and roll up into finger-shaped and -sized packets, tucking the ends of the leaves in from the start. Pack fairly closely in a casserole. Pour the wine over and add water to cover the sarmis. Cook over low heat, 40–45 minutes, or bake in a 300° oven, 40–45 minutes, adding water from time to time to keep the sarmis covered, until the cooking is almost done; then allow to brown a little with an additional sprinkling of olive oil. Makes about 40 finger-sized sarmis. (Serves 10–12 persons, figuring 3–4 sarmis per person.)

HAMIM DI FAGIOLO (ITALIAN CHOLENT)   *Shabbat*

The Jews of Italy are nearly all descendants of Spanish Jews who fled the Inquisition. This Sabbath dish called "hamim" is from the Hebrew word for "hot." But while the cholent or shalet (as it is sometimes called) has a German influence on its flavor, the "hamim" is definitely Italian-inclined, just as the dish of the same name in North Africa is highly spiced, like all their other foods.

1 *pound beans, broad or*	*3 eggs*
navy	*3 tablespoons breadcrumbs*
1 *cup tomato sauce*	*2 tablespoons minced parsley*
(*see* Index for Capelleti	*3 tablespoons oil for frying*
Freddi)	*1 onion, chopped*
4 cups water	*salt and pepper to taste*
2 pounds minced meat	

Soak the beans overnight. Make a tomato sauce as in the recipe for Capelletti Freddi. Put the drained beans in a heavy pot with the sauce and the water, and bring to the boil. Mix the chopped meat, egg, breadcrumbs, and parsley and form into four or five balls (which are cut up for serving). Fry the meat balls in the oil with the onion. When the sauce in the beans begins to thicken, season to taste and put the meat, oil, and onion on top. Cover the pot tightly. Put on low heat and cook overnight. (Serves 6–8.)

KEFTEDES WITH TAHINA *Succot*

The keftede, or kufta, is a little round flat hamburger, either grilled or fried, which tastes different in the homes of Bulgarian immigrants (who spice it strongly with cumin), in the homes of Moroccans (who make it fragrant with cinnamon), and at the tables of immigrants from Syria (who use allspice and/or mint). On Saturday nights, in the immigrant villages of Israel, whole families go to outdoor restaurants to eat keftedes. It is quite an event, with the aromas of barbecuing keftedes grilling over the embers and plates of hot hamoutzim pickles and piquant bean salads tantalizing one and all.

3 tablespoons water
1 teaspoon powdered
   chicken soup
1 slice white bread
   (without crust)
1 pound chopped beef or
   lamb
1 onion, chopped fine
1 clove garlic, crushed
   salt and pepper to taste

1 or 2 teaspoons chopped
   mint (if desired)
1 egg, well beaten
   dash of either cumin,
   allspice or cinnamon,
   to taste
½ cup dry breadcrumbs
1 cup tahina paste
   (see Tahina Paste,
   introductory note)

Mix the water with the chicken soup powder and soak the bread in it. Add the meat, onion, garlic, salt, pepper, mint, and egg. Mix well. Use either cumin, allspice, or cinnamon for spicing further. Form the mixture into small flat cakes and fry until just brown on both sides. Or grill them. Put the keftedes into a baking pan or griller. Mix the breadcrumbs with prepared tahina and spread over the top of each keftede. Put under the grill or in the oven until the topping is golden. Serve hot. (Serves 4.)

HONEYED CHICKEN (JEDJAD IMER) *Passover*

The English have always been hearty beef eaters, but they also liked fowl and during the Middle Ages they ate swans and served peacocks if the king was coming. One of their delicacies was to roast meat or chickens with honey. The Crusaders brought the dish to Palestine and Arabs in the Middle East still make it today, calling the dish "Jedjad-Imer."

salt
1 4-pound chicken
½ lemon
6 tablespoons margarine

3 tablespoons honey (more
    if you have a sweet
    tooth)

Salt the chicken. Rub with the lemon. Melt the margarine and mix it with the honey. Brush the bird inside and out with the sweetener. Roast in a 350° oven until the bird is done (1½ to 2 hours), basting occasionally with more of the honey-margarine mixture. (Serves 5–6.)

SESAME FRIED CHICKEN *Independence Day*

Sesame seeds have come to Israel from its neighboring lands. This nut-flavored seed is used in a wide variety of dishes, from bread to confections.

1 cup flour
1 cup sesame seed
2 tablespoons favorite herbs,
    chopped
2 teaspoons sweet paprika

2 teaspoons salt
1 fryer (about 2½ pounds)
1 egg
1 cup stock or water
    oil for frying

Mix the flour, sesame seed, herbs, paprika, salt, and pepper in a paper bag. Cut the chicken into serving pieces and shake in the bag. Beat the egg and add to the stock. Dip the chicken in this liquid and shake again in the flour mixture. Heat the oil in a heavy pan and fry the chicken until golden. Transfer to a casserole and bake in a 325° oven half an hour, or until tender.

Independence Day
CITRUS CHICKEN—POULET MAROCAIN AU CITRON

Chicken is used more than any other flesh food in Israel, and with the abundance of citrus fruits, the combination of the two has led to many succulent dishes. This one, based on a lemon-chicken dish from Morocco and an orange-duckling dish from France, can by now be termed truly Israeli.

1 roaster (about 4 pounds)	salt and pepper to taste
lemon, kumquat, or orange	dash of coriander
conserves or marmalade	water or orange juice
olive oil to cover roasting pan	

Put the conserve (2 small lemons or 4 kumquats or 1 orange) into the body of the chicken. Heat the olive oil. Sprinkle the bird with the salt, pepper, and coriander and place in a roasting pan with the hot olive oil. Roast 1¾ hours in a 350° oven. Baste during roasting, adding a little orange juice or water for sauce. The fowl comes out aromatic and delicious. (Serves 4.)

NOTE: Every Israeli who owns a citrus tree makes preserved citrus fruit. This is done by soaking the cut skins or even the whole fruit for a day and then boiling them three times, with a fresh change of water each time. The fruit or skins are then weighed and cooked with an equal weight of sugar until glazed. If whole fruits are used, they must be very small.

CHICKEN STUFFED AND DRUNK   *Shabbat*

1 large roasting chicken	dash each of pepper,
4 tablespoons chicken fat	paprika, ginger,
⅔ cup raw rice	cinnamon
2 tablespoons chopped	1 tablespoon chopped
pecans	parsley
2 tablespoons chopped dates	1 cup dry white wine
1 tablespoon dehydrated	1 cup tomato juice
chicken soup	water, if needed
1 teaspoon salt	

Sprinkle the bird with salt and spread, inside and out, with the fat. Set aside while you mix the stuffing of rice, nuts, dates, de-hydrated soup, and salt. Add a dash each of pepper, paprika, ginger, and cinnamon. Stir in the chopped parsley. Fill the cavity of the chicken and sew up. Put the chicken into a roasting pan and surround with the wine, tomato juice, and chopped onion. Cover and cook in a moderate oven until the chicken is tender. Baste the chicken from time to time. If the sauce is absorbed before cooking is finished, add a little more wine with water. Remove the lid for browning the chicken at the end. (Serves 4–6.)

ISRAEL FRIED CHICKEN
à la Southern or Backhendl!　　　　　　　　　*Succot*

Now really, what is the difference (except in price, I mean) between Israel-fried chicken, American Southern-fried chicken and Vienna backhendl? Only the spicing, nothing much else. Israelis like a hot hint of cayenne, Americans are content with salt, and the Austrians want a taste of lemon and bay leaf. Have it my way—the ingathered recipe.

2 broiler-fryers	dash of paprika
juice of 1 lemon	dash of cayenne
2 eggs, beaten	dry crumbs
½ cup flour	oil for frying
salt and pepper	

Cut the chickens into frying pieces. Drizzle with lemon juice and set aside. Beat the eggs. Mix together the flour, salt, pepper, parika, and cayenne. Roll the chicken in this mixture and shake off the excess. Dip the pieces in beaten eggs and then in the dry crumbs. Fry the chicken in a little oil until golden. Then reduce heat and continue to cook covered, for 25–30 minutes. Drain. Serve with lemon wedges. (Serves 4–6.)

MOROCCAN CHICKEN—JEDJAD ZEITOON　*Yom Kippur*

1 3-pound broiler-fryer	1 cup green olives
4 tablespoons olive oil	1 sweet pickled lemon
¼ teaspoon turmeric	water to cover

Cut the chicken into serving pieces. Brush with the oil and sprinkle with turmeric. Put the chicken into a heavy pot and cover with the olives and slices of lemon. Cover with water and simmer until the chicken is tender (about 30 minutes). (Serves 4.)

LEMON GRILLED CHICKEN *Purim*

The Israel outdoor kumzits, *with its campfire barbecue, has instilled into Israelis a passion for grilled instead of pan- or oven-cooked food. This dish of Queen Anne's—and her great-grand-father's, Charles II, too—was called Chicken Surprise, ". . . served with a sauce of butter and gravy and squeezed lemon and Your Garnishing fry's Parsley and cut Orange." It could go very well into a menu in Tel Aviv today.*

2 2-pound broilers	salt and pepper
juice of 3 large lemons	orange slices and parsley
½ cup margarine	for garnish

Split each chicken into 4 pieces and set aside for an hour in the lemon juice. Rub generously with margarine and sprinkle with salt and pepper. Put the pieces (skin side down) about 6 inches from broiler heat. Sprinkle the flesh with lemon juice and broil. Baste if necessary with the pan juice and more lemon juice. Grill for about 15 minutes, then turn and sprinkle again with lemon juice. Baste until brown. If you have a rotisserie you can keep them turning for another 20 minutes. If not, put into a 350° oven, with the juices from the dripping pan, and bake for about 20 minutes more. Serve with orange slices and parsley for a queenly dish. (Serves 6.)

COCK IN THE POT *Ju Besh'vat*

A Jewish legend relates that at the time of Methuselah, children were born after a few days pregnancy and could walk and talk right after birth. Once a newborn babe, running to fetch a light whereby his mother might cut the navel string, met the chief of the demons, and a combat ensued.

Suddenly a cock crowed and the demon made off, crying out to the child, "Go and report unto thy mother, if it had not been for the crowing of the cock, I had killed thee."

Whereupon the child retorted, "Go and report unto thy mother, if it had not been for my uncut navel string, I had killed thee."

1 tablespoon chicken fat	salt, pepper, paprika, to
3 onions, sliced	taste
1 cock (well, it could be a	
pullet!) cut up	

Put the chicken fat and onions in the pot and the chicken pieces on top. Sprinkle with salt, pepper, and paprika. Close the pot tightly and cook very slowly on top of the range. Water generally is not required unless the fowl is fat, and even then only a few spoonfuls should be added at a time. Cook until the chicken is tender (2½ hours for the cock!).

CHICKEN CURRY *Rosh Hashana*

Since the founding of the state of Israel, a new Jewish community has been ingathered: the Jews of Cochin, India. The ancestors of this community are believed to have emigrated from Palestine after the second destruction of the Temple. Although their culture (including a caste system) and even their skin coloring has become indistinguishable from that of their Hindu neighbors, they never forsook their Jewish heritage. Their food, chiefly rice and curries, is like that of the Indians, except that they strictly maintain the kashrut laws.

1 2-pound chicken	1 (or more) tablespoons curry powder
3 tablespoons olive oil	1½ tablespoons flour
3½ cups water	3 cups chicken stock (or coconut milk)
5 large onions, chopped	
2 cloves garlic, mashed	2 tablespoons grated coconut (optional)
4 large tomatoes, chopped	
1 cup chopped celery	1½ teaspoons salt
2 apples, peeled and cubed	cayenne pepper to taste
2 tablespoons sugar	
1 teaspoon ground ginger	

Cut the chicken up and fry lightly in the oil. Remove from the oil and simmer in the water until tender (about ½ hour). (Use the liquid as the soup stock for the curry.) Fry the onions, garlic, tomatoes, celery, apples, sugar, ginger, and curry powder in the oil. Sprinkle on the flour, mix well, and add the chicken stock or coconut milk, coconut, and seasonings. Add the chicken and cook 10 minutes more. Serve hot with rice. (Serves 4.)

ORIENTAL CHICKEN *Purim*

1 chicken (about 3 pounds)	1 green pepper, chopped
½ cup olive oil	1 teaspoon pine nuts
1 clove garlic, minced	1 cup water
2 onions, chopped	dash of curry (optional)
2 cups chopped tomatoes	

Cut the chicken into serving pieces and brown in the oil. Put into a casserole with the oil. Add the remaining ingredients. Bake in a 375° oven until the chicken is tender (about 30 minutes). (Serves 4.)

CHICKEN CELERIAC TUNISIAN   *Rosh Hashana*

*Oh, how I long for a crisp white stalk of American celery, which
we do not get in Israel! However, we do have something better
for cooking—our celeriac, or celery root! This is a green celery,
the big root of which goes into soups and cooked-vegetable salads;
the stalk and leaves are used for flavoring every kind of fish,
fowl, and flesh dish. Wild celery was used even by the ancient
Romans as an appetizer, and was well known in the Middle Ages
as a seasoning. American white celery was developed only a century ago, after the Spaniards introduced the wild plant to
Mexico. We eagerly await its culture in Israel.*

1 3-pound young chicken	salt and pepper to taste
oil for browning	1 cup water
2 cups small onions	2 bundles celery, stalks
1 pound celery root, cubed	and leaves
½ cup tomato purée	

Brown the whole chicken in oil and put into a casserole with the
onions, celery root, tomato purée, seasoning, and water. Cover
the whole chicken with wet leaves and stalks of celery and close
the pot tightly. Cook over very low heat until the vegetables and
chicken are tender (1 to 1½ hours). If necessary, wet the celery
leaves from time to time with a sprinkling of water. (Serves 4.)

Tu Besh'vat
CHICKEN FRICASSEE IN BLACK AND WHITE

*Rina Nikova brought ballet to Israel long before anything but
the rugged* hora *folk dancing was acceptable. She took her
Yemenite Biblical ballet group to Paris, where they performed
in the palace of Baron Maurice de Rothschild. After the perform-
ance the young girls were feted at a fourteen-course dinner of the
finest French cuisine, including* la fricassée de poulet. *Unaccus-
tomed to subtle flavors, and longing for their familiar fiery
sauces, the girls shocked the staff when they began to cure their
food. When the fricassee was snowed under a heavy sprinkling
of salt and highlighted with spoonfuls of pepper, they began to
enjoy their food, which was thereafter referred to by the above
title. Louis XIV, who made the original dish popular, may have
turned in his grave as a result.*

1 stewing chicken	2 tablespoons margarine
4 cups water	2 tablespoons flour
1 onion	3 egg yolks
1 clove	¼ pound sliced mushrooms,
1 carrot, sliced	boiled

> bouquet of herbs
>   (parsley, celery, etc.)
> salt and pepper to taste

> 10 small onions
> 1 teaspoon lemon juice

Cut the chicken into pieces and cook in the water with the onion (stuck with the clove), carrot, herbs, salt, and pepper. Simmer gently for one hour, skimming the soup of all froth and fat. When the chicken is tender, strain off the stock. In another pan melt the margarine and stir in the flour. Add 1½ cups of the stock slowly and stir while it cooks. Beat the egg yolks, add a little stock to them, and beat them into the stock. Add the mushrooms and onions, and then the lemon juice. Pour this sauce over the hot chicken. (Serves 4–6.)

NOTE: Don't do what the Yemenite girls did—all that salt and pepper!

KOSHER CHICKEN A LA KING   *Shabbat*

Since the kosher laws prohibit the cooking of milk with meat or fowl, chicken à la king was a forbidden dish until clever cooks found out how to omit the cream and still succeed with the taste. This recipe, created by Chef Otto Gromer of the Sheraton Tel Aviv Hotel, is fit not only for a king, but even for a rabbi.

> 1 large chicken
>   (about 5 pounds)
>   water
> 7½ tablespoons margarine
> 3 tablespoons flour
> 1½ cups chicken stock
> ½ cup white wine

> ½ clove garlic, minced
>   dash of white pepper
>   dash of mace or nutmeg
> 1 fleshy green pepper
> 1 red pimiento
> 1 cup sliced mushrooms
> 2 egg yolks

Cut up the chicken and cook in a shallow pan with water to cover about 35 minutes, or until the meat can be removed from the bones and diced into 1-inch chunks. Reduce the stock to 1½ cups by boiling briskly. Melt 3 tablespoons of margarine, add the flour, and when the mixture bubbles, stir in the chicken stock and wine. Flavor with the garlic, white pepper, and mace or nutmeg. Dice the pepper and pimiento, add the mushrooms, and sauté in 3 more tablespoons margarine. Add to the chicken and keep hot. Put the chicken stock sauce into a blender. Slowly add the remaining margarine and the egg yolks and blend until the mixture is white. Add this sauce to the remaining ingredients and mix carefully. Serve in patty shells. (Serves 6.)

GEORGIAN STUFFED CHICKEN *Shabbat*

This recipe won Geulah Shemueli fame at the Israel Culinary Contest, where it was judged one of the nine choicest dishes.

2 medium onions, finely chopped	light dash of allspice
2 tablespoons oil for frying	1 teaspoon salt
½ cup water	1 cup pomegranate juice
½ pound chopped beef	1 tablespoon sugar
heavy dash of freshly ground pepper	3 tablespoons lemon juice
heavy dash of cinnamon	1 3-pound roasting chicken
	½ lemon
	grape juice, if desired

Fry the onions in the oil until golden. Add the water to the meat, stir into the onions, and cook until the water is evaporated, stirring from time to time. Drain off any fat left in the pan. Add the spices and salt to the meat mixture. Pour in the pomegranate juice and add the sugar and lemon juice. Rub the chicken inside and out with the lemon and then fill with the meat stuffing. Lightly brown the chicken. Pot roast it on very low heat for about 3 hours, adding grape juice, if you wish, and more pomegranate juice from time to time, to flavor, gild, and glaze the bird. (Serves 3.)

CHICKEN À LA SABRA *Purim*

This recipe was created by Willeta Bar-Ilan for the Tel-Aviv Sheraton Hotel.

10 oil-cured whole olives, plus ½ cup pitted and slivered	1 cup margarine
	2 cups orange juice
	1 cup dry red wine
¾ cup water	2 large red onions, sliced
2 3-pound broilers	2 teaspoons salt
flour for coating	¼ teaspoon black pepper
salt, pepper, and paprika for coating	1½ teaspoons powdered thyme

Simmer the whole olives in the water for 10 minutes. Strain. Have the chickens cut into quarters. Coat the chicken pieces with a mixture of flour, salt, pepper, and paprika. Melt the margarine in the skillet; add the chicken, and brown lightly. Remove the chicken from the skillet and place in a large flat casserole. To the skillet add the orange juice, wine, olive liquor, onions, salt, pepper, and thyme. Simmer 3 minutes. Pour the sauce over the chicken and bake 1 hour in a 350° oven, basting occasionally with the sauce. Spread the ½ cup pitted, slivered olives over the chicken. Continue baking the chicken 30 minutes more, or until tender. (Serves 6–8.)

LE COQ AU VIN   *Shabbat*

2 *2-pound frying chickens*   *4 small onions*
flour   *2 cups dry wine*
margarine   *(white or red)*
½ *pound mushrooms*   *salt and pepper*
parsley, celery (tied
together)

Cut the chickens into serving pieces, roll in flour, and sauté in margarine. Add the mushrooms, herbs, and onions, cover the pan and simmer until almost tender (about 20 minutes). Remove the parsley and celery. Add the wine and cook until done (about 10 minutes more). Season to taste. (Serves 4.)

NEW WAVE CHICKEN   *Shabbat*

This dish, which won second prize in the Israel Culinary Contest, may read like an abstract composition, but the flavors blend harmoniously and succulently. The dish is an original creation of Mrs. Mathilde Alkilay, an immigrant from Bulgaria.

1 *3-pound chicken*   ½ *bunch celery stalks and*
4 *tablespoons cooking oil*   *a few celery leaves,*
3 *tomatoes, diced*   *chopped*
7 *cloves garlic*   5 *whole black peppercorns*
½ *cup cognac*   *pinch of ginger*
2½ *cups dry white wine*   12 *green olives*
1 *teaspoon salt*   2 *oranges, sliced*
4 *bay leaves*   *(unpeeled)*

Cut the chicken into serving pieces and brown well in the oil. Add the tomatoes and 2 cloves of the garlic. Cook on low heat 30 minutes. Add the cognac, white wine, salt, bay leaves, celery stalks and leaves, black peppercorns, ginger, olives, and the remaining garlic. Continue cooking for another 30 minutes. When the chicken is tender, surround with the orange slices and keep on the heat for a few minutes more. Serve with Oriental rice. (Serves 4.)

CHICKEN PAPRIKA $\mathcal{S}habbat$

Thanks to our ingathering of Hungarians, this dish has become an Israeli specialty.

4 large onions, finely chopped	2 green peppers, diced
4 tablespoons fat	1 teaspoon salt
(chicken or margarine)	1 teaspoon flour
1 tablespoon paprika	2 tablespoons water
2 young chickens, cut up	

Put the onions and fat in a heavy skillet over very low heat and stew until the onions are almost dissolved. (They should not fry.) Add the paprika, and after 5 minutes the cut-up chicken. Cover and continue to stew for about 20 minutes. Add the green peppers and salt. Stew until the chicken is tender (about 10 minutes). Add the flour mixed with the water, bring to a boil, and serve with dumplings. (Serves 4.)

STUFFED PIMENTO $\mathcal{T}u$ $\mathcal{B}esh'vat$

Letters in reply to my food column in the Jerusalem Post *repeatedly ask, "What is a pimento?" Once upon a time "pepper" simply meant "spice." The Spanish word for pepper is "pimiento," which lost an* i *in English (a mere printer's error!). The word "pimento" stuck to the berry of the allspice tree, when housewives began to use more spices and to label them, and "pepper" was kept for the many hot berries and fruits we know by that name. However, just to confuse you more, the bell peppers of the nightshade family (with cousins like the tomato, eggplant, and potato) are as varied in shapes and sizes as the squash family. And one of their offspring is a tomato-shaped and deep red (when ripe) pepper from which sweet paprika is made, and it is—guess what?—a pimento!*

P.S. *Consult the encyclopedia for the pepper family tree.*

10 medium sweet red peppers	3 cups ground cooked
2 onions, chopped	chicken
3 tablespoons oil for frying	salt to taste
1 clove garlic, crushed	1 egg
1 tablespoon chopped	½ cup water
parsley	

Cut the tops off the peppers and remove the seeds. Fry the onion in the oil. Add the garlic, parsley, chicken, salt, and egg. Fill the pimentos. Put into a casserole with the water. Bake in a 375° oven for about 30 minutes. (Serves 10.)

CHICKEN PILAU (RICE)

Shabbat

This is a Sabbath dish among the Iraqi immigrants to Israel. They learned it from their Moslem neighbors who make it thus.

1 4-pound chicken	3 cups rice
water to cover	½ cup almonds
salt and pepper to taste	oil as needed
3 tablespoons tomato paste	¾ cup raisins
few grains saffron	

Brown the chicken on all sides in oil. Cover with water, add salt and pepper, and cook until the chicken is done (about 45 minutes). Remove the bird. Add the tomato paste and saffron to the stock. While the chicken cooks, soak the rice in cold water (this is essential, to prevent the rice from sticking in a mass later on). Add the soaked rice to the stock. If necessary, add more water to cover the rice. Bring to the boil, then reduce heat as low as possible, so that the rice cooks slowly and soaks up the stock. Remove the meat from the chicken in as large pieces as possible. Sauté the slivered almonds in oil. Add the raisins for a moment. Pour the oil over the rice. Arrange the rice in a casserole and top with the chicken, almonds, and raisins. (Serves 6–8.)

CHICKEN ROLLS WITH ORÉGANO

Purim

The hyssop referred to in the Bible did not grow in Palestine. The origanum looks almost like it and is believed by researchers to have been the plant used in purification ceremonies. Today it is found in Israeli food, after its introduction through the Neapolitan pizza in Tel Aviv.

3 chicken breasts, cut into	salt and pepper
six pieces	1 teaspoon orégano
6 tablespoons margarine,	(or sweet marjoram)
melted	6 mild sausages

Bone the chicken breasts and pound until flat. Brush with the margarine and season with salt, pepper, and a sprinkling of orégano. Roll up each piece of chicken around a sausage. Fasten with toothpicks. Put into a greased baking dish. Brush with more margarine. Cover the casserole and bake in a 350° oven for one hour. (Serves 3 or 6, depending upon appetites.)

IRAQI HAMIM   *Shabbat*

1 cup lima or other beans
1 fat chicken
½ cup rice
3 tablespoons oil for frying
10 large tomatoes, diced
   dash of cinnamon

dash of cardamom
sale and pepper to taste
5 medium potatoes
   water to cover
3-4 tablespoons chicken fat
   (optional)

Soak the beans overnight. Skin the chicken from below the wings, to include the wings and skin of the neck. Fry the rice in the oil until golden, add four of the diced tomatoes with a dash of cinnamon, cardamom, and salt. Fill the cavity of the skin about ⅓ full and sew up.

Put the drained beans in a pot, with the skinned chicken, and the stuffed skin next to it. Surround with the potatoes. Sprinkle with more cinnamon, cardamom, salt, and pepper. Top with the remaining tomatoes. Cover with water. If the chicken is lean, add 3 or 4 tablespoons of chicken fat. Cover well and simmer on very low heat overnight. (Serves 6.)

ROMANIAN KEFTELE   *Passover*

1 pound chicken breast
5 onions
   oil for frying

12 pears, cut up
   water to cover
6 eggs, beaten

Put the chicken breast and onions through a mincer and fry in oil. Peel and core the pears. Cover with water and cook 15 minutes. Drain. Add to the chicken mixture with the eggs. Fry like pancakes. (Serves 8.)

NOTE: On Passover serve this with the traditional beetroot-horse-radish sauce.

GALANTINA DI POLLO—PRESSED CHICKEN *Yom Kippur*

The Italian housewife has brought to Israel her tradition of devoted homemaking. She, more than anyone else, is ready to spend hours preparing a special dish, of which the following is one. If boning the chicken is hard for you, get your butcher to do it.

1 5-pound roasting chicken	½ ounce goose sausage or
1 ½-pound veal cutlet	salami
1 chicken breast	½ cup blanched pistachio
olive oil	nuts
2 hard-cooked eggs	chicken stock

Remove all flesh and bone from the skin of the chicken (but leave the wings intact). Marinate the veal and chicken in the oil. Then mince all ingredients and mix well. Pack the mixture back into the skin of the chicken, but not too tightly. Sew up the skin and puncture it in several places with a needle. Cook very gently in chicken stock for 1 hour. Remove and cool, covered with a plate and a weight. This jells in its own juices and is served cold. (Serves 6.)

SUPER-MOCK GEFILTE FISH *Shabbat*

My friend Arona Berold told me how her late mother, Annie Cohen, once visited a friend in the desert who longed for gefilte fish on Friday night. Due to the heat and transport problems fish was risky. "But there's a Jewish proverb," said Annie, "which says if you can't have chicken on Friday night, have fish. Let's reverse that: if you can't have fish, serve chicken— and I'll make it taste like gefilte fish!" And she did.

1½ pounds chicken breasts,	3 teaspoons salt
boned	1 teaspoon pepper
5 onions (3 of them sliced)	chicken bones
3 eggs	3 carrots, sliced
½ cup cold water	½ pound celery root, sliced
3 tablespoons matzo meal	

Grind the chicken breasts with the 2 unsliced onions, very fine. Stir in the eggs, water, matzo meal, salt, and pepper. In a large pot put the chicken bones, carrots, the 3 sliced onions, and celery root. Cover with water and a fish rack and bring to a boil. Form the chopped chicken mixture into balls and place next to one another on the rack (or use a bed of onions instead). Liquid should just come to the bottom of the "fish." Bring to a quick boil and then reduce heat to very low. Simmer for 3 hours, adding a little boiling water at the side of the pot from time to time. Remove the "fish" onto a platter and serve cold. (Serves 4.)

TURKEY STEAKS P_{urim}

My neighbor Rivka Kirsch, who is a native Israeli, knows why turkey is such a popular dish on Purim in this country. When she was little, the children living around would go to the nearest barnyard and ask the turkey: "When is Purim?"

The gobbler, of course, answered, as ever: "Adar-Adar-Adar."

And indeed, on the fourteenth of Adar the turkey comes to the table for the Purim feast!

2 pounds turkey breast	salt and pepper
1 egg, beaten	fat for frying

Have the butcher cut the turkey breasts into steaks ½ inch thick and pound them lightly with a mallet. Dip the steaks in beaten egg, sprinkle with salt and pepper, and roll in breadcrumbs. Fry the steaks on rather low heat until tender (about 20 minutes). (Serves 4.)

Y_{om} K_{ippur}
POLPETTONE DI TACCHINO—STUFFED TURKEY BREAST

Many housewives prefer a cold supper after a hot soup as the break-fast meal of Yom Kippur. This is a typical Italian festive cold cut, served after consuming the soup in which it was cooked.

Buy a whole breast of turkey without the wings. Get the butcher to remove most of the flesh. Mince the meat, mix with a few bread crumbs, 2 or 3 eggs, salt, pepper, and nutmeg. Fill the skin and sew it up. Puncture it with a needle so the skin will not burst during cooking. Stew in chicken stock 1¼–1½ hours. Serve cold, garnished with hard-cooked eggs and parsley. (Serves 4.)

TURKEY CUTLETS S_{uccot}

A young man gave up his worldly life to become a porush, to live a self-imposed, monastic-like existence of Biblical study and poverty. Only on Sabbath and festivals did he emerge from solitude to be a guest among the citizens.

*One day a turkey entered his garret and sat smilingly in the corner. Her presence distracted the porush from his mystical ponderings, and he began to consider giving the disturbing turkey as a gift to any poor man who would invite him to dine on Purim. But the longer the bird stayed on, the more attached he became to her, until he began to hope that a rich man would invite him for Purim and the bird need not be given away and sacrificed. By the second day, when the porush's bread, water **and** groats*

were sent up, he so loved the turkey that he put his plate down for her to eat, while he remained hungry.
                    —*from* WHENCE A PROVERB *by* ISAAC LOEB PERETZ

8 *celery stalks, cut up*	2 *turkey breasts*
chicken fat	3 *eggs*
3 *slices white bread, crust*	1 *teaspoon salt*
removed	*dash of nutmeg*

Fry the celery stalks in the chicken fat until soft but not brown (about 10 minutes). Soak the bread in water and squeeze dry. Grind the meat and add the bread, eggs, and seasonings. Form into cutlets and place on the fried celery. Add just a little water and simmer the cutlets until done (about 1 hour), turning them once or twice. (Serves 6–8.)

Rosh Hashana
ROAST TURKEY WITH SWEET STUFFING

Turkeys in Israel are bred almost exclusively by American settlers.

The Bird

Stuffing

1 *10-pound turkey*	2 *cups rice*
salt	½ *cup margarine*
margarine	1 *cup orange or other fruit juice*
	1 *cup raisins*
	1 *onion, grated*
	2 *apples, chopped*
	grated rind of 1 lemon
	6 *tablespoons sugar*
	dash of cinnamon or nutmeg

Rub the turkey with salt and soft margarine, inside and out. For the stuffing: Fry the rice in the margarine until golden, and adding the orange juice, parboil the rice for 8–9 minutes. Add water if needed; the rice must not be mushy. Add the remaining stuffing ingredients and put into the cavity of the bird. Sew up or fasten cavity with skewers. Roast the turkey, with a little water in the pan, in a 300° oven until browned and tender, basting occasionally. About half an hour is required for each pound of turkey. (Serves 6–8.)

EL AL ISRAEL WINGS

Succot

6 turkey wings
3 tablespoons olive oil
1 large onion, chopped
   dash of coriander
2 teaspoons salt

1 cup orange juice
1 cup dry white wine
1 tablespoon glazed orange
   rind
water to cover

Cut the turkey wings at the joint. Brown in the oil. Add the onion and sauté until transparent. Transfer to a casserole. Sprinkle with the spice and salt. Add the remaining ingredients, with just enough water to cover. Bake in a 325° oven until the meat is tender (45–60 minutes). Serve on rice. (Serves 6.)

ROAST DUCK

Shabbat

1 4- to 5-pound duck
   salt and pepper
   celery stalks, leaves, and
   root

1 onion
1 apple

Clean the duck. Rub the body cavity and skin with a little salt and sprinkle with pepper. Put the celery leaves, stalks, and cut-up root, onion, and apple into the cavity of the duck to flavor it (these are removed before serving). Place the bird on a rack and roast in a 325° oven 1½ hours. Unless the duck is very lean, do not baste it. Do not prick the skin of the duck or it will dry out. (Serves 3–4.)

DUCK IN WINE

Shabbat

1 4- to 5-pound duck
   margarine
1 onion, diced
1 carrot, diced
½ pound celery root, diced

1 parsley root, diced
1 leek, diced
   salt and pepper to taste
1 cup red wine
10 black olives

Brown the duck in a little margarine and put it in a roasting pan. In the same fat brown all the vegetables. Put into the duck's cavity and sew up. Sprinkle the duck with salt (very little, if the olives are salty) and pepper. Place on a rack in a roasting pan. Add the wine and olives. Roast in a 325° oven, basting from time to time, until the duck is tender and golden (about 1½ hours). (Serves 3–4.)

DUCK IN ORANGE SAUCE *Shabbat*

salt and pepper to taste
1 5-pound duck
1 orange
1 cup orange juice plus
   juice of 2 oranges
½ cup sugar
1 tablespoon wine vinegar

4 tablespoons curaçao
   grated ring of 1 orange
1 tablespoon flour,
   if desired
shredded peel of 1 orange
orange slices, for garnish
parsley, for garnish

Sprinkle salt and pepper on the duck, put a small orange in its cavity, and roast it in a 325° oven for about 1 hour, or until the duck is almost cooked (somewhat rare, at this stage). Baste with the cup of orange juice during the remaining cooking (about 30 minutes). Remove the duck and keep warm.

Skim the fat off the gravy in the roasting pan. Mix the sugar and vinegar in a pan on low heat until the mixture begins to gild and caramelize, then add juice of 2 oranges, the curaçao, and the grated orange rind. Add to the liquid in the pan and bring to the boil. If you wish, you can thicken the sauce with 1 tablespoon flour. Add the shredded orange peel and pour over the duck. Garnish the bird with orange slices (leave the peel on for color effect) and parsley. (Serves 3–4.)

ROAST GOOSE STUFFED WITH APPLES *Hanuka*

In Holland, on Hanuka, Jewish children play a game of chance called "ganzenbord," since gans—goose—is the traditional fowl of the festival. This doubtless came to be because Hanuka falls at the time when geese are at their best. For the same reason, goose is the favorite Christmas fowl in many parts of the world.

1 8-pound goose (young)
   salt and pepper
   ginger (optional)

whole apples, peeled and
   cored

Rub the goose, inside and out, with salt, pepper, and ginger. Fill the cavity with the apples. Place the bird on a rack, breast side down. Roast in 325° oven for 3–4 hours, turning the goose over after about 2 hours. The fat should be drained off as it accumulates, about every hour. Do not baste the goose, as geese usually are quite fat enough at Hanuka time. (Serves 4–6.)

GLAZED GOOSE (DUAZ FEHNJOH) *Hanuka*

"The goose goes so often to the kitchen that at last she is fastened to the spit" is a Danish proverb. Glazed goose (Duaz Fehnjoh) is a very festive dish introduced to Israel from Persia, with a typical recipe.

1 8-pound goose	8 almonds
4 tablespoons honey	6–8 teaspoons sugar
⅛ teaspoon cloves or	4 tablespoons icing sugar
¼ teaspoon cinnamon	candied cherries,
8 very small apples	if desired
(6 if somewhat larger)	mint sprigs for garnish

Rub the goose, inside and out, with honey and sprinkle with cloves or cinnamon. Core the apples (do not peel) and fill the holes with blanched almonds and sugar. Stuff into the goose's cavity. Fasten with skewers. Roast the goose on the spit 2–2½ hours (or in a 350° oven about 2 hours and 40 minutes). When done, sprinkle with icing sugar, and garnish with candied cherries and sprigs of mint. If you wish to serve the goose cold you can cover it with a regular cake frosting and decorate this with candied fruits and nuts. (Serves 4–6.)

SMOKED GOOSE *Hanuka*

Artist Reuven Rubin tells how, in his father's house, the chimney was perforated in the freezing attic through which it passed so that the smoke could get through to cure the geese hanging under the straw roof. Smoked fowl and beef were eaten in the days of the Hasmonaeans, as meat so prepared could thus be preserved and transported in the hottest weather. Today in Israel the ambitious farmer's goodwife can take her goose to the butcher (who takes it to the sausage maker) for smoking, after making the following preparations:

1 7-pound goose	3 tablespoons coarse salt
2 cloves garlic	1 tablespoon saltpeter
1 tablespoon sugar	20 whole peppercorns

Cup up the goose, using only the fleshy parts such as the legs, breast, and thighs (the bony parts can be kept for soup). Rub the meat with garlic and sprinkle with the sugar, salt, peppercorns, and saltpeter. Pack the meat into a crock, put a heavy weight on it, and refrigerate for a week. A brine will rise to cover the meat, which will have to be turned daily so that all parts receive equal immersion. After seven days, remove the meat and send it for smoking. It can then be eaten uncooked or grilled on the spit as they do in the Balkan countries. Or it can be boiled and served sliced cold. (If you boil the smoked goose, use the liquid for making pea soup.) (Serves 4–5.)

KOSHER CHOW MEIN   *Tu Besh'vat*

Chow mein noodles became exceedingly popular in Israel before any hotel or restaurant served chow mein or before people knew what is was. Now the dish, altered to meet the kosher laws and the available Israel ingredients, is becoming a party favorite.

1 *cup raw veal, cut into* *strips*	2 *cups chicken stock*
3 *tablespoons oil for frying*	2 *cups cooked chicken,* *cut into strips*
½ *cup kohlrabi, cut into* *1-inch strips*	2 *tablespoons cornstarch*
1 *cup sliced onions*	3 *tablespoons soy sauce*
1 *cup celery stalks, cut into* *1-inch strips*	4 *cups boiled rice*
1 *cup sliced mushrooms*	1 *cup or more fried chow* *mein noodles*

Lightly fry the veal in the oil, then remove. Fry the kohlrabi, onions, celery, and mushrooms for three minutes (they should not be raw, but still crisp). Add the chicken and bring to the boil. Dissolve the cornstarch in the soy sauce and add to the mixture. Cook only until the sauce is thick and clear (about 2 minutes). Serve on rice, and top with fried chow mein noodles. (Serves 6.)

QUAIL   *Shabbat*

The Sabbath zmirot—the gay table hymns—praise the menu's fare of "ducks and quail and fish, and all the finest things."

6 *quail*	½ *cup broth*
salt and pepper	6 *tablespoons white wine*
3 *tablespoons margarine*	

Salt and pepper the quail, and spread with margarine. Put them into a heavy pot with the broth. Cover tightly and stew for 15 minutes. Add the wine and baste the birds with the sauce. Cook until tender (10–15 minutes longer). (Serves 3 or 6.)

STUFFED PIGEONS *Tu Besh'vat*

Although pigeons are not mentioned in the Old Testament as food, but only as birds of love, harmlessness, and gentleness, and as sacrifices of purification, it seems clear from the annals of the New Testament that pigeons, like oxen and sheep, were being dealt in as stock for the approaching Passover. Although pigeons are festive fare among Jews in Western Europe, they have not come into much use as such in Israel, perhaps because of the tender Biblical associations with this fowl.

The Birds

  4 *pigeons*
     salt, pepper, paprika
     parsley
 16 *mushrooms, chopped*
  1 *carrot, chopped*
 ½ *pound celery root,*
     chopped
  2 *cups stock*
  1 *tablespoon flour*
  1 *tablespoon margarine*
 ¼ *cup sweet sherry*

The Stuffing

  4 *pigeon livers*
  2 *egg yolks*
  2 *tablespoons chicken fat*
     salt and pepper
 ½ *cup fresh breadcrumbs*
  2 *tablespoons orange juice*
     grated rind of ½ orange

Season the pigeons with salt, pepper, and paprika. Mix all the ingredients for the stuffing. Fill the cavities of the birds about ⅔ full and sew up. Place the pigeons in a casserole or roasting pan with the vegetables. Add the stock and cook in a 350° oven until the birds are light gold (45–60 minutes). Thicken the sauce with the flour and margarine mashed together. Add the sherry. Serve hot. (Serves 4.)

CRACKLINGS (GREBEN) *Hanuka*

Ah! The smell of goose cracklings in the making, frying in their fat with diced onions on a sleety winter's day! Being the only Jewish family in our village in northern Saskatchewan, we had to bring the shochet, the ritual slaughterer, from the nearest city (a hundred miles away!) just before Hanuka, when he would kill the geese to make the Passover shmaltz (fat), which required special pots and dishes to conform with the kashrut. Two women came in to pluck geese all day. Mama skinned the fat off the birds, and the flesh was frozen for our winter's fowl, along with all the other cuts of meat hanging, since the coming of the frost, in the screened-in verandah.

fat of a goose	*water as needed*
skin of a goose	*salt*
onions	

Cut the fat and skin into one-inch squares or cubes. Dice the onions. Put the fat, skin, salt, and onions on low heat with a little water so that the fat melts out and the cracklings do not burn. After some time the water will evaporate and the cracklings and the onions will be brown and crisp. Remove them and drain off the fat for separate use. Cracklings keep very well when stored in a cool place.

PASSOVER STUFFING FOR CHICKEN   *Passover*

I. *Savory*

II. *Sweet*

5 *matzos*	5 *matzos*
soup stock	*soup stock*
2 *eggs*	2 *eggs*
4 *tablespoons grated celery*	4 *tablespoons raisins*
root or onion	3 *tablespoons chicken fat*
1 *tablespoon chopped parsley*	1 *tablespoon sugar*
4 *tablespoons chicken fat*	*pinch of salt*
dash of ginger or nutmeg	*dash of cinnamon or lemon*
salt and pepper	*rind*
	1 *teaspoon grated lemon rind*

Break up the matzos and dampen in the soup stock. Beat the eggs and mix with the remaining ingredients. Let the mixture rest for 15 minutes. Fill the chicken. Sew up. (This will fill one very large or two very small chickens.)

PIPIKLACH—GIZZARDS   *Purim*

Roast "pipiklach" are a specialty at Café Kassit, the artists' rendezvous center in Tel Aviv.

30 *gizzards*	2 *onions, chopped*
water to cover	5 *tablespoons chicken fat*
salt and pepper to taste	

Cover the cleaned gizzards with water and simmer until tender. When almost all the water has evaporated (45–60 minutes), add the seasoning, onions, and fat and let the meat cook until the gizzards are brown but not hard. Serve with rice. (Serves 6.)

GIBLETS WITH RICE   *Succot*

Rice is believed to be as old as time, and for half the people of the world rice, rather than wheat, is the staff of life. No food is more versatile in its possibilities in cooking, going into every course from appetizer to dessert.

1 *pound giblets, diced*	*salt and pepper*
2 *onions, diced*	*water to cover*
3 *tablespoons chicken fat*	1¼ *cups rice*

Brown the giblets and onions in the fat, add the seasoning, cover with water, and simmer 45 minutes. Add the rice and boiling water to cover. Cook until the meat and rice are tender (20–25 minutes). (Serves 4.)

CHICKEN LIVERS AND ONIONS   *Purim*

Heinrich Heine scoffed at those who praised an actor because he could draw tears from an audience, for, said he, "the smallest onion has the same talent!"

In order to conform with kashrut, livers must be grilled to let the blood run off. This often results in their being somewhat dry, and the following recipe overcomes that difficulty.

6 *chicken livers*	*salt and pepper*
6 *onions, sliced thin*	*mushrooms, if desired*
4 *tablespoons chicken fat*	

Dip the livers in cold water before grilling (this prevents them from hardening). While the livers are under the broiler for a minute or two, fry the onions in the chicken fat, covering the pan, as the onions should not be crisp. Season with salt and pepper. Sliced mushrooms may be added if you wish. When the livers are grilled, add them to the pan and smother them in the onions. Cover well and cook a few minutes more. Serve hot. (Serves 4.)

FRIED GOOSE LIVERS   *Hanuka*

In Yugoslavia and some of the surrounding Balkan countries, geese are nailed down through the webs of their feet in order to keep them immobilized, and are fattened by forced feeding, so that their costly livers will swell to double and triple normal size. This cruelty is not practiced in Israel, and so our goose livers are neither as large, fat-loaded, or tender as those that go into the world-famous pâté de foie gras.

1 pound goose livers	½ pound onions
goose fat as required	¼ pound mushrooms
(about 4 tablespoons)	salt and pepper to taste

Dip the livers in ice-cold water and then brush them with goose **fat.** Grill for a few minutes. Then cut the livers into four and **fry** together with chopped onions and mushrooms in enough fat to keep the livers from sticking, but not enough to make the dish too greasy. Salt and pepper to taste. (Serves 3–4.)

CHICKEN HELZEL—TURKISH STYLE *Hanuka*

Turkey abounds in chestnuts, walnuts, almonds, and pistachios, which find their way into endless delicious dishes. I cannot recall the name of this Jewish dish which was served to me in Istanbul, but the ecstatic flavor will live on forever on my palate.

3 slices white bread, crust	chopped parsley
removed	salt and pepper
2 eggs	1 skin of chicken (or
½ cup chopped walnuts	turkey or goose) neck

Soak the bread in water and squeeze dry. Add the eggs, nuts, **parsley,** and seasoning. Stuff into the fowl's neck, sew up, and **roast** next to the chicken in the pot. Serve as a side dish. The chicken may be filled with the same stuffing. (Serves 1 or 2, depending on which bird has been used.)

HELZEL *Shabbat*

2 tablespoons matzo meal	3 tablespoons raw chicken
2 tablespoons soy flour	fat or margarine,
5 tablespoons chopped onion	chopped
⅛ teaspoon pepper	1 skin of chicken neck
¼ teaspoon salt	

Mix all the ingredients for the stuffing and loosely fill the chicken neck, sewing up both ends. Roast next to meat or chicken, basting the neck with the gravy in the pan from time to time. The helzel **needs** the same roasting time as the fowl.

TURKEY HELZEL—STUFFED TURKEY NECK *Hanuka*

It seems utterly incredible that this recipe for stuffed capon's neck existed five hundred and fifty years ago, for it is almost exactly like the Jewish-Eastern recipe used today for stuffing a turkey neck, except for one main ingredient—flour!

Pudding of capon's neck. Take parsley, gizzard, liver, and heart and parboil them in water; then chop them small, put two or three yolks of eggs thereto, and chop again forthwith. Take mace and cloves, and put thereto, and saffron and a little powdered pepper and salt; and fill him up and sew him and lay him along the capon back and prick him thereon and roast him and serve forth.

3 onions, chopped fine
3/4 cup chicken fat
   (or more to taste)
2 teaspoons chopped parsley
   dash of saffron
   dash of nutmeg or cinna-
    mon (Middle Eastern
    Israelis prefer cinna-
    mon)

1 teaspoon salt
1/2 teaspoon pepper
   cooked liver, heart, gizzard
    of turkey, chopped
2 cups flour
8 whole hard-cooked eggs
1 turkey neck, including
   chest skin and wings

Lightly fry the onions in the fat and mix the seasonings, giblets, and flour. Pack some of this flour mixture into the neck and then put in the hard-cooked eggs, filling with flour mixture to surround them. Sew up the helzel and breast skin and roast in a 350° oven as you would a fowl, with fat, vegetables, and a little water for 1 hour. Or, preferably, roast alongside the bird. Prick the skin. The egg will come out as a central garnish with each slice of the helzel when served. (Serves 4.)

GANS-HELZEL—STUFFED GOOSE NECK *Hanuka*

The poverty-stricken Jewish masses of Eastern Europe had to make the most out of every morsel, and the women were quick to realize that while the neck and feet and gizzard of the goose would make a good soup, the skin of the neck could be filled for a meal. And indeed, they did this with such success that helzel has become a special dish, often served as a first course at a feast. Sometimes the helzel is stuffed like derma (see Index), but this is more festive.

1 large onion, diced	½ teaspoon pepper
3 tablespoons cooking oil	chopped parsley
1 cup flour, sifted, or white	(optional)
crumbs	1 skin of goose neck
¼ pound chopped beef	2 large onions, sliced
salt to taste	

Fry the onion in the oil until golden. Mix with the flour or crumbs, meat, salt, and pepper. Add chopped parsley if you wish. Fill the skin loosely and sew up both ends. Roast on a bed of sliced onions with just a little water, in a 350° oven (or in a pot on top of the stove) for about an hour, or until the helzel is tender and brown. Baste or turn from time to time. (Serves 2.)

SALADS AND SALAD DRESSINGS

TOSSED GREEN SALAD *Rosh Hashana*

Fresh salads are on the table at every meal in Israel—including breakfast (but not the leafy kind for this meal)!

1 clove garlic
1 teaspoon prepared
    mustard
1/2 teaspoon salt
    dash of pepper
    dash of paprika
1/3 cup olive oil
    juice of 1 lemon
2 hard-cooked eggs,
    chopped

1 large head lettuce
1 bunch parsley, chopped
1 bunch chives, chopped
1 red pimiento, chopped
    or sliced
1 green pepper, chopped
2 red radishes, sliced
1 small carrot, finely sliced

Rub a wooden bowl with the garlic. Add the mustard, salt, pepper, paprika, olive oil, lemon juice, and eggs and mix well. Put plastic or wooden servers in the bowl to keep the dressing from touching the salad. On top of the servers, arrange whole or torn leaves in the shape of a lettuce head. Garnish each layer of lettuce with the parsley, chives, pimiento, green pepper, radishes and carrot. Mix the salad at the table to ensure its crispness. (Serves 6–8.)

ZEVULUN LETTUCE SALAD

It took the seafaring imagination of Zim Shipping Lines' Chef Cymbalista to create this exciting salad, which was on the prize-winning menu he entered in Israel's Wizard-Chef Contest. The lettuce looks like ocean waves, the bananas like flying dolphins, the white horseradish sauce like foam upon the water, and the floating peanuts like flotsam on the sea.

1 1/2 heads of lettuce
3 bananas
1/3 cup sour cream
2 tablespoons freshly
    grated horse-radish

1/2 cup mayonnaise
4 tablespoons water
    juice of 1 1/2 lemons
2 tablespoons sugar
1/2 cup salted roast peanuts

Cut the lettuce heads into quarters and put into a salad bowl, round side up. Cut the bananas in half lengthwise and put between the lettuce, after dipping the fruit in lemon juice. Mix the sour cream with the horse-radish, mayonnaise, water, lemon juice, and sugar. Pour this over the lettuce, top with a sprinkling of peanuts, and serve. (Serves 6.)

SALAD WITH LEBEN (YOGHURT)　　　*Shavuot*

Leben (or yoghurt), the richer lebeniya, and the still richer light sour cream, were foods in Israel and the Near East millennia ago. Job refers to curdled milk, the stage right after leben coagulation.

The dish is eaten plain, in salads, as a garnish for many summer soups, and with cereals. It is most refreshing, particularly with its regular partner, mint, in many salads.

1 large cucumber, sliced thin	1 cup leben or lebeniya
	mint sprigs, for garnish
3 or 4 red radishes, sliced thin	mint leaves (fresh), if desired
1 small clove garlic or chives, chopped	

Mix the cucumber and radishes with the garlic or chives. Pour on the leben or lebeniya and garnish with sprigs of mint. A few mint leaves may also be chopped into the salad. (Serves 4.)

MINT HERB SALAD　　　*Independence Day*

Since the Biblical times, mint has been a favorite aromatic herb, eaten with the native lamb and used as medicine, too.

tomatoes	snipped parsley
cucumbers	fresh mint, chopped
radishes	snipped dill
pimientos	olive oil
green peppers	lemon juice
young onions	salt and pepper
garlic	

Proportions do not matter in this recipe. Cut the vegetables into small cubes of the same size. Mix with a hint of crushed garlic, quite a bit of snipped parsley and dill, and a great deal of chopped fresh mint. Dress with olive oil and lemon juice, and add salt and pepper to taste. Chill. The mint flavor must predominate.

THE KIBBUTZNIKS' SALAD *Purim*

Making salads in a kibbutz has become a ritual. On the tables are bowls of tomatoes, cucumbers, peppers, onions, garlic, schoog-relish, leben (yoghurt), sour cream, salt, pepper, oil, parsley, coriander, plus other vegetables so plentiful that the surplus has to be tackled in the dining room. Motke will dice his salad finely and dress it in oil, Hannah will slice her combination and use sour cream dressing. The greatest gourmets everywhere mix their salads at table; at the kibbutz each one does his own to save the kitchen staff extra labor. And every kibbutznik takes pride in his own combination. So there's a great tradition, but no recipe. You just have to make up your own!

TABOULAH SALAD *Shavuot*

⅓ cup burghul (cracked
    wheat)
2 cups diced cucumbers
1 tablespoon chopped mint
    or other herbs
2 green onions, chopped
½ teaspoon cumin

3 tablespoons olive oil
    salt and pepper to taste
1 tablespoon lemon juice
1 tablespoon honey or
    syrup
    lettuce and tomato wedges,
    for garnish

Soak the burghul in water overnight. Dice the vegetables and mix with the burghul. Make a dressing of the remaining ingredients and pour over the salad. Serve on lettuce with tomato wedges. (Serves 4.)

THE EMIR'S PEARLS—ORANGE-ONION-OLIVE SALAD

This tri-toned salad of the Middle East is as bold and tasty as the contrasting combinations in American salads. The legend of how it came to be is lost, but some say that its beauty is comparable to kingly gems, others that Aladdin's find of jewels gave the dish its name. In any case, we do know that Anatole France introduced the dish to the West. It is most appreciated among Westerners in Israel, although it is a native Middle Eastern dish.

4 oranges, skinned and
    thinly sliced
4 sweet onions, thinly sliced

black olives
olive oil
lemon juice

On top of each orange slice, put a slice of sweet onion. Garnish with black olives and drizzle with olive oil and lemon juice. (Serves 4–6.)

FASOULIA—GREEK HARICOT BEANS   *Succot*

1 cup dried beans	1 bay leaf
½ cup olive oil	1 clove garlic
salt and pepper	1 lemon
1 cup bean liquid	1 onion, finely chopped
2 tablespoons tomato purée	

Soak the beans overnight. Cover with fresh water and cook until almost tender (1–2 hours), then drain, reserving the liquid. Heat the oil and add the beans, pepper and salt. Brown well. Add about 1 cup of the liquid from the original cooking, the tomato purée, bay leaf, and garlic and simmer until the beans are soft and the sauce thick. Add the lemon juice and finely chopped onion. Cool and serve as a salad course. It is also good hot. (Serves 3–4.)

RED CABBAGE SALAD   *Passover*

1 clove garlic	1 onion, sliced paper thin
salt	olive oil
4 cups shredded red cabbage	pepper

Rub a salad bowl with the garlic. Sprinkle the salt on the cabbage and toss in the onion slices. Add olive oil and pepper to taste. Stir and serve. (Serves 4.)

CABBAGE-ROSE SALAD   *Shavuot*

1 small head red cabbage	1 cup diced celery stalks
1 small head white cabbage, shredded	½ cup mayonnaise
	½ cup sour cream
1 grapefruit, skinned and diced	½ cup pecans or almonds, slivered
2 apples, diced	2 pimentos, shredded

Remove the outside leaves of the red cabbage and cut off the stalk close to the leaves. Fold back the next layer of leaves and cut out the center of the cabbage. This leaves a shell of red cabbage leaves which will serve as a rose-petal container for the salad. Put this cabbage bowl into cold water for an hour and then drain it. Mix remaining ingredients and fill the shell. Dress with more mayonnaise if you like, garnished with more shredded pimento. (Serves 6–8.)

WALDORF-COLE   *Tu Besh'vat*

2 cups diced apples
  lemon juice for sprinkling
  salt
2 cups shredded white
  cabbage
1 cup mayonnaise
½ cup (or more) sour
  cream

sugar, if desired
1 cup diced celery
6 tablespoons broken
  walnuts
  sprinkling of raisins,
  if desired

Sprinkle the diced apple with lemon juice to keep it white. Salt
the cabbage. Thin out the mayonnaise with the sour cream, adding a nip of sugar if you like. Mix all the ingredients together
and serve on crisp lettuce or in a nest of red cabbage leaf.
(Serves 6.)

RADISH-TURNIP SALAD   *Hanuka*

*The radish, turnip, olive, and onion were the vegetables most
used, as historic evidence shows, among the people of Israel in
the days of the Maccabees. This salad has been a Jewish favorite
in Russia, Poland, and neighboring lands since time immemorial,
and the emigrants took it to the New World. It stayed on in the
Holy Land as a much-relished salad.*

2 cups coarsely grated black
  or red radishes and/or
  turnips
2 tablespoons chopped
  onions (1 tablespoon
  to a cup of radish
  mixture)

3 tablespoons chicken fat
  or olive oil
  salt and pepper to taste
12 ripe olives

Grate the radishes (black ones are first peeled, the red are only
washed well) and/or the turnips (they are good mixed together).
Fry the onion in chicken fat or olive oil. Mix with the radish
mixture, season to taste, and serve with ripe olives as a garnish.
(Serves 6.)

Independence Day
GEZER-HAI: (ORANGE-CARROT SALAD)

This is a newborn Israeli dish called "Living Carrots."

1 pound firm, fresh carrots
  juice of 3 oranges
  juice of ½ lemon

dash of ginger (optional)
salt and sugar to taste

Peel the carrots and grate coarsely. Cover with the orange and lemon juice, adding sugar and salt to taste. Add a dash of ginger if desired. Refrigerate for several hours (this salad improves with keeping up to three days) so that the carrots absorb the juices. Serve on crisp lettuce leaves or in lemon baskets garnished with a sprig of mint. (Serves 4–6.)

CAULIFLOWER SALAD   *Shavuot*

The cauliflower was developed by the ancient Greeks when they held sway over the Middle East. It was hardly known in Europe until the Crusaders brought it back, calling it "Cyprus cabbage."

The Cauliflower	*The Dressing*
1 *medium head cauliflower*	2 *tablespoons olive oil*
3 *cups water*	1 *cup wine vinegar*
2 *teaspoons salt*	*salt and white pepper*
	1 *teaspoon mustard*
	dash of sugar

Separate the florets of the cauliflower and cook rapidly in salted water about 8 minutes. Drain well.

Make the dressing by shaking together all the ingredients. Pour this over the cauliflower and chill thoroughly. (Serves 4–5.)

LUBIYA BEAN SALAD   *Hanuka*

This North African salad fills the culinary role in Middle Eastern countries that the potato salad does in the West. Lovers always eat it together; otherwise they would be unable to tolerate each other's kisses (due to love of garlic, not to lack of love for each other)

2 *pounds cowpea beans*	6 *tablespoons olive oil*
salted water to cover	*juice of 1 or 2 lemons*
4 *cloves garlic, crushed*	*chopped parsley*
1 *red chili pepper, finely*	
chopped	

Soak the beans overnight. Drain, cover with salted water, and cook until the skins burst and swim to the top (2–3 hours). Remove the skins and drain. Cool. Add the crushed garlic and finely chopped chili pepper and dress with olive oil, lemon juice, and chopped parsley. Serve cold. (Serves 4–6.)

EGGPLANT-PEPPER SALAD   *Purim*

The measure of a worthwhile bride among the Arabs of Palestine was the number of eggplant dishes she knew how to prepare. One hundred dishes made the bride a costly one, worthy of an effendi; fifty brought her within the financial reach of a hawajah; and if she knew only twenty-five, even a poor fellah could afford to buy her.

2 pounds eggplant	*1 tablespoon chopped parsley*
juice of 1 lemon	*dash of cayenne*
4 sweet green peppers	*salt and pepper to taste*
2 sweet red peppers	*mayonnaise or tahina*
2 cloves garlic, chopped	

Put the eggplants over an open flame until soft, turning once or twice to roast evenly. Remove the charred skin under running water, slit the eggplant, and let the juices drain off. Break up the eggplant with a wooden spoon and beat with the lemon juice. Chop up the peppers very fine. Add with the remaining ingredients, using just enough mayonnaise to hold the vegetables together. (Serves 8–10.)

CHARRED EGGPLANT SALAD   *Independence Day*

Romanian immigrants in Israel make quite a protocol of the preparation and serving of this dish in its simplicity. Others have come to offer this Balkan hors d'oeuvre in Israel dress—with garlic and tahina or mayonnaise, and gaily garnished. But the originators insist on the pungent charred flavor being maintained above all, and serve it with chopped onions and oil, added at the table. They use only wooden bowls and choppers in the preparation, and offer the dish with wooden spoons, for even the touch of metal is said to alter the taste.

1 large eggplant, (about	*salt and pepper to taste*
1 pound)	*red pimiento, chopped*
1 clove garlic, crushed,	*(optional)*
or 1 green onion, chopped	*mayonnaise or tahina*
1 tablespoon lemon juice	*(optional)*
4 tablespoons olive oil	

Put the unpeeled eggplant on the open flame and turn it when the skin begins to char. When all the skin has been blackened and the eggplant is soft, put it on a board, make an incision, and let the excess juice drain off. Wash the eggplant under the tap to remove the charred skin. If you are a great gourmet you will now open the eggplant and remove the seed sections also. Add garlic (if you do not intend to use onion) and lemon juice during the chopping, until the mixture is pure white. Some people add the olive oil during the chopping, but the ceremony calls for adding it at the table, along with chopped onions and salt and pepper to taste. Non-Romanian Israelis serve this course in green pepper boats, garnished with red chopped pimiento, on a lettuce leaf and with or without mayonnaise or tahina stirred in. (Serves 4–6.)

"NAHIT AND BOB" SALAD   *Purim*

Chick-peas and fava beans—known as "Nahit and Bob"—are eaten with a salad dressing on Purim. Reason: Queen Esther lived largely on legumes in order to observe kashrut in the court of King Ahasuerus.

1 cup chick-peas	pepper to taste
1 cup broad (fava) beans	French dressing (see
water, as needed	Index)
1 teaspoon salt	

Soak the chick-peas and beans separately, overnight. Cook each separately in water to cover 2–3 hours. When the peas and beans are tender, drain. Mix them together and add salt and pepper. Pour the dressing over while the legumes are still hot. Cool. (Serves 6–8.)

PRESSGURKA—CUCUMBER SALAD   *Rosh Hashana*

6 cucumbers	2 tablespoons chopped dill
1 teaspoon salt	1 tablespoon water
2 tablespoons sugar	½ cup mild vinegar
1 teaspoon black pepper (mild)	

Slice cucumbers as thin as possible. Sprinkle with salt and mix. Place a plate and a weight on the cucumbers for an hour, to extract the liquid. Drain. Mix the remaining ingredients, pour over the cucumbers, and marinate them for about 15 minutes. (Serves 6–8.)

STUFFED CUCUMBERS *Shavuot*

4 large cucumbers
1 green onion
⅓ cup flaked lox
(smoked salmon)

1 cup creamed cottage
cheese
½ cup sour cream
tomato slices, for garnish

Cut the cucumbers in half lengthwise (leave the skin on if the cucumbers are freshly picked). Scoop out the seed pulp, leaving the firm border of cucumber. Chop up the seed pulp, onion, and lox and mix with the cottage cheese (no salt is required). Fill the cucumber cases and top with sour cream. Serve with tomato slices. (Serves 8.)

FINOCCHIO SALAD RINGS *Shavuot*

Helen Morgenthau Fox, the international authority on herbs, calls the finocchio (in its more formal name of Florence Fennel or Foeniculum dulce) as one of the "forgotten vegetables." Recorded in America as far back as 1806, the vegetable-herb was little known outside of Italy in years thereafter. It grows wild in Israel but has only recently been cultivated and is speedily gaining popularity in salads, or on its own with olive oil and salt, or stewed or sauced and baked au gratin.

1 large finocchio (fennel)
dash of celery salt
½ pound Bel Paêse cheese
1 medium tomato, diced

4 black olives, sliced
lettuce
olive oil

Separate the thickened stalks at the base of the finocchio. Sprinkle with celery salt. Put slices of the soft Bel Paêse cheese on each stem, and press in pieces of tomato and black olive. Fit 3 stalks together to make a roll. Chill and then cut into ½-inch rings. Serve on lettuce with a little olive oil. (Serves 8.)

POTATO SALAD (KARTOFFELSALAT) *Purim*

Potato salad has become about as international as boiled potatoes. With the German immigration to Israel just before the war, the demand for the dish was so great that a local factory had to begin making mayonnaise. The German Jews taught all Israel how to make it their way, and that's about the only way one can get it in a restaurant now—and as a native of Canada, with less passion for sour cucumbers, I object and will take it (if I get time) to the Committee of Human Rights at the United Nations!

2 pounds potatoes boiled in   3 tablespoons vinegar
    their skins and peeled   ½ cup mayonnaise (more
1 large dill pickle   if desired)
2 tablespoons chopped onion   salt and pepper
1 large sour apple

Dice all the ingredients, dilute the mayonnaise with the vinegar,
stir into the salad, add salt and pepper, and *Guten Appetit!*
(Serves 4–6.)

PEA-CHEESE SALAD   *Shavuot*

*This dish is colorful, zesty, and hearty and much more interesting
than potato salad, which it replaces. It improves with keeping up
to four days, as the flavors mellow and blend.*

¼ pound mild cheddar   ⅓ cup sweet pickles
    cheese   2 cups drained, canned
½ cup mayonnaise   peas

Dice the cheese and fold into mayonnaise. Cut up the pickles and
add with the peas. Mix lightly. The dish should marinate for at
least a few hours for the blending of flavors. (Serves 4.)

RADISH CREAM SALAD   *Shavuot*

*Israel's minister of foreign affairs, Mrs. Golda Meir, tells the
story of a rabbi who was invited by the elders of a neighboring
village to advise them on the appointment of a new leader for
their community, as their own rabbi had passed away. The honored visitor was placed at the head of the table and, as custom
decreed, he was the first to be offered the bowl of radish salad.
The rabbi ate the whole bowlful! A second bowl was brought and
again he did not take a mere portion and pass the dish around,
but once more ate it all himself! The astonished elders decided
not to consult the rabbi on their problem, since he had been so
rude and greedy. But some time later they learned the reason
for the strange behavior of the rabbi. The radish had been so
oversalted that it was almost impossible to eat it, and fearing
that his hostess might be scoffed at for her culinary failure, the
old rabbi determined that no one else at the table should taste
the radish salad!*

20 red radishes   1 tablespoon sugar
    salt to taste   1 tablespoon vinegar
1 cup sour cream

Slice the radishes and salt them. Mix the sour cream, sugar, and
vinegar and stir into the radishes. (Serves 4–6.)

KOHLRABI SALAD   *Succot*

4 young kohlrabi	*2 teaspoons olive oil*
½ teaspoon salt	*black olives*

The kohlrabi must be young and fresh or they will get woody and lose their sweetness in a day. Peel and slice very thin, sprinkle with the salt, dress with the olive oil, and serve with the black olives.

KISHUYIM—SQUASH IN MAYONNAISE   *Purim*

Mayonnaise—which was unknown in these parts fifty years ago— is today as much used as tahina, the sesame oil dressing for salads. What would Richelieu have thought if he could foresee that his dressing, in which he took so much pride because his name was associated with its origin, would one day conquer the Holy Land? And, moreover, that it would be used on the Biblical "cucumbers" (which were really summer squashes according to the Hebrew translation of "kishuyim")?

10 small squash	*½ cup mayonnaise*
1 teaspoon salt	*herbs for garnish*
½ cup sour cream	

Wash (do not peel) the squash. Cut in two lengthwise. Sprinkle with salt and cook in just enough water to keep them from scorching, until just past the raw stage. Do not allow them to get soft. Chill thoroughly. Mix the sour cream with the mayonnaise and spread over the squash. Garnish with herbs and serve very cold. (Serves 10.)

KUSA-LEBEN SALAD—SQUASH-YOGHURT SALAD   *Shavuot*

10 small summer squash	*1 tablespoon chopped fresh*
water to cover	*dill*
1 tablespoon chopped fresh	*salt and pepper*
mint leaves	*2 cups leben (yoghurt)*

Cut the squash very thin. Just cover with water, bring to a boil, and remove from heat (squash should only be parboiled). Drain. Chill thoroughly, sprinkle with herbs and seasoning, pour the yoghurt over, and serve very cold. (Serves 6–8.)

TAHINA CHEESE SALAD   *Shavuot*

The valley along Mount Zion in Jerusalem was known as the Tyropoeon Vale—which means the "Valley of Cheesemakers." In ancient times cheese was referred to as "curds" or "cuts of milk" and was very likely similar to our cottage cheese today.

¼ cup prepared tahina (see Index)	2 tablespoons sour cream salt and pepper to taste
1 green onion, chopped fine	6 medium cucumbers dash of paprika
½ pound creamed cottage cheese	lettuce and tomato slices, for garnish

Mix the tahina, green onion, cottage cheese, sour cream, salt, and pepper. Cut the cucumbers in half, lengthwise. Scoop out the seed section and chop coarsely, then add to the cheese mixture. Pile the filling into the cucumber boats and sprinkle with paprika. Serve on lettuce with tomato slices. (Serves 12.)

NOTE: Green peppers may be substituted if cucumbers are not in season.

LAKSHMI RICE SALAD   *Rosh Hashana*

The Jewish community from India now living in Israel have discarded their beautiful saris and taken on our Western dress. In exchange they have given us Indian curry dishes that are becoming increasingly popular. This salad is named for a Hindu goddess, worshiped for prosperity, beauty, and love. Western dressings with curry powder, are used for sauce. Pistachio nuts belong in this salad, but Israel's wonderful peanuts are substituted locally in the dish.

1 clove garlic	3 green onions, chopped
1 teaspoon curry powder French dressing or mayonnaise	2 green peppers, chopped
	1 pimiento, chopped
4 cups cold cooked rice	4 tablespoons chutney (optional)
½ cup salted peanuts or pistachio nuts	

Rub mixing bowl with garlic. Add the curry powder to the French dressing or mayonnaise. Mix all the remaining ingredients and add. Garnish with lettuce. (Serves 8.)

RUSSIAN SALAD   *Hanuka*

A Russian Jewish description of an all-right, okay guy is: "Now, he's the right sort of pepper." And to make this salad right, you should use freshly ground good pepper. This is a very popular salad in Israel.

1 cup diced cooked potatoes	3 hard-cooked eggs, diced
2 dill pickles, diced	mayonnaise mixed with
1 cup cooked peas	sour cream, to taste
½ cup diced cooked beans	salt and freshly ground
1 cup diced cooked carrots	pepper

Toss the vegetables together with the mayonnaise and sour cream. Add salt and plenty of pepper. Serve instead of potato salad. (Serves 6.)

TONGUE AND CELERY SALAD   *Yom Kippur*

Although this dish came to Israel with the German immigration, it was originally a French dish—that is, it was an Italian dish introduced by Catherine de' Medici from her home town of Florence to Paris, where she came to live as wife to the future Henry II.

1 pound ox tongue, cooked	1 tablespoon chopped capers or pickles
1½ pounds celery root,	1 tablespoon chopped olives
2 small tomatoes	salt and pepper to taste
1 cup mayonnaise	
1 pimiento, chopped	

Cut the tongue and the vegetables into julienne strips. Mix the mayonnaise with the pimiento, caper, and olives, and stir into the meat mixture. Serve on lettuce.

CHICKEN OR MEAT SALAD   *Passover*

2 cups diced cooked chicken, beef, veal, or sweetbreads (or mixed)	mayonnaise
	salt and pepper
3 hard-cooked eggs, diced	6 avocado halves or sectioned tomatoes
1 onion, chopped	olives for garnish
3 stalks (inner, tender) celery, chopped	

Avocado quarters or halves are ideal for this salad. Or you can cut a tomato into six sections, without severing the bottom, and open it out like a flower for the filling. Lightly mix all the ingredients for the salad, being careful that it does not get mushy. Put into the avocados or tomatoes and serve on lettuce with a few black, green or stuffed olives. (Serves 6.)

SWEDISH PLATE   *Shavuot*

"Platah Shvedi!"—"Swedish Plate!"—is the call heard in restaurants large and small throughout Israel. It has come to be a national stand-by snack or brunch plate. The variety of salty and savory foods has given it the Swedish title.

slices of smoked "lakerda" *(great tuna)*	*potato salad*
slices of red "lox" (cured or smoked tuna or lox)	*sliced tomato*
	dill pickle
fillets of herring	*cottage cheese with caraway*
sardines	*cut of salt goat cheese*
hard-cooked egg, halved, with mayonnaise	*slices of assorted yellow cheeses*

All beautifully garnished, served with a roll and butter, downed with a cup of coffee. There's no rule about what to remove or to add.

AVOCADO-CITRUS SALAD   *Tu Besh'vat*

pomelo segments *	*French dressing (see Index)*
grapefruit segments	
orange segments	*ball of cottage cheese*
avocado wedges	*grating of yellow cheese*
tomato wedges	*lettuce*

* If not obtainable, add more grapefruit.

Remove the membranes from the pomelo, grapefruit, and orange segments and arrange in a circle with wedges of avocado filled with wedges of tomato. Place the cottage cheese, topped with the grated yellow cheese, in the center of the circle. Pour French dressing (use lemon juice instead of vinegar in the dressing) over the fruit and vegetables and garnish with lettuce.

POTATO AND CELERIAC SALAD *Passover*

5 slices sausage
1 tablespoon oil for frying
1 onion, chopped
3 tablespoons vinegar

salt and pepper
3 cups diced cooked potatoes
2 cups diced cooked celery root

Cut the slices of sausage into fine slivers and fry until crisp in the oil. Remove from heat and add the onion, vinegar, salt, and pepper. Stir in the potatoes and celery root. Toss together and serve on lettuce. (Serves 4–6.)

SARDINE SALAD *Shavuot*

1 can silver sardines
  juice of 1 lemon
1 green onion, chopped
2 hard-cooked eggs, chopped
1 teaspoon parsley, chopped

1 dill pickle, chopped
salt and pepper to taste
lettuce and radish roses, for garnish

Mash the sardines, without the oil, drizzle on the lemon juice, and mix. Add the chopped onion, eggs, parsley, dill pickle, and salt and pepper to taste. Pile on lettuce and garnish with radishes cut into roses. (Serves 2–3.)

SHAMROCK LAKERDA SALAD *Shavuot*

During World War II for many months there was practically no available protein food in Palestine except the smoked giant tuna from Turkey known as "lakerda." Nutritionist Lilian Cornfeld and I then worked out fifty recipes on how to use lakerda for dishes such as finnan haddie, gefilte fish, Irish stew, patties, schnitzels, casserole bakes, blinis, caviar, sandwich loaves, and everything, it seems, except jam! I still use that cookbooklet for salad snacks such as this one:

3 green peppers
1 cup cottage cheese
4 tablespoons chopped salt
  lakerda (tuna)
1 small pimento, diced

9 almonds, slivered
orange slices, for garnish
lettuce for garnish
9 black olives, for garnish

Mix all the ingredients except the peppers and garnishes. Cut the tops from the peppers and remove the seeds and filters. Stuff with the filling. Chill for a few hours. When ready to serve, slice thin with a bread knife. Place each "shamrock" on an orange slice and then on a lettuce leaf, with an olive on the side. (Serves 4–6.)

FISH SALAD   *Shavuot*

Although fish thrive in the Sea of Galilee and the Jordan River, they all die as soon as they swim into the Dead Sea. In Biblical times fish had to be cured, either by sun-drying or salting, for sale at the famous Fish Gate in Jerusalem, as there were no lakes or ponds nearby. The Phoenicians became the chief suppliers of cured fish to Judea. Today in Israel even the giant tuna, which our fishermen get from the Atlantic, is sold fresh or frozen.

2 *cups flaked cooked tuna*	2 *green onions, chopped*
2 *tablespoons capers*	*salt and pepper*
2 *tablespoons lemon juice*	*dash of cayenne*
1 *green pepper, chopped*	1/2 *cup sour cream*
1 *red pimento, chopped*	1/2 *cup mayonnaise*
1 *cucumber, diced*	*lettuce and tomato*
1 *stalk celery, chopped*	*wedges, for garnish*

Toss together all the ingredients (do not mix too much or the fish will get mushy) except the garnishes. Serve on lettuce with tomato wedges. (Serves 4.)

MAYONNAISE   *Passover*

1 *teaspoon mustard*	1 *egg*
1 *teaspoon salt*	1¾ *cups cooking oil*
1 *teaspoon sugar*	4 *tablespoons vinegar*
1/2 *teaspoon cayenne*	

Chill an egg beater, a bowl, and the ingredients in the refrigerator. Put all the dry ingredients in the bowl, add the egg, and begin beating with the rotary beater or mixer. Drip in the oil slowly—otherwise it will not emulsify. Beat constantly. After the emulsion begins to thicken you can pour instead of drip in the oil, but do this slowly too. Toward the end of the oil, begin alternating with dribbles of vinegar. Beat until thick and smooth. Should the emulsion break up during beating, take another egg yolk, beat it, and then slowly pour in the mayonnaise, beating constantly.

SHAVUOT FIRST-FRUITS SALAD   *Shavuot*

*The following salad is made up of fruits mentioned in the Bible
and known to have grown in the Holy Land in ancient days. "The
goodly tree" was the citron, and today all citrus fruits—the
orange in particular—are our goodly trees. The "apple" is believed to be the "apricot."*

grapes (Isaiah 5:2)
figs (Proverbs 27:18)
dates (Joel 1:12)
pomegranates (Deuteronomy
  8:8)
apples (Song of Solomon
  2:3)
apricots (called apples
  Joel 1:12)
almonds (Ecclesiastes
  12:5)

peanuts (Genesis 43:11)
walnuts (Song of Solomon
  6:11)
sycamore figs (Amos 7:14)
citrus (Leviticus 23:40)
mulberries (II Samuel 5:23)
melons (Numbers 11:5)
oranges (Proverbs 25:11)
honey (II Samuel 17:29)
cream (Judges 4:19)

As this recipe grew out of a game my husband played with the
children, to test their Bible knowledge, there are no set rules
about amounts of each fruit to be used. Toss the cut fruits together and dress with honey and cream. A sprinkling of cinnamon may be added if your children can locate the spice in the
Book (Proverbs 7:17).

FRENCH DRESSING   *Tu Besh'vat*

*My five-year-old Sherry observes every nuance in fine cooking.
Ever since she saw the chef in the Maccabean Room make us a
salad, she insists that I omit garlic from the dressing and rub it
on the bowl to let it lurk, half-detected, "because that's what
makes that salad so very-very good!" French dressing is the
most popular of all for salads in Israel.*

  6 *tablespoons olive oil*
  3 *tablespoons wine vinegar*
  1 *teaspoon sugar*
½ *teaspoon mustard*
  1 *clove garlic, crushed*

¼ *teaspoon salt*
  pinch of paprika
  grain of cayenne
  pinch of pepper

Put all the ingredients into a bottle. Shake well.

SAUCES

HILBEH—FENUGREEK SAUCE *Rosh Hashana*

Fenugreek is a legume that was little known in Israel until the lost Yemenite tribes brought it in with their mass immigration after the birth of the state. Although most of them had never even seen a wheel in their abode so distant from civilization, they were not surprised by the sight of the El Al planes that brought them from Aden, to which they had trekked for weeks on foot. For they knew the Bible, and were aware that they would return to the Promised Land on the wings of eagles.

This sauce is combined with fiery and flavored spices, and is as much used by the Yemenites as butter or margarine is by people of the West. An ancient—and still maintained—Arab belief is that the fenugreek legume keeps women plump and highly fertile, and makes horses fleet-footed. They therefore fed it to their harems and their steeds.

The seeds of fenugreek are pounded in a mortar to make flour. This flour is put in water overnight, and in the morning the water is poured off (the flour sinks to the bottom of the jug). The flour is mixed, a little at a time, with more water to make an emulsion. It is then flavored with schoog (*see* Index) and salt and used as a dressing on salads or a sauce on vegetables, meat, and other dishes, or as a dip with Middle-Eastern bread.

TOMATO SAUCE (ORIENTAL) *Succot*

Fire-eaters are not only in circuses. I have seen westerners in Israel eating chili peppers and fiery tomato sauce, with stomachs unused and unarmored to such delights, and the perspiration rolled so copiously off their faces one didn't know if it was tears or just Nature's way of opening a fire extinguisher.

1 pound ripe tomatoes	1 teaspoon sugar
3 hot chili peppers	1/2 teaspoon salt
pinch of black pepper	1 clove garlic, crushed

Put the tomatoes and chilis through the meat grinder. Bring to the boil, with remaining ingredients, and cool 2 minutes. May be used as a relish or sauce.

TAHINA SAUCE WITH VEGETABLES *Succot*

The kosher laws forbid the eating of milk with meat, and therefore milk sauces cannot be used on vegetables in many meals. Middle Eastern immigrants in Israel have given us a tahina sauce for vegetable dishes.

1½ tablespoons flour   *3 cups cooked vegetables*
  1 cup tahina (see Tahina
     Paste, introductory note)

Sprinkle the flour into the prepared tahina and mix well. Bring to a slow boil. Add the vegetables and heat through. Serve in patty shells as a first course, or as a side dish with meats, or over hard-cooked eggs on toast. (Serves 4–6.)

SPANISH SAUCE *Hanuka*

This is not to be confused with sauce espagnole, that rich brown sauce of vegetables, spices, tomatoes, meat, mushrooms, and wine that the French use all the time. No, ma'am—this one is the Israeli version, which our Sephardic (that is, once-upon-a-time, before 1492 Spanish) community likes.

2 green bell peppers, cut   *4 tablespoons oil*
  very small   *2 tablespoons chopped*
2 sweet red peppers, cut   *parsley*
  very small   *2 pounds tomatoes, diced*
1 chili pepper, chopped   *2 teaspoons salt*
2 onions, chopped   *black pepper*
1 clove garlic, chopped

Lightly fry the chopped peppers, onions, and garlic in the oil. Add the parsley, then the tomatoes and the seasoning. Cook on low heat until the tomatoes become a pulp (about 30 minutes).

BÉCHAMEL (OR WHITE) SAUCE *Shavuot*

Marquis Louis de Béchameil was a courtier in the service of Louis XIV, and his lord steward. He is said to have invented a white sauce which the king named for him. But there are so many variations of the Béchamel sauce that few know which is the original. It can be flavored with onion or nutmeg or bay leaf or mustard, enriched with cream or egg yolks, and it can be made partly of chicken stock. (In Israel we have a pareve—that is, neutral, not meat or dairy—chicken-tasting soup powder which is used for reasons of kashrut instead of chicken stock, in this sauce.)

For Cream Soups

1 cup milk
1 small onion, cut in two

1 tablespoon margarine
1 tablespoon flour
salt and pepper to taste

Heat the milk with the onion. Melt the margarine and add the flour. When the margarine mixture begins to bubble, add about half of the hot milk and stir until it boils. Add the remaining milk gradually and stir until thickened. Add salt and pepper and any other desired seasoning. Remove the onion. (Makes one cup.)

For dressing fish or vegetables: as above, but use twice the amount of margarine and flour.

For croquettes: as above, but use 4 tablespoons margarine and 5 tablespoons flour.

For soufflés: as above, but use 3 tablespoons margarine and 3 tablespoons flour.

Rosh Hashana

CHESTNUT SAUCE FOR BOILED CHICKEN

2 teaspoons sugar
1 cup puréed, cooked
    chestnuts
2 tablespoons chicken fat

2 tablespoons flour
1 cup hot chicken stock
    salt and pepper
2 egg yolks

Add the sugar to the chestnuts. Melt the chicken fat and mix in the flour. Add the hot stock, salt, and pepper and cook until thick, stirring often. Beat the egg yolks. Pour a few tablespoons of the hot sauce over the beaten yolks and mix well. Then stir this mixture back into the remaining sauce and heat up, but do not boil, stirring constantly. Now add the puréed chestnuts, mix well, and serve with the chicken or over it.

WINE SAUCE

1/2 cup cherry liqueur or
        white wine
1/2 cup water
3/4 cup sugar

2 eggs
1 tablespoon lemon juice
    grated rind of 1/2 lemon

Mix the liqueur or wine with the water and sugar and heat to the boiling point. Beat the eggs and slowly whip in the diluted hot wine. Add the lemon juice and rind. Cook over hot water, stirring constantly, until the mixture is rather thick. Serve hot or cold on any dessert that requires a topping.

PEPERONI-TYPE ITALIAN SAUCE   *Succot*

What's sauce for the goose is sauce for the gander is true enough.
But what is sauce for an Italian may not be sauce for an Israeli.
Except in this case: Israelis love peppy foods like peperoni sauce!

6 ounces spicy sausage, chopped	orégano or basil
1 tablespoon olive oil	2 cloves garlic, crushed
½ pound minced beef	3 cups diced tomatoes
1 onion, chopped	½ pound tomato purée
½ pound sliced mushrooms	2 bay leaves
6 tablespoons chopped parsley	dash of cayenne
	½ teaspoon salt
	2 cups water

Put the sausage in a frying pan and let the fat sizzle out of it.
Add the olive oil and the beef and fry briefly. Add the onion,
mushrooms, parsley, orégano, garlic, tomatoes, tomato purée, bay
leaves, cayenne, and salt. Add the water and cover the pan well.
Simmer for 2 hours. Remove the bay leaves.

SOUR CREAM SAUCES

Sauce for Desserts

1 cup sour cream
2 teaspoons sugar
few drops vanilla

Dressing for Salads

1 cup sour cream
salt and pepper
juice of ½ lemon
mayonnaise (optional)
1 teaspoon prepared mustard or grated horse-
radish

Mix ingredients thoroughly.

RELISH AND PICKLES

CHRAIN—HORSE-RADISH RELISH *Passover*

This is often served, with sliced dill pickles in it, on Passover as a relish for meat, fish, and pancakes.

½ cup grated fresh horse-
    radish
½ cup citrus vinegar
1 teaspoon salt

2 cups grated boiled beets
2 tablespoons sugar
   pinch of pepper

Grate the horse-radish root out-of-doors or it will draw more tears than a bushel of onions. Mix all the ingredients together.

PASSOVER ROSSEL—BEET SOUR *Passover*

5 pounds beetroot   boiling water

Cut the raw beets into quarters and pack into a crock or glass jars. Cover with boiling water and a closely bound cloth. Remove the scum after a few days and repeat about twice a week. The rossel is ready for use in about three weeks' time.

SCHOOG—SPICY YEMENITE RELISH *Rosh Hashana*

This Yemenite relish is used, along with hilbeh, by the people who brought it to Israel. It has become an extremely—and surprisingly—popular dish among the Israeli youth in the army and the kibbutzim *(the collective settlements) who use it on salads or as a spread on cottage cheese or just plain margarine sandwiches.*

garlic
hot chili peppers
black peppercorns
cumin

cardamom seed
coriander
salt
2 pounds tomatoes, chopped

Mix the tomatoes with the above spices in quantities to suit your taste. Then mix with hilbeh (Fenugreek Sauce, *see* Index) or tahina (sesame seed oil, *see* Index).

AMBA—MANGO CHUTNEY   *Rosh Hashana*

*The B'nai Israel from Cochin, India, flavor dishes with a mango
chutney called amba, now becoming popular throughout the land.*

4¼ pounds firm mangoes	2 teaspoons salt
1½ cups vinegar (or more	½ teaspoon coriander
if needed)	2 teaspoons chopped
1 cup sugar	candied ginger
½ cup raisins	1 teaspoon cumin
2 cloves garlic, chopped	2 teaspoons turmeric
3 red chili peppers,	6 threads saffron
chopped	

Put all the ingredients except the mangoes into a pot and bring
to the boil. Reduce the heat to very low. Peel the mangoes, cut
them into strips, and add. Cook very gently until the mangoes are
no longer raw, but still firm. Pour into jars and seal. Serve with
rice, meat, or vegetable dishes.

EGGPLANT PICKLES   *Independence Day*

*Jews from Middle Eastern countries like pickles very sour and
peppery. They preserve turnips, radishes, tomatoes, and cucumbers as described below, and serve them with hors d'oeuvres such
as homos, and with rice dishes.*

2 pounds very small	2 cups wine vinegar
eggplants	1 chili pepper
2 cups water	4 bay leaves
4 teaspoons salt	10 peppercorns
2 tablespoons sugar	

Select the slim type of baby eggplant. Wash but do not peel.
Boil the water, salt, sugar, vinegar, chili pepper, bay leaves, and
peppercorns for 5 minutes. Put in the eggplants and cook until
just done, but still firm. Store in jars.

PICKLED LEMONS   *Shabbat*

*The Greeks and Romans ate the inner peel of citrons pickled in
vinegar. The tradition of the dish seems to have remained, for in
the twelfth century an Arab native of Seville wrote on the fruits
of Spain, telling how to pickle lemons with the addition of honey
and saffron. The dish is made today by Middle Eastern Jews who
have come to Israel.*

12 lemons	12 whole peppercorns or
salt	1 chili pepper
paprika to taste	½ cup olive oil
3 bay leaves	

Bring the whole lemons to a boil and simmer for about 20
minutes. The lemons should still be firm. Remove and drain. Cut
each lemon into quarters. In a jar put the lemon quarters in
layers, topping each layer with a sprinkling of salt and all the
other spices. Continue until the jar is full. Add the oil. Cover
with waxed paper and close the jar. A brine will form in a few
days, sealed by the oil on top. This will be ready to eat in six
months.

CURRY SAUCE (RELISH)   *Succot*

*"Kari" means "sauce" in southern India, and these sauces vary
from district to district and dish to dish, but all of them contain
turmeric. Coriander, ginger, cardamom, cumin, fenugreek, peppers, and all sorts of other things are sometimes added, even
carrots and apples and onions and bananas and tomatoes and
raisins and . . . So westerners mixed up some of these things,
particularly the turmeric, and called the powder curry. Ditto in
Israel.*

1 large onion	1 teaspoon curry powder
1 large bell pepper	dash of grated lemon rind
2 ripe tomatoes	dash of cumin
1 clove garlic	1 tablespoon chopped
⅛ teaspoon cayenne or	parsley
1 small chili, ground	3 tablespoons oil
1 teaspoon salt	2 tablespoons citrus vinegar

Put the onions, bell pepper, tomatoes, and garlic through the
meat chopper. Add the seasonings and liquids and beat well. With
a little water added, this relish may be used for cooking curry
dishes.

PICKLED PLUMS   *Succot*

2 pounds plums	1 teaspoon cinnamon
2 cups sugar	½ teaspoon whole cloves
⅔ cup citrus or wine vinegar	dash of ginger

Prick the plums with a fork. Boil the remaining ingredients together. Add the plums. Simmer for 20 minutes and seal in jars.

DILL PICKLES AND THEIR RELATIVES *Succot*

A few women (one being my chic ever-youthful neighbor, Freda Bloch), unafraid of revealing their pre-refrigeration-days age, will tell—oh, so nostalgically—of the cellars of their childhood days. But the men of Israel get positively sentimental when they tell you of the barrels of sauerkraut and dill cucumber pickles, baby watermelons and green tomatoes in brine, red gambas and green peppers with chermitchi (what can it be?) seed, big apples perfuming the air in their liquor, and honeyed mead and home-made wines restless in their aromatic fermentation, as the listener gets mouth-wateringly ecstatic. Without cellars, and with fresh vegetables all year round and factories putting out first-rate Grandma-flavored pickles, the Israel housewife makes only a few jars of dills at a time (perhaps to win favor in her husband's eyes), which can be seen standing on the back-porch window of almost every flat.

24 small cucumbers	3 tablespoons vinegar
3 bay leaves	(optional)
6 small cloves garlic	9 cups water
a fistful of fresh dill	9 tablespoons coarse salt
3 chilis (optional)	

Wash the cucumbers and fit them closely into three 1-quart-sized jars. Top each jar with a bay leaf, 2 cloves of garlic, a chili pepper, if desired, and sprigs of washed fresh dill. Mix the water, salt, and vinegar (boil it if you like, but cool it before pouring on the cucumbers) and pour over the cucumbers. Place the jars in the sun, but be sure the cucumbers are kept under the brine; it may be necessary to add water as it evaporates. The cucumbers turn yellowish in a few days and are then ready to eat. (These cucumbers do not keep for more than a few weeks, as do those which are made with boiling brine and sealed in sterilized jars.)

PICKLED CHILIS *Hanuka*

The red-hot pickled chili is a favorite in Israel, but it takes a cast-iron digestive system and a fire extinguisher to eat more than one.

2 cups water	2 teaspoons salt
2 cups vinegar	1 pound chili peppers
sugar, if desired	

Bring the water, vinegar, sugar, and salt to a boil. Drop in the chilis, without cutting the pods. Bring to a boil. Pack into jars and seal well.

SWEET PICKLED LEMONS   *Shabbat*

"The goodly tree" in the Bible is believed to be the citron or its near relative, the lemon. Pickled lemons, whether sweet or sour, is so ancient a condiment in Middle Eastern fare, that its source is obscure.

6 *small lemons*   4 *cups, or more, sugar*

Wash and quarter the lemons, then pack in a large crock with layers of sugar between them. Cover the jar and keep in a cool place. After some time, fermentation will begin. Remove any scum that may rise, and see that the lemons remain covered with sugar. They will be ready in about 6 months' time. The lemons are used as pickles and in some Middle Eastern dishes.

PICKLED TURNIPS (IRAQI STYLE)   *Passover*

This dish is a "must" on Passover in Iraqi-Jewish households.

2 *pounds turnips*   *water to cover*
6 *tablespoons salt*

Peel and quarter the turnips. Pack into a jar and put the salt on top. Pour cold water to the top and close. In a fortnight the turnips turn light pink.

WATERMELON PICKLES   *Passover*

7 *cups watermelon rind*	7 *cups sugar*
1½ *tablespoons salt*	1 *teaspoon whole cloves*
7 *cups cold water*	3 *inches cinnamon stock*
1 *cup mild vinegar*	1 *small piece ginger root*

After cutting out the red flesh of the watermelon for food, remove the green rind, too. Cut the white rind into uniform cubes. Cover with water and salt and let stand overnight. Drain and cover with ice water for an hour. Drain again and cover with boiling water and cook until peel just begins to be tender. Drain and cook with the remaining ingredients until the melon rinds are transparent. Let stand for a day. Boil up once more and pack into jars.

HAROSETS OF MANY KINDS   *Passover*

Haroset is a mixture of fruits, spices, wine, and matzo meal which is on the Seder dish on Passover eve. It is supposed to look like the mortar on which we worked as slaves in Egypt. Some people make it taste almost like mortar. Others make it so good that the children in the family put an end to a huge bowlful of the haroset before the night is over.

What decides a Haroset? The fruits which are available, the nuts which are plentiful, go into the making of each community's Haroset. The spices used must color (if color be needed) the pulp to look like bricks. The wine must be red—in remembrance of the Red Sea. Matzo meal is used to give bulk to the paste and often to hold it together; more is used in a haroset when there is little money for expensive nuts and fruit.

"Sabra" Israel Type Haroset

2 apples, peeled and cored	*1 cup dry red wine*
6 bananas	*matzo meal as needed*
1 lemon, juice and rind	*4 tablespoons candied peel*
1 orange, juice and rind	*2 teaspoons cinnamon*
20 dates	*sugar to taste*
1 cup peanuts	

Put the fruit and nuts through the meat grinder. Add the wine and fruit juice. Then add enough matzo meal to soak up the wine, to the consistency you like (some like it thick, some like it thin). Mix in cinnamon and sprinkle on sugar to taste.

Central European Haroset

1 cup apples, grated	*2 teaspoons cinnamon*
½ cup chopped almonds	*dry red wine*

Mix the ingredients together, using just enough wine to make it into a liquidy paste.

Yemenite Haroset

30 dates, chopped	*matzo meal as desired*
20 dried figs, chopped	*dry red wine*
2 tablespoons sesame seed	*1 chili pepper (optional)*
2 teaspoons hot ginger powder	

Mix the fruits and spice. Add matzo meal and wine to make a firm paste.

Iraqi Type Haroset

1 cup almonds	1 cup pine nuts
1 cup walnuts	3 tablespoons red wine

Grind the nuts together and add the wine.

Italian Type Haroset

4 apples, chopped	6 walnuts, chopped
6 dates, chopped	½ cup raisins, chopped
3 hard-cooked eggs, chopped	matzo meal
1 cup almonds, chopped	lemon juice

Mix all the ingredients together, adding matzo meal and lemon juice as desired.

North African Type Haroset

2 ounces pine nuts	½ cup chopped walnuts
1 hard-cooked egg yolk	1 lemon, grated rind and
1 apple, grated	juice
½ cup sugar	cinnamon and ginger to
½ cup ground almonds	taste

Mix all ingredients together.

Turkish Type Haroset

20 Smyrna dates	½ cup almonds
1 cup raisins	red wine
1 cup walnuts	

Put the fruit and nuts through the meat chopper. Mix with wine.

VEGETABLES

ARTICHOKES WITH TARTARE SAUCE *Shavuot*

Maurice Szillend Curnonsky, one of the world's leading specialists in gastoronomy, wrote of the artichoke: "This is, perhaps, more subtle of flavor, more delicate of texture, than any other green vegetable. Besides, it's fun to eat!" The flavorful, delicate morsel consists of one nibble at the base of each leaf (plus the tasty heart, which one has to reach through a thistled cap). Pluck off the leaf and dip it in tartare sauce (or Hollandaise or just mayonnaise or sour cream), then with one baby-bite you are rewarded.

The Artichokes

8 artichokes
4 quarts water
2 tablespoons salt
2 tablespoons vinegar

The Tartare Sauce

½ teaspoon chopped tarragon
1 cup mayonnaise
4 tablespoons sour cream
   (optional)
1 tablespoon chopped
   pickles or capers
1 tablespoon chopped
   chives
1 tablespoon chopped
   parsley

Trim the spikes (if there are any) off the top of the artichokes. Bring the water to a boil and add the salt and vinegar. Cook the artichokes for 40–50 minutes (leaves should pull out easily). Drain, cool, and serve cold.

Mix the ingredients for the tartare sauce. (Serves 8.)

NOTE: Artichokes can also be served hot, with butter or hollandaise sauce (*see* Index).

FILLED ARTICHOKE HEARTS *Passover*

Boil artichokes until tender. Remove the leaves (which can be served separately). With a sharp knife cut off the choke (it is easily removed in one piece). The artichoke heart, very sweet and succulent, is shaped like a small deep saucer. Fill as for Pazie (Stuffed Stems) (*see* Index) and cook as directed in that recipe.

CARCIOFI ALLA GIUDAICA
ARTICHOKES—JEWISH STYLE *Passover*

When artichokes are in season in Rome, it is an experience to go into one of the small restaurants in or near the Ghetto. All Italians love this dish and the Jews serve it especially on Passover. The restauranteur's whole family will be seated in the dining room with huge buckets full of young artichokes, and baskets full of the trimmings, working away to make a perfect ball of each artichoke thistle. The frying garlic of the battuto *emanates from the kitchen and the animated conversation of the family, waiters and cooks, about the quality of the artichoke is most titillating to the appetite.*

12 *small artichokes*	2 *tablespoons chopped*
2 *cloves garlic, crushed*	*mint*
(optional)	1 *cup olive oil*
2 *tablespoons chopped*	*lemon wedges*
parsley	*salt*

Trim the tops off the artichokes, working around and around so as to retain the shape. Soak in salt water for an hour, then drain dry. Meanwhile lightly fry the garlic and herbs (this is a *battuto*) in a tablespoon of the oil ond tuck a little of this mixture into the center of each artichoke. Heat the remaining oil and place the artichokes in it, upside down, 2 or 3 at a time. Cook until crisp on the outside (about 10 minutes) and serve hot with lemon wedges and salt. The artichokes open up like a rose, are crunchy on the outside and tender within. (Serves 6.)

TURKISH ARTICHOKES *Shavuot*

10 *artichoke hearts*	¼ *cup olive oil*
juice of 1 lemon	1 *small clove garlic*
1 *teaspoon salt*	2 *teaspoons sugar*
½ *cup water*	1 *tablespoon cornstarch*

Soak the artichoke hearts in the lemon juice, salt, and water for an hour. Put them, and the liquid in which they were steeped, into a little pot with the oil, garlic, and sugar. Simmer gently until tender (about 30 minutes). Remove the artichokes to a serving dish. Thicken the sauce with cornstarch and pour over the hearts. Cool. Serve cold. (Serves 4.)

THE PRIZE ARTICHOKES   *Purim*

Seventy years from the day of its giving, a gift of Baron de Roths-
child's bore the finest fruit in Israel. The French artichoke,
brought to Israel in 1893, created the prizewinning dish in the
Culinary Contest of 1963. Mrs. Abbalah Mazawi, a Christian
Arab woman of Nazareth, wife of a restauranteur, mother of four,
and herself one of six sisters who competed in creative cooking,
is so gifted in the field that two of her dishes were selected out of
1,400 for the finals. Although this dish has definite nuances of
Arab flavor, it is very similar to the old traditional Jewish-
Sephardic stuffed artichoke. It is very delicate in spite of what
seems like a lot of fat in the recipe.

3 pounds young	*2 ounces pine nuts*
artichokes	*1 tablespoon salt*
⅔ pound margarine	*¼ teaspoon pepper*
2 large onions	*1 teaspoon cinnamon*
1¼ pounds lamb	*4 cups water*

Remove the outer leaves of the artichokes until you get to the
tender inner leaves. Remove the chokes and put the artichokes
into cold water. Melt the margarine. Lightly fry the artichokes in
this fat and then arrange them on a shallow baking dish. Chop
the onions and grind the meat, and then fry in the fat. Add
the pine nuts, salt, pepper, and cinnamon. Fill each artichoke
with this mixture. Add the water and bake in a medium oven for
1½ hours, adding more water, if necessary. (Serves 6–10.)

ASPARAGUS WITH HOLLANDAISE   *Shavuot*

In his meditations on food, the great gastronome Brillat-Savarin
comes to a strange conclusion about asparagus. "Experience," he
writes, "founded on millions of observations, has taught us that
food determines dreams. Generally, all foods that are slightly
exciting, cause people to dream, such as brown meat, pigeons,
ducks, game, and above all, hare. This property is also recognized
in asparagus. . . ." Here's to happy dreams!

The Asparagus

2 bunches asparagus,
trimmed
water as required
1 teaspoon salt

The Hollandaise Sauce

½ cup butter
3 egg yolks
1 tablespoon lemon juice
¼ teaspoon salt
½ cup hot asparagus liquid
cayenne pepper, if desired

Cook the trimmed asparagus, standing up, in quickly boiling water with the salt. The tips should not be in the water, but should be steamed for about 15 minutes by putting a smaller pot over the top of the one with the water. Drain well, reserving the liquid.

For the sauce, work the butter until creamy, adding the egg yolks one at a time, then the lemon juice and salt. Just before serving, add the asparagus liquid and stir quickly. Cook in top of a double boiler until thick, stirring constantly. Add a dash of cayenne pepper if you wish. Serve over the drained asparagus. (Serves 6–8.)

BAKED BEANS WITH APPLES *Succot*

The bean has a very ancient history. The Romans of yore not only ate the legume, but used it in gathering votes of the people and in electing magistrates: A white bean was "for" and a black or brown bean "against." It also had a role in the Lemuria and Parentalia, in which ceremony the head of the house threw black beans over his head and repeated the words: "With these beans I redeem myself and my family."

1 cup white navy beans	1 teaspoon salt
3 large apples, peeled and quartered	dash of cinnamon
	½ cup red wine
1 cup sugar	2 tablespoons wine vinegar
¼ pound fat	

Soak the beans overnight, change the water, and cook until tender (2–3 hours). Drain, add the remaining ingredients, and stew gently over low heat for 1 hour. (Serves 4–6.)

ROSEMARY-BEETS IN ORANGE *Tu Besh'vat*

1 tablespoon margarine	salt to taste
1 tablespoon cornstarch	1 teaspoon grated orange peel
1 cup orange juice	
4 tablespoons sugar	1 teaspoon rosemary
2 cups cooked beets, sliced thin	

Melt the margarine, add the cornstarch, and stir. Mix the orange juice and the sugar and add. Bring to a boil and stir constantly until smooth and thick. Add the remaining ingredients and heat through. Serve hot. (Serves 4.)

BEANS IN TOMATO SAUCE *Hanuka*

This Middle Eastern dish has caught on so well in the kibbutzim of native youth that it is the first food to be emptied off the trolleys that are moved from table to table (in turn by every settler, for not one of them would give up land work to become a waiter) in the huge dining halls. They learned to like the dish in the army, where the large number of soldiers from surrounding countries need it more than bread.

3 cups white navy beans	*4 tablespoons olive oil*
3 large onions	*water*
3 cloves garlic	*½ cup chopped parsley*
3 carrots	*dash of paprika or cayenne*
6 large tomatoes	*salt and pepper to taste*

Soak the beans overnight. Boil 2–3 hours, or until tender. Drain. Cut up the vegetables fine and fry in oil until golden. Add a very little water and cook to a pulp (about 10 minutes). Add the seasonings. Put the sauce into the beans and simmer together for about 15 minutes more. (Serves 8–10.)

"PUL" IN POD—GREEN BROAD BEANS

Vicia faba—"the bean of history"—or the broad bean, or the butter bean, or the horse bean, or the field tick, or windsor, or the fava bean, or pul (as it is popularly called in Israel)—belongs in Asia and dates back to antiquity. In Israel, when it is freshly harvested, the bean is eaten in multiple ways with its fleshy pod.

4 cups fresh fava beans	*dash of cumin (optional)*
½ cup chopped onion	*4 tablespoons oil*
1 clove garlic, crushed	*½ cup water (about)*
2 tablespoons chopped dill	*tomato sauce, if desired*
salt and pepper to taste	

Wash the beans and remove the strings. Slice sliver thin, pod and young bean together. Put into a heavy skillet with all the remaining ingredients except the water. Let the beans "stew in their own juice" and add a little water only if they begin to dry or to stick. Cook on low heat until the beans are done (about 30 minutes). Any desired tomato sauce may be added if you like, but the above is very good without further additions.

BROWN BEANS   *Shabbat*

Because of the poverty of most of Europe's Jews through the ages, and because in most lands they were not allowed to till the soil, fresh vegetables were almost an unknown food to them. The bulk of their food was cereals, pulses and legumes. And these came even to the Sabbath table, but this time enhanced with the flavor of meat and often with sugar added.

2 cups brown beans, butter beans or other water as required	2 teaspoons salt pepper
1 cup sugar	1 cup wine vinegar 3 tablespoons chicken fat

Soak the beans overnight. Cook the beans in fresh water until tender (2–3 hours), on low heat. Add the remaining ingredients and stew gently for 30 minutes. (Serves 4–6.)

B'OB—FAVA BEANS   *Shabbat*

1 pound fava or butter beans (dried)	salt

Soak the beans overnight in cold water. Drain. Cook in fresh water over low heat for about 45 minutes. Drain and sprinkle with salt while still warm.

LIMA BEANS WITH HONEY   *Rosh Hashana*

The American Indians are supposed to have first thought of cooking beans with a sweet—in their case, maple syrup. The American white colonists soon switched to using molasses in the making of baked beans. But who taught the Jews of Eastern Europe to cook lima or other beans with honey?

2 cups dried lima or other beans water to cover	4 tablespoons suet or other fat ½ cup honey
2 onions, cut up	2 teaspoons salt

Soak the beans overnight, cover with water, and cook over a low heat until beans are soft (2–3 hours). Drain off the water. Fry the onions in the fat, then add the honey and salt and mix with the beans. Bake in a 350° oven for about an hour, or until beans are glazed. (Serves 6–8.)

BEANS FROM DAMASCUS—FUL MEDAMAS *Succot*

The colors of this dish look like the robes of an Arab in a blue-and purple-tiled mosque. The dish must be garnished glamorously with the small brown beans turned somewhat purple in the cooking, the eggs mealy from long boiling, the white tahina sprinkled with red cayenne and surrounded with much green parsley.

2 cups small brown beans	*1 cup prepared tahina*
6 cups water	*(sesame seed paste)*
6 eggs	*(see* Index*)*
salt and pepper to taste	*juice of ½ lemon*
3 tablespoons olive oil	*dash of cayenne*
3 cloves garlic	*parsley*
	dash of turmeric

Put the beans, water, unshelled raw eggs, salt, and pepper in a heavy pot and bring to the boil. Add the oil and the garlic. Simmer, covered, overnight on very low heat. Serve the beans with the whole eggs, shelled, and next to it the tahina sprinkled with lemon juice and garnished to taste, with parsley and a sprinkling of cayenne. Sprinkle turmeric on the egg. (Serves 4–6.)

HARVARD BEETS *Rosh Hashana*

The remains of a century-old Russian-Jewish cookbook in my possession gives a recipe for beets under the title of "tzimmes" for Rosh Hashana: it is almost exactly the same dish as Harvard beets. Is this not proof how distances and time have no effect upon the culinary tastes of man? Beets are part of the traditional Rosh Hashana Sephardic fare as they are one of the ten foods blessed on that occasion at table.

8 medium beets	*½ cup sugar*
2 tablespoons margarine	*⅓ cup lemon juice*
1 tablespoon flour	*salt and pepper to taste*

Boil the beets in their skins until they can be pierced with a fork (30–60 minutes). Remove the skins and slice with a lattice or other fancy cutter. Melt the margarine and bring to bubbling. Add the flour. Add the sugar mixed with the lemon juice and cook until thick and transparent, stirring constantly. Add the beets, season to taste, and heat through. You can use a little water to dilute the lemon juice if you prefer it less piquant. (Serves 6–8.)

BRUSSELS SPROUTS WITH HONEY   *Rosh Hashana*

In Wadi Hunein—the Valley of Roses—near my home in Israel, there lived in the last century a German Christian, drawn here, with his wife and many children, by the Messianic belief. The swamps of the area infected the family with malaria, and all but the father died on the farm. Broken-hearted, he left Palestine, exchanging his poor farm for one in Russia equally as poor, owned by Reuven Lehrer and his wife Feige, who were about fifty years old. Reuven was deathly ill and decided to spend his last few years, or perhaps months, in the land of his forefathers, and be buried in the holy soil. Poverty-stricken, they lived on the cabbages they grew, and on wild honey, and later the honey they produced in a small apiary. Wadi Hunein is now called "Ness Ziona"—the "Miracle of Zion"—and no wonder, for Reuven lived to be a hundred (he died in 1938) and Feige danced the hora on her 106th birthday!

"To what do you attribute your longevity when others died like flies here?" asked reporters.

"To the fact that we had only cabbage and honey to eat, for we were so poor."

On that day Feige ate Brussels Sprouts with Honey (and meat in it too!).

1 2-pound brisket of beef	*1 onion, chopped*
3 tablespoons cooking oil	*1 pound Brussels sprouts*
water to cover	*½ cup honey*
1 teaspoon salt	

Sear the meat in the oil, add water, salt, and onion and simmer, covered (about 1½ hours). Pour boiling water over the Brussels sprouts to blanch them. Add to meat with honey, enough water to cover and cook until meat and vegetables are tender (10–15 minutes). (Serves 4–6.)

RED CABBAGE WITH APPLES   *Succot*

1½ pounds red cabbage	*salt and pepper*
4 tablespoons cooking oil	*3 tablespoons sugar*
3 sour apples, peeled and cubed	*3 tablespoons wine vinegar*

Shred the cabbage and soak in cold water 30 minutes. Drain. Fry lightly in the oil. Add the apples, salt, pepper, sugar, and vinegar. Cover the pot tightly. If necessary, add a little water to keep the cabbage from burning. Cook on very low heat for 15–20 minutes. (Serves 4–6.)

ZESTY BEETROOT
Shavuot

*The ancient Romans are believed to have developed the beetroot
as a table vegetable; they even succeeded in breeding the scarlet
color into it. In any case, the beetroot was held in the highest
esteem in those days, for the Greeks paid homage to Apollo by
serving him beetroots on a silver platter.*

8 *small beets*	*2 tablespoons sugar*
1 *teaspoon salt*	*1 bay leaf*
2 *medium onions, thinly*	*6 peppercorns*
sliced	*lettuce*
2 *teaspoons grated horse-*	*mayonnaise*
radish	*sour cream*
1 *cup mild or diluted vinegar*	

Cook the beets in their jackets. Peel and slice very thin. Sprinkle
with salt, then mix with the onions and horse-radish. Boil the
vinegar with the sugar, bay leaf, and peppercorns, and while very
hot, add to the beet mixture. Allow to marinate for a few hours.
Serve on lettuce dressed with mayonnaise mixed with sour cream.
(Serves 4–6.)

NOTE: This dish may also be used as a mild pickle.

BRUSSELS SPROUTS
Hanuka

*Greens were considered "poor stuff" and scorned, as were most
vegetables in the thirteenth century, when people indulged
themselves gluttonously on meat foods. But the Belgians toyed
around with the cabbage plant and developed the delectable
Brussels sprouts. The vegetable was not grown commercially in
Israel until recent years, but is now much favored.*

6 *cups trimmed Brussels*	*6 tablespoons butter or*
sprouts	*1½ cups white sauce*
2 *teaspoons salt*	*(see below) or 1 cup*
3 *quarts boiling water*	*hollandaise sauce*
	(see Index)

Soak the Brussels sprouts in water to cover, with the salt, for
about 15 minutes. Discard the water. Cook in the boiling water
until just tender (10–15 minutes). Do not overcook—the sprouts
must not be mushy. Drain and serve hot with butter, or hollandaise sauce, or the following white sauce. (Serves 6–8.)

White Sauce

2 tablespoons margarine
2 tablespoons flour
1 cup hot milk

salt and white pepper to
    taste
dash of nutmeg
    (optional)

Melt the margarine and add the flour. When the mixture begins to bubble, stir in the hot milk and cook, stirring constantly, until thick and creamy. Add the seasoning.

STUFFED CABBAGE (HOLISHKES, PRAAKES, HOLIPCE OR GALUPTZES)   *Succot*

The holishke (also called "holipces" or "praakes") family is divided into two branches: those that wear grape leaves and are simmered with wine, and the more bourgeois cousins rolled in cabbage. The former are usually called "sarmi" (see Index*) and are as elegant as ladies' fingers (and therefore shaped that way). Plain holipces are plump and round and are stewed in tomato sauce. (These two cousins have a very lowly, plebeian Romanian relative, never served on a holiday, which is dressed in sour cabbage, stuffed with coarse cornmeal and fried onions, and served with sour cream. It does not even have a name!) Every member of this family is a delight to the palate.*

10 cabbage leaves
 1 pound chopped beef
½ cup raw rice
 2 onions, minced
 1 parsnip, peeled and grated
   salt and pepper to taste

1 egg
4 tablespoons cooking oil
1 cup tomato paste
5 tablespoons sugar
3 tablespoons vinegar
1 clove garlic (optional)

Pour boiling water over the cabbage leaves and allow them to soften for a few minutes. Mix the meat, rice, onions, parsnip, salt, and pepper and put a heaping tablespoon or two (depending on the size of holishkes desired) into the center of each leaf. Fold over and roll up, tucking in the edges as you go along. Place in a heavy pot. Pour the remaining ingredients, well mixed, over. Bake in 450° oven for 20 minutes, then reduce heat to 300° and cook 40 minutes longer. Add water if needed in the early parts of cooking, but most of the sauce should have been absorbed at the end. (Serves 5.)

NOTE: This dish may also be cooked on top of the range, on high heat for 20 minutes, then simmered for 40 minutes.

CABBAGE WITH CHESTNUTS   *Succot*

In the Hoshanah Rabba prayers of Succot, the phrase "Kol Me-Vasser"—"A voice heralds"—is read. And as a play of words upon that phrase, a symbolic dish called "Kohl mit Wasser" (cabbage—kale—with water) is usually served on Succot. However, as boiled cabbage is everyday fare in German-speaking countries, the dish served instead is cabbage with chestnuts.

1/4 cup vinegar	1/2 cup sweet red wine
1/2 cup water	1 cup blanched chestnuts
1 medium red cabbage	1 tablespoon sugar
2 tablespoons margarine	4 tablespoons currants or
salt, pepper, and allspice	raisins
to taste	1 tablespoon flour

Heat the vinegar and water. Shred the cabbage and pour the hot liquid over. Drain, reserving the liquid. Melt the margarine, add the cabbage and seasonings. Then add the wine and simmer for a few minutes. Meanwhile cook the chestnuts in the reserved vinegar and water with the sugar and currants or raisins. Sprinkle the flour over the cabbage and add to the chestnut mixture. (Serves 6.)

RED CABBAGE WITH WINE   *Tu Besh'vat*

1 medium head red cabbage	dash of cinnamon
1 cup dry red wine	salt and pepper
5 tablespoons margarine	1/2 cup dark red jam
4 tablespoons lemon juice	2 tablespoons water
1 apple, grated	1 tablespoon flour

Shred the cabbage and mix with all the ingredients except the water and flour. Cook on low heat, stirring occasionally. If necessary, add a little water to keep from scorching. Before serving, mix the water and flour and thicken the sauce. (Serves 6-8.)

Rosh Hashana
CARROT-KNAIDLE TZIMMES—CARROT DUMPLING DISH

That greatest of Yiddish writers, Sholom Aleichem, describes the joys of being a shadchan, a marriage-broker, and the grand manner in which he is received when invited to a prospective bride's home to arrange a shiduch—that is, make a match. "At the table they serve me the best portions of meat and feed me tzimmes even on weekdays!"

Carrot-knaidle tzimmes is different from the glazed carrot

*tzimmes made especially for Rosh Hashana. Nonetheless, this
tzimmes will appear on many boards during this festival, and
will indeed comprise the whole main course of the dinner, since
it includes meat, vegetables, and a dumpling.*

Meat and Vegetable Pot

2 pounds beef brisket or
    other fat meat
2 tablespoons oil
6 carrots, sliced
6 medium sweet potatoes,
    sliced
½ cup honey
    salt and pepper to taste

2 tablespoons flour

The Knaidle

1 cup self-rising flour,
    sifted
½ cup margarine or suet
    salt and pepper to taste
¼ cup water
    dash of nutmeg

Brown the meat in oil in a heavy pot. Pile the vegetables around
the meat and add the honey, salt, and pepper. Cover with water
and bring to the boil. Reduce heat as low as possible and cook
slowly for 12 hours. Meantime, mix knaidle ingredients and
form into a ball. When the meat is done, remove from the pot.
Put in the knaidle; add water if necessary. Cover pot and simmer
2 hours. Before serving, brown the 2 tablespoons of flour and
stir into the tzimmes to thicken. Serve hot with the meat. (Serves
4–6.)

NOTE: The knaidle may be cooked overnight with the meat.

CARROT TZIMMES (GLAZED) *Rosh Hashana*

*Rosh Hashana carrot tzimmes should be glazed and made with-
out the usual flour sauce. Carrots are served on Rosh Hashana
because of their symbolism: round and golden like coins, for
man's prosperity, and honeyed, for a sweet year.*

8 large carrots
    salted water to cover
½ cup honey
4 tablespoons sugar

4 tablespoons cooking oil
lemon rind
dash of ginger
    (if desired)

Cut the carrots into slices and just cover with salted water. Boil
10 minutes. Add the honey, sugar, and oil. Cook gently until the
liquid is absorbed and the carrots slightly glazed (about 30
minutes). Sprinkle with lemon rind and ginger, if desired.
(Serves 6–8.)

SAUERKRAUT—ISRAEL STYLE *Hanuka*

Where are the days when, with the onset of winter, six women arrived with twelve sacks of cabbage, three wooden barrels, metal tubs, and cutting boards, to bend over the grating of cabbage and ensure that the kraut would be ready by Hanuka? As in the days of the Maccabees, when the cabbage core was prized as the daintiest morsel, Mother saved the "katchelkihs" for the children. After the cabbage was grated, the barrels were coated and smeared with honey and the cabbage was packed into them, along with salt and water, and sometimes a few apples. Each barrel was covered with a board and a heavy stone, and examined daily to see that the brine was covering the vegetable. Oh, the perfumes, the uneasy stirring of bubbles, the taste . . .

Today women in Israel make kraut in batches of 3 or 4 jars at a time, out of purely nostalgic reasons, for it is locally canned and exported over the world.

1 *large head of cabbage* (*about 5 pounds*)	*2 tablespoons coarse salt* *water as needed*
1 *teaspoon caraway seed* (*optional*)	

Cut the cabbage fine. Pack into jars, with a sprinkling of salt and caraway seed between each layer. Pack the cabbage down as tightly as possible. Add water to overflowing. Close the jar with a glass top and screw cap on loosely. Add water each day if needed to keep jar full. The kraut will be ready in about a week's time if kept at room temperature.

CAULIFLOWER WITH BUTTERED CRUMBS *Tu Besh'vat*

Dr. Sarah Bawly, who has done a gigantic job in teaching nutrition in Israel, had to cope with many unique and tough situations. When our small population was being doubly and trebly multiplied with poverty-stricken immigrants from the four corners of the earth, it was startling to discover that most of them did not know how to use a primus burner for cooking or how to cope with our products for food. Nutritionists were sent out to all the communities and cooking demonstrations were improvised in tents, schoolrooms, homes, and hostels. When I attended such a lesson to report it as a journalist, I also learned how to prepare this simple dish, along with Yemenite women in embroidered trousers and tunics, ultra-Orthodox Polish women with wigs and kerchiefs, Libyan women laden with silver jewelry and wearing multi-colored robes, Indian women in saris, and German women in trimly pleated skirts and white blouses.

1 large cauliflower	1 cup margarine
10 cups water	½ cup dry breadcrumbs
1 teaspoon salt	

Boil the cauliflower in the water, with the salt, until tender but not too soft (8–20 minutes). Fry the breadcrumbs in margarine over low heat so they will not burn, stirring all the time. When the crumbs are golden, spread them over the cauliflower and serve hot. (Serves 6.)

SAUERKRAUT WITH SAUSAGE   *Succot*

4 tablespoons margarine	½ cup water
1 cup chopped onions	dash of pepper and
4 cups sauerkraut	paprika
1 teaspoon caraway seed	8 smoked sausages
1 teaspoon sugar	

Melt the margarine and add the onions. Fry until light gold. Add the remaining ingredients (except the sausages) and cook on low heat for about half an hour. Add the sausages and cook until heated through. (Serves 4.)

HOT SWEET SAUERKRAUT   *Hanuka*

So good is sauerkraut that even its juice was held in the highest esteem in Europe. Peasants, who made the kraut at home, drained off the juices and sold it as a tonic—or even a medicine —to townfolk at the markets in Romania.

1 1-pound, 13-ounce can	1 onion, chopped
sauerkraut	4 tablespoons brown sugar
6 tomatoes, cut up	raisins, if desired
2 cups tomato soup	

Put all the ingredients into a heavy pot on very low heat. Simmer for about six hours, or overnight. Serve hot. (Serves 6–8.)

NOTE: This dish is good, but not as remarkable, if cooked for only an hour.

CAULIFLOWER, CRÈME DU BARRY   *Rosh Hashana*

Comtesse du Barry was a French courtesan who became the mistress of Louis XV. She loved cauliflower as much as the king loved her, and so gave her name to many dishes in which the vegetable is featured. Madame du Barry lost her own head, but her name lives on in the glory of a cauliflower.

1 *cauliflower*	*dash of nutmeg*
2 *tablespoons margarine*	*salt and pepper*
2 *tablespoons flour*	*chervil or other herbs*
1 *cup chicken stock*	

Cook the cauliflower in salted water 8–10 minutes or until tender. Melt the margarine and stir in the flour smoothly. Add the stock and cook, stirring constantly, until thick and smooth. Season and pour over the cauliflower. Garnish with chopped chervil or other herbs. (Serves 4–6.)

CAULIFLOWER WITH MOCK HOLLANDAISE   *Purim*

The Cauliflower

1 *cauliflower*
   pinch of sugar
   pinch of salt
8 *cups boiling water*

The Sauce

3 *tablespoons butter*
2 *tablespoons flour*
1 *cup hot water*
   salt
2 *tablespoons lemon juice*
2 *egg yolks, well beaten*

Boil the cauliflower, with sugar and salt, in an open pot in rapidly boiling water, until tender but not mushy (8–20 minutes). Drain.

To make the sauce, melt the butter, add the flour, and mix. Gradually add the hot water as you cook the sauce over very low heat or in a double boiler. Stir continuously until thick. Add salt and lemon juice. Pour the mixture over the egg yolks, stir very well, and pour over the cauliflower. Serve at once. (Serves 4–6.)

CAULIFLOWER CREOLE   *Purim*

1 *medium head cauliflower*	1 *or 2 green peppers,*
½ *cup chopped onion*	*chopped fine*
6 *tablespoons butter or*	*salt and pepper to taste*
margarine	1 *tablespoon chopped*
3 *cups chopped tomatoes*	*parsley*
3 *tablespoons flour*	

Divide the cauliflower into florets and boil in plain water. Meanwhile brown the onion in some of the butter, add the tomatoes, and stew about ½ hour to make a smooth sauce. Mix the flour with the remaining margarine to thicken. Add to the sauce. Put in the green pepper and stew a few minutes. Season and add the cauliflower, to heat through for 5 minutes. Garnish with the chopped parsley. (Serves 4–6.)

CHICK-PEAS (HOMOS) WITH HONEY   *Rosh Hashana*

Chick-peas were a common food, along with many other leguminous plants, in the days of the Maccabees. As honey and cinnamon (or cassia) were equally well known at the time, it seems very likely that a dish such as this one was not unknown to the ancient Israelis.

2 cups chick-peas	2 teaspoons salt
2 tablespoons suet or	½ cup honey
other fat	water to cover
1 teaspoon cinnamon	

Soak the chick-peas overnight and then cover with fresh water and simmer 2–3 hours, or until tender. Drain off the water. Mix with the remaining ingredients and bake in a 350° oven about 1 hour, or until peas are glazed. (Serves 6–8.)

NAHIT AND RICE TZIMMES   *Shabbat*

Although this dish is a newcomer to Israel, having been brought along with mamiligi from Romania, one wonders if its original home could have been here. For evidence dating back two millennia shows that the people of Israel used chick-peas and honey and even rice, and this combination is a very plausible one.

1 cup chick-peas	1 cup honey
2 cups water	½ cup sugar
1 pound fat meat, cubed	salt to taste
(optional)	1 cup rice

Soak the chick-peas overnight and then cook them in the 2 cups (fresh) water until soft (2–3 hours) (add more water if needed). Drain. Combine with remaining ingredients and cook until the meat (if used) is tender, the rice is done, and the mixture quite golden (30–40 minutes). (Serves 6.)

GARBANZOS (CHICK-PEAS) IN TOMATO SAUCE *Purim*

Godey's Lady's Book, *written about a hundred and thirty years ago, describes the tomato as tasty and nutritious but is shocked at the fact that it is served only half cooked. "It should be cooked three hours, for it cannot be cooked in one!" is the conclusion. For this dish, indeed, it needs long cooking.*

2 cups garbanzos
  (chick-peas)
water to cover
3 tablespoons olive oil
1 onion, chopped
1 clove garlic, crushed

1 cup tomato sauce, either
  Spanish sauce or
  Oriental sauce
  (see Index)
salt and pepper to taste

Soak the peas overnight. Cover with fresh water and bring to the boil. Simmer slowly with the olive oil, onion, and garlic. When the peas begin to get tender, add the tomato sauce and finish cooking. Season to taste. (Serves 6–8.)

NOTE: The chick-peas should be just covered with water during cooking.

IMAM BAYILDI—"THE IMAM FAINTED" *Succot*

Turkish immigrants in Israel tell you that this dish got its name because a priest passed out with delight when the aroma of the eggplant reached his nostrils at the end of the Ramadan fast.

3 large tomatoes
5 large onions
1 clove garlic
3 large eggplants
2 tablespoons chopped
  parsley

1 teaspoon coriander or dill
  or other herb
½ cup olive oil
1 teaspoon salt
¼ teaspoon pepper
1 tablespoon sugar

Chop the tomatoes, onions, and garlic into small pieces. Cut the eggplant into 1½-inch-thick slices. Slit a pocket into each slice by cutting through part of the skin and working the knife around the slice, inside the pulp. Stuff this pocket with the cut-up vegetables and herbs. Arrange the eggplant slices in a casserole. Add the remaining ingredients and water to cover. Cover the casserole and cook briskly at first, then reduce heat and simmer for about 1½ hours. (Serves 8–10.)

CORN ON THE COB   *Tu Besh'vat*

Corn is supposed to be an American vegetable, cultivated by the Indians long before the white man set foot on the North America shores. But in Israel, where corn on the cob is sold (salted but unbuttered) on the streets from huge metal drums with hissing, red-hot primus underneath, there is a legend about corn dating back to the Queen of Sheba. The visiting empress tested Solomon's wisdom by dressing eunuchs and women alike and then challenged him to tell which was male and which female. Solomon offered them ears of corn: the men, not being bashful, seized the corn eagerly with their bare hands, while the women hesitatingly took the corn with gloved fingers. Whereupon Solomon correctly exclaimed: "Those are the males, these the females."

Remove the tassels and husks from the corn. Drop quickly into boiling water for no more than 2 minutes, to set the milk. Remove from heat, but keep in the hot water to complete cooking, 2 or 3 minutes more. Serve with butter, salt, and pepper.

EGGPLANT CHATELAINE (STUFFED)   *Shavuot*

The Sauce

2 tablespoons butter
2 tablespoons flour
1 cup rich milk (part
     cream if you wish)
     dash of pepper
¼ teaspoon salt

The Topping (optional)

   grated yellow cheese

The Filling

3 small eggplants
6 tablespoons oil
6 mushrooms, chopped
1 tablespoon salt
2 cups tuna or other fish
     dash of pepper
2 tablespoons mild prepared
     mustard
   dash of garlic salt

To prepare the sauce, melt the butter, add the flour, and bring to a bubble on the stove. Stir in the milk and cook until smooth and thickened. Add the seasoning.

For the filling, cut the eggplants in halves and fry (cut side first) for a few minutes in the oil. Lightly fry the mushrooms. Scoop half of the flesh out of the eggplant (save it for another dish). Mix the remaining ingredients of the filling with the sauce, and pile into the eggplant shells. Put into a casserole and bake in a 400° oven for about 15 minutes. If you wish, this can be topped with grated yellow cheese to make a flavorful crust.

CHICK-PEAS AND CHARD   *Shabbat*

We love taking tourist friends to the Jerusalem Restaurant in our capital city because it is so "amcha"—of the people. This is one of our favorite dishes there:

1 pound chick-peas	salt, pepper, and paprika
1 pound Swiss chard	to taste
2 large onions, diced	1 clove garlic
½ cup oil for frying	1 cube or 2 tablespoons
	chicken soup powder

Soak the chick-peas for 4 hours in lukewarm water. Simmer in fresh water for 1 hour. Cup up the Swiss chard as for salad. Fry the diced onions in the oil. Add the seasonings. Mix all the ingredients together and cook on a very low heat overnight. (Serves 4–6.)

LUBIYA—COWPEAS   *Rosh Hashana*

This bean (Vigna sinensis) *is so prolific that it has become a symbol of fruitfulness at the Rosh Hashana service among Middle Eastern families. It is an Asian legume eaten all year by the poor masses in the Middle East, but on Rosh Hashana this gift of plenteous food is sweetened and blessed.*
  The dish is eaten with meat.

1 cup lubiya (cowpeas)	2 tablespoons honey
water to cover	1 tablespoon sugar
2 tablespoons oil or meat fat	½ teaspoon salt

Soak the beans overnight. Cover with fresh water and bring slowly to the boil. Reduce to a simmer. Add the remaining ingredients and simmer very slowly until beans are soft and all liquid absorbed (about 3 hours). (Serves 4.)

SHULAH'S EGGPLANT   *Tu Besh'vat*

Created by my neighbor Shulah Braudo for her husband, who agreed to become a vegetarian by marriage.

6 small eggplants	1 package (4 tablespoons)
2 tablespoons cooking oil	dehydrated mushroom
6 tablespoons ground nuts	soup powder
(any kind)	2 onions, chopped and fried
	salt and pepper to taste

Boil the eggplants and cool. Cut them in halves, lengthwise, and scoop out most of the pulp. Drizzle a little oil into each shell and bake them in a 400° oven for a minute (to crisp the shells). Mix the eggplant pulp, nuts, mushroom soup, and onion. Season. Put into the shells. Bake 10 minutes longer. Serve hot or cold. (Serves 6.)

EGGPLANT BAKED IN CHEESE SAUCE

My neighbor Etta Chalfon taught her child the Jewish blessings on bread, fruit, and wine. But when it came to eggplant there was violent protest: "On eggplant—phooey—no blessing!"

2½ pounds eggplant	1 cup milk
oil for frying	½ cup grated yellow cheese
1 tablespoon flour	salt and pepper to taste
1 egg	

Slice the eggplant thick (do not peel). Fry in very hot oil and remove before slices are soft. Put them into a casserole and dust each with flour. Mix the egg and milk, add the grated cheese and seasoning, and pour over the eggplant. Bake in a moderate oven until the eggplant is soft and the dish set in the sauce. Good hot or cold. (Serves 6–8.)

EGGPLANT IN TOMATO SAUCE   *Succot*

Centuries ago, the eggplant was considered poisonous, and perhaps for that reason was called "the mad apple." The unknown hero who first dared to eat it could never have guessed how widespread the vegetable has become and what varied delectable dishes are today made from it.

2 large eggplants	2 eggs
salt and pepper	oil for frying
1½ cups flour	2 cloves garlic, crushed
⅔ cup water	tomato sauce

Slice the eggplant (leave the skin on) fairly thin. Sprinkle with salt and put in the sun to sweat out the moisture. Make a batter of the flour, water, and eggs. Dry the eggplant slices with a towel, dip in batter, and fry in hot oil. Arrange the slices in a casserole with a sprinkling of salt and pepper and the garlic (or garlic salt). Cover with any favorite tomato sauce and bake in a 350° oven for 30 minutes. Serve cold, preferably, although it is very good hot in chilly weather. (Serves 6–8.)

EGGPLANT MUSHROOMS   *Succot*

The dearly loved mushroom is dearly priced when it is culti-
vated, and so the imaginative Israeli housewife has discovered
how to make this expensive-tasting dish with fine flavor but at
low cost.

1 large eggplant	*dash of salt*
3 tablespoons butter	*1 cup sour cream*
1 chopped onion or 2 table-	
spoons powdered mush-	
room soup	

Peel the eggplant. Cut out balls with a melon cutter or cut into
cubes. Melt the butter. Lightly fry the chopped onion and then
add the eggplant. Stir often during frying. When the eggplant
is slightly golden, put it into a baking dish, sprinkle with salt,
and sour cream. Heat in a 375° oven for 10–15 minutes. (Serves
4–6.)

NOTE: If you wish to use mushroom soup powder, omit the
onions and add the soup powder to the sour cream before inserting into the oven.

EGGPLANT WITH TAHINA PASTE   *Purim*

"Spread the table and contention will cease," said Ben-Syra, the
great Hebrew sage of yore. This seems to be universally accepted,
and particularly so in the Middle East among the Arab peoples.
When a serious tribal quarrel is brought to an end, a "sulha" or
"peace feast" is held, attended by all the villagers or tribes.
Mounds of rice, whole roast lambs stuffed with chickens that are
stuffed with birds, minted salads, and endless cooked and per-
fumed vegetables and conserves come to the "table" (usually
enormous brass trays set on low stands, as all sit on the carpeted
floor of the sheik's tent). A favorite dish, now adopted by all the
Israel community, is eggplant with tahina, which the Arabs call
"baba gannoy."

2 eggplants	*1 clove garlic, crushed*
½ cup tahina paste (see	*salt and pepper to taste*
Tahina Paste, intro-	*lemon juice to taste*
ductory note)	*tomatoes and chopped herbs*
dash of cayenne	*for garnish*

Grill the eggplants over an open flame until the skin is charred.
Remove the burnt skin under running water. Beat the eggplant
with a wooden spoon and work in the tahina paste. Flavor with
the remaining ingredients. Garnish with sliced tomatoes and
chopped herbs. (Serves 8–10.)

EGGPLANT STUFFED WITH MEAT   *Succot*

*"I've been your food fan for years," said Mrs. Becky Goldzweig-
Mino to me just as I was clipping the following recipe, which
she wrote, for I am a fan of hers! She became a runner-up (one
out of nine finalists out of 1,400 contestants) in the Israel National Culinary Queen Contest, with this dish. That "little difference" of flare and flair in her recipe of this otherwise well-known
dish was due to the little flamelike flavor from the chili-pepper-
flavored oil.*

2 pounds eggplant (very small variety)	2 tablespoons chopped parsley
½ pound lamb, diced into ½-inch cubes	1 teaspoon sugar
2 medium onions, chopped	2 tablespoons chili-flavored oil (see NOTE, below)
4 tablespoons cooking oil	¾ cup rice
2 teaspoons salt	2 tablespoons chopped roast peanuts
¼ teaspoon black pepper	2½ tablespoons tomato purée
1 tomato, peeled and chopped	

Remove the tops of the eggplants and scoop out the flesh, leaving
the skin intact. Fry the meat and onion in 2 tablespoons of the
oil. Remove from heat and add half the salt, the pepper, tomato,
parsley, ½ teaspoon of the sugar, and 1 tablespoon of the chili-
flavored oil. Add the rice, peanuts, and 1 tablespoon of the
tomato purée. Half fill the little eggplants. Place them in a shallow pan and fry in the second 2 tablespoons of oil. Cover with
water and add the chicken fat, the second tablespoon of chili-
flavored oil, the rest of the salt, the rest of the sugar and the rest
of the tomato purée. Cook over medium heat for 30 minutes,
then remove to a baking dish and bake in a 400° oven for 20
minutes, basting from time to time. (Serves 6.)

NOTE: To make chili-flavored oil, grind dried chili peppers and
put into a jar with an abundance of salt. Pour the oil over. Re-
plenish the oil in the jar each time some is used.

Rosh Hashana
PRASAH-ZEYTLINIS—LEEKS AND OLIVES

The leek is one of the oldest known vegetables, longed for in Bible days, "well loved" in Chaucer's Canterbury Tales, *and referred to as "poor man's asparagus" (and indeed, it tastes like asparagus) in modern French culinary vocabulary.*

10 *leeks, cut into 4-inch lengths*
3 *tablespoons olive oil*
2 *tablespoons margarine*
1 *tablespoon cornstarch*
1 *cup chicken stock*

2 *tablespoons tomato purée*
salt and pepper to taste
2 *tablespoons sugar*
juice of 1 lemon
1 *cup large black olives*

Blanch the leeks for a few minutes in boiling water. Drain and dry thoroughly. Fry lightly in the oil. Melt the margarine, stir in the cornstarch and add the stock. Cook, stirring constantly, until thick. Add the tomato purée, seasoning, sugar, and lemon juice. Pour the sauce over the leeks and cook until the vegetables are soft (about 15 minutes). Add the olives at the end, to cook for about 10 minutes. Remember that the olives will be salty; therefore very little salt should be added for seasoning. (Serves 6–8.)

KHUBEISA (HAALAMIT) CUTLETS *Independence Day*

3 *cups khubeisa or other leaf greens*
2 *tablespoons parsley, chopped fine*
1 *cup dry bread crumbs*

3 *tablespoons flour*
salt and pepper to taste
dash of nutmeg
3 *eggs, lightly beaten*
oil for frying

Wash the khubeisa or other greens and cook with very little water until greens are wilted and almost tender (about 5 minutes). Drain. Chop the greens coarsely and add the parsley, crumbs, flour, salt, pepper, and nutmeg and stir in the lightly beaten eggs. Drop from a tablespoon into hot fat. Fry until golden on both sides. Serve hot.

SWEET-SOUR GREEN BEANS *Tu Besh'vat*

The French, or haricot, bean is probably of South American origin and was introduced to Europe only after the discovery of America. Seeds of the bean have been found in Peruvian tombs so ancient they could not be definitely dated. This Jewish Alsa-

tian dish is based upon the French custom of eating beans while still young.

1 pound green beans	1 tablespoon flour
water to cover	salt and pepper
1 teaspoon salt	2 tablespoons sugar
2 tablespoons fat	2 tablespoons lemon juice

Wash the beans and split them lengthwise through the pods. Cook until tender in just enough water to cover (15–20 minutes). Drain, reserving liquid, and add the salt. Melt the fat and add the flour, then 1 cup of the liquid in which the beans were cooked (add water if necessary to make up 1 cup), then the remaining ingredients. Add to the beans and heat through. (Serves 4.)

PRASAH—LEEKS IN LEMON *Independence Day*

Leeks, notwithstanding their bland taste, are much loved by the Middle Eastern peoples, who generally highly spice their food. They are sometimes made with tomato sauce and olives, but this is the favorite recipe. They look much like green onions, but taste more like asparagus.

1 pound leeks	1 tablespoon cornstarch
water to cover	2 tablespoons olive oil
1 teaspoon salt	juice of 1 large lemon

Clean the leeks well. Cover with water, add salt, and cook until tender (15–20 minutes). Drain off the liquid. To two cups of the hot liquid add the cornstarch, and cook, stirring constantly, until thick. Add the lemon juice and oil and pour over the leeks. Cool, then chill. Serve cold. (Serves 3–4.)

LENTILS AND BARLEY *Succot*

2 onions, chopped	1 cup lentils
1 cup diced tomatoes	½ cup pearl barley
3 tablespoons margarine	½ teaspoon salt
1 clove garlic, crushed	

Fry the chopped onion and tomatoes in the margarine. Add the garlic. Cook the lentils and barley in water until almost tender (about 45 minutes). Drain off all but 1 cup of the liquid. Add the onion, tomatoes, garlic, and salt to the pulses and liquid and cook until done (10–15 minutes). (Serves 6.)

FAKE STEAK   *Tu Besh'vat*

During the austerity years in Israel, when our first duty was to feed the thousand-a-day refugee immigrants coming into the country, meat could not be obtained by the settled population, but was available only for newcomers' camps. We did get a small sausage ration and a meat-tasting soup seasoning that went into the making of this dish, which has remained because it is so good.

6 thick (1-inch) slices of
    eggplant, unpeeled
6 thin slices of salami
    salt and pepper
1 clove garlic

oil for frying
1 tablespoon flour
1 tablespoon powdered
    chicken soup
1 cup water

On the side of each slice of eggplant, cut a small pocket, large enough to insert a salami slice. Sprinkle with salt and pepper. Put the clove of garlic into the oil and heat, then fry the eggplant slices until deep brown. To the oil add the flour, powdered soup, and water, to make a gravy. Pour over the fake steak. You can use chopped meat instead of, or along with, the sausage. Serve on Tu Besh'vat, to celebrate Israel's bountiful blessing of food today! (Serves 6.)

PRASAH KEFTEDES—LEEK PANCAKES *Rosh Hashana*

This is a Rosh Hashana dish enjoyed by Greek immigrants in Israel. Although it is very good hot, it is generally eaten cold. Leeks were a favorite vegetable in Bible times and have so remained in the land of the Bible.

1 pound leeks
1 teaspoon salt
    water to cover
1 slice white bread,
    without crusts
3 eggs

1 pound minced meat
½ cup chopped walnuts
¼ teaspoon pepper
    olive oil for frying
    juice of 2 lemons

Strip the leeks of the coarse outside leaves, dice into very small pieces and just cover with salted water. Cook until the water has evaporated (about 15 minutes). Add the slice of white bread to absorb the moisture, then break it up into crumbs. Beat in the eggs, meat, walnuts, and pepper. Form into patties and fry in fairly deep hot olive oil. Put the keftedes into a casserole, sprinkle with the lemon juice, and cover. Place over low heat or in a 325° oven for about 10 minutes to allow the keftedes to steam in the lemon juice. (Serves 4.)

"THE GREEN THING"   *Independence Day*

"What is the green thing on our plate?" asked guests at President Ben-Zwi's table on Independence Day.

"It is khubeisa—'haalamit' in Hebrew—which comes from the Arabic word for bread, for it is the bread of the starving, pasture for which the goats range over the mountains in search of every green thing."

During the siege of Jerusalem, when Mrs. Ben-Zwi was cut off from the city with the children of her agricultural school in the suburb of North Talpiot, she gathered this herb, under gunfire, for their food. As a botanist she knew what a good herb it was. "News of khubeisa spread from mouth to mouth, but could not be broadcast or printed, for then the enemy would have known how hungry we were," said Mrs. Ben-Zwi. "We have it always now on Yom Atzmaut in the President's house, as a symbolic commemorative dish. It is served either plain boiled or blanched for salad, as in the siege, or in the following way."

One can use Swiss chard, spinach, or other leaf greens to replace khubeisa.

GRILLED MARINATED PEPPERS   *Succot*

This Romanian speciality quickly captured the spice-loving Israelis. It is served all during the pepper season, which lasts much of the year due to the varied climates and altitudes in the little land of Israel. The fleshy dark green peppers and sweet red peppers are best for this dish.

green peppers	*citrus or wine vinegar*
sweet red peppers	*olive oil*
salt and pepper	*sugar to taste*

Hold each pepper on a fork over an open flame, and when it is charred, turn to scorch the other side. This charred touch adds a delightful flavor to the dish. Rinse the peppers under cold water to blanch them. Put them into a bowl, sprinkle with salt and pepper and pour a little oil over each pepper. Prepare a marinade of citrus or wine vinegar and sugar to taste, and pour this over the peppers. After a few hours in the refrigerator the peppers will be ready. They keep very well for days. Some people add a hint of garlic to the marinade.

SAUTÉED MUSHROOMS IN SOUR CREAM *Hanuka*

To think of it! According to the writings in Antiquities of the Talmud, *cabbage was considered the greatest delicacy in the days of the Maccabees, whereas mushrooms and truffles were poor man's fare. Today the reverse is true. Whether sautéed (and then delicious with meat and fowl) or sauced in sour cream (wonderful with fish), mushrooms are certainly superduper.*

1 *pound mushrooms*	1 *cup sour cream*
2 *tablespoons margarine*	*salt and paprika to taste*
or butter	

Peel and slice the mushrooms and sauté in the margarine for 10 minutes, stirring often. Add the sour cream and cook five minutes more. Add the seasoning. These mushrooms are wonderful on toast. (Serves 4.)

ONION MACHSHI *Succot*

Although the onion is mentioned only once in the Old Testament (and then as a succulent delicacy), it was widely known in the Middle East at that time. Many Egyptian monuments are decorated with the emblem of the onion. In Israel the Philistines named the city of Ashkelon for the ascalonica onion (the shallot).

12 *large onions*	2 *tablespoons ground*
½ *pound chopped beef*	*almonds*
dash of allspice	1 *egg*
chopped parsley	2 *tablespoons flour*
salt and pepper to taste	3 *tablespoons cooking oil*
	water to cover

Cut the onions in half and scoop out the hearts (the effort is worth the tears involved). Chop about 3 tablespoons of these hearts and add to the meat with the allspice, parsley, salt, pepper, almonds, and egg. Fill the onions with this mixture. Dust the tops of the onions with flour and fry them (meat side first) in the oil. Put the remaining onion hearts into the bottom of a heavy pot. Pour on the oil left in the pan and add just enough water to cover this onion bed. Put the golden fried stuffed onions on the onion bed. Cover the pot and simmer slowly until the onions are soft (about 50 minutes), adding a very little water from time to time if needed. (Serves 12.)

OLIVES—HOME CURED
Succot

Olives are one of the oldest foods of the Middle East. They are not used as relish or mere garnish, but form one of the main dishes of Middle Eastern Jews and appear in almost every Israel household at breakfast and supper. There are many olive trees in Israel over a thousand years old, and still producing fruit. Anyone with an olive tree in his yard plucks and cures the olives for home use. Green olives are treated differently from black.

Green Olives: If you want the olives cured within a month, hammer each one lightly with a wooden mallet. If you are ready to wait a year, do not hammer them. Put the olives to soak in water for 3 days, changing the water daily. Make a salt solution of 1 cup coarse salt to every 12 cups water. Pack the olives into jars with any flavoring you like—garlic, lemon slices, peppercorns, chili peppers, bay leaves, lemon leaves, or any combination of these—and then pour the brine over. Be sure that the olives are kept under brine for a whole month (if they are exposed to air they spoil at once). After the fermentation process finishes (3 or 4 weeks), remove the scum, cover with brine, and seal.
Black Olives: The olive must be ripe right through, black to the pit. For every 2¼ pounds of olives you will need 2 cups of coarse salt. Wash and dry the olives. Pack alternate layers of olives and dry salt in a jar. After one month the olives will be cured and ready to eat.

MINTED GREEN PEAS
Passover

If a menu has the words Saint-Germain added to the name of a dish, you can be almost certain that there are green peas in it (but don't be too sure, for this does not always apply). But in Israel there's no riddle about peas: you know if they are buttered American-style, or dressed with olive oil, a bit of basil, and a hint of sugar as the Italians do, or show the North African touch as in this wonderful dish.

2 pounds fresh peas in pod	10 sprigs fresh mint or
boiling water	1 teaspoon dried mint
2 teaspoons sugar	2 tablespoons olive oil
	salt to taste

Shell the peas and cover with the boiling water. Add the sugar and mint and cook on low heat until just tender (10–25 minutes). Drain the peas and add the olive oil and salt to taste. (Serves 4.)

BAMIA—OKRA IN TOMATO SAUCE *Yom Kippur*

There is a legend that King Solomon ordered a hundred dishes for the feast welcoming the Queen of Sheba. The king's chef could think of only ninety-nine and went out to the fields in search of something new. There for the first time he saw the okra pod and immediately named it "bamia" for "Ben-Maiyah," which means "the hundredth." Iraqi Jews in Israel serve this dish at the close of the Yom Kippur fast.

1 *pound minced meat*	2 *pounds fresh tomatoes*
1 *clove garlic, minced*	2 *teaspoons sugar*
1 *cup olive oil*	*salt and pepper to taste*
2 *onions, chopped fine*	*juice of ½ lemon*
2 *pounds young fresh okra*	

Mix the meat with the garlic and make into meat balls the size of marbles. Fry in the oil. Remove the meat balls. Fry the onions. Remove. Cut the stem top and tip from each pod and fry lightly in the oil. Grate the tomatoes and add. Season with the sugar, salt, and pepper. Cook until the okra is almost soft (12–15 minutes). Stir in the lemon juice, then cover with the meat balls. Cover the pot and simmer over very low heat until the sauce is thick (about 30 minutes). Serve hot or cold, with rice that has been cooked in chicken broth. (Serves 8.)

ONIONS AND PRUNES *Hanuka*

Brillat-Savarin in his Physiology of Taste, *that near-holy textbook of the gourmet, records: ". . . gastronomic science advanced gradually; the Crusaders gave her the shallot, plucked from the plains of Ascalon . . ."*

What inroads the onion has made into cookery! This dish, for instance, comes from the French Jews of Alsace, who really know how to prepare a good thing. They used fruits along with vegetables as an accompaniment to meat long before the Americans took to the idea.

1½ *pounds firm onions*	1 *pound prunes*
4 *tablespoons margarine*	

Select onions about the size of prunes. Peel and sauté them gently in the margarine over low heat. Soak the prunes for half an hour and then add to the onions. Cook until tender (20–30 minutes). If necessary, a very little water may be added to keep the ingredients from frying quickly. (Serves 6.)

STUFFED PEPPERS
Succot

This dish is so delicious that one usually eats it until filled to the brim like the pepper. Pimentos—bright red tomato-shaped peppers—are usually filled and cooked along with the green ones to make an effective garnish in the casserole. It is an ideal dish for Succot since it contains all the ingredients of a meal and is hot and hearty in the chill outdoors, as well as easy and attractive to serve.

12 *bell peppers and/or*	1 *pound minced meat*
sweet red peppers	*salt and pepper to taste*
1 *onion, chopped*	¼ *cup tomato ketchup*
1 *cup raw rice*	*water to cover*
2 *tablespoons oil*	

Wash the peppers, cut off the caps and scoop out the seeds. Fry the onion and rice in the oil and then mix with the raw meat. Add the seasoning. Fill the peppers half full, cover with caps, and fit closely into a casserole. Mix the ketchup with enough water to cover the peppers. Bring to the boil and then stew for 1 hour. Or bake in a 375° oven 15 minutes, then reduce heat to 325° and bake for 1 hour more. Add water if necessary during cooking. (Serves 12.)

POTATO AU GRATIN
Shavuot

It is no good planting boiled potatoes.
—C. H. SPURGEON

Nor is it any good crying over spilt milk. But spill the milk into boiled potatoes, and you'll end up with a good dish!

2 *pounds potatoes, cooked*	1 *cup grated yellow cheese*
in their jackets	6 *eggs*
2 *tablespoons butter*	2 *cups milk*
salt and pepper	

Remove the skins from the boiled potatoes. Cut into slices. Grease a casserole with the butter. Alternate layers of potato, sprinkled with salt and pepper, with layers of cheese, ending with a layer of cheese. Beat the eggs, pour over the potatoes, add the milk, and bake in a 350° oven about 30 minutes. (Serves 6–8.)

ROAST POTATOES   *Hanuka*

3 *pounds potatoes*   *salt and pepper*

Pare the potatoes and cut into even-sized pieces (halves or quarters). Sprinkle with salt and pepper and put into a pan with a pot roast or covered oven roast. The potatoes must roast in the juice of the meat. Turn occasionally. The potatoes should be soft and golden. (Serves 8.)

SARATOGA CHIPS AND FRENCH FRIES   *Passover*

Every restaurant in Israel sells more chips that all other vegetables combined. Sometimes they are even served along with rice dishes in Oriental restaurants. My children consider me a pagan when I sprinkle vinegar over my plate of chips (a Canadian touch), feeling that I am desecrating an Israeli dish. Little do they know that the chips are the creation of an American Negro chef from Saratoga Springs.

2 *pounds potatoes*   *deep fat for frying*
2 *teaspoons salt*   *salt for sprinkling*
  water to cover

Slice the potatoes very thin. Sprinkle with the salt and cover with water. After half an hour, drain and dry the potatoes thoroughly between towels. Have the deep fat very hot (400°) and fry a few potatoes at a time. Drain on paper and sprinkle with salt. Put the chips into the oven to crisp them for a few minutes. Serve hot or cold.

French fried potatoes are made in much the same way, except that the potatoes are cut into strips (about eight to a potato) and served right after frying in deep hot fat.

ETHIOPIAN POTATOES   *Passover*

How the Laurus nobilis got into Ethiopian cookery I know not, but how it invaded Israel I can tell you. Marjam, governess in the royal Ethiopian household, came to Palestine with Emperor Haile Selassie's entourage as a refugee during the Italian invasion. She remained in the country, became nursemaid to my children and taught me this dish, which quickly won popularity through my food column. Though retired and on Government pension (on the side she is a "Shabbas goy" who turns off the lights for the ultra-Orthodox in the Mea Shearim quarter of Jerusalem), Marjam still comes to prepare the dish for our Passover Seder.

20 *medium peeled raw*   20 *bay leaves*
        potatoes   *salt and pepper*
    oil for deep frying

Potatoes must be of the same size for uniform frying. Cut them
in half and fry in deep 350° oil, a few at a time, together with a
bay leaf for each potato, until golden brown (15–20 minutes).
Arrange the potatoes in a baking dish, a bay leaf next to each.
Sprinkle with salt and pepper. These potatoes can be warmed up
for later serving (that is why we have them on Passover night,
apart from their delicious flavor). (Serves 20.)

POTATOES IN SOUR CREAM   *Shavuot*

1 *pound potatoes*   ½ *cup sour cream*
1 *large onion*   1 *tablespoon dill*
1 *tablespoon butter*   *salt and pepper*

Partially cook the potatoes (about 5 minutes). Drain and slice
thickly. Brown the chopped onion in the butter and add the potatoes with the remaining ingredients. Cover the pot and cook
over very low heat until the potatoes are done (20–30 minutes).
(Serves 4–6.)

LYONNAISE POTATOES   *Hanuka*

*This is my favorite potato dish, psychologically in any case (for
Lyons was my maiden name). Many people believe the potato to
be of Irish origin, but it was discovered in Peru by a Spanish
priest. The Spaniards thought the tuber had aphrodisiac qualities, and that's what started it on its popular career.*

3 *cups cold, sliced, cooked*   4 *tablespoons margarine*
        potatoes   1 *onion, chopped*
    salt and pepper   2 *tablespoons chopped*
    dash of powdered chicken   *parsley*
        soup (optional)

Sprinkle the potatoes with the salt, pepper, and powdered
chicken soup. Heat the margarine, add the onion, and cook until
light golden. Add the potatoes and fry until all the fat is absorbed and the potatoes brown in spots (the more the tastier).
Add the chopped parsley, heat together well, and serve. (Serves
4–6.)

CARAWAY POTATOES

Succot

8 *medium potatoes*
3 *tablespoons butter*
     salt and pepper
     dash of paprika

1 *teaspoon carraway*
½ *cup sour cream*
     (optional)

Boil the potatoes in their jackets, then peel and slice thickly.
Heat the butter. Sprinkle the potatoes with salt, pepper, and, if
you wish, a dash of paprika for color and extra flavor. Fry until
golden. Sprinkle on the caraway seed, cook a minute more, and
serve plain or with heated sour cream for a topping. (Serves
8–10.)

O'BRIEN POTATOES

3 *tablespoons margarine*
     or butter
4 *cups cubed, cooked potatoes*
1 *onion, chopped*
1 *large green pepper, finely*
     cubed

2 *sweet red peppers, finely*
     cubed
     salt and pepper to taste
2 *teaspoons chopped parsley*

Heat the fat and brown the potato cubes. Add the onion and
peppers and fry together, being careful not to break the potatoes.
(Or you can fry the peppers and onions separately from the
potatoes, and then stir together for a heating through.) Serve
hot, seasoned to taste, and sprinkled with parsley. (Serves 6–8.)

POTATO-TOCH OR KARTOFLANIK

Succot

*Even in Tudor times savory potato pie was considered a great
luxury, for the tuber was a rarity and had been brought to
Britain only by Sir Walter Raleigh. Potato-toch or kartoflanik
is a savory potato loaf, which was one of the early Jewish potato
specialties in Galicia. It is sold as a specialty in Israel restaurants, and made at home by women hailing from Poland.*

1 *ounce fresh yeast*
     (or 2 packages dry)
¼ *cup warm water*
1 *large onion, chopped*
2 *tablespoons cooking oil*
2 *cups flour, sifted*

1 *teaspoon salt*
     dash of pepper
1 *egg, beaten*
2 *pounds raw potatoes,*
     finely grated

Dissolve the yeast in the water. Fry the chopped onion in the oil. Sift together the dry ingredients. Mix the yeast with the egg and add to the fried onion and the potato. Stir in the flour mixture and knead well on a floured board. Put into a warm bowl, cover and set to rise until almost doubled in bulk. Put into a well-greased pan and bake in a 350° oven until the loaf sets off from the sides of the pan. Serve hot with any main dish. (Serves 6–8.)

POTATO KAESEL *Passover*

My neighbor Dvora Zadikoff inherited this dish from her great-great-grandmother.

goose or chicken fat	1 tablespoon potato flour
4 eggs	salt and pepper
4 medium raw potatoes, grated very fine	2 tablespoons water

Heat the fat in a casserole. Beat the eggs until fluffy and beat in the grated potato. Dissolve the potato flour, with the salt and pepper, in the water and beat into the first mixture. Bake in a 400° oven for about 30 minutes. The kaesel puffs up soufflé fashion, and should be served at once. (Serves 6.)

POTATO KUGEL *Shabbat*

Although the kugel is recorded as a Sabbath dish eight hundred years ago, the potato, which was discovered only about five hundred years ago, entered Jewish cooking centuries later. A generation ago Sholom Aleichem wrote of the luscious potato kugel: "Ah, you know what an aroma that has when you lift the lid off the pot, and oh, the flavor of it, you know what that's like. . . ."

10 medium potatoes	1 teaspoon salt
1 large onion, chopped	dash of pepper
4 tablespoons chicken fat	5 eggs, separated

Boil and mash the potatoes. Lightly fry the onion in the chicken fat and add to the potatoes with the salt and pepper. Beat the egg yolks well and whip into the potatoes. Beat the egg whites until stiff and fold into the potatoes. Bake in a greased baking dish in a 350° oven until the kugel is golden (about 30 minutes). (Serves 6–8.)

POTATO GOULASH   *Hanuka*

3 large onions, chopped fine   *8 potatoes, cooked in their*
4 tablespoons cooking oil   *jackets*
2 green or sweet red peppers,   *1 teaspoon salt*
      chopped   *2 teaspoons paprika*
3 tomatoes, chopped   *dash of caraway seed*

Put the onions into the oil and simmer on very low heat. When
they begin to color, add the peppers and tomatoes and continue
to simmer. Skin the boiled potatoes, cut into cubes, sprinkle with
salt and paprika, and add to the sauce. Heat through, with a
sprinkling of caraway seed on top. Serve hot. (Serves 8–10.)

GRATED POTATO KUGEL   *Yom Kippur*

6 medium potatoes   *1 cup flour*
1/2 pound celery root,   *3/4 teaspoon salt*
      peeled and grated   *1/2 teaspoon pepper*
2 onions, grated   *1/2 teaspoon celery salt*
1 carrot, grated   *6 tablespoons fat*
4 eggs

Peel and grate the potatoes and squeeze out as much of the
liquid as possible. Add all the remaining ingredients except the
fat, which should be heated in two pie pans. Pour in the batter
and bake in a 375° oven until golden (about 45 minutes). Serve
in wedges like pie. (Serves 6–8.)

POTATO—PRUNE TZIMMES   *Rosh Hashana*

1 pound prunes   *salt and pepper to taste*
2 pounds brisket of beef   *dash of cinnamon*
2 tablespoons cooking oil   *1/2 cup brown sugar*
2 pounds potatoes, peeled   *juice of 1 lemon*

Soak the prunes overnight. Sear the meat in the hot oil. Surround with potatoes and prunes, sprinkle on the seasoning,
sugar, and lemon juice. Cover with water. Covering pot tightly,
bring to a boil and then put on the lowest possible heat so that
the mixture just simmers slightly. Cook 12 hours, or until the
meat is tender. Do not stir, but add water if required. This dish
is also very good if cooked, covered, in a 200° oven (after bringing to the initial boil) for about 12 hours. (Serves 8–10.)

POTATO HALKES   *Shabbat*

The "Dough"

3 large raw potatoes
1 cooked potato
2 tablespoons chicken fat
1 tablespoon chopped onion
5 tablespoons matzo meal
2 eggs
½ teaspoon salt
½ teaspoon cinnamon
   dash of pepper

The Filling

1 cup ground meat
1 onion, chopped
   salt and pepper
   dash of cinnamon

For the "dough," grate the raw potatoes fine and let them drain in a sieve, squeezing from time to time to expel the liquid. Mash the cooked potato and add. Mix with the remaining ingredients. Form into one or two large balls. Hollow out the balls, and after mixing all the filling ingredients, put the filling into the balls and seal. Cook the halkes in a bed of raw carrots (as done in Carrot Tzimmes, *see* Index) or other raw vegetables or in gravy alongside of the meat. (Serves 4.)

KUSA—SQUASH IN TOMATO SAUCE   *Hanuka*

Although the squash ("kishuyim," in Hebrew) is spoken of in the Bible and has for millennia been a Mediterranean dish, the Americans have named it the "Native Son of the Golden West"! However, since the United States produces a score of varieties from the small Israel-type summer squash to the massive pumpkin, I am sure they had no intention of infringing on Israel's ancient agricultural copyright.

2 tablespoons chopped onion
3 tablespoon margarine
2 tablespoons flour
2 cups tomato juice
2 teaspoons bouillon cube,
   crushed
1 teaspoon salt
   dash of paprika
1 teaspoon sugar
10 small squash
1 teaspoon chopped parsley

Fry the onion in the margarine. Add the flour, and when the mixture bubbles, add the tomato juice and stir until thickened. Add the bouillon cube, and the seasonings. Slice the squash (do not peel) and put into a casserole. Sprinkle with the parsley and cover with the sauce. Bake in a 375° oven 30 minutes, or until the squash are tender. (Serves 6.)

Independence Day
ZUCCHINI FRITTI—FRIED SUMMER SQUASH

The poetic English translation from the Bible refers to cucumbers instead of the Hebrew word of "squash" (kishuyim). Both belong to the family of Cucurbitacea, and both are still liked as much as the onions and the leeks and the melons and the garlic by people in these parts.

6 small summer squash, sliced	1 cup tomato pulp
½ cup olive oil	1 chopped sweet red or green pepper
2 onions, chopped	salt and pepper to taste

Fry the squash in the olive oil until golden, then remove. Add the onions to the oil and cook until transparent; then add the tomato pulp and sweet pepper, salt and pepper. Cook until the sweet pepper is soft (about 20 minutes). Serve the squash in this tomato sauce. (Serves 3–4.)

SPINACH SOUFFLÉ
Tu Besh'vat

Henrietta Szold, one of the greatest Jewish women of all time, was known as the mother of 100,000 children, snatched from the burning through Youth Aliyah. But her most individual child was Emma Ehrlich, who was with her everywhere and every day, as private secretary and companion. After most of a lifetime of adoration, Emma disagreed with Miss Szold about only one thing. She wrote to me:

Miss Szold enjoyed good food but ate sparingly, her first concern being health and the energy to work hard. She had an exquisitely keen and acute sense of taste and smell and deeply appreciated good cooking and seasoning. I remember her trying to influence me to try spinach with eggs—a real delicacy, she said, which she enjoyed very much when properly prepared. The stuff was anathema to me. Although usually ready to yield to her gentle persuasion, I balked at spinach in any form, and steadfastly refused to even touch it. She did like spinach!

2 tablespoons butter	1 tablespoon minced onion
4 tablespoons flour	2 cups spinach purée
2 tablespoons chopped parsley	4 large eggs
	salt and pepper

Melt the butter, stir in the flour, and cook until the mixture begins to bubble. Add the parsley, onion, and spinach purée and cook until thick. Cool the mixture and then stir in the beaten eggs yolks and seasoning. Beat the egg whites until stiff and fold in. Place in a buttered baking dish and bake in a 350° oven 45–55 minutes. Serve at once. (Serves 4.)

SAVORY SPINACH *Purim*

1 *pound spinach*
1 *clove garlic, chopped*
1 *teaspoon salt*

1 *tablespoon lemon juice*
1 *teaspoon sugar*

Wash the spinach, sprinkle with the garlic and salt, and put into a well-covered pot without water. As soon as the spinach has fallen into a mass and cooked in its own steam (8–10 minutes), add the lemon juice mixed with the sugar. Serve at once. (Serves 3.)

NOTE: This dish is very good sprinkled with grated cheese.

SPONGUHS—SPINACH CHEESE DISH *Shavuot*

Mrs. Simcha Sopher reached the culinary contests finals with this traditional "Old Yishuv" gold and green dish.

2 *pounds spinach*
1 *teaspoon salt*
6 *tablespoons cooking oil*
6 *eggs, lightly beaten*

½ *pound salt goat cheese*
  (zefatit), finely grated
½ *teaspoon black pepper*

Chop the spinach and mix with the salt. Allow to drip for 5 minutes. Pour on the oil and spread on a shallow baking pan. Add the eggs and the pepper to the finely grated cheese. Make six hollows in the spinach and put the cheese mixture in each. Bake in a 400° oven for 30 minutes. (Serves 6.)

SPINACH AND RICE *Tu Besh'vat*

½ *cup olive oil*
1 *cup chopped onions*
2 *pounds spinach*
1 *cup rice*

1 *cup diced tomatoes*
1 *clove garlic, chopped*
  salt and pepper
2 *cups hot water*

Put the oil and onions in a pan, cover, and let stew for about ten minutes. Wash and cut up the spinach, and put over the onions. Cover with the rice. Put the tomatoes and garlic over the rice, add the salt and pepper, and pour in the water. Cover and simmer about an hour. (Serves 6.)

STUFFED PUMPKIN

Succot

This unwieldy monster makes a terrific impression before a large crowd, as it did at the Israel Culinary Contest finale, when Mrs. Sabiha Ma'alam became a runner-up. The filling is fabulous. For family size use a hard-type squash or even a melon instead of a pumpkin.

1 3-pound pumpkin	4 tablespoons tomato purée
2 pounds meat	red wine (about 2 cups)
1/2 cup cooking oil	salt, sugar, and lemon
1 large onion, chopped	juice to taste
6 cloves garlic, chopped	dash each of pepper, all-
3/4 cup rice	spice, cinnamon,
1/2 cup raisins	turmeric, cardamom,
1/2 cup chopped peanuts	cumin
chopped parsley	

Peel the whole pumpkin. Make an opening the size of a cup at one end. Clean out the whole cavity, wash, and then soak the pumpkin in salt water for 10 minutes.

For the filling, cube one fourth of the meat into very small pieces and grind the rest. Put the oil into a pan and fry the cubed meat over medium heat, until lightly browned. Add the onion and garlic. Stir. Add the rice and fry for five minutes. Add the ground meat, raisins, peanuts, parsley, and flavorings including the wine. Simmer until the wine is absorbed (14–15 minutes). Put the mixture into the pumpkin and close up the hole. Stew in a large pot on very low heat until the pumpkin is done, but still firm enough to be taken out and put on a platter (about 2½ hours). (Serves 6–8.)

MILTON'S MARROWS

Passover

The secret of this dish is that you must use peanut oil and that you must not fry the marrows for more than 2 or 3 minutes. In fact, they should still be crisp and almost raw, but hot, Chinese style.

8 small very fresh young	2 tablespoons caraway seed
marrows (squash)	salt
4 tablespoons peanut oil	
(about)	

Skin the marrows and cut into 6 strips lengthwise. Heat the oil. Put in the marrows and keep tossing them so they will just heat through without browning or softening. Sprinkle on the caraway seed and salt, turn the marrows, and serve at once. (Serves 4.)

SQUASH ALIAS ASPARAGUS   *Shavuot*

12 small summer squash	2 packages powdered
2 tablespoons margarine	asparagus soup
	2 cups milk

Peel the squash and cut into asparagus-sized strips. Put into individual casseroles. Dab with a bit of margarine. Boil the dried asparagus soup and milk (or used canned asparagus soup, diluted to sauce consistency). Pour over squash and bake in a 350° oven 30 minutes. The dish tastes like asparagus. (Serves 6.)

Independence Day
KUSA MIMULA—STUFFED SQUASHES

Stuffed squashes, known as "kusa," are made delectably in Israel. They are filled with savory meat mixtures, rice and meat fillings, or rice and vegetable fillings. Eggplants can also be filled in the same way.

20 very small squashes	dash of chili pepper
(vegetable marrows)	1 cup raw rice
3 tablespoons oil	1 pound ground meat
2 onions, chopped	½ teaspoon cinnamon
1½ pounds tomatoes,	1 tablespoon chopped
chopped	parsley
1 teaspoon sugar	salt and pepper to taste
1 teaspoon salt	

Hollow out the squashes with an apple corer. Do not peel. Put most of the pulp, reserving the rest, into a skillet with the oil, onion, and tomato and fry lightly. Add the sugar, salt, and chili pepper. This tomato mixture will be used as a sauce in which to stew the stuffed squashes. Mix the rice, meat, cinnamon, and parsley with salt and pepper to taste. Fill the squashes with the meat mixture, leaving each about half-empty, and seal with a piece of the squash pulp. Put the squashes in a saucepan in layers, with the tomato sauce in between. If necessary, add water to cover. Simmer very gently, uncovered, until sauce is almost all absorbed and the rice cooked (about 35 minutes). Excellent hot or cold. (Serves 4–5.)

MEDYAS—AROMATIC FILLED SQUASH *Rosh Hashana*

Sephardic Jews in Israel have come from many lands, although their place of origin was Spain. From each country of their sojourn, they took on local nuances of cooking. Thus the summer squash (zucchini, vegetable marrow), which was even a Biblical favorite, takes on many different flavors.

2 pounds baby squash	1 egg diluted with
2 slices white bread	1 tablespoon water
1 cup ground meat	oil for frying
½ teaspoon cinnamon	juice of 1 lemon
salt and pepper to taste	1 tablespoon sugar
1 tablespoon flour	water to cover

Cut the squash in half lengthwise and scoop out the seeds. Moisten the bread and squeeze dry. Mix the bread with the meat and add spice and seasoning. Put the mixture into the hollowed-out marrows. Dip the filled marrows first in flour and then in the diluted egg. Fry the marrows on the meat side only. Put into a shallow casserole and sprinkle with the lemon juice and sugar. Just cover with water. Cook gently until squashes are tender and most of the sauce absorbed (35–40 minutes). (Serves 4–6.)

SQUASH MEDYAS (SLIT AND STUFFED) *Shavuot*

Cheese is today curdled with rennet, taken from the membrane of calves' or lambs' stomach. This discovery—so the legend goes —was made when a Bedouin filled his water goatskin with fresh milk and discovered to his dismay that it turned at once to cheese. However, he was able to drink the refreshing whey and also eat the curds of cheese.

This dish is typically Middle Eastern, but prepared in an oven instead of an open fire, and topped with sour cream instead of sour milk.

12 small summer squash	2 cups cottage cheese
(vegetable marrow or	4 eggs
zucchini type)	salt and pepper
2 tablespoons grated yellow	butter (optional)
cheese (optional)	½ cup sour cream

Cook the unpeeled tender squash in as little water as possible, and drain them while still firm. Slit lengthwise ("medyas" means "cut in two") and remove the seed section, leaving a scooped-out boat shape for filling. Mix the cheeses and eggs with salt and pepper and fill the cavities. Put the scooped-out seed sections in a well-buttered casserole and place the medyas on top. Dab each medyas with a little butter if you wish. Bake in a hot oven until the filling has set. Top with sour cream and bake 5 minutes more. Delicious hot or cold. (Serves 12.)

KUSA—SQUASH SOUFFLÉ *Shavuot*

A natural food partner for the soufflé—the ever-popular summer squash of Israel.

4 egg yolks	*4 tablespoons milk*
1½ cups grated summer	*2 tablespoons chopped*
squash	*parsley*
6 tablespoons mayonnaise	*1 tablespoon grated onion*
4 tablespoons flour	*1 teaspoon lemon juice*
dash of salt and pepper	*4 egg whites*

Beat the egg yolks into the grated squash. Mix the mayonnaise, flour, salt, and pepper. Add the milk slowly. Stir in the squash mixture, then the parsley, onion, and lemon juice. Beat the egg whites until stiff. Fold the squash mixture in carefully. Pour into a greased baking dish and bake in a 300° oven 45 minutes. Serve immediately. (Serves 4.)

KARAH—BOTTLE SQUASH *Rosh Hashana*

The devoutedly religious Jew seeks an opportunity to bless God at every turn, even when it involves a play on words. Karah— Hebrew for the green bottle squash (Leganaria vulgaris)—is a very ordinary dish. But since it sounds like the word "yikarahtu" in the phrase "Yikarahtu oyveinu"—"May our enemies be chopped down"—the bottle squash comes in for a special blessing in Middle Eastern homes on Rosh Hashana. They make it very palatable on this festive occasion.

6 bottle squash (small), or	*salt to taste*
other winter squash	*dash of ginger*
dash of cinnamon	*water*
honey to taste	

Cut the squashes into cubes and sprinkle with all the seasonings and honey. Add a very little water and cook until the vegetable is soft and the liquid absorbed (about ½ hour). (Serves 4–6.)

SQUASH MOCK APPLE COMPOTE   *Passover*

1¼ cups sugar
 3 cups water
 rind and juice of
   2 lemons

1 or 2 cloves
1 pound firm young
   summer squash
1 apple, diced (optional)

Make a syrup of the sugar and water. Add the lemon rind and cloves. Peel and dice the squash fine (without the inner pulp, unless very firm) and drop into the syrup. Cook only until the squash begins to get clear. Remove from heat and add lemon juice. Serve very cold. If you add a diced apple it adds to the flavor and can hardly be distinguished from the squashes. (Serves 4.)

CANDIED SWEET POTATOES   *Rosh Hashana*

3 pounds sweet potatoes
1 cup orange juice
1 teaspoon salt

dash of ginger or
   cinnamon
1 cup brown sugar
½ cup margarine

Boil the sweet potatoes in their jackets. Skin and slice thickly and arrange the slices attractively in a greased baking dish. Pour the orange juice over. Sprinkle with the salt, ginger, and sugar and dot with margarine. Bake in a 375° oven until the sweet potatoes are candied (about 45 minutes). (Serves 8–10.)

SWEET POTATO KUGELACH   *Hanuka*

Columbus discovered America: granted. But was it he who discovered the sweet potato—still called "batata" in Israel? For he wrote to the Spanish king: ". . . I have brought back a kind of batata with flesh not unlike that of a carrot, but not as sweet."

3 cups mashed sweet
   potatoes
5 tablespoons chicken fat
3 eggs, beaten
½ cup brown sugar

¼ cup honey
1 cup water
1 teaspoon salt
rind and juice of 1 lemon
dash of ginger

Mix all the ingredients together and put into greased muffin tins, ⅔ full. Bake in a 350° oven for about half an hour and serve hot as a side dish for fowl. (Serves 6.)

CALABASH WITH NAHIT
(WINTER SQUASH WITH CHICK-PEAS)   *Succot*

2 *cups chick-peas*   *salt and pepper*
2 *pounds brisket of beef*   *water to cover*
¼ *cup oil*   *2 pounds winter squash or*
1 *teaspoon cinnamon*   *pumpkin (calabash)*

Soak the chick-peas overnight. Sear the meat in the hot oil. Add
the chick-peas and the seasonings. Cover with water and simmer
until the meat and chick-peas are almost done (2–3 hours). Cut
the squash into serving pieces, leaving on the skin. Put on the
bottom of a casserole. Cover with the meat, chick-peas, and
liquid and put into a 350° oven. Bake until the liquid is almost
all absorbed and the ingredients are tender (about 1½ hours).
(Serves 6–8.)

CALABASH AND DUMPLINGS   *Succot*

*The calabash—or calabassah as it is commonly called (in Hebrew
the name is "dla'at"—is Israel's pumpkin-like giant squash. Its
size and abundance make it symbolic of the bountiful harvest,
and it is therefore served on Succot (particularly on Hoshanah
Rabba day) with dumplings. As there are no cellars in Israel,
these huge, orange, tough-skinned vegetables are stored where
neither sun nor rain nor frost can harm them.*

The Vegetable   *The Dumplings*

2 *pounds calabash (or any*   ¾ *cup flour*
    winter squash)   2 *tablespoons semolina*
4 *tablespoons brown sugar*   *pinch of salt*
½ *teaspoon salt*   ½ *cup water or milk*
¼ *teaspoon cinnamon or*
    nutmeg
5 *tablespoons margarine*
    water

Cut the calabash into 1-inch cubes, sprinkle with sugar and
seasoning, dot with margarine, and half cover with water. Cook
until the vegetable is soft (about 1½ hours). Mix all the
dumpling ingredients and drop by the teaspoonful into boiling
water. Cook for 5 minutes. Serve with the calabash. (Serves
about 6.)

BKEILA—SWISS CHARD AND BEANS *Rosh Hashana*

This Tunisian dish is served on Rosh Hashana because Swiss chard, being of the beet family—"selek" in Hebrew—is a play of words upon the blessing "Lesalek oyveinu"—"to get rid of our enemies." The yellow beans are a symbol for the first fruit of the harvest.

½ pound diced head meat
2 onions, chopped
2 cloves garlic, chopped
6 tablespoons cooking oil
1 pound dried beans

salt and pepper to taste
pinch of ground coriander
water to cover
1 pound Swiss chard (or spinach)

Fry the meat with the onions and garlic in the oil. Add the beans and seasoning and just cover with water. After cooking for about 20 minutes, add the chopped chard or spinach. Cover the pot and finish the cooking on very low heat (about 1½ hours). (Serves 4.)

RUTABAGA TURNIP TZIMMES *Shabbat*

2 pounds fat beef
2 pounds diced turnips
water to cover
salt and pepper to taste

½ cup brown sugar or honey
2 tablespoons cooking oil
2 tablespoons flour

In a heavy pot, brown the meat to seal it. Add the turnips, cover with water, and bring to the boil. Reduce heat to very low and add the salt, pepper, and sweetening. Cook very slowly, shaking the pot from time to time. When the meat is done (about 2–3 hours) and the turnips golden, mix the oil and flour and add to thicken the sauce. Cook a few minutes more and serve hot. (Serves 6.)

HARVEST FESTIVAL (HAG HA-ASIF) TZIMMES *Succot*

One of the many names of Succot is "Hag Ha-Asif," or the Harvest Holiday, and it is fitting that harvest dishes be served this week. A typical dish is this one, symbolic of the fruits that grow in the earth and on the vine and tree.

1 pound cooked sweet potatoes
1 pound firm apples, pared and cored
1 pound parboiled winter squash (or pumpkin)

salt to taste
4 tablespoons fat
½ cup honey or orange marmalade
½ cup water
½ cup white wine

Slice the potatoes, apples, and squash thickly and place in alternate layers in a casserole. Mix the remaining ingredients and pour over. Cover and bake in a 350° oven until the apples are done and the sweet potatoes glazed (about 30 minutes). (Serves 4–6.)

FRUTADAS—VEGETABLE PANCAKES   *Rosh Hashana*

This Sephardic Rosh Hashana dish is in three colors—white, gold, and green—to symbolize the variety of the harvest.

⅔ cup chopped, cook leeks	½ cup flour
⅔ cup chopped, cook spinach	2 eggs
⅔ cup chopped, cook pumpkin	2 teaspoons sugar
	salt to taste
	cooking oil

The vegetables should be cooked separately, then chopped. Mix the flour, eggs, sugar, and salt and divide amongst the vegetables. Form into small patties and fry in deep hot oil. (Serves 4–6.)

VEGETARIAN GEFILTE "FISH"   *Shabbat*

The Sauce

1 large onion, sliced
1 carrot, sliced
2 cups water
1 teaspoon cooking oil
salt, pepper, and sugar
to taste

The "Fish"

4 tablespoons soy flour
2 tablespoons matzo meal
salt and pepper to taste
¼ cup boiling water
1 onion, chopped
1 tablespoon oil
1 hard-cooked egg, mashed
4 slices white bread, soaked
in water and crumbled
1 raw egg, separated

Put all the ingredients for the sauce into a pot and bring to the boil. Prepare the "fish" by mixing together the soy flour, matzo meal, salt, and pepper, then adding the boiling water. Fry the chopped onion in the oil and add to it the hard-cooked egg and soaked, crumbled bread. Beat the raw egg yolk and add. Beat the egg white until stiff and fold in. With wet hand, form into balls and drop into the boiling sauce. Reduce the heat and simmer gently for 1 hour. Cover the pot after 30 minutes of cooking. (Serves 4.)

Rosh Hashana
TURLU—GIUVETCH—VEGETABLE MEDLEY

This vegetable medley is very popular among all peoples of the Balkan countries and in Turkey; the Jews there serve it on Rosh Hashana. The vegetables are sometimes stewed together with a joint of mutton or a combination of meats. It is often made as a purely vegetarian dish. Any vegetables in season may be used.

6 tablespoons olive oil	2 tablespoons chopped
1 pound meat, diced	fennel
2 cups water	3 tomatoes, diced
1 cup cut green beans	1 cup diced potatoes
½ cup green peas	1 cup diced summer squash
½ cup cauliflower florets	1 cup diced eggplant
½ cup diced celery root	½ cup whole okra
⅓ cup diced turnips	1 cup diced leeks
⅓ cup diced turnips	6 tablespoons lemon juice
2 tablespoons chopped	
parsley	

Heat the olive oil and brown the meat cubes. Add the water and cook until tender, if necessary adding more liquid. Remove the meat and cook the sauce down to half a cup. In a casserole, arrange the vegetables in layers and pour the liquid over. Simmer 15 minutes, add the lemon juice, and bake, covered, in a 250° oven until all the vegetables are tender (45–60 minutes). Remove the cover and cook 10 minutes longer. (Serves 8–10.)

NOTE: The meat may be layered with the vegetables or eaten separately as a side dish.

Rosh Hashana
PAZIE—MACHSHI—HARSHOUF—STUFFED STEMS

This dish is always served on Rosh Hashana in Israeli-Sephardic homes, when a blessing on a variety of foods makes up a fascinating ceremony. On that occasion the stems of beet or chard are used. During the rest of the year stems of swiss chard, artichokes, or celery are used. It is an unusually tasty dish, served as an hors d'oeuvre.

20 broad stems of either	2 eggs
artichoke, celery,	salt and pepper
chard, or beet	dash of cinnamon
½ pound meat, minced	(optional)

2 *tablespoons breadcrumbs*   *flour as needed*
1 *tablespoon chopped*   1 *tablespoon water*
   parsley   *lemon juice to taste*
1 *tablespoon oil*

Cut the artichoke, celery, chard, or beet stems into five-inch lengths. Mix the meat with the breadcrumbs, parsley, salt and pepper, oil, 1 egg, and the seasonings (North African Jews add a dash of cinnamon too; some like nutmeg, others nothing). Fill the stems. Roll in flour. Dilute the remaining egg with the water and dip the floured stems in this. Fry in hot oil just to seal and then put the filled stems into a casserole (meat side up) and almost cover with water flavored with lemon juice. Cover pot and cook over low heat about 1½ hours. Just before finishing cooking, add more lemon juice if you like. Serve hot or cold.

NOTE: If you cannot get the required stems, you can use celery stalks for this.

FRUIT

Rosh Hashana

SUESSAPFELGEMUSE—VEGETABLE APPLES

Somehow the apple, even more than the Biblical pomegranate, has become the symbolic "first fruit" of Rosh Hashana. It therefore goes into the making of countless dishes both in Eastern and Western lands for this festival. The following is a Swiss-Jewish dish that is eaten instead of vegetables with the main dish, since sweet foods are eaten in every course on Rosh Hashana.

3 pounds apples	*4 tablespoons water*
4 tablespoons fat	*1 cinnamon stick*
4 teaspoons brown sugar	

Wash, slice, and core apples, but do not peel. Heat the fat and put in the brown sugar. Add the apple slices and toss. Put in the water and the cinnamon stick and cook over low heat until the apple slices are tender but not mushy (10–20 minutes). (Serves 8–10.)

COMPOTE

Shabbat

How a French title ever came to crown an ancient Jewish dish, I know not. The Sabbath dessert of dried prunes, pears, and apples, stewing slowly on the back of the stove, is something every Jewish child remembers all his life for its aroma. Fresh fruits are used for this dessert in Israel, be they apples, pears, plums or peaches in season. Sugar is adjusted according to the sweetness or the sourness of the fruit used.

1 cup sugar	*2 whole cloves or piece of*
2 cups water	*cinnamon stick*
12 apples or other fresh fruit	*1 tablespoon lemon juice*

Bring the sugar and water to the boil. Peel and core the apples and cut into rather thick slices. Add the spices to the syrup and then the apples. Cook gently until the fruit just begins to soften. Remove from heat and let the fruit cool in the syrup. More water may be used if a thin sauce is preferred. Add the lemon juice. Serve cold. (Serves 8–10.)

APPLE MUNCH

Succot

*"An apple a day keeps the doctor away" is an adage on which
I was brought up in apple-bountiful Canada. And now, what do
you think?—in Israel, the land where an apple was once worth its
weight in gold, the above boost for the apple growers is now
used—but in Israel they say "Eat two apples a day to keep the
doctor away!"*

8 large apples, peeled	1½ cups brown sugar
6 tablespoons water	¾ cup margarine
juice of ½ lemon	1 cup flour
½ teaspoon cinnamon	

Slice the apples and pile them in a buttered baking dish. Mix the
water and the lemon juice and sprinkle on the apples. Rub together the cinnamon, sugar, margarine, and flour to form
crumbs. Sprinkle the mixture over the apples and bake in a 350°
oven about 35 minutes. Serve either hot or cold. (Serves 6–8.)

NOTE: The dish is very good with sweet cream poured on if it is
hot, and topped with whipped cream if it is cold.

CANDIED APPLES

Succot

*On Simhat Torah children in the synagogues wave flags topped
with apples on which lighted candles have been placed.*
*And indeed, candied apples, with the Biblical cinnamon flavor
added—are special for children everywhere. They are sold on
the streets at the harvest time of Succot.*

⅔ cup honey (or syrup)	few drops red food
⅔ cup sugar	coloring
½ teaspoon cinnamon	12 small apples
	12 lollipop sticks

Put the honey and sugar in a deep pan over low heat and stir
until the sugar melts. Add the cinnamon and food coloring. Do
not stir further. Cook until a few drops harden in a glass of cold
water—250° to 266° on a candy thermometer. Remove the pan
from the heat and put it over hot water or on a low-heated electric plate. Fasten a stick into each apple and dip them into the
candy. Fasten them into a flower holder or put them upright in
glasses until the candy coating hardens.

APPLES CHÂTEAUX   *Shabbat*

6 apples, peeled	juice and rind of ¼ lemon
1 cinnamon stick	½ cup cornstarch
¼ cup sugar	sugar to taste
water (about 1 cup)	3 egg yolks, beaten
2 cups dry white wine	

Put the whole apples, with the cinnamon stick and sugar, in a
pot and add just enough water (about 1 cup) to cook the apples
without making them mushy. Simmer about 20 minutes and
remove the apples. To ½ cup of the apple liquid add the wine,
lemon juice and rind, sugar to taste, and the cornstarch. Mix
well. Beat the yolks and stir in. Cook the sauce over very low
heat, stirring constantly until thick. Pour the sauce over the
apples and serve hot or cold. (Serves 6.)

AVOCADO DESSERT   *Passover*

4 medium avocados	3 tablespoons sour cream
6 teaspoons lemon juice	or 1 tablespoon of
¼ cup sugar	liqueur, if desired

Select ripe avocados, peel, seed, and press them through a sieve.
Add the lemon juice and sugar, and if you like, the sour cream
or liqueur. Mix very well. Chill thoroughly (do not freeze).
(Serves 8.)

BANANA IN A BLACK NIGHTGOWN   *Hanuka*

*"Yes, we have no bananas" is something no Israeli believes, for
we bury our surplus crops!*

6 tablespoons butter	6 tablespoons water
6 bananas	½ cup white sugar
½ cup brown sugar	dash of salt
2 squares unsweetened	½ teaspoon vanilla
chocolate	

Melt 3 tablespoons of the butter in a skillet. Peel the bananas and
roll in the brown sugar, then fry until golden in the butter. Set
aside to cool. Mix the chocolate and water over low heat. Add the
white sugar and salt and cook until the mixture begins to thicken,

stirring constantly. Add the rest of the butter and the vanilla. Pour the hot sauce over the cooled bananas and serve. Or chill before serving. (Serves 6.)

BANANA SAUTÉ   *Tu Besh'vat*

6 *bananas*
2 *teaspoons lemon juice*
6 *tablespoons brown sugar*

3 *tablespoons butter or*
  margarine
4 *tablespoons wine*
  (*optional*)

Sprinkle the bananas with lemon juice, roll in sugar, and fry in the butter until golden. Serve hot or cold. If you wish, add wine toward the end of the cooking. If you let the bananas cool in the wine, the sauce becomes jelly-like and the fat remains in the pan. (Serves 6.)

BANANA FOOL   *Passover*

2 *cups mashed bananas*
1 *teaspoon lemon juice*
4 *egg yolks, beaten*

2 *tablespoons banana*
  liqueur or brandy
½ *cup whipping cream*

Mash the bananas with the lemon juice and whip. Add to the egg yolks with the liqueur or brandy. Pour into sherbet glasses and top with whipped cream. (Serves 4.)

BROILED GRAPEFRUIT   *Rosh Hashana*

It is believed that Confucius collected the ancient writings called Shu-King (500 B.C.E.). Oranges and shaddocks (parent of the grapefruit) are mentioned in these works, so perhaps the following dish was no stranger to the Oriental ancients. To the Japanese the sour orange (called Dei-dai) was most symbolic, for it meant "from generation unto generation." The grapefruit is a wonderful fruit heritage indeed.

4 *grapefruit*
8 *tablespoons sugar or honey*

4 *tablespoons butter*
8 *cherries and mint sprigs*

Cut the fruits in half, and loosen each section from the skin and membranes. Fill the core with butter and sprinkle the sugar or honey well over the fruit. Broil for 15–20 minutes, 3 to 4 inches from low heat. Serve hot, garnished with a cherry in the core and a sprig of mint. (Serves 8.)

STUFFED BAKED ORANGES   *Hanuka*

As long ago as 1547, at a Christmas dinner in Venice, a dish of stuffed oranges was served. Whether this was an orange shell filled with fresh fruits, or one stuffed and cooked in honey with the candied citrons they used so much in those days, remains a riddle. In any case, this dish—being both sweet and piquantly bitter—would surely have found favor in those days as it does today at special Hanuka affairs, when the ignited oranges look like the festive candles.

8 small oranges	*1 cup sugar*
hot water to cover	*½ cup honey*
8 dates	*juice of ½ lemon*
8 almonds or walnuts	*8 cubes sugar dipped in*
butter	*brandy, if desired*
¾ cup sugar	

Grate the outer rind (zest) off each orange, all over the fruit. Cover the fruit with hot water and simmer half an hour. Remove from the water and cool. Core a deep hole in each orange. Pit the dates and fill them with whole nuts. Pack the dates, with pieces of butter, into the holes in the oranges. Put into a casserole.

Boil together the sugar, water, and honey for 2–3 minutes. Add the lemon juice and pour over the oranges. Bake for about 1¼ hours in a 375° oven, basting from time to time with the syrup. Cool and chill. Serve very cold. A piece of sugar dipped into brandy can be put on top of each orange and the dessert ignited at the table. (Serve 8.)

BROILED ORANGE SLICES   *Hanuka*

In 1457, the Hungarian ambassador Comte de Foix was sent to Paris to ask for the hand of Madeleine, daughter of Charles VII, for the seventeen-year-old King Ladislas. He gave a lavish banquet at which fried oranges were served together with leveret (young rabbit) pies. Today oranges are broiled instead of fried, but they are still loved as an accompaniment to fowl or meat.

4 oranges	*3 tablespoons brown sugar*
4 tablespoons margarine	*dash of ground ginger*

Cut each orange into ½-inch slices, leaving the peel on. Put a dab of margarine in the center of each slice. Mix the brown sugar with the ginger and sprinkle over the orange slices. Broil until bits of gold begin to appear on the orange slices. (Serves 4.)

ORANGE HONEY   *Tu Besh'vat*

The first mention of citrus fruits is in the ancient writings of the Chinese. This is only to be expected, as the source of the fruit was in the area between China and India. Their literature relates how they preserved the fruit in honey; each ingredient must have benefited from the intermingling of flavors and perfumes.

2 cups fresh orange juice	*1½ cups sugar*
grated rind of 2 oranges	*½ cup honey*

Mix all the ingredients and cook gently until the mixture is thick as honey (about 10 minutes).

ORANGE BITTER SWEET   *Tu Besh'vat*

Records show that even before the year 1500 women had a coy way of tantalizing the men they loved. Oranges, like valentines today, were messages of love and it was customary for fair ladies to throw the fruit at their swains, or would-be swains. The custom prevailed for two centuries, and its practice has come down to us in stories and poetry. Ronsard, poet of the French Renaissance, wrote: "Oranges and citrons are the symbols of love." Well, you'll love this orange dish—for it is as bittersweet as love itself.

4 tablespoons grated coconut	*4 tablespoons water (more*
(optional)	*if needed)*
1 pound oranges	*2 cups sugar*

Grate some of the rind off from the oranges (leave about a fourth, here and there on the oranges). Cut into quarters and soak in water overnight. Weigh the fruit and add sugar of equal weight if you intend to serve this dish within a week (keep it refrigerated). If you intend to glaze the orange for keeping longer, use sugar of 1½ times the weight. Add just a little water to keep the sugar from scorching and cook gently until all the liquid is absorbed and the fruit soft. Depending on many factors, this can take from 30 minutes to 2 hours. Serve very cold, garnished with shredded coconut.

AMBROSIA *Passover*

1 *pomela (shaddock) or*	½ *cup fine or powdered*
2 *grapefruit*	*sugar*
6 *oranges*	1 *cup sweet shredded*
3 *tablespoons curaçao*	*coconut*
liqueur	

Cut the pomela or grapefruit into sections, remove all membranes, and flake. Slice the oranges very thin. Into a glass bowl or in sherbet glasses put alternate layers of pomela flakes and orange slices. Drizzle a little curaçao on each layer of oranges and dust with sugar. Just before serving top generously with shredded sweet coconut. (Serves 6–8.)

CITRUS AMBROSIA *Tu Besh'vat*

"Sweet oranges strewn with powdered sugar" were served at a Christmas banquet as long ago as 1529 in Italy. This is a very common tasty way of serving the fruit today. It is very decorative, and like nectar and ambrosia, fit for the gods.

8 *grapefruit slices*	8 *dates, pitted*
8 *orange slices*	*coconut, shredded*
powdered sugar	*sprigs of mint*

Remove the peel and outer membrane from the grapefruit and oranges and slice thickly. Sprinkle sugar over the grapefruit slices and cover with the thick orange slices. Sprinkle with more sugar. Put a pitted date on each orange. Sprinkle shredded coconut over the fruit and garnish with sprigs of mint. (Serves 8.)

Tu Besh'vat
CANDIED CITRUS PEELS (POMERANTZEN)—ORANGES, LEMONS, CITRONS, GRAPEFRUITS, POMELOS

Festive dinners in the days of the Renaissance sometimes ran to twenty courses and a hundred dishes; at all of these the citrus had its honored place, from the hors d'oeuvres down to the dessert. Candied citrus peel also went into the preparation of many dishes, and were served as tidbits, too. Here is the dessert on a menu in Italy dated 1529: "Spanish olives, jellies, peas, Parmesan cheese, Oranges, Candied Citrons, and Citrons covered with sugar."

6 *citrus fruits*	1½ *cups water*
3 *cups sugar*	

This recipe is for fruits the size of a large orange. If you use larger or smaller citrus fruits, judge sugar and water measures accordingly. (Weight for weight of peel and sugar is satisfactory.) Wash and dry the fruit and remove the skins in sectors. Cut the peel into strips about a quarter of an inch thick. Cover with water and bring to a boil. Change the water and boil again. Do this five or six times. Drain, then put in the 3 cups sugar and 1½ cups water and cook slowly until all the syrup has been absorbed. Drain and roll the peels in sugar. Let dry for a day before storing.

POMEGRANATE KIBBE

Succot

Because of its many pips, the pomegranate was an ancient symbol of fertility among the Israelites. This dish is a favorite among Kurdistan families, in which the men are tough and virile (all the porters in the country seem to come from Kurdish stock), the women robust and prolific, the children many and healthy. You can use the kibbe batter (see Index) for the coating in this dish, or the following combination created by the Soy Bean Council of America in its Israel testing kitchen:

The Filling

2 cups chopped beef or lamb
1 onion, chopped
4 tablespoons cooking oil
1 cup pomegranate pips
2 tablespoons raisins
  (optional)
dash of cinnamon
salt and pepper to taste

The Coating

1 pound burghul (cracked wheat)
½ cup cooking oil
2 tablespoons salt
3 tablespoons tomato purée
1 teaspoon paprika
2 teaspoons ground fennel
¼ cup flour
1 cup soy flour
1½ cups water
oil for frying

For the filling, fry the meat and onion slightly in the oil. Add all the other ingredients and set aside.

For the coating, mix the burghul and oil. Add salt, tomato purée, paprika, fennel, flour, and soy flour. Mix well. Knead, adding water from time to time. Set aside for half an hour and then divide into 30 balls. Press a hole in the center of the dough and work around the inside to make a hollow. Pack in the filling, seal up the coat, and fry in deep oil until golden. (Serves 4–6.)

MEAT-FILLED DATES

Rosh Hashana

The Hebrew word for date is "tamar," and as this word sounds like "yitahmu" in a Rosh Hashana blessing meaning to be cleansed of sin and, moreover, as the date is also a sweet fruit for a sweet New Year, this dish is served as a garnish to the fowl that is usually on the menu on this festival. The dish is also often served on Passover because it is so delectable.

50 dates
1/4 pound chopped meat
1/4 teaspoon salt
1 egg yolk

small amount of oil, for
    frying
juice of 1 lemon
water to cover

Stone the dates. Mix the meat, salt, and egg yolk and pack into the dates (they may be left open). Fry the dates in the oil on low heat until they puff up. Add lemon juice, cover with water, and simmer for about an hour.

TEHAINIM MITUKIM—SWEET FIGS

Rosh Hashana

"Yitahmu Hatayim min Haaretz"—"May there be an end to sin in the land"—is one of the Rosh Hashana blessings at the Jewish board in Israel. As "tehainim" (figs) sounds like "yitahmu," the fruit is on the table as a symbol, deliciously concocted in the Arabic way. Fresh figs are available at the Rosh Hashana season in Israel, but dried figs can be used after soaking for a few hours.

4 cups water
1 1/2 cups sugar
    dash of ginger and/or
        cinnamon

1 1/2 pounds fresh or 1 pound
        dried figs
    juice of 1 orange and
        1/2 lemon
    pine nuts

Make a syrup of the water and sugar and add the spices (preferably a piece of fresh ginger root and cinnamon stick). Add the figs and cook gently until the syrup is quite thick (10–15 minutes). Add the orange and lemon juice. Remove from heat and add a sprinkling of pine nuts. Serve cold. (Serves 4–6.)

GRAPE COMPOTE

Succot

1/2 cup sugar
3 cups water

1/2 cup Concord wine
4 cups grapes

Boil the sugar and water. Add the wine. When the sauce comes back to the boil, remove from the range and add the grapes. They will cook sufficiently by steeping in the hot sauce. Cool and chill. Serve cold. (Serves 6–8.)

MANGO MÉLANGE   *Succot*

When I first saw—and in a very fashionable Boston restaurant at that—the waiter put a bib around an athletic customer's neck, I was sure he had ordered mango—but no, it was lobster. Eating mango requires special tools (available only in South America where the fruit is much loved), unless you are willing to discard the flesh around the seed. And who could bear to throw away even one succulent mouthful? The fruit is so good some people even consume the leathery skin.

mangoes   *whipped cream (if you insist*
any other fruits   *on spoiling the dish)*

Cut the mangoes into halves and top with any diced fruit, such as melons, papaws, or peaches. Chill and serve with whipped cream on the side (for those pagans who don't know better).

YOTVATA MELONS   *Hanuka*

One of the delightful surprises in experimental farming at Kibbutz Yotvata (where my daughter Varda and her family live), in the torrid rainless desert around Elath, is that melons thrive only out of season, enabling their export when all melon crops are finished elsewhere. But I doubt if the Yotvata farmers have done as well as those of Salome in the United States, which records in its literature: "Everything grows well in Salome. But melons don't do very well becuz the vines grow so fast they wear the melons out dragging them around the ground—and in dry years we sometimes have to plant onions in between rows of potatoes and then scratch the onions to make the potatoes' eyes water enough to irrigate the rest of the garden . . ."

2 melons   *sugar*
  lemon juice   *diced oranges*

Cut the melons in wedges and scoop out the seeds. Sprinkle with lemon juice and sugar. Pile the diced oranges into the melon cavities. Serve chilled, on grape leaves. (Serves 4.)

MINTED PEARS

"Offer not the pear to him who gave the apple" is a rather ungenerous old proverb. Professor and Valita Backus introduced minted pears to the tables of Israelis, who had rarely partaken of this new-grown fruit.

1 1-pound, 4-ounce can Bartlett pears	peppermint oil or a handful of fresh mint and
juice of ½ lemon	1 tablespoon pear brandy
½ cup sugar	green food coloring

Prepare the day before serving.

Allow at least 2 pear halves per serving. Drain the pears (reserving the juice for another use). Combine the lemon juice, sugar, a few drops of peppermint oil and enough of the vegetable food coloring to give the syrup a delicate green tint. (Be cautious about the oil, as a little goes a long way. If you have no peppermint oil you can use the mint sprigs and tablespoon of pear brandy, or any colorless liqueur, as mentioned above.) Boil uncovered for ten minutes and cool. Put the fruit in a large flat dish. Pour the syrup over the pears and refrigerate. Turn the pears three or four times so they will color evenly. Very good topped with coconut if you wish to serve the pears as a dessert. (Serves 4–6.)

Rosh Hashana

FLOHMEN COMPOTE—FESTIVE STEWED PRUNES

Stewed prunes were served as the Sabbath dessert in Russian Jewish homes, and this compote has become traditional the world over.

½ pound prunes	4 tablespoons blanched almonds or prune kernels
4 cups water	
4 tablespoons honey	
1 lemon	

Put the prunes to soak for a few hours in the water. Add the honey and the lemon, cut in two, and cook very gently and slowly until the prunes are soft (20–30 minutes). Add the blanched almonds or prune kernels just before the compote is finished. Remove the lemon (the rind gives the dish a wonderful flavor). Cool. Chill and serve cold. (Serves 4.)

BAKED QUINCE

Yom Kippur

Jews from Iraq break the Yom Kippur fast with this fruit dish.

6 quinces	1 cup sugar
raisins	spice as desired
2 cups water	

Pare and core the quinces and put into a casserole. Fill the cavities with raisins. Mix the water, sugar, and spice and pour around the fruit. Bake in a 300° oven 3 hours, or until the quinces are rosy red. If the syrup evaporates too much, add a little water. (Serves 4–6.)

QUINCES STUFFED WITH CHICKEN

Passover

This Persian dish is delightful with a ruddy meat course such as roast beef.

6 small quinces	dash of salt
2 chicken breasts	margarine
2 tablespoons matzo meal	sprinkling of sugar
clove or cinnamon	

Peel the quinces. Core them, leaving the bottom intact but the top as wide as possible. Grind the meat, mix with the matzo meal, and flavor with clove or cinnamon and a dash of salt. Fill the quinces with this mixture and with a pat of margarine. Put the quinces into a baking dish with just a little water on the bottom. Sprinkle with sugar and spice and bake in a 400° oven until the quinces are pink and done (about 1½ hours).

RHUBARB SAUCE

Shavuot

The rhubarb roamed in ancient days from Southern Siberia to China. Its odyssey by camel took it back as far as Rome, in days of yore. It reached Israel only after the founding of the Jewish state in 1948.

2 pounds rhubarb	½ cup water
1 cup sugar	

Sprinkle the sugar over the rhubarb and set aside for 10 minutes. Add the water and cook on low heat until tender (15–20 minutes). Serve cold, with sour cream. (Serves 8.)

SABRAS—PRICKLY PEARS   *Succot*

The "sabra" is the cactus fruit known as the prickly pear. Israeli natives have been nicknamed "sabras" because, like the fruit, they are prickly on the outside, sweet on the inside. Sabra fruits are sold on street corners in season, the barbs removed by the rubber-gloved vendors and the peeled fruit kept on ice for chilling. At home it can be more glamorously served.

24 sabras
  lemon juice

powdered sugar
strawberries

Chill the peeled sabras. Sprinkle with lemon juice and powdered sugar and garnish with sugared strawberries. (Serves 4–6.)

SABRA COMPOTE   *Rosh Hashana*

Sabra is generally eaten raw, but also makes a fine compote. This recipe is from Hanan Ephraim, chef of the ORT Culinary School in Israel.

1 cup sugar (or more
    to taste)
4 cups boiling water

15 whole sabras, peeled
    juice of 1 lemon
4 tablespoons broken pecans

Add the sugar to the boiling water, and when it bubbles, add the fruit, Cook for a few minutes only. Remove from heat and add the lemon juice. Serve chilled with a garnish of pecans. (Serves 4.)

SUCCOT FRUIT CUP   *Succot*

If an apple hanging from a tree tempted Adam and Eve, how much more tantalizing are the boughs of the succah laden with hanging pomegranates, custard apples, bananas, guavas, tangerines, apples, quinces, persimmons, lemons, avocados, grapefruits, pomelos, pears, oranges, grapes, and dates, the harvest fruits of the season. To keep even adults from eating the decorations, this California-type fruit cup has come into popularity in Israel as a first course or even a dessert.

sections of 2 grapefruit
sections of 3 tangerines
    or oranges
1 avocado, cubed

seeds of 1 pomegranate
juice of 1 lemon
2–3 tablespoons honey
    (to taste)

For color and texture effect, make a base of yellow grapefruit sections from which the membranes have been removed. Cover with a layer of tangerine sections. On top of that place the green avocado cubes, and sprinkle with the cerise-red pomegranate seeds. Dress with the lemon juice to which a little honey has been added. The fruit cup looks lovely and tastes even better. (Serves 6.)

WATERMELON BOWL OF FRUITS   *Rosh Hashana*

The physician to Francis I wrote in a delighted and surprised letter to a friend: "In Provence . . . they serve, during meals, an exquisite dish, fresh or dried figs, grapes and raisins, and even citrons, oranges, lemons, and shaddocks, which everywhere else are considered merely as seasonings. . . ."
   If the royal doctor were to drop into an Israel home in the early autumn with its first fruits, he might recognize the dish. New fruits are served on Rosh Hashana as a symbol for having lived, and a blessing to that effect is made over them.

1 *watermelon*	*lemon slices*
1 *cantaloupe*	*mint sprigs*
1 *mango, if obtainable*	*fresh figs*
papaws, if obtainable	*early sweet oranges*
blue grapes	*tangerines*
green grapes	*persimmons*
red grapes	*pears*
guavas, if obtainable	

Cut a cap off the blossom end of the watermelon. Scoop out the flesh with a ball cutter, discarding the seeds. Fill the melon bowl with balls of watermelon, cantaloupe, mango, papaws, grapes, and guava. Garnish with lemon slices and mint sprigs. Surround with fresh figs, orange and tangerine sections, persimmons, and pears, garnish with mint.

NOTE: Several of these fruits are rarely, if ever, obtainable in the U.S. Substitute any you like for filling or decoration for an equally appetizing effect.

STRAWBERRIES IN SIMPLE GLORY   *Passover*

big strawberries, unhulled	*blanched almonds, slivered*
powdered sugar	*sprigs of mint*

Serve the chilled unhulled strawberries, dusted with powdered sugar, sprinkled with blanched almonds, and garnished with sprigs of mint, on glass plates.

PAPAW FRUIT SALAD   *Shavuot*

4 cups cubed papaw   2 oranges, diced
   (papaya)   2 bananas, sliced
   lemon juice and sugar to   whipped cream, for
   taste   garnish
½ cup granadilla pulp
   and/or berries

Cube the papaws and sprinkle with lemon juice and sugar to taste. Add the granadilla pulp (you can use berries instead, or also, if you like), the diced oranges, and the sliced banana. Serve well chilled, with sugared whipped cream for garnish on the side. (Serves 6–8.)

ORANGE FRUIT SALAD   *Independence Day*

The orange is called "tapuach zahav"—golden apple—in Hebrew; it is the chief fruit of Israel and the basis of its most luscious desserts.

6 oranges, thinly sliced   6 plums, cut up
3 tablespoons sugar   6 apricots, cut up
3 bananas, sliced   6 strawberries
6 loquats, cut up   6 sprigs of fresh mint
1 cup mulberries   sweet white wine

Sprinkle the orange slices with sugar. Arrange the fruit in six cocktail goblets in layers of oranges, bananas, loquats, mulberries, plums, and apricots. Pour a little sweet white wine into each goblet. Top with a strawberry and a sprig of fresh mint. Serve chilled. (Serves 6.)

CHESTNUTS WITH APPLES   *Rosh Hashana*

Chestnuts are festive fare throughout Central Europe, and are used in all manner of vegetable and dessert dishes. This dish is used much as Americans use applesauce, as a garnish to fowl or other meat on Rosh Hashana.

1 pound chestnuts   sugar to taste
   water to cover   juice of 1 lemon
1½ pounds apples

Remove the shells and skins from the chestnuts. Cover with water and boil gently, covered, until tender (8–20 minutes). Peel, core, and cut up the apples. Cook over low heat with sugar 20–30 minutes. Put through a sieve with the chestnuts. Add the lemon juice.

Like applesauce, this dish can be used as a dessert, in which case vanilla would be used instead of lemon and there would be a whipped cream topping. (Serves 6–8.)

PERSIMMON-POMEGRANATE-POMELO SALAD   *Hanuka*

Solomon lauded the loveliness of Sheba's rosy cheeks by comparing them to pomegranates. The very sight of this salad would have driven him, as it does a gourmet, into love ecstasies.

1 pomelo (or grapefruit)	juice of ½ lemon
1 cup sour cream	2 firm Chinese persimmons
1 avocado	pips of 1 pomegranate

Peel and remove the membranes from the flesh of the pomelo or grapefruit and break up the sectors. Mix with the sour cream and pile into a glass bowl. Cut the avocado into eight wedges and sprinkle them with the lemon juice. Around the pomelo mixture, arrange wedges of persimmon alternately with wedges of avocado. Center the salad with the pips of a red pomegranate. Serve chilled. (Serves 6.)

GRAPE AND MELON CUP   *Shavuot*

The eroded terraces around the mountains of Judea were a sorry sight even a decade ago. Today many of these barren hills have been reclaimed with reforestation, after two thousand years of neglect. Many have been re-terraced by new immigrants and replanted with vineyards. The sight that dazzled the spies of Moses may yet return to Israel—grapes so great and abundant that it would take two men to carry a single branch.

2 cups honeydew melon balls	6 tablespoons honey
2 cups watermelon balls	6 tablespoons lemon juice
2 cups purple grapes	mint sprigs

Toss the melon balls with the grapes. Dress with the honey dissolved in the lemon juice. Garnish with sprigs of mint (put some leaves in the dressing for flavor and aroma) and serve chilled in sherbet glasses. (Serves 8–10.)

DESERTS

CARAMELIZED CUSTARD
Shavuot

1½ cups sugar
 4 eggs
 ¼ teaspoon salt

4 cups hot milk
1 teaspoon vanilla

Melt 1 cup of the sugar until brown and quickly pour into 8 individual baking cups, tilting each round until evenly coated. Whisk the eggs slightly, add the remaining sugar and the salt, and mix well. Slowly add the hot milk, stirring constantly. Add vanilla. Pour the custard into the caramel-coated cups. Place the cups in a pan of hot water in a 350° oven until the custards are done (about 30 minutes). Test with a knife: if it comes out clean, the custard is cooked. Do not overcook. (Serves 8.)

PAREVE CRÈME CARAMEL
Shabbat

Caramelized custard has become so popular in Israel that chef Max Cymbalista of the S.S. Theodor Herzl created this non-dairy version of the dish, so he could serve it with meat meals on the Sabbath, without violating the kosher laws.

1½ cups (*plus 2 tablespoons*)
     water
 4 tablespoons margarine
 ½ vanilla bean
     pinch of salt

4 tablespoons cornstarch
½ cup sugar for caramel
⅔ cup sugar
8 eggs

Boil the water with the margarine, vanilla bean, and salt. Remove the vanilla bean. Dissolve the cornstarch in 2 tablespoons water and stir into the hot mixture. In a long-handled pan, cook ½ cup of the sugar until golden. Remove from heat; carefully add half of this caramel to the thick mixture, with a long-handled spoon (as it often spurts and can burn your hand). Pour the remaining caramel into a greased baking dish, and swirl it around to coat the bottom evenly. Mix the remaining ⅔ cup sugar with the eggs and beat together only long enough to make a smooth mixture. Slowly pour the cornstarch mixture into the egg mixture, stirring constantly. Now pour this over the caramel coat in the baking dish. Put the baking dish into a pan of hot water and bake in a 300° oven until the mixture is set (about 45 minutes). Never let the water in the pan boil (add more cold water if necessary), but only simmer, or the custard will come out full of holes. Prepare a day ahead, serve chilled and un-molded. (Serves 6–8.)

TIPSY TRIFLE *Shavuot*

sponge cake or white cake   custard
sherry wine   whipped cream
preserved cherries   blanched almonds
red gelatin dessert   sprigs of mint

In individual sherbet glasses or a large glass bowl, put a thick layer of sponge or white cake. Slowly spoon on sherry wine, until the cake is saturated but not liquidy. On this put a layer of pre-served cherries or other fruit. Cover the fruit with the gelatin dessert. Put a few slivered almonds on top and cover with any rich wine- or brandy-flavored custard. Garnish the custard with a sweetened whipped cream and decorate with sprigs of mint. Serve very cold. A simplified trifle may be made of the cake and wine layer, a layer of jam and a topping of sweetened whipped cream.

SABAYON OR ZABAGLIONE *Tu Besh'vat*

The French are the creators of sabayon, and the Italians learned it from them (in return, perhaps, for all the dishes that the Italians taught the French). A number of excellent Italian res-taurants in Israel have brought the dessert to the local public, and it is quickly taking hold of the community, not only because it is so good, but because we have such an abundance of eggs and wine that the delicacy is within reach of the common budget.

1 cup egg yolks   1 cup muscatel wine
1 cup sugar

Put the yolks and sugar in the top of a double boiler and beat with a rotary beater until light and fluffy. Slowly add the wine, beating constantly. Put the pan over hot water and cook, beating continuously, until very thick. Serve at once in sherbet glasses, warm. (Serves 6–8.)

MULHAALIBIYA—ORANGE CUSTARD   *Shavuot*

An Arab superstition of the twelfth century still persists: if a woman eats an orange, it will banish all evil thoughts from her mind. This dish excites only nice sweet thoughts.

½ *cup brown sugar*   ¾ *cup white sugar*
1 *tablespoon hot water*   3 *cups hot milk*
2 *oranges*   ½ *teaspoon salt* (*optional*)
6 *eggs*

Butter a baking mold. Melt the brown sugar, add the water, and cook a moment. Cut the oranges into sections, removing the membrane, place the sections in the buttered mold, and pour the melted sugar over. Beat the eggs, add the white sugar, and mix in the hot milk gradually. Add the salt, if desired (the Arabs also add a dash of pepper!). Pour into the mold. Put the mold into a pan of hot water and bake in a 350° oven until a knife comes out clean when inserted into the custard (50–60 minutes). Serve very cold. (Serves 6.)

NOTE: Caramelized white sugar may be substituted for the melted brown sugar.

ORANGE PUDDING   *Independence Day*

Cornstarch custards (with or without eggs and with or without milk) are called puddings in Israel. They come in milk, chocolate, coffee, and all fruit flavors.

⅔ *cup sugar*   2 *egg yolks, beaten*
5 *tablespoons cornstarch*   2 *egg whites, stiffly beaten*
   pinch of salt   1 *teaspoon lemon juice*
3 *cups orange juice*   *honey for topping*

Mix the sugar, cornstarch, and salt. Heat the orange juice and mix well with the dry ingredients. Cook over boiling water in a double boiler, or over very low heat, stirring constantly, until thick and bubbly. Remove from heat. Add some of the hot custard mixture to the egg yolks, a spoonful at a time, stirring well. Then put the egg mixture into the remaining custard and cook two minutes more over boiling water, stirring constantly. Add the lemon juice and mix. Fold in the stiffly beaten egg whites.

Pour into six individual sherbet glasses. Chill. Top each glass with a teaspoon of honey and serve with ice cream wafers. (Serves 6.)

CHOCOLATE MILK PUDDING   *Independence Day*

This dish, very much like chocolate blanc mange, is as familiar to to the Israeli as milk with honey must have been to Solomon. Tender babies are nourished on it, rugged halutzim *in the kibbutzim get it almost daily, and yet the dish remains festive enough even for Independence Day.*

3 tablespoons cocoa
3 tablespoon cornstarch
⅓ cup sugar
2 cups milk

1 tablespoon margarine or
     butter
     honey for sauce

Mix the cocoa and the cornstarch and stir in the sugar. Stir in ½ cup cold milk. Heat the remaining milk and gradually add the cornstarch mixture. Cook over low heat until thick. Add the margarine and continue cooking for 10 minutes. Put into 4 serving glasses and chill. Serve with a topping of honey. (Serves 4.)

RÖD GRÖD—STRAWBERRY PUDDING   *Passover*

God could have made a berry better than the strawberry, but never did.

—PROVERB

4 cups whole strawberries
     sugar to taste
2½ cups water
2 tablespoons potato flour
     (for Passover) or
     instant strawberry
     pudding

½ teaspoon vanilla
     sweetened whipped cream

Boil 2 cups of the strawberries, with sugar to taste, in 2 cups of the water. Put through a sieve. Dilute the potato flour or strawberry pudding in the remaining water and add to the first mixture. Add the other 2 cups of whole strawberries and cook for 5 minutes. Add the vanilla. Pour into sherbet glasses. Chill thoroughly and top with sweetened whipped cream. (Serves 6.)

WINE FLOAT P_{urim}

Zechariah's words, "and their heart shall rejoice as through wine," are brought to mind whenever one imbibes this two-tone dessert, like a sailboat afloat on a purple sea.

2 cups red table wine	3 tablespoons cornstarch
¾ cup water	juice of 1 lemon
1 stick cinnamon	3 stiffly beaten egg whites
½ cup sugar (or more, to taste)	

Bring the wine and water to the boil with the cinnamon stick. Mix the sugar, cornstarch, and lemon juice and stir in. Cook over low heat, stirring constantly, until thick. Take out the cinnamon stick. Remove from heat, and while still warm but not hot, fold the stiffly beaten egg whites into one-third of the pudding. Pour this fluff over the remaining pudding, in individual glasses or a glass bowl. Serve cold. (Serves 4.)

CHESTNUT VERMICELLI $Rosh\ Hashana$

A royal French recipe, dated 1662, reads: "For roasted chestnuts—pour orange juice on them, this being their true sauce; and powder them with sugar. If you have no orange juice, use lemon juice or a good sweet wine or orange blossom water or rose water."
    This is a Rosh Hashana dessert or coffee-time treat brought to Israel from Switzerland. It is similar to many chestnut delicacies so loved in Western Europe.

3 cups blanched chestnuts	1 teaspoon vanilla
orange juice to cover	2 tablespoons confectioner's
½ cup sugar	sugar
3 tablespoons brandy	6 cherries for topping
1 cup whipping cream	

Cook the chestnuts in orange juice to cover, covered, 8–20 minutes, or until tender. Put them through a ricer. Add the sugar and brandy, and mix well. Put the mixture through the ricer again, to get a vermicelli effect. Whip the cream and add the vanilla and confectioner's sugar to it. Gently fold the cream mixture into the "vermicelli" chestnuts and pile into sherbet glasses. Chill for a few hours and serve topped with cherries. (Serves 6.)

WINE CREAM—CRÈME AU VIN   *Independence Day*

This dessert has come to Israel from many sources: it is closely related to the Italian zabaglione, and very much like the Dutch and Alsace-Lorraine wine cream, and the Spanish Bavarian cream. In any case, it is an ingathered gourmet recipe.

2½ tablespoons gelatin	1½ cups sweet light red wine
½ cup cold water	rind of 1 lemon
4 egg yolks	2 teaspoons lemon juice
dash of salt	4 egg whites
¾ cup sugar	

Soak the gelatin in the cold water for five minutes. Beat the egg yolks, salt, and sugar together until light. Heat the wine with the lemon rind and juice (do not boil). Add to the yolks and stir well. Cook in a double boiler or over hot water, stirring constantly, until the mixture coats the spoon. Add the gelatin and stir until dissolved. Set in a pan of cold water and stir until the mixture begins to thicken. Fold in the stiffly beaten egg whites. Turn into a mold that has been dipped in cold water. Chill until firm. (Serves 6.)

YUSSUF EFFENDI ORANGE JELLY   *Hanuka*

In Middle Eastern markets, the red-orange tangerine and the blood orange are called "Yussuf Effendi" or "Joseph the Feudal Lord." Before Joseph became a lord in Egypt, he was the major-domo in Potiphar's household. His master's wife became enamored of him, and one day she invited her lady friends to see her handsome servant. Joseph served them oranges with fruit knives, but they were so entranced by his good looks that they cut their fingers instead of the fruit, which was quickly colored red with their blood.

1 package orange- or	1 cup orange juice
lemon-flavored gelatin	1 cup whipping cream
¾ cup hot water	4 egg whites, beaten stiff
4 egg yolks, beaten	

Dissolve gelatin in the hot water and stir well. Beat the egg yolks and stir in the gelatin mixture. When cool, add the orange juice and refrigerate until firm. Beat the cream until it begins to thicken and then beat in the gelatin. Fold in the stiffly beaten egg whites and chill until firm. (Serves 4–6.)

SCODELINE ITALIAN DESSERT

Passover

1 cup almonds
8 eggs, separated, plus
   2 extra egg whites

1 cup sugar
⅓ cup water
rind and juice of ½ lemon

Blanch and grind the almonds. Beat the egg yolks and fold in the stiffly beaten whites. Meanwhile, heat the sugar, water, and lemon rind and juice. When the sugar is dissolved, add the almonds. Bring to a boil. Remove from heat and stir in the eggs. Put over low heat and stir for a few minutes. Remove from heat and continue stirring until the mixture is cool. Serve in individual glass bowls. (Serves 8.)

LEMON CREAM MERINGUE

Shabbat

4 egg whites
½ teaspoon cream of tartar
1½ cups sugar
4 egg yolks
3 tablespoons lemon juice

2 teaspoons grated lemon
   rind
1 cup cream, stiffly
   whipped

Beat the egg whites until foamy. Add the cream of tartar and 1 cup of the sugar gradually, during beating. When the mixture is stiff enough to hold its shape, spread in a lightly buttered cake tin and bake 40 minutes in a 300° oven. Cool while making the filling. Beat the egg yolks until thick and pale. Beat in the remaining sugar, lemon juice, and lemon rind. Cook in a double boiler until thick. Cool. Spread a layer of whipped cream on the baked meringue crust, then add a layer of filling and top with another layer of whipped cream. Chill in the refrigerator overnight before serving. (Serves 6–8.)

LEMON CREAM CLOUD

Purim

2 cups water
   juice of 2 lemons
½ cup sugar

1 tablespoon cornstarch
3 eggs, separated

Mix the water, lemon juice, sugar, and cornstarch. Beat the egg yolks well and add. Cook in a double boiler over hot water, stirring constantly, until the mixture is thick. Remove from the heat. Beat the egg whites until stiff and fold into the first mixture, while still warm but not hot. Serve in sherbet glasses, well chilled. (Serves 4–6.)

LEMON CREAM   *Shabbat*

Rich yet refreshing, this dessert was introduced to Israel by women from Vienna, and it is now often on the menus of the best restaurants, pensions and hotels and a special treat for the Sabbath meal.

8 eggs, separated	*juice of 2 lemons*
½ cup margarine	*grated rind of 1 lemon*
½ cup sugar	

Combine the egg yolks, margarine, sugar, and lemon juice in the top of a double boiler and cook over hot water (just under the boiling point), stirring constantly, until thick and creamy. Be careful not to overheat. Remove to a mixing bowl and beat until foamy. Beat the egg whites until stiff and fold into the yolk mixture. Mix in the grated rind.

The dessert is now ready for serving, but you can go one step further for double glamour. Pour the mixture into a casserole lined with waxed paper. Place the dish on a trivet in a pan of hot water and bake in a 300° oven 1½ hours. To unmold, loosen the edge of the dessert with a knife, cover with a serving dish, and turn the casserole upside down. Let it stand until the custard unmolds of itself. Serve cold. (Serves 6.)

LEMON CURD   *Passover*

Lemon curd, which is never curdled unless it is spoiled, is a smooth English spread for cakes and bread. Due to the strict Passover dietary laws, manufactured jams and marmalades were not purchased by Jews for Passover; instead, they made this as a spread for matzo.

3 eggs	*1 cup sugar*
6 tablespoons butter	*2 lemons, rind and juice*

Beat up the eggs slightly and add the butter, sugar, finely grated lemon rind, and lemon juice. Place the bowl over a pan of boiling water and stir until the mixture is thick and smooth. Pour into warm jars, cover, and cool. This is best kept in the refrigerator.

TORTA DI MANDORLE E CIOCCOLATA—
CHOCOLATE MERINGUE   *Yom Kippur*

½ pound almonds   1⅓ cups sugar
6 ounces milk chocolate   8 egg whites, stiffly beaten

Blanch the almonds and chop fine. Grate the chocolate and add the sugar. Fold all the ingredients into the egg whites. Butter and flour a pan, spread on the meringue mixture and bake in a 350° oven 30 minutes.

RICE KUGEL   *Shabbat*

1 cup rice   ½ cup raisins
1 teaspoon salt   ¼ cup almonds
3 cups boiling water   6 tablespoons chicken fat
1 cup diced apples   or margarine
4 eggs, beaten   dash of ginger or
½ cup sugar   cinnamon

Cook the rice, with the salt, in the boiling water until almost done (about 10 minutes). Drain. Mix with the remaining ingredients and bake in a greased casserole for about 1 hour. (Serves 4–6.)

RICE-DATE PUDDING   *Shavuot*

Among Persian Jews, Shavuot is called "The Feast of the Roses" —rose petals are strewn on the Holy Scrolls and rose water is sprinkled on members of the congregation during prayers. Accordingly, this festival dish is flavored with rose water.

2 eggs   ¼ cup sugar
2 cups milk   4 tablespoons butter
3 cups cooked rice   1 teaspoon rose water or
1 cup chopped dates   vanilla
½ cup chopped blanched
   almonds

Beat the eggs well and add the milk, then the rice and the remaining ingredients. Serve cold, garnished with red roses (for symbolism) if you wish. (Serves 6.)

RICE LIKE A L'IMPERATRICE   *Shavuot*

This Israeli dessert may be a stepchild of the green- and red-flecked rice dish named for Empress Maria Alexandrovna, but what does it matter? In Israel it is a popular simple dessert, garnished with raspberry fruit syrup (also comes in mandarin, orange, lemon and mixed juices).

sugar to taste	4 cups hot cooked rice
red and green candied	1½ cups sour cream
citrus peels	4 tablespoons raspberry
1 teaspoon vanilla	squash

Mix sugar with the citrus peels, vanilla, and boiled rice, and pack into a ring mold and chill. Unmold. Whip the sour cream (not too long, or it will turn to butter) and add the raspberry squash. Pour the sauce over the cold rice and serve. (Serves 8.)

POTATO-CARROT SWEET KUGEL   *Rosh Hashana*

This is a variation on the mock plum pudding that Canadian homesteaders used to make when candied fruits were beyond their purse. I believe that it was I who brought it to Israel, and from my food column in the Jerusalem Post, *it became a Rosh Hashana dish in Israel.*

1 cup coarsely grated apples	1 cup brown sugar
1 cup coarsely grated yams	1 teaspoon baking soda
1 cup coarsely grated raw	1 teaspoon salt
potatoes	1 teaspoon ginger
1 cup coarsely grated raw	1 teaspoon cinnamon
carrots	1 tablespoon brandy
1 cup raisins and nuts and	1 orange, rind and juice
candied fruits (or less	1 lemon, rind only
as desired)	1 teaspoon other mixed
1 cup flour	sweet spices
1 cup suet or margarine	

Roll the fruit and nuts in the flour, then mix with all remaining ingredients. Put into a pudding form or a tin that can be sealed firmly, filling only ⅔ full. Cover, put into boiling water, and cook at a simmer overnight. This kugel improves with keeping (refrigerated) for a few weeks. It can be warmed over and over. Serve with any fruit sauce. (Serves 8–10.)

SOUTLIASH *Shavuot*

Soutliash is the rice pudding for all festive occasions in the Balkans, Greece and Turkey. Sometimes it is made with whole grain rice, often with ground rice; sometimes it is caramelized and sometimes it is garnished with rose-petal jam.

2½ cups milk	1 teaspoon rose water or
4 tablespoons ground rice	vanilla
4 tablespoons sugar	rose petal (or cherry)
2 tablespoons butter	jam for garnish
dash of salt	

Heat the milk. Gradually add the ground rice and sugar, and stir until thick. Add the butter and salt and cook over very low heat for 15 minutes, being careful the rice does not stick. Add the rose water or vanilla. Pour into molds and chill. Unmold and serve with the garnish of rose petal jam. (Serves 4.)

SWEET LOKSHEN (NOODLE) KUGEL *Rosh Hashana*

½ pound broad egg noodles	¼ cup candied citrus peels
8 cups boiling water	dash of ginger
1 teaspoon salt	dash of cinnamon
4 tablespoons sugar	1 cup orange (or other)
3 eggs, lightly beaten	juice
6 tablespoons margarine	
½ cup raisins and almonds,	
chopped	

Boil the noodles in the water with the salt for 7–8 minutes. Drain and mix with the remaining ingredients. Bake, in a well-buttered pan, in a 400° oven for about three-quarters of an hour, or until golden-tipped on top. (Serves 4–6.)

LOKSHEN KUGEL
(DAIRY NOODLE KUGEL) *Shavuot*

When Marco Polo left Venice to travel half the world (before the days of El Al jets!) by caravan, he was as strongly attracted by the wealth of exotic dishes as by the priceless jewels of the Far East. It was from C' ina that Marco Polo brought pasta and taught the Italians the art of making it. Since then macaroni, noodles, lokshen, and itriot, have become favorite dishes throughout most of the world.

1 pound medium-width
   egg noodles
1 tablespoon butter
2 cups milk
2 eggs

½ cup sugar
1 teaspoon salt
¼ cup sultana raisins
1 teaspoon vanilla

Parboil the noodles in plenty of water. Drain (do not rinse). Mix all the remaining ingredients and stir in the noodles. Bake in a well-buttered casserole in a 350° oven until the kugel is done (about 30 minutes). (Serves 6.)

PASSOVER CARROT KUGEL
Passover

½ cup margarine
5 tablespoons matzo meal
¼ cup potato flour
½ cup red wine
2 cups grated raw carrot
¼ cup raisins

½ cup chopped dates
½ cup sugar
1 teaspoon cinnamon and
   ginger, mixed
grated rind of 1 lemon

Cream the margarine and matzo meal. Dissolve the potato flour in the wine. Mix all the ingredients together. Put into a well-greased casserole and bake in a 375° oven for about 1 hour. (Serves 4–6.)

BETTER-THAN-FIG KUGEL
Rosh Hashana

2 cups flour
2 eggs
½ cup margarine
   cloves, whole
   white wine

Filling

½ cup raisins
½ cup chopped nuts
¼ cup sugar
½ teaspoon cinnamon
   dash of cloves and
   allspice

Mix the flour, eggs, and margarine to make a dough. Roll into small balls. Mix all the filling ingredients and, making a dent in each ball, pack in some filling. Shape each ball like a fig and tuck a clove in the "stem" end of the mock fig. Fit the "figs" into a very well buttered baking dish that has been sprinkled with sugar. When all the "figs" have been put into the dish in rows, bake in a 375° oven 20–25 minutes, or until golden. When the dish is done, baste all the "figs" with the white wine and serve hot. (Serves 6–8.)

EL AL'S BIBLICAL KUGEL *Independence Day*

". . . a land of wheat and barley, and vines and fig trees and pomegranates; a land of olive trees and honey. . . ."
— *Deuteronomy 8:8*

½ cup pearl barley
1 cup self-rising flour
2 cups raisins
2 cups dates
½ cup figs
½ cup candied citrus
    peels
½ cup chopped almonds
½ cup sugar
2 teaspoons cinnamon
½ teaspoon ginger

½ teaspoon cloves or
    allspice
1½ teaspoons salt
½ cup olive oil
1 cup honey
3 eggs
1 cup pomegranate syrup
    (or other light fruit
    syrup)
brandy

Cook the barley, in water to cover, on low heat about an hour. Sift the flour over the chopped fruit and nuts. Mix together the remaining ingredients and then add to the floured fruit and barley. Pour into greased molds, each of them two-thirds full. Cover and put into a steamer. Surround with boiling water and steam from four to eight hours (depending on the size of the molds). This kugel keeps for weeks in the refrigerator and is excellent warmed over. Serve with lemon sauce, or pour on brandy and ignite it. (Serves 10–12.)

APFELSCHALET—DEEP APPLE KUGEL *Yom Kippur*

This dish is very much like a deep apple pie and is therefore sometimes referred to as "Apfelschalet." As a dessert it is eaten hot. A typical Shabbat dish that can be cooked overnight, it is a traditional pre-fast Yom Kippur dessert in Switzerland.

The Pastry

3 cups flour, sifted
1 cup margarine or suet
4 tablespoons sugar
    rind and juice of 1 lemon
2 egg yolks
4 tablespoons water

The Filling

3 pounds apples
½ cup brown or white sugar
½ teaspoon cinnamon
    peel and juice of
    ½ lemon
½ cup raisins
2 tablespoons flour
¼ cup chopped almonds

Mix all the ingredients for the pastry and roll out. Cover the sides and bottom of a deep pie dish or casserole with the pastry. Peel the apples and cut into thin sections. Dust with the sugar and cinnamon and sprinkle with the rind and lemon juice. Wash the raisins and roll in the flour. Then add, with the nuts, to the filling mixture and put it into the pastry. Cover with more pastry dough, and prick with a fork. Dab the top with margarine. Bake in a 350° oven for about an hour. (Serves 8–10.)

NOTE: The kugel can be baked overnight if the oven is at its lowest heat.

Tu Besh'vat
APFEL KUGEL MET WAATZ—APPLE KUGEL WITH WHEAT

This Dutch kugel is something very special. It is served on Shabbat Beshalach and can therefore cook overnight in a warming oven. Pearl barley can be substituted for wheat, if you wish.

3 pounds apples	or 1 teaspoon ginger powder
1½ cups sugar (part brown, if desired)	¾ cup almonds
2 teaspoons cinnamon	½ pound chopped suet or margarine
¼ teaspoon salt	1½ cups lukewarm water
1 teaspoon grated lemon peel	⅓ cup cracked wheat (burghul)
4 cups flour	red wine (optional)
1 cup raisins	
4 ounces preserved ginger	

Peel and slice the apples. Line an iron pot or deep casserole with the fruit. Sprinkle with half the sugar and dust with half the cinnamon, salt, and lemon peel. Sift the flour over the raisins. Add the ginger, remaining sugar, cinnamon, salt, and lemon peel, nuts, and suet. Put the mixture into the nest of apples and cover with more apple slices, so that the filling is completely hidden. Pour the lukewarm water around the kugel, covering it entirely. Sprinkle the wheat over the top. Cover tightly and simmer for at least 2 hours, and then complete the cooking in a 250° oven for 2 hours or more. Water (or red wine) may have to be added from time to time, as the kugel must cook rather than bake. It improves with keeping and recooking for about a week. (Serves 8.)

PASSOVER APPLE KUGEL   *Passover*

*Sholem Aleichem tells a story of a Jewish schoolmaster finally
getting home for Passover, when he would traditionally sit among
the cushions at the head of the table, like a king. En route he sent
a telegram to his wife, and was arrested at the station on arrival. For the telegram read: "I have money. Prepare the kugel
and kugelach. I am coming to reign." In Yiddish "kugel" means
a baked or boiled pudding, and "kugelach" are individual little
kugels—festival favorites. But in German they mean "cannon-
ball" and "bullets."*

4 large apples	4 eggs, separated
4 tablespoons sugar	1½ tablespoons matzo
1 teaspoon cinnamon	meal
juice of ½ lemon	½ cup almonds

Slice the apples thin and add the sugar, cinnamon, and lemon
juice. Then add the egg yolks, well-beaten, matzo meal, and
almonds. Beat the egg whites stiffly and fold in. Pour into a well-
greased pan and bake in a 350° oven 45 minutes. (Serves 6.)

THE OLDEST SHABBAT KUGEL   *Shabbat*

*Many writings of the Middle Ages refer to the kugel as casually
as to bread, for it was an established Sabbath dish. Since then
the kugel has been changed to include fruits and nuts and to be
made of ingredients other than bread. A century ago Saphir
wrote of the dish: "Something goes into it besides flour and fat,
an elusive something emanating from the oven itself and pene-
trating into the kugel." For the Shabbat kugel cooked for about
twenty hours in the baker's oven.*

6 white rolls	1 teaspoon cinnamon
½ pound chicken fat or suet	½ teaspoon salt
½ cup sugar	2 tablespoons soup or
2 eggs, beaten	water
rind of 1 lemon, grated	fresh fruit, if desired

Soak the rolls in water, squeeze out the water and crumble them.
Mix with all the remaining ingredients and put into a greased
heavy pot or earthen casserole. Cover tightly and bake in a 225°
oven from just before sundown on Friday until Sabbath midday.
The warm kugel will be crisp on the outside and mellow within.
(Serves 4–6.)

NOODLE FANZ

Succot

This is a rich dessert called "fanz" which is so "constructed" with povidle (plum jam), nuts, and poppy seed, as to resemble the succah, the booth or tabernacle, lacy and open at the top like the boughs through which one sees the sky.

½ *pound broad noodles*	½ *cup sugar*
2 *cups milk*	⅓ *cup poppy seed*
3 *egg yolks, beaten*	½ *cup chopped nuts*
½ *cup butter*	½ *cup plum jam (povidle)*
3 *stiffly beaten egg whites*	
2 *large apples, sliced*	
very thin	

Cook the noodles in the milk 9 minutes. Cool. Add the egg yolks and butter and stir, then fold in the stiffly beaten egg whites. Sprinkle the apples with the sugar. In a buttered baking dish alternate layers of the noodles with layers of sugared apples, poppy seed, chopped nuts, and jam. Top with a lattice of noodles so that the fruit, poppy seed, nuts, and jam show through. Bake in a 350° oven 30 minutes. (Serves 4–6.)

Rosh Hashana
CHARLOTTE AUX POMMES—APPLE CHARLOTTE

Princess Elizabeth-Charlotte of France, daughter-in-law of Louis XIV, was much loved and soon came to be called "Liese-Lotte." This succulent dish was named for her. The original calls for buttered bread crusts to be used as pastry to encase the filling, but the Jews of France, and those from France who have come to Israel, make it in the following manner on Rosh Hashana and on all festive occasions.

8 *slices challah bread*	1 *cup sugar*
4 *eggs, separated*	*dash of cinnamon*
4 *tablespoons cooking oil*	6 *tablespoons raisins*
2 *pounds apples*	*juice and rind of*
pinch of salt	1 *lemon*
½ *cup rum*	¼ *cup chopped almonds*

Soak the bread in water and squeeze out the liquid. Add the egg yolks and remaining ingredients, folding in the stiffly beaten egg whites last. Bake in a well-greased casserole in a 375° oven for about an hour. Serve warm, either plain or with a wine sauce. (Serves 6.)

SABBATH SEVEN-LAYER SHALET *Shabbat*

"Shalet" or "cholent" was a well-known Jewish dish as long ago as the twelfth century. As the dish was kept hot by slowly cooking overnight, some say that the name came from "chald" or "chaud," which in French means "hot." Others say the word comes from the German "Shul ende" (end of synagogue) as the dish was eaten when the family returned home from morning services. The seven-layer shalet is symbolic of the seventh day, the day of rest. This dessert "shalet" may well be the mother of the "Charlottes" and is quite different from the overnight-cooked bean-meat "shalet."

1 *recipe any pastry dough*
    (*see* Index)
any seven kinds of fillings
    (*fruits or nuts*)

sugar, spices for sprinkling
margarine

Roll out any desired pastry dough (whether it be flaky, noodle, yeast or cookie dough does not matter) into eight circles or rectangles. Place the bottom layer into a well-greased baking dish. Sprinkle it with sugar, spices, and any desired fruit and dab well with margarine. Fill each layer with a different filling of fruits and nuts, or if you prefer, with the same filling. The top of the shalet should be of pastry. Pour water along the edge of the shalet, cover closely, and put in a 225° oven to bake overnight. This can also be made on low heat on top of the range.

PEAR SHALET *Shabbat*

Heinrich Heine, a convert from Judaism to Christianity, was quite a satiric philosopher, for he wrote: "This dish (shalet) is superior and how regrettable that the Christian Church, which adopted so many good things from Judaism, failed to include the schalet! . . . When that will happen the Jews will adopt Christianity out of conviction . . . for it is shalet and shalet alone that binds them to their ancient faith."

The Pastry
  4 cups flour, sifted
  1 egg
  4 tablespoons breadcrumbs
  1 cup sugar
    pinch of salt
  1 cup water
  ½ cup suet or margarine
  2 tablespoons cooking oil

The Filling
  10 small or 6 large pears
    red wine to cover
    dash of cinnamon
    sugar to taste

Mix the pastry ingredients (except the oil) and roll out to a thickness of ½ inch. Put the oil into a deep casserole, fit in the dough, and bake in 375° oven 20 minutes.

Meanwhile, cook the pears, halved or quartered, in just enough wine to cover them, with cinnamon and sugar. When the pastry is almost done, moisten with the pear sauce and fill with the pears. Bake in a 225° oven about 3 hours. Serve warm. (Serves 6–8.)

TAMBOUR—ALSATIAN APPLE LAYER PUDDING   *Purim*

This dish, between a pudding, cake, and pie, reminds one of the fruit dishes of the Middle Ages in England, when "ovens" first came into use. An oven was a big space in a thick wall with an iron door. Bundles of faggots were put inside and lit. When all the sticks burned out the door was opened and the ashes raked to one side. Then the baking was put in and the door was shut, and by the time the oven walls had cooled, the puddings, pies, cakes, or bread were baked. Heavy metal pots were used, often first heated right on the flame.

½ cup margarine   ½ cup sugar

The Pastry (Muerbe Teig)   *The Filling*

¾ cup margarine   2 pounds apples, sliced
3 cups flour, sifted   1 cup brown sugar
3 tablespoons sugar
3 egg yolks
  dash of salt

Grease a heavy iron pan with the ½ cup margarine and sprinkle with the ½ cup sugar. Mix all the Muerbe Teig (or any other pastry) ingredients together and roll out to a thickness of about ¼ inch. Line the bottom and sides of the pan with this dough. Put in a layer of the apple slices and sprinkle with brown sugar. Put in another layer of pastry. Follow with another layer of filling, until all the dough and filling are used up. The top should be pastry. Put the pan over heat on top of the stove, so the bottom will caramelize a bit. After the pot is hot and the cooking can be detected by the aroma, remove from heat. Carefully turn the pudding out into a plate and then back into the casserole with a little more sugar and margarine for caramelizing the layer that was originally on the top. Then bake in a 375° oven about 1¼ hours, until the house is filled with the perfume of the pudding. (Serves 6.)

SERVIETTEN KNOEDEL—BAG PUDDING *Ju Besh'vat*

½ loaf stale bread, white
    or dark
2 tablespoons fat
5 eggs
1 cup sugar

2 tablespoons chopped suet
  juice and rind of
    1 lemon
½ cup raisins or other
    dried fruit

Soak the bread in water and squeeze out thoroughly. Heat the fat, and when hot, add the bread, stirring until smooth and dry. Beat the eggs, and add the bread and the remaining ingredients. Grease a very large napkin or bag, place the pudding in it, and tie up. Be sure to leave plenty of room for the pudding to swell. Put the bag in boiling water and cook for 2 to 3 hours. Serve hot, with any favored dessert sauce. (Serves 6–8.)

ASHURE—NOAH'S PUDDING *Shavuot*

When Noah's Ark came to rest on Mount Ararat in Turkey, it was certainly occasion for a celebration. But there were not enough supplies left for a proper feast and so the scraps were put together, and lo and behold, this wonderful ashure (so goes the legend) was created. It takes a lot of preparation (and can be simplified by omitting the legumes and using extra rice) but the results are interesting.

7 tablespoons rice
4 tablespoons chick-peas
6 tablespoons dried beans
1 cup burghul (cracked
    wheat)
8 quarts water
3 cups milk
1 cup sugar

½ cup dried apricots
1 cup dried figs
¼ cup currants
1 cup raisins
½ cup rose water
1 cup blanched almonds
1 tablespoon halved walnut
    meats

Soak the rice, chick-peas, and beans overnight, each in a separate bowl. Put the burghul and rice, beans, and chick-peas in a very large saucepan, cover with the water, and cook for 6 hours, then put through a strainer. To the pulpy liquid add the milk and sugar and continue cooking until the mixture is like a thick soup. Wash the fruits, cut into small pieces, and add. Cook until the mixture is further thickened and all the fruit soft. Add the rose water. Remove from heat and add the almonds and walnuts. Pour into individual glasses and cool. The result is a thin custard, very rich, which may not appeal greatly to Western tastes. (Serves 8–10.)

MATZO KUGEL IN WINE   *Passover*

8 *matzos*	½ *cup walnuts or pecans*
1½ *cups rosé wine*	½ *cup pine nuts*
water as required	1 *cup sugar*
8 *tablespoons melted*	*cinnamon*
margarine	6 *egg whites, stiffly*
½ *cup raisins*	*beaten*

Soak the matzos in ¾ cup of the wine diluted with just enough
water to soften all the matzos. In a buttered casserole put alternate layers of matzos, drizzled with melted margarine, and the
raisins and nuts mixed, sprinkled with sugar and cinnamon. Put
a layer of beaten egg white on top of the raisins and nuts. Continue in this way, using up all the matzos, fruit and nut mixture,
and egg white, to the top of the casserole. Bake in a 375° oven
for 30 minutes, then pour on the remaining ¾ cup of wine and
return to the oven for a few minutes. Serve, if you wish, with
château sauce (*see* Index for recipe for Apples Château). (Serves
8–10.)

CITRUS-NUT KAESEL   *Passover*

*The custom of eating nuts on Passover goes back to the days of
Rabbi Akiba in the second century. To keep children at the Seder
from falling asleep as a result of the wine in the four cups, nuts
were given to them to crack and eat, and keep their interest in
the service keen. On this Festival the Song of Solomon is read,
telling of Solomon's visit to the garden of nuts, to see the fruits
of the valley.*

1 *large orange*	4 *tablespoons matzo meal*
1 *large lemon*	6 *tablespoons ground*
4 *eggs*	*walnuts*
⅔ *cup sugar*	

Put the orange and lemon, in their skins, into hot water. Bring
to the boil. Drain, and change the water. Repeat this process
three times and then cook the fruit until tender. Cut the orange
and lemon open and let them cool. Remove the seeds and then
put the fruit (skin, rind, pulp and all) through a meat grinder.
Beat the eggs with the sugar and add the matzo meal and nuts.
The mixture should be foamy. Add the fruit. Put into a greased
casserole and bake in a 375° oven about 45 minutes. Serve hot or
cold. (Serves 4.)

SHABBAT PASHDIDA   *Shabbat*

An old legend tells of a little Jewish boy captured by brigands in Germany on a Friday night. He wept so much and so loud for his Sabbath pashdida that his cries were heard by his seekers; whereupon the boy was discovered and ransomed. The "pashdida" was a favorite Sabbath dish in central Europe in the Middle Ages, and the word "pasteten" (meaning "pastries") has remained in Germany, while the word "pashdida" (for baked puddings) is in the Hebrew language today. The dish is much like the German snitz kloes or hutzle, but kept warm overnight in order to avoid cooking on the Sabbath.

4 cups dry breadcrumbs	salt to taste
½ pound chopped suet	dash of ginger
3 eggs	sprinkling of cinnamon
1 cup sugar (white or brown)	2 cups dried fruit or 4 cups fresh fruit
½ cup flour	2 cups water
1 tablespoon baking powder	

Mix the breadcrumbs, suet, eggs, sugar, flour, baking powder, salt, and spices, and form into a ball. Put the fruit and water in a heavy pot and cook. Place the ball of crumb mixture on a heatproof plate and set it on the fruit. Bring to a boil, reduce heat, and simmer, tightly covered, on very low heat or in a 225° oven, overnight. (Serves 8.)

TURKISH DELIGHT FLADEN— FLADEN RAHAT EL HALKUM   *Succot*

Rahat el Halkum is the gelatinous-starchy luscious sweetmeat known as Turkish delight throughout the world. In Israel it is often put into dried-fruit flaky strudels and into the Succot–Simhat Torah fladen. It is very rich, very wonderful in small pieces.

The Pastry	*The First Filling*
4 cups flour	2 cups dates
3 teaspoons baking powder	¾ cup brown sugar
1 cup sugar	½ cup water
1 cup butter	½ cup chopped nuts
1 egg	juice and rind of
milk	½ lemon

The Second Filling

milk
dash of cinnamon
about 2 cups
   Turkish delight
     (*see* Index)

For the pastry, sift the flour, baking powder, and sugar together. Cut in the butter. Add to the mixture the egg, beaten in a cup and with enough milk added to fill the cup. Divide into three equal parts and roll each part out thin. Spread one sheet of dough on the bottom of a buttered baking pan and cover with the following.

For the filling, cook the dates, brown sugar, and water for 5 minutes. Remove from heat and add the chopped nuts and lemon juice and rind. Spread this mixture on the bottom pastry and cover with another sheet of pastry. Moisten the pastry with a little milk and sprinkle with cinnamon. Cover with Turkish delight, then cover with the top pastry. Bake in a 300° oven for 1½ hours. The fladen comes out like a solid fruit cake.

KIRSCH AUFLAUF—CHERRY SOUFFLÉ *Rosh Hashana*

This light yet nourishing soufflé is a Swiss favorite for Rosh Hashana, when one may cook. There is no symbolism attached to this dish; it is merely so very good, and easy to make at the harvest of the cherry crop.

½ cup butter	1 teaspoon cinnamon
½ cup sifted flour	3 cups pitted fresh or
3 cups milk or water	stewed cherries, well
4 eggs, separated	drained
½ cup sugar	cherry brandy or kirsch

Melt butter. Stir in flour smoothly. Add milk and cook in a double boiler or over low heat until thick. Beat in the electric mixer, then cool. When cool, beat in the egg yolks, sugar, and spice, and then fold in the stiffly beaten egg whites and the cherries. Put into a buttered angel-food pan or soufflé dish and bake in a 375° oven until golden brown on top (35–40 minutes). Serve with a little kirsch or cherry brandy. (Serves 4–6.)

ROLY-POLY SOUFFLÉ

Succot

Beware of this soufflé—it's so good you'll eat too much of it! I first had it on an Israeli ship.

1 cup flour	1 teaspoon vanilla
⅔ cup margarine	½ cup candied fruit peels,
½ cup sugar	diced
1 cup water	pinch of salt
8 egg yolks	8 egg whites, beaten stiff
1 teaspoon grated lemon	with ⅓ cup sugar
rind	

Mix the flour, margarine, and sugar into a smooth paste. Bring the water to the boil, add the paste, and mix on very low heat until smooth. After cooling, add the egg yolks one at a time, mixing after each addition. Add the lemon rind, vanilla, candied peels, and salt. Fold in the egg whites. Pile into a greased and sugared pudding mold. Put into a pan of hot water and bake in a 375° oven for 45 minutes. Unmold and serve at once with any dessert sauce (*see* Index). Or, if you like, you can dilute apricot jam with fruit juice, warm it somewhat, and use as a sauce. (Serves 6.)

BANANA SOUFFLÉ

Shavuot

Mrs. Blanche Cohen, one of the runners-up in the finals of Israel's Culinary Contest, added just the needed zest in this American dish. Hopes are high that the growing popularity of this recipe may save Israel from burying more of its surplus banana crop!

5 large firm bananas	3 egg yolks, beaten thick
1½ tablespoons butter	pinch of salt
½ cup sugar	¼ teaspoon cream of
⅓ cup white wine	tartar
1 tablespoon lemon juice	3 egg whites, beaten stiff
1 tablespoon orange rind	
zest	

Boil the bananas in their skins. When tender (about 10 minutes), remove the skins and put the fruit through a sieve. Add the butter and sugar to the hot pulp and mix well. Add the wine, lemon juice and rind, beaten egg yolks, and salt and beat all together. Add the cream of tartar to the egg whites and fold in. Place the mixture in a buttered form and bake in a 350° oven 25 minutes. (Serves 4.)

FLADEN OR FLUDEN   *Succot*

If any dessert is symbolic of the plentiful harvest, it is this one, with its row upon row of fruits and nuts. It is sometimes made of the thinnest strudel dough, so that one can hardly tell where a fruit layer begins or ends, or it may have this more substantial pastry. The dish was already a traditional one of Judeo-German cooking in the twelfth century!

The Pastry

4 cups flour, sifted
3 teaspoons baking powder
1 cup sugar
¼ cup cooking oil
2 eggs, beaten
⅓ cup water

The Filling

1 cup sugar
1 teaspoon cinnamon
1 cup chopped nuts
⅔ cup apricot jam
1 cup shredded coconut
½ cup raisins
3 apples, sliced

For the pastry, sift the flour, baking powder and sugar. Add the oil, eggs, and water and mix a little. Divide the dough into five parts (one of them somewhat larger than the others). Roll out each part. Place the largest piece in a baking pan, covering the sides and bottom. Mix filling ingredients; spread one-fourth of the filling ingredients on the dough. Fit in the next piece of dough and proceed with the layering until all ingredients are used up. Sprinkle the top pastry with a little sugar and spice and bake in 300° oven about 1½ hours. Cut into serving pieces.

BANANA ICE CREAM WHIP   *Shavuot*

2 medium bananas
milk as needed
1 package chocolate ice cream mix

¾ cup heavy cream
grated chocolate or whipped cream, for topping

Mash the bananas and put into a cup. Fill to the top with enough milk to make 1 cupful. Stir vigorously in a bowl with the ice cream mix. Whip the cream until stiff and fold into banana mixture. Pour into refrigerator trays and freeze until firm. Serve with a topping of grated chocolate or whipped cream. (Serves 4.)

TUVIA'S BAVARIAN CREAM

4 cups hulled strawberries
1 cup sugar
3 teaspoons powdered gelatin
3 tablespoons boiling water
1 tablespoon lemon juice

2 cups heavy cream, whipped
½ package strawberry jelly
  powder
¾ cup boiling water

Slice berries and sprinkle with 1 cup sugar. Soak gelatin in 3 tablespoons water and then dissolve in 3 tablespoons boiling water. Stir in the berries and sugar mixture. Add lemon juice. Refrigerate until thick, almost set, then stir in the whipped cream. Put into a mould or sherbet glasses. When this mixture is firm, dissolve the strawberry jelly powder with the ¾ cup boiling water. Cool, then use it to top the strawberry mould. Chill well. (Serve 8.)

APRICOT SHERBET   *Passover*

"Boukra fil mish-mish" literally means "Tomorrow, when the apricots are ripe" in Arabic. Its application however, could better be translated as "Maybe one day, we'll see." Jews from Arab lands living in Israel use the phrase as an idiom.

2 cups apricots
1½ cups water
¾ cup sugar

2 egg whites, beaten stiff
½ cup sweet cream,
  whipped

Peel apricots, remove stones, and cook to a pulp in the water. Add the sugar (more if apricots are not very sweet) and cook until rather thick and syrupy. Cool. Put into trays and freeze until firm. Remove and beat until light, add the egg whites and whipped cream and refreeze to ice cream consistency. (Serves 6.)

AVOCADO VELVET ICE CREAM   *Shavuot*

This is a sour-cream ice cream unique in flavor. The abundant avocado is so new to Israel's agriculture that it hasn't yet been given a Hebrew name!

1 cup mashed avocado
  juice of 1 lemon
1 package vanilla ice cream
  mix

1 cup sour cream
lemon squash (syrup)
  mixed with lemon juice,
  for topping

Mash the ripe avocado and cover at once with the lemon juice. Mix in the ice cream mix and then add the sour cream. Whip up to a smooth mixture and freeze at the coldest temperature of the refrigerator. Top with a spoonful of lemon squash to which a few drops of fresh lemon juice have been added. (Serves 4.)

LEMON SHERBET *Shavuot*

It is no wonder that ice cream was invented in the Mediterranean basin, where the sun shines warmly for so many months a year. The Italians created the dish; Catherine de' Medici introduced it to France. Packaged ice cream powder, packaged bricks in the shops, and cones at every kiosk have made it a favorite dish in Israel.

1¾ cups sugar
  grated rind of ½ lemon

½ cup lemon juice
4 cups milk

It is vital that this sherbet be mixed in the order listed above. If you add the ingredients differently you will finish up with cheese. So, mix in the above order and freeze. It is the lightest, most refreshing of all summer ices. (Serves 6.)

PAREVE LEMON ICE CREAM *Passover*

2 eggs
2 tablespoons sugar
  juice of 2 lemons

1 cup water
1 cup lemon squash
  (syrup)

Put the eggs, sugar, and lemon juice into the top of a double boiler. As the mixture cooks over boiling water, beat until creamy. Mix the water with the lemon squash and add. Cool. Put into the refrigerator to freeze at the coldest setting. When hard around the edges, remove from the trays. Whip up well and re-freeze. (Serves 4.)

STRAWBERRY ICE CREAM MOUSSE *Shavuot*

1½ cups fresh strawberries
1 cup milk
1 package ice cream mix

2 egg whites
½ cup heavy cream

Turn the temperature of the refrigerator to its coldest point. Crush the strawberries. Mix the milk with the ice cream mix and stir in the berries. Beat the egg whites until stiff and fold into the berry mixture. Whip the cream and fold in. Pour into freezing trays, and when half firm, stir once in the tray and continue to freeze until firm. (Serves 4.)

MOCHA DATE ICE CREAM

Shavuot

Soft rich dates make this ice cream dish chewy and sweet in a surprise of taste.

1 cup cold milk
1 package mocha ice cream
    mix

½ cup heavy cream,
    whipped
15 dates, cut up
    shredded coconut

Stir the milk into the ice cream mix. Freeze until the edges begin to harden. Remove from the tray and beat. Fold in the whipped cream and chopped dates. Freeze until firm. Serve with a topping of shredded coconut. (Serves 4.)

ORANGE ICE CREAM

Shavuot

Among the many wonderful things that Marco Polo brought back with him from the Far East was a recipe for "milk ice" from Japan. That perhaps gave the Italians the fillip to proceed in their making of "ices," adding milk and cream, so that today they have the most lavish variety of ice creams in the world.

2½ cups strained orange
    juice
    juice of 1 lemon

1¼ cups sugar
3 cups whipping cream

Combine the juices with the sugar and let stand for 15 minutes, stirring from time to time so that the sugar will dissolve. Whip the cream stiff. Stir the juice into the whipped cream (not the cream into the juice as it may curdle). Pour into refrigerator trays and freeze. Stir two or three times during freezing, but do not beat. (Serves 6.)

ORANGE MILK SHERBET

Shavuot

This ice cream is so light and so refreshing it's almost unbelievable.

1 cup fine sugar
2 cups milk

juice of 2 oranges
juice of 1 lemon

In order to dissolve the sugar it will be necessary to heat it with the milk. Set aside to cool, then put into refrigerator tray. When it begins to harden at the edges, remove to a cold mixing bowl, add the fruit juices gradually and beat with electric beater until fluffy. Return to the tray and freeze. (Serves 4.)

PEACHY ALMOND ICE CREAM   *Succot*

Peaches, pears, or guavas can be used in making this refreshing ice cream.

1 package almond ice
   cream mix
1 cup cold milk
½ cup whipped cream
1½ cups sieved peaches,
   pears, or guavas

4 tablespoons fine sugar
3 peaches, pears, or
   guavas, halved
   slivered almonds

Prepare the almond ice cream by combining the mix with the milk. Freeze until the edges begin to harden. Remove and beat. Fold in the whipped cream and sieved fruit mixed with the sugar. Put to freeze until firm. Serve a scoop of this ice cream on a halved fruit and top with slivered almonds. (Serves 6.)

NON-CREAM PAREVE ICE CREAM   *Purim*

This recipe is the creation of the Accadia Hotel's chef Shmuel Werner who has dubbed it "Bombe Sarah Bernhardt" for the great actress. Without the special emulsifier used by him, the ice cream is hard to make, but worth the effort. It is as creamy as if it were made of pure cream, but can be eaten at meat meals. This recipe is for 25 servings.

1 pound 7 ounces
   margarine
3¼ cups water
10 egg yolks
1 cup sugar

2 cups chopped nuts
   (optional)
9 ounces chocolate, melted
1 whole egg

Whirl the margarine in a blender, adding water gradually until it is light and fluffy. In an electric mixer, whip the egg yolks and beat in the sugar gradually. Add the nuts and chocolate. Put in the top of a double boiler and cook, whipping constantly for 3 minutes. Do not allow to boil. Remove from heat and fold in the margarine mixture. Whip the whole egg and fold it in at the last. Put into the freezer (do not stir) at lowest setting and freeze. (Makes 4 trays [25 servings].)

STRAWBERRY ICE *Passover*

Ices that do not contain any milk or other dairy products may be taken as dessert at the end of meat meals.

4 cups strawberries
1½ cups sugar

2 tablespoons lemon juice
2 egg whites

Mash the strawberries and mix the pulp with the sugar and lemon juice. Beat the egg whites until stiff and fold in. Freeze until almost stiff. Stir with a fork once or twice, or better still, remove and beat up with a rotary beater and then freeze until firm. (Serves 4–6.)

GELATO DI ZABAGLIONE—ITALIAN ICE CREAM *Shavuot*

Slave runners, in the days of the great glory of Rome, used to rush snow and ice down from the mountains to freeze pomegranate juice; this may have been the first step in the making of ice cream. The Italians developed the art and still make the most fabulous combinations—the bisque tortonis and tutti fruttis. This one, based on their famous zabaglione, is easy to make at home.

8 egg yolks
8 tablespoons sugar

1 cup muscatel or other
   sweet white wine
2 cups heavy cream

Beat the egg yolks and sugar, then beat in the wine. Cook over hot water, stirring constantly, until the mixture is quite thick (about 5 minutes). Cool the zabaglione over ice, beating it all the time. Whip the cream, stir into the cooler egg mixture, and freeze in trays. (Serves 6.)

MELON SUNDAE *Independence Day*

In Israel a new variety of melon called "yokneam" has been developed, with a peach-pineapple-melon flavor that is outstanding, but cantaloupe can be used for this dish.

2 cantaloupes
8 balls vanilla ice cream
   juice of ½ lemon

strawberries
fresh mint

Chill the melons and cut into quarters. Drizzle with lemon juice. Put a ball of ice cream on each piece, garnish with fresh strawberries and sprigs of mint. (Serves 8.)

CHOCOLATE PARFAIT   *Shavuot*

chocolate ice cream   chocolate sauce
peppermint candies   whipped cream
salted peanuts   sprigs of mint

Into a tall glass put a scoop of chocolate ice cream and top with crushed peppermints. Put on another scoop of ice cream and top with salted peanuts. Pour chocolate sauce over this. Garnish with a dab of whipped cream and a sprig of mint.

STRAWBERRY PARFAIT PIE   *Shavuot*

The Filling   *The Crust*

1 package strawberry-   1½ cups cookie crumbs
   flavored gelatin   ½ cup margarine
                                  2 tablespoons sugar
1 cup hot water
2 cups vanilla ice cream
1 cup sliced, sugared
   strawberries

For the filling, mix the gelatin and hot water. Add the ice cream slowly and stir until melted. Chill until thick but not yet set. Fold in the sliced berries.

   For the crust, mix the cookie crumbs, margarine, and sugar and pat into a pie pan. Put the gelatin mixture into the crust. This parfait becomes a "solid pudding" very quickly. (Serves 4–6.)

MUESLI PORRIDGE   *Shavuot*

5 tablespoons honey or   ½ cup chopped nuts
   sugar   2 cups fresh fruits, such as
½ cup raisins   bananas, berries, peaches,
2 cups raw oatmeal   pears, oranges, etc.
2 cups milk   2 cups light sour cream

Mix the honey or sugar, raisins, oatmeal, and milk and refrigerate for a few hours (overnight is best if you want it for breakfast on a hot summer morning). Just before serving, stir in the remaining ingredients. (Serves 6–8.)

FRUITED COUSCOUS—EL MISTOUPHA *Tu Besh'vat*

1 cup boiling water
½ teaspoon salt
1 pound semolina
20 pitted dates
20 almonds
1 cup nuts
   grated rind of 1 orange

1 cup raisins or currants
½ cup sugar
4 tablespoons olive oil
   juice of 1 orange
1 teaspoon vanilla or
   curaçao
4 tablespoons raisins

Pour the boiling water, with the salt, over the semolina and stir in one direction. Place in a sieve over rapidly boiling water and steam for 30 minutes, stirring once or twice. Fill the dates with whole almonds and put on top of the semolina to soften. Meanwhile, pound or grind together the nuts, orange rind, raisins or currants, sugar, and olive oil. Add the orange juice and flavoring. When the couscous is done, fold in the pounded fruits and form into the shape of a pyramid. Garnish with the stuffed dates and a sprinkling of raisins. (Serves 6–8.)

SEMOLINA SURPRISE *Shabbat*

Semolina is called "cream of wheat" in the U.S.A. and is perhaps the "fat of the kidneys of wheat" referred to in the Bible (Deuteronomy 32:14). It is a product resulting from the milling of the finest flour. This dish—made of almost raw semolina—is a refreshing surprise, and therefore called by that name in Israel.

1½ cups water
1½ cups orange juice
   (or water)
¾ cup semolina

   grated rind of 3 lemons
1 cup sugar
½ cup lemon juice

Boil the water. Mix the orange juice (or water) with the semolina and add to boiling water. Stir and bring just to the boil. Put into the mixer, add the remaining ingredients, and whip until mixture has cooled off. Serve chilled. (Serves 4.)

SUFFAH—GREEK WHEAT DESSERT *Tu Besh'vat*

1 cup cracked wheat
   (burghul)
4 figs, chopped
6 dates, chopped
½ cup raisins

½ cup broken walnuts
½ cup pomegranate seeds
   (optional)
2 tablespoons honey
1 cup white wine, chilled

Boil the wheat until tender, then stir in the fruits. Cool. Serve chilled, with a dressing of honey mixed with white wine. (Serves 4–6.)

TRIGO KOTCHO—WHEAT AND FRUIT   *Tu Besh'vat*

What better symbols than wheat—the staff of life—and raisins and figs—the fruits of Biblical promise—are there for the New Year of the Trees, Israel's Arbor Day? This dish comes from Turkey, but it is Sephardic in origin.

1 cup sugar	3 tablespoons pine nuts
1 cup water	1 tablespoon rose water
1 cup cracked wheat	(or other essence)
1 cup chopped dried figs	1 teaspoon cinnamon
½ cup raisins	

Boil the sugar and water 2–3 minutes. Add this syrup to the wheat and heat through. Cook gently until the wheat has swollen several times in size. Stir in the remaining ingredients and serve hot or cold on Tu Besh'vat. (Serves 4–6.)

TEL KADAYIF CAKES   *Hanuka*

In Turkey, the general population makes tel kadayif in the form of a large pie. The Turkish Jews serve it on Hanuka (and have introduced the dish to Israel) with the noodles shaped into flat round cakes. Most industrious Jewish housewives prepare their own vermicelli and use it before it is dry (so that the process of dampening is not necessary, as in the following recipe). Shredded wheat may also be used in place of vermicelli in this recipe.

¾ pound fine vermicelli	1½ cups melted butter
or shredded wheat	2¾ cups sugar
1 cup or more chopped	3 cups milk
nuts	

Dip the vermicelli into boiling water and drain at once. Wrap in waxed paper and refrigerate overnight. Butter a pan and form each vermicelli skein into a round, filling the center with chopped nuts. Pour the melted butter over these cakes and then cover with a plate to press down the vermicelli. Remove the plate and bake in a 375° oven for about 30 minutes, or until crisp. Meanwhile, cook the sugar and milk together 5 minutes. When the tel kadayif in the oven is crisp, take it out and drain off the butter. Pour the milk syrup over the hot cakes, and when cool, put a plate over them and turn them over. (Serves 4–6.)

CABBAGE STRUDEL (SWEET OR SAVORY)   *Succot*

A poor man who had heard of strudel asked his wife to make some.
   "But we have no apples, or money to buy them," she said.
   "So make it without apples," he said.
   "We have no eggs either."
   "So leave out the eggs," he said.
   "And what about the sugar and the raisins?"
   Well, his wife used cabbage and dough, and when her husband ate it he remarked, "I wonder why rich people like strudel so much?"
   But don't worry—this version of a poor man's cabbage strudel is good!

strudel or noodle dough (see Index)	½ cup (or more) raisins
6 cups finely grated cabbage	1½ cups sugar
½ cup cooking oil	2 teaspoons cinnamon
	½ cup chopped nuts
	melted margarine or oil

Prepare strudel or noodle dough. Put the cabbage and oil into a heavy frying pan and sauté for about 20 minutes, stirring often. Cool and mix with the other filling ingredients. Spread on the strudel or noodle dough and roll up. Brush the top with melted margarine or oil. Place on a generously buttered pan and bake in a 350° oven about 45 minutes, or until golden. Serve hot, as dessert. (Serves 8–10.)

NOTE: Cabbage strudel can also be made as a savory by omitting the sugar, spice, nuts, and fruit and adding chopped onion with a seasoning of salt and pepper.

BROAD BEANS WITH HONEY   *Hanuka*

Strange to relate, this dish is a dessert. It is much loved by the Israelis who hail from Romania, who have succeeded in getting it into the local repertoire of bean dishes.

1 cup dried broad beans	½ teaspoon salt
6 tablespoons honey	

Soak the beans overnight. Change the water and put the beans to cook over low heat for 2–3 hours. When the beans are almost tender, add the honey and salt and continue to cook until the beans are soft and golden. (Serves 4.)

CRIMSEL—FILLED *Passover*

Crimsel or Gremsjelies or Chremslach, as various communities call this delectable dish, are all basically of a matzo meal batter or a batter of soaked and squeezed matzos, with eggs. Crimsel may be filled with fruit, like fritters, or you can put nuts and dried fruits (see recipe for Chremslach) and spice right into the batter. This is the filled variety.

The Batter

1 cup water
½ cup hot fat
3 cups matzo meal
¾ cup sugar
3 eggs, well beaten
½ teaspoon salt
  dash of ginger or
  cinnamon

The Filling

1 cup fruit preserves
  (any kind)
½ cup chopped nuts
1 to 2 tablespoons matzo
  meal

fat for frying

To make the batter, boil the water and fat and pour over the matzo meal mixed with sugar. Let stand 30 minutes, then add the eggs, salt and spice. Form into flat cakes.

For the filling, mix the preserves, nuts, and as much matzo meal as necessary to prevent the filling from being too liquid. Put a spoonful on each cake. Pinch together and pat flat again. Fry in hot fat until golden. Serve hot or cold, plain or with wine sauce (*see* Index). (Serves 6.)

MATZO CHREMSLACH *Passover*

3 matzos
  juice of 1 orange, diluted
    with water
4 eggs, separated
4 tablespoons sugar

2 ounces chopped nuts
  grated rind of 1 orange
  dash of cinnamon
  dash of salt
  fat for deep frying

Soak the matzos in the orange juice diluted with water. Squeeze dry and force the pulp through a sieve. Beat the egg whites stiff. Mix all the ingredients together, folding in the whites at the last. Drop the mixture by spoonfuls into deep hot fat (wet the spoon each time). Serve hot or cold with a sauce of honey. (Serves 6.)

HELMA'S GREMSJELIES

Passover

3 matzos
3 eggs
  salt
  sugar to taste

grated rind of 1 lemon
2 tablespoons raisins
1 large apple, grated
oil for frying

Soak the matzos in water and then squeeze dry. Beat well with the eggs. Add the remaining ingredients and drop by spoonfuls into hot oil. Fry until golden. Be careful not to burn the gremsjelies, as they catch easily—particularly if you have a sweet tooth and put in a lot of sugar or raisins. (Serves 5–6.)

PASSOVER CREPES SUZETTE

Passover

Just imagine (for it is true): a prince—who later became Edward VII of England—orders crepes in Paris. By mistake, the liqueur sauce catches fire, but it is too late for the cook to do anything about it and he serves the dish. It is divine, because of the burnt flavor. The cookboy becomes world famous Henri Charpentier, and the dish is named for the prince's lady guest, the first to eat them. And today in Tel–Aviv you can get kosher-for-Pesach Crepes Suzette!

The Crepes

1 cup potato flour
2 eggs
1¼ cups water or milk
1 tablespoon sugar
  pinch of salt
  whiff of vanilla
  grated rind of 1 lemon

The Sauce

4 tablespoons margarine
  or butter
⅓ cup sugar
1 tablespoon grated orange
  rind
½ teaspoon grated lemon
  rind
½ cup strained orange juice
1 ounce Cointreau
1 ounce brandy

For the crepes, mix the potato flour, eggs, most of the water (or milk), sugar, salt, vanilla, and lemon rind and beat until very smooth. Add the remaining water. Butter a pan lightly, pour in about 4 tablespoons of batter and tilt it quickly to distribute the batter. When cooked on one side, turn the pancake. Pile up the crepes and keep warm while you prepare the sauce.

    The sauce is usually prepared at the table in a chafing dish, for the aroma is too wonderful to keep in the kitchen. Put the margarine and sugar in the pan and let it just begin to brown.

Add the grated rind and then the orange juice. When the sauce begins to bubble, put in the crepes, one at a time, and fold up to envelope shape, in the simmering sauce. When they are all folded, pour in the liqueurs and light with a match. Serve the crepes with sauce. (Serves 6.)

APFEL BEIGNETS—APPLE FRITTERS   *Hanuka*

Apfel beignets—or apple fritters—as its married name of both French and German implies, is a dish of Switzerland. Being a fried pancake, it has become a Hanuka favorite. Did it come to be from the recipe in Leviticus 7:12, which reads: ". . . a thanksgiving . . . unleavened cakes mingled with oil . . . of fine flour, fried"?

1 teaspoon cinnamon	*3 egg yolks, beaten*
6 tablespoons sugar	*3 tablespoons cooking oil*
8 apples, peeled and cut	*1⅔ cups light beer*
into slices (¼ inch)	*3 egg whites, stiffly beaten*
2 cups flour	*fat for deep frying*
2 teaspoons baking powder	*powdered sugar*
½ teaspoon salt	

Mix cinnamon and sugar, and sprinkle on the apples. For the batter, mix and sift the dry ingredients. Add the egg yolks and oil. Stir in the beer carefully and slowly and beat well to prevent lumps. Fold in the stiffly beaten egg whites. Dip the apple slices into the batter. Fry in deep hot fat until golden brown. Drain and sprinkle with powdered sugar. (Serves 8.)

ORANGE CINNAMON TOAST   *Hanuka*

Four hundred years ago—in 1533 to be exact—Sir Thomas Elyot wrote of an appetizer that is similar to a tea or supper snack today: "a slice of toasted bread dipped in lemon juice, strewn with powdered sugar, mint and a little cinnamon."

oranges	*cinnamon*
butter	*sugar, brown and white*
slices of soft toast	*mint sprigs*

Peel the oranges and slice very thin. Butter the toast and sprinkle with cinnamon and brown sugar. Cover with the thin orange slices centered with dabs of butter and sprinkled with white sugar. Put under the grill for just a minute to glaze. Garnish with mint sprigs and serve with lemon tea.

ORANGE FRITTERS

Hanuka

Among the hundreds of fabulous dishes served at a banquet at the Villa d'Este—where even the toothpicks were perfumed— is one so noble that it receives special mention in a record of the menu: orange fritters with sugar and cinnamon!

3 medium oranges	*2 teaspoons baking powder*
sugar for sprinkling	*dash of salt*
1 egg, well beaten	*cinnamon for sprinkling*
⅔ cup orange juice	*(optional)*
1⅓ cups flour, sifted	*fat for deep frying*

Peel the oranges, removing all membrane, slice ½ inch thick, and sprinkle with sugar. To make the batter, mix the egg with the orange juice and add to the dry ingredients. Drain the orange slices, dip into the batter, and fry in deep hot fat for about two minutes. Drain and serve with a sprinkling of sugar, and if you wish, a dash of cinnamon. (Makes about 15 fritters.)

CAKE

SPICY CAKE

Now that cake mixes are available in Israel, I never turn my hand to labor over a Spice Cake. But this is the recipe I used to make, and I still think it is good.

1½ cups flour
¾ cup white sugar
¼ cup brown sugar
1 teaspoon baking soda
  pinch of salt
2 teaspoons mixed cake
  spices such as ginger,
  cinnamon, cloves, all-
  spice

1 cup sour cream or
  yoghurt
⅓ cup margarine if you are
  using sour cream,
½ cup margarine if
  you are using yoghurt
2 eggs

Sift the dry ingredients together into the bowl of the electric mixer. Add the remaining ingredients and beat until smooth. Bake in a 350° oven for about 45 minutes.

CAROB SYRUP CAKE (DIBBS CAKE)

"Dibbs" is the Arabic word for carob or date syrup. It was the only sweetener we had in the austerity days just after the founding of the State of Israel.

4 cups flour, sifted
1 tablespoon baking soda
2 eggs
5 tablespoons sugar

⅓ cup oil
½ pound carob, date, or
  other syrup or honey
¾ cup orange juice

Sift the flour and baking soda. Beat the eggs and gradually beat in the sugar. Beat in the oil, syrup, and orange juice, then stir in the flour mixture. Grease a loaf pan and pour in the batter. Bake at 325° F for about 1½ hours, or until browned on top and a straw inserted into the cake comes out clean. Cool on a rack before removing from the pan.

RICH GUGELHUPF

Yom Kippur

There used to be as many gugelhupfs in the Jewish homes of Austria, Switzerland, and Germany as there were families to eat them. This yeast cake came to Israel with the first refugees from Europe before the war. It is a cake baked often for Sabbath but always to have with coffee after the fast of Yom Kippur. This is a rich version of the plain cake.

1 cup butter	½ ounce dry yeast
10 egg yolks	(*2 packages*)
2 cups flour, sifted	½ cup lukewarm milk
4 tablespoons sugar	sprinkling of cornstarch
dash of salt	sprinkling of cinnamon
raisins and nuts, if	
desired	

Cream the butter, then add the egg yolks and flour alternately, beating well. Add the sugar and salt and mix well. If you wish, you can put in chopped nuts and raisins, floured a bit. Dissolve the yeast in the milk and add. Mix well. Grease a gugelhupf or angel food pan and dust with the cornstarch and cinnamon. Place the dough in the pan. Cover and allow to rise in a warm place until double in bulk (30–45 minutes). Bake in a 350° oven for about 1 hour.

KUBAHNEH—YEMENITE YEAST CAKE

Shabbat

This Yemenite yeast cake is served after synagogue service on Sabbath morning, along with hawadijz—coffee highly scented with cardamom pods and fired up with ground ginger. As the Yemenites use very little sugar in their cookery, the kubahneh is more like bread than cake, and, having cooked overnight, comes out more like a kugel than a bread.

½ cup sugar (*optional*)	6 tablespoons melted butter
1 ounce compressed yeast	1 cup milk or water
(*2 packages dry*)	4 cups flour
1 cup lukewarm water	¼ teaspoon salt

Dissolve the sugar, if desired, and yeast in the lukewarm water and then add the melted butter and the milk or water. Sift the flour into the liquid with the salt and mix well. Put to rise in a warm place for 4 hours. Put the mixture into a well-buttered thick pan with a heavy cover. Cover closely and bake in a 200° oven overnight. The kubahneh is served warm.

NOTE: In Israel this is always "baked" on top of the range over very low heat.

BOLAS—CAKE OF BREAD   *Shabbat*

For those who could not afford to bake cake for the Sabbath there was still the delicious bolas—cake made from the Sabbath challah dough. Josephus, in his Antiquities of the Jews, *sees in the legend of Gideon the low state of Israel, because of the cake of barley bread, symbol of poverty. Yet this cake turned the camp of the Midianites upside down and brought victory to the Jews.*

challah dough (see Index)
1 cup brown sugar
1 teaspoon cinnamon or
  ginger

chopped candied peel
½ pound margarine or
  butter
1 egg

Pinch off enough challah dough to roll into a foot-square sheet. Sprinkle with brown sugar, candied peel, and spice and drizzle on the melted fat. Roll up the dough and cut into finger-thick pieces. Place on a well-greased baking sheet and set to rise again. Brush with diluted egg and bake in a 350° oven about 45 minutes.

BAKAU RAHAT KUCHEN   *Shavuot*

2 ounces fresh yeast or
  4 packages dry
4 egg yolks, beaten
  pinch of salt
1 cup warm milk
1 teaspoon vanilla

1⅚ cups flour, sifted
¾ cup butter
4 tablespoons sugar
½ cup Turkish delight
  (see Index)

Mix the yeast, egg yolks, salt, milk, and vanilla. Stir in 1½ cups of the flour and stir (slow speed). Cover and set aside for 15 minutes while you cream the butter and sugar. Spread the remaining ⅓ cup of flour on a board and then pour the dough onto the board. Fold over and over, working in the flour on the board. Then form into a ball and roll out to a thickness of ½ inch. Make a rope of the Turkish delight and put it along the edge of the dough. Spread the rest of the dough with the butter mixture. Roll up like a jelly roll and cut into 10 thick slices. Set, cut side up, in a greased round cake pan. Bake in a 325° oven about 45 minutes. This cake should be eaten within 24 hours.

BUNDT KUCHEN

Shabbat

½ cup margarine
1 cup sugar
4 eggs
  grated rinds of 1 lemon
    and 1 orange

1 teaspoon almond essence
2¼ cups flour, sifted
2 teaspoons baking powder
1 cup milk
½ cup blanched almonds

Cream the margarine and sugar, add the eggs, one at a time, and beat well. Add the rind and flavoring. Mix the flour and baking powder and stir in alternately with the milk. Put the almonds in the bottom of the greased bundt form (or angel-cake pan), pour in the batter, and bake in a 350° oven for about 45 minutes.

SAND TORTE

Shabbat

1 cup margarine
1 cup sugar
6 eggs, separated
3 teaspoons baking powder

1 cup flour
1 cup cornstarch
  rind and juice of
    1 lemon

Cream the margarine and sugar. Beat the egg yolks and add. Mix the remaining dry ingredients and sift into the mixing bowl, stirring and alternately adding the lemon juice and rind. Beat the egg whites until stiff and fold in. Bake in a buttered cake pan in a 350° oven about 45 minutes.

CROWN KOLACH

Shavuot

This Czechoslovakian pastry comes in a large variety of shapes and sizes and with different fruit or cheese fillings. It has been popular all over Europe for a number of generations. French Jews serve it on Shavuot, with the kolaches shaped into crowns to represent the silver crowns on the Torah scrolls in the synagogues.

4 tablespoons sour cream
2 cups cottage cheese
⅓ cup sugar
2 eggs
½ cup white raisins

4 tablespoons blanched
  almonds
1 teaspoon vanilla
  any rich yeast dough
  (see Index)

Mix all the ingredients for the filling. Shape the dough into egg-sized balls and then roll out into ovals. Put a little filling into each, fold over lengthwise and seal the edges with a fluted cutter.

Bring the two pointed edges together to make the shape of a crown. Decorate by pricking with a fork. Put to rise until doubled in bulk. Brush with egg yolk and sprinkle with sugar. Bake in 400° oven for about 15 minutes, or until golden.

ONEG SHABBAT MARBLE CAKE
Shabbat

¾ cup margarine
2 cups sugar
4 eggs
3 cups flour, sifted

3 teaspoons baking powder
1 cup water or milk
1 teaspoon vanilla
8 tablespoons cocoa

Cream the margarine and sugar and add the eggs, one at a time, beating well. Mix the flour with the baking powder and add alternately with the milk or water. Add the vanilla. Put half the batter in another bowl and mix in the cocoa. Into a greased pan pour alternate layers of the white and chocolate batter. Bake in 350° oven 45 minutes.

LEKACH—HONEY CAKE
Rosh Hashana

Old folk saying: "When a miser becomes a spendthrift, he eats his borscht with lekach."

Countries of Western as well as Eastern Europe make almost the same festive honey cake for Rosh Hashana, whether it be pierniki luckie in Poland or honingkoek in Holland, which is rather unusual for lands with very different dishes. In Israel the coffee is often omitted and water used in its stead, and more accent is put upon citron peel than spice, to blend with our unusually fine orange blossom honey.

1¾ cups honey
1 cup strong coffee
2 tablespoons brandy
4 eggs
4 tablespoons cooking oil
1 cup brown sugar
3½ cups flour
3 teaspoons baking powder

1 teaspoon baking soda
2 teaspoons spices (cinnamon, cloves, ginger, allspice, nutmeg)
1 cup chopped almonds, raisins and citron peel

Add the coffee to the honey and bring to a boil. Cool. Add the brandy. Beat the eggs and stir in the oil, then the sugar. Sift the dry ingredients and add the nuts and fruits to them. Stir into the egg mixture alternately with the honey mixture. Mix well and place in a greased loaf pan. Bake in a 300° oven for about one hour. When done, invert the pan and cool.

CIAMBELLA DI PURIM—PURIM HONEY CAKE *Purim*

This is the Italian version of the Polish lekach:

9 cups self-rising flour,
   sifted
1½ pounds honey
½ pound ground almonds
   or walnuts
2 ounces chopped citron
   peel

1 tablespoon orange juice
2 tablespoons olive oil
1 teaspoon ginger

Mix all the ingredients together. Fit into a round baking pan. Bake in a 350° oven about 1 hour.

THE SABBATH SPONGE CAKE *Shabbat*

Judge Seymour Levine of New York wrote in one of our regular to-and-fro letters: "With what vividness I remember the hush which descended on our house each Friday afternoon, as if by alchemy the noise and bustle of weekday world could dissolve in the thinness of air. Coming home from school I would find the house, which normally would be cluttered with all the paraphernalia that boys can bring to a house, transformed into majestic, quiet beauty. To be sure, there would be newspapers on the floors (they had just been washed). The curtains on the windows would exude the freshness of starch, the candles would stand silently awaiting the first spark to ignite them into radiance, the white linen cloth on the table, the dishes and the silverware gleaming in expectancy—but more pervading was the aroma—the delicious aroma of the Sabbath sponge cake being baked."

1 cup flour, sifted
   pinch of salt
7 eggs, separated
   grated rind of 1 lemon

2 teaspoons lemon juice
1 cup fine sugar
½ teaspoon cream of tartar

Sift the flour with the salt 4 or 5 times. Beat the egg yolks until light yellow and quite thick, then slowly beat in the lemon rind, lemon juice, and half the sugar. Beat the egg whites, and before they are stiff, add the cream of tartar. Continue beating until stiff. Fold the remaining sugar into the egg whites. Fold the egg white mixture into the egg yolk mixture, and then fold in the flour. Pour into an ungreased pan and bake in a 325° oven for an hour. Turn the pan over (this will stretch the cake) on a cake rack until cool.

STRAWBERRY CHANTILLY CAKE   *Passover*

*Cream was offered as a present in Biblical days, and it remains
a specialty even in these days in Israel. Strawberries are bountiful in season, and they are very often served with whipped cream,
as follows:*

1 sponge cake (regular
    or Passover) · (see
    Index)
3 cups strawberries
	½ cup sugar
	    whipped cream
	    sugar to taste
	    vanilla

Split a sponge cake. Hull the strawberries and cut in two. Sugar
them and let them stand a few hours. Pour the juice from the
strawberries over the cake, on both layers. Whip and sugar the
cream to taste and add a few drops of vanilla. Fill the cake with
a layer of whipped cream and strawberries. Top the cake with
whipped cream and decorate with whole hulled berries, and a
garnish of mint sprigs. Serve chilled. (Serves 6.)

MY STORE CAKE   *Shavuot*

*The biggest cooking compliments I get are for a standard store
cake which I always keep on hand called "sponge" or "torte" or
even "lekach" (depending on whether you come from England,
or Germany or Poland). I deck it out in minutes when unexpected
guests arrive.*

1 round 9-inch sponge cake
½ cup syrup from peaches
6 tablespoons curaçao or
    brandy
1 1-pound, 4-ounce can
    sliced peaches
	1 cup heavy cream
	3 tablespoons fine sugar
	1 teaspoon vanilla

Cut the cake into 4 layers (use only 2 if you like, and then serve
larger wedges). Mix the syrup with the curaçao or brandy and
sprinkle it, a little at a time to prevent sogginess, over each layer
of cake. Arrange the peach slices in a pattern over the brandied
cake. Whip the cream with the sugar and vanilla. Spread a thin
layer of whipped cream over the fruit. Pile up the layers. Decorate the top layer with peach slices, whipped cream in the center.
Add other frills if you like (sprigs of mint, cherries), arranging
them into coronets around the cream. Chill before serving. The
cake improves with keeping and chilling for a day.

ENGLISH CAKE—ISRAEL STYLE   *Shabbat*

*In the household of Charles II of England, sugared orange peel
was used in baking, and to make the high perfume even headier,
rose water was added, just as it is in the Middle East today.
These fragrant ingredients went into all manner of baking and
desserts—apple tarts, lemon jellies, and creams, including chocolate creams. No wonder it highlights this English cake, much
loved in Israel today:*

1¼ cups sugar	1 cup walnuts, broken up
1 cup margarine	grated rind of 1 lemon
2¾ cups self-rising flour,	1 cup orange juice
sifted	3 eggs
1 cup candied citrus peels	1 teaspoon rose water
and raisins, mixed	(optional)

Cream the sugar and margarine. Sprinkle some of the flour on
the fruit, nuts, and lemon rind. Add the orange juice and remaining flour alternately to the sugar mixture, until all is used up,
mixing continuously. Beat in the eggs, one at a time. Toss in the
fruit and nuts and mix well. Add rose water, if desired. Butter
two loaf pans well, line with waxed paper and pour the batter
into the pans. Bake in a 350° oven 45 minutes.

NOTE: This is not as heavy or rich as the English pound cake,
but is as good and known only as "English cake" in Israel.

THE FREEDOM FRUIT CAKE   *Hanuka*

*During the siege of Jerusalem, no food came into the city for
weeks. The gardens, too, shriveled for lack of water, as the piped
sources to the city had been cut off. Mrs. Ben-Zwi, wife of the
President, went into the fields and gathered the dried figs on the
trees, the dried carobs, the hawthorn apples, and the grapes that
had scorched into raisins. These she mixed with a little flour
that was left in the larder and fed the boys and girls under her
care at the isolated agricultural school at North Talpiot. This
cake was born of the experience and those fruits.*

2 cups self-rising flour	2 large apples, chopped
½ cup water	1 teaspoon cinnamon
1 egg	dash each of ginger,
1 cup raisins	allspice, and cloves
1 cup chopped dried figs	1 cup sugar
½ cup grated carob or	powdered sugar for
chopped dates	topping

Mix the flour, water, and egg and let the dough rest for a few hours. Roll it out and stretch it as thin as possible. In a greased baking dish, alternate layers of the dough with layers of the fruits, sprinkling the fruit with spices and sugar. Bake in a 350° oven 50–60 minutes. Sprinkle the top pastry with powdered sugar immediately after it is baked. Cut while the cake is still warm.

APPLE CAKE WITH CREAM SAUCE　*Rosh Hashana*

This is one of the most luscious apple cakes imaginable, and it is therefore served at teatime on Rosh Hashana in the homes of immigrants from Germany. The topping may be omitted, but in any case, this cake will prove to be the apple of your eye!

The Pastry	*The Filling*
½ cup margarine	6 apples
2 egg yolks	1 egg
4 tablespoons sugar	2 tablespoons sugar
2 cups flour, sifted	1 to 2 tablespoons lemon
1½ teaspoons baking powder	juice
2 tablespoons brandy	1 tablespoon cornstarch
	½ cup sweet cream

The Topping

1⅓ cups flour
½ cup margarine
½ cup sugar

For the pastry, with the electric mixer mix together the margarine, egg yolks, sugar, flour, and baking powder, until crumbly. Add the brandy and mix. Pat this into a buttered springform pan, on the bottom and halfway up the sides.

For the filling, peel the apples and slice fine. Put into the pan, on top of the pastry. Mix the egg and sugar and stir in the lemon juice. Dilute the cornstarch in the cream and add the lemon juice mixture slowly. Pour this over the apples.

To make the Streussel topping, rub the flour, sugar, and margarine together to form crumbs, and sprinkle over the top of the cake.

Bake in a 350° oven until done (45–60 minutes). (Serves 6.)

CARROT CAKE
Rosh Hashana

1 pound carrots
2 cups nuts
8 eggs, separated

2 cups sugar
rind of an orange
juice of ½ orange

Boil the carrots and grate them. Chop the nuts very fine (if you use almonds, blanch them first in hot water). Beat the egg yolks until thick and pale. Add the sugar gradually, then the orange rind and juice, carrots, and nuts and mix well. Fold in the stiffly beaten egg whites and bake in a 350° oven 45 minutes. Top with whipped cream.

DATE NUT LOAF
Tu Besh'vat

3 cups flour, sifted
4 tablespoons baking
   powder
½ cup sugar
1 teaspoon salt
1 cup chopped dates

¼ cup (or more) chopped
   walnuts
1 egg, beaten
1½ cups milk
2 tablespoons melted
   margarine

Sift together the flour, baking powder, sugar, and salt, then add the dates and nuts and mix. Beat the egg, milk, and margarine together and add to the flour mixture. Work together. Turn into a buttered loaf pan and let stand for 30 minutes. Bake in a 350° oven for about 1½ hours. Cool on a rack. Serve sliced, with a spread of butter.

BECKY'S ORANGE CAKE
Tu Besh'vat

3 medium eggs
1 cup sugar plus 4 table-
   spoons
pinch of salt
1 teaspoon vanilla

2 cups self-rising flour,
   sifted
1 cup orange juice
rum or brandy to taste
1 cup sweetened whipped
   cream

Beat the eggs and the 1 cup of sugar in an electric mixer. Add the salt and vanilla, then the flour. The batter must be very thick. Put into a greased pan and bake in a medium oven for 45 minutes. Meanwhile, prepare a syrup of the orange juice and the 4 table-spoons of sugar. Remove from heat when the mixture is about to boil, and add the brandy or rum. As soon as you take the cake out of the oven, spoon on the hot syrup, slowly. Chill the cake thoroughly before serving, and top it with whipped cream.

ORANGE-FIG CAKE   *Independence Day*

Orange cakes are made all year round in Israel, even when the season is over and bottled juices are used. This cake is often served as a chilled dessert in the summertime.

3 eggs, separated	*pinch of salt*
2 cups sugar	*2 cups orange juice*
⅔ cup margarine	*fresh or canned figs*
3 cups sifted flour	*for garnish*
3 teaspoons baking powder	*whipped cream*

Cream the egg yolks, 1½ cups of the sugar, and the margarine together. Mix and sift the flour, baking powder, and salt, then add to the first mixture alternately with 1 cup of the orange juice. Beat the egg whites until stiff and fold into the mixture. Pour into two 9-inch cake pans and bake in a 375° oven 30 minutes. Remove from the oven. Make a syrup of the remaining cup of orange juice and ½ cup of sugar cooked together. Very slowly spoon the syrup over the cake and return it to the oven for 5 minutes. Cool, then chill. Serve with a filling of sliced fresh or canned figs and whipped cream that has been sugared to taste and flavored with a little grated orange rind. Top the cake with figs and whipped cream. This cake can also be baked in a single layer and topped only.

JAFFA CAKE   *Rosh Hashana*

This Italian nut-meringue-wafer is to remind one of Jaffa, the ancient city of Israel where Jonah went to take a ship for Tarshish. Jaffa is today a conglomerate of ancient buildings and new ones, narrow alleys and broad highways, old ruins and new nightclubs. Its flea market is a colorful corner full of shining brass and copper pots for sale.

1½ cups unblanched	*2 egg whites, stiffly*
almonds	*beaten*
1 cup sugar	*wafer sheets*
2 tablespoons brandy	

Grind the almonds and add the sugar, brandy, and egg whites. Butter a pan, line with wafer sheets, top with the meringue mixture, and bake in 275° oven until the tips of the meringue are brown (45–60 minutes). (Serves 4–6.)

Rosh Hashana
YEAST ZWETSCHGEN KUCHEN—YEAST PLUM CAKE

*This is the German version of the Rosh Hashana plum cake.
It was once baked in pans so huge that they had to be taken to
the village baker's oven unless the housewife was equipped for the
ravenous appetites that met this dish. The following recipe has
been reduced to present-day family consumption.*

1 ounce yeast	2⅓ cups sugar
1 cup milk (or less)	½ cup butter or margarine
4 cups sifted flour	3 pounds plums (ripe)

Dissolve yeast in lukewarm milk with ⅓ cup of the sugar. Mix
with flour and the melted fat to make a dough. Knead well and
put to rise in a warm place until double in bulk. Roll the dough
out fairly thin. Cut each fresh plum into four "petals," trying to
keep the bottom unsevered so that when the stone is removed
the plum can be pressed down fan-shaped into the dough. Put the
plums as close together as possible. Put the cake into a cold oven.
Turn the heat on to 350° and bake until crust is done and plums
soft. Remove from the oven and sprinkle very generously with the
2 cups sugar immediately, so that it melts right on the fruit for
a succulent glazed topping.

GUAVA UPSIDE-DOWN CAKE   *Rosh Hashana*

*The taste for guavas must be cultivated because of their over-
whelming exotic perfume. There are a number of varieties, sweet
and sour, pink fleshed (the strawberry guava) and creamy inside
(the large lemon guava that looks and tastes like a pear), but all
of them are so highly aromatic that one is inclined to believe they
have been soaked in eau de cologne. It is a cheap and bountiful
fruit in Israel. When cooked, its flavor remains but its smell
evaporates.*

3 tablespoons butter or margarine	candied cherries
1 cup brown sugar	any plain or sponge cake batter (see Index)
6 guavas	

Melt the butter in a heavy frying pan and spread evenly with the
sugar. Peel, halve, and pit the guavas. Arrange, with the cherries, in an ornamental pattern on the skillet. Pour on the cake
batter. Bake in a 350° oven about 50 minutes. Turn upside down
while the cake is still hot. Serve cold, garnished if you like with
whipped cream. (Serves 6–8.)

NOTE: The same cake can be made with any fruits in season, particularly peaches, apricots, plums, and pears.

PEACH UPSIDE-DOWN CAKE
Succot

When the peach harvest is on in our village, friends who have orchards bring us pails and baskets of the fruit. And at that time I recall again and again the story of our first President, Chaim Weizmann, whose heart and soul were so much in the Zionist cause that even on his honeymoon he left his bride to attend a Zionist meeting. Knowing that she would surely be annoyed, he returned to his hotel room with a basket of peaches, which is a very good way of wooing a wife.

3 tablespoons butter	12 glazed cherries
1 cup brown sugar	sponge or other cake
6 peaches	batter (*see* Index)

Butter a rectangular cake pan very well and sprinkle with the brown sugar. Cut the peaches in half and stone them. Put a cherry in each cavity and arrange the fruit (cut side down) on the pan. Pour the cake batter over this and bake in a 350° oven about 50 minutes. Turn the cake over as soon as you remove it from the oven or the caramel topping will stick to the pan. (Serves 6-8.)

BANANA CHIFFON CAKE
Shabbat

2¼ cups flour, sifted	1 cup mashed bananas
1½ cups sugar	1 tablespoon lemon juice
3 teaspoons baking powder	8 egg whites
½ teaspoon salt	dash of cream of tartar
5 egg yolks	whipped cream
½ cup cooking oil	sliced bananas

Blend together the flour, sugar, baking powder, and salt. Beat in the egg yolks, one at a time, then the oil, bananas, and lemon juice. Beat the egg whites, with the cream of tartar, until stiff. Fold the banana mixture into the egg whites. Bake in an ungreased angel cake pan in a 325° oven about 1 hour. Turn the pan upside down and set it on the neck of a bottle, as soon as you remove it from the oven. This will stretch the cake and give it the chiffon texture. Remove from the pan only when cold. Serve with whipped cream and sliced bananas.

ORANGE CUSTARD CAKE   *Purim*

Mrs. Sarah Eckstein, member of the very Orthodox kibbutz of Hafetz Haim, prepared this orange custard cake at the regional competition at the King David Hotel, in the Israel Culinary Contest. It is something different, and very good indeed.

2 cups flour	4 tablespoons cornstarch
⅓ cup sugar, plus 7 table-	2 cups orange juice
spoons	3 oranges, peeled and
2 teaspoons baking powder	sectioned
1 cup margarine	3 egg whites

Sift the flour, ⅓ cup sugar, and baking powder and cut in the margarine. Pat into a spring pan and bake in a 350° oven until golden (about 20 minutes). Mix the cornstarch with a little of the orange juice. Bring the remaining juice to the boil with 4 tablespoons of the sugar and add the dissolved cornstarch. Stir until thick. Remove from heat. When the pastry is done put the orange sections on top of it and pour the sauce over. Whip the egg whites with the remaining sugar, spread on the cake, and put into a 450° oven until the meringue is golden (10–15 minutes). Serve cold. (Serves 8.)

CHOCOLATE FUDGE CAKE   *Shavuot*

½ cup butter	1 teaspoon baking soda
1¾ cups sugar	1 teaspoon baking powder
2 eggs	1 cup sour cream
1 tablespoon vinegar	3 ounces chocolate,
1¾ cups flour, sifted	melted

Cream the butter and sugar, then add the eggs, one at a time, beating vigorously after each. Add the vinegar. Sift the dry ingredients together and add alternately with the sour cream. Stir in the melted chocolate. Bake in a medium oven (350°) for 45 minutes. When cool, ice with any chocolate frosting or this one (my favorite):

Walnut-Fudge Frosting

2 ounces chocolate	1¼ cups white sugar
½ cup milk	2 tablespoons butter
½ cup brown sugar	1 teaspoon vanilla
	½ cup broken walnuts

Melt the chocolate, add the milk and both kinds of sugar, and boil until a few drops form a soft ball in a glass of cold water. Add the butter and vanilla. Set aside to rest for a few minutes. Beat until cool and thick enough to spread. Stir in the nuts.

HONEY CHOCOLATE CAKE   *Shabbat*

2 cups cake flour	2 eggs
1½ teaspoons soda	3 squares unsweetened
½ teaspoon salt	chocolate, melted
½ cup margarine	⅔ cup water
1¼ cups honey	1 teaspoon vanilla

Sift the flour, soda, and salt together 3 times. Cream the margarine and work in the honey gradually, beating well. Add a few tablespoons flour and beat until smooth. Add the eggs, one at a time, beating after each addition. Add the chocolate and blend well. Add the remaining flour in thirds, alternately with the water, beating well after each addition. Add the vanilla. Bake in a 350° oven in 2 layer pans, for a little over 30 minutes. Fill and frost as desired.

CHEESECAKE—POLISH TYPE   *Shavuot*

The Pastry	*The Filling*
1 cup butter	4 cups cottage cheese
1 cup blanched, ground	½ cup sour cream
almonds	⅓ cup melted butter
1 cup sugar	3 egg yolks
3 eggs	⅔ cup sugar
2 cups flour, sifted	2 tablespoons rum
	½ cup blanched almonds
	½ cup candied orange peel
	3 egg whites, stiffly beaten

For the pastry, cream the butter and combine with the nuts, sugar, eggs, and flour. Mix well. Roll out thin and cover two greased pie plates with it. Bake in a 350° oven until light gold (about 10 minutes).

To make the filling, put the cheese and sour cream through a sieve. Add the butter, then the egg yolks, one at a time, mixing well. Cream in the sugar. Add the rum and continue beating, while adding the almonds and peel. Fold in the egg whites last. Spread evenly on the pastry and bake in a 350° oven for about 20 minutes. This is a heavy but very tasty cheesecake.

DOLCE REBECCA—ITALIAN MOCHA CAKE *Yom Kippur*

4 cups flour, sifted	*½ cup margarine or butter,*
3 teaspoons baking powder	*melted*
½ teaspoon cinnamon	*1 cup strong cool coffee*
½ cup cocoa	*1 cup milk*
1 cup sugar	*2 eggs*
	1 teaspoon vanilla

Mix the dry ingredients and sift together. Add the butter, coffee, and half the milk and mix together. Beat well and add the remaining milk and each egg separately, beating well after each addition. Add the vanilla and beat again. Pour into a buttered and floured cake pan and bake in a 350° oven 50–60 minutes. Cover with white icing, decorate with nuts and glazed cherries.

POPPYSEED ROLEY-POLEY   *Purim*

1 recipe yeast plum cake	*2 tablespoons sugar*
dough (see Index)	*½ cup almonds or walnuts,*
1 cup poppy seeds	*chopped*
1 cup milk	*1 tablespoon candied peel*
½ cup raisins	*1 teaspoon vanilla*
2 tablespoons honey	*2 tablespoons butter, melted*

Prepare the dough and roll out thin. Cover with a cloth, away from drafts, and allow to rise while you prepare the filling. Put the seed through the meat chopper (if not purchased already ground) and then boil with the milk, raisins, honey, and sugar. When the mixture is thick, remove from heat and add the nuts, candied peel, and flavoring. Cool the mixture and then spread it over the dough. Roll up like a jelly roll and put into a greased pan. Set in a warm place to rise again until double in bulk. Spread the top with the melted butter and bake in a 300° oven until golden (about 1 hour and 15 minutes).

SALLY'S ALMOND PUDDING CAKE   *Passover*

This pudding or cake, made by my sister Sally Rothberg, is flourless and as eggy and as light as a soufflé. Measurements must be exact, and when it is in the oven don't bang the door or shout at your children or even sneeze—for the cake will sigh and sink if you do.

4 eggs, separated　　　　　*4 ounces fine sugar*
4 ounces ground almonds

Beat the yolks and whites separately, then together, until very light. Add the ground almonds and sugar and beat for another 15 minutes by hand or 3 minutes with the electric mixer. Turn into a greased dish and bake in a 350° oven about 30 minutes or until the cake is no longer sticky at the touch of a finger.

POPPY SEED TORTE *Purim*

The abundance of poppy seed in this cake is symbolic of the blessing of the manna in the desert. The seed has a light nutty flavor, and when dispersed through this fluffy cake, gives it a cloudlike airy effect.

¾ cup margarine　　　　　*¼ cup cornstarch or*
1 cup sugar　　　　　　　　　*potato flour*
3 egg yolks　　　　　　　*2 tablespoons milk*
6 ounces poppy seed,　　*2 tablespoons brandy*
　　ground　　　　　　　　*3 egg whites, stiffly beaten*
¼ cup flour

Cream the margarine and sugar. Beat in the egg yolks, then mix in the ground poppy seeds. Sift the dry ingredients together and add alternately with the liquids. Fold in the egg whites. Pour into a greased tube pan and bake in a 350° oven for 45 minutes to 1 hour.

THE DIPLOMATIC CHEESECAKE *Shavuot*

5 eggs, separated　　　　*½ cup heavy cream*
1 cup sugar　　　　　　　　*grated rind of 1 lemon*
1 tablespoon flour, sifted　*1 teaspoon vanilla*
1 pound cottage cheese,　*½ cup raisins*
　　sieved　　　　　　　　*cracker crumbs*

Cream the egg yolks and sugar until light yellow. Add the flour, cheese, and cream and mix very well. Add the lemon rind, vanilla, and raisins and mix vigorously. Beat the egg whites until stiff and fold in. Pour into a spring-form pan that has been well buttered and dusted with finely crushed cracker crumbs. Bake in a 375° oven for about 45 minutes. Do not open the oven before that. Turn off the heat and let the cake cool in the oven.

SOUR CREAM CHEESECAKE *Shavuot*

This cake is so luscious one suspects that if it were not the prize of Shavuot, a festival would have to be created to feature it. This creamy delight, which came to Israel from America, is quickly pushing all the old-fashioned heavy cheesecake concoctions of Europe into limbo. Serve it plain (it isn't a bit plain!) or topped with sugared strawberries and sprigs of mint.

The Crust

1 cup cookie crumbs
4 tablespoons melted
    margarine

The Filling

2 heaping cups cottage
    cheese
1 cup light sour cream
½ cup sugar
2 eggs
1 teaspoon vanilla
2 tablespoons flour

The Topping

1 cup sour cream
2 tablespoons sugar
1 teaspoon vanilla

To make the crust, mix the cookie crumbs and the margarine and pat into a spring-form pan. Chill.

For the filling, mix all the ingredients well. Pour into the crust and bake in a 350° oven for 20 minutes. Remove from the oven. Turn the heat up to 450°.

Mix the ingredients for the topping well and spoon gently onto the cake. Return the cheesecake to the 450° oven for just 5 minutes. Remove from the oven. The topping will set as it cools.

JELLIED CHEESECAKE *Shavuot*

On Shavuot, homes in Israel are garlanded with spring boughs, and jugs of the bountiful gladioli fill the rooms. For Shavuot has agricultural as well as religious meaning, like most Jewish festivals. The symbol of planting and spring is carried even into foods, which are often garnished to represent flowers or first fruits.

1 cup crumbled biscuits
3 tablespoons margarine
3 eggs, 2 separated
¾ cup sugar
    pinch of salt

½ cup cold water
1½ cups cottage cheese,
    sieved
    juice and rind of
    1 lemon

4 tablespoons milk
3 tablespoons lemon-
   flavored gelatin

½ cup heavy cream
   candied cherries and
   citron peel, for garnish

Mix the biscuit crumbs with the margarine and pat into the bottom and sides of a spring-form pan. Mix the whole egg, yolks, ½ cup of the sugar, salt, and milk and cook in the top of a double boiler until the mixture coats a spoon. Dissolve the gelatin in the cold water and stir into the custard. Cool a little. Add the cheese and the lemon juice and rind. Beat the cream until stiff and fold in. Beat the egg whites stiff, with the remaining sugar, and fold in. Turn into the crumb crust and chill in the refrigerator. Garnish with candied cherries cut to look like flowers and leaves made of citron peel.

TIROPETA—GREEK CHEESECAKE   *Shavuot*

5 tablespoons rice
6 eggs
6 cups cottage cheese
5 tablespoons sour cream

10 pastry sheets (see Index
   for strudel dough), or
   millefeuille pastry (see
   Crème Schnitte)
2 cups melted butter

Cook the rice in boiling water for 14 minutes. Drain and set aside. Beat the eggs until light and whip in the cottage cheese mixed with the sour cream. Then fold in the rice. Butter a baking pan and put in 5 sheets of the dough, brushing each layer with melted butter. Pour in the cheese mixture and top with the remaining sheets, also buttered. Bake in a medium oven for 45 minutes. Serve hot or cold. Use less butter if you wish, though the Greeks use more! (Serves 6–8.)

PASSOVER SPONGE CAKE   *Passover*

6 eggs, separated
1 cup sugar
   rind and juice of
   1 lemon

4 tablespoons potato flour
   pinch of salt
½ cup sifted matzo meal

Beat the egg yolks with the sugar until light in color. Add the lemon juice and rind. Sift the potato flour and salt into the matzo meal. Fold into the batter. Beat the egg whites until stiff and fold in. Pour into a deep pan. Bake in a 350° oven about 40 minutes.

PASSOVER NUSSTORTE (NUT SPONGE) *Passover*

4 eggs, separated	*rind and juice of*
1 cup sugar	*½ lemon*
1 cup ground nuts	*dash of cinnamon or*
½ cup matzo meal	*ginger*

Beat the egg yolks until light yellow, and cream in the sugar. Add the nuts and matzo meal and mix well. Add the lemon juice and rind and cinnamon or ginger. Beat the egg whites until stiff and fold in. Bake in a 350° oven 30 minutes.

Rosh Hashana
ESH ES SIRAYA—EGYPTIAN PALACE BREAD

This has a few crumbs of bread merely to make its name modest. The dish is served with "kaymuk," the skim of milk boiled so long that it becomes a paste, which can be cut. In Israel, former Egyptians top the cake with sour cream or eat it plain.

½ pound honey	*1 cup white breadcrumbs,*
½ cup margarine	*or more*
½ cup sugar	

Heat the honey, margarine, and sugar in a pan until melted and then add the crumbs. Cook together gently, stirring often, until the whole is one mass (5–10 minutes). If necessary add more crumbs. Pour out onto a plate and cool, then cut into individual cakes. (Serves 4–6.)

GHIHINOON—YEMENITE CAKES *Tu Besh'vat*

6 cups flour, sifted	*1¼ cups water*
½ cup sugar	*nuts or jam or cottage*
1 teaspoon coarse salt	*cheese, if desired*
1 pound butter or	
margarine	

Rub the flour, sugar, and salt with half the butter until smooth. Pour in half the water and mix, then gradually add the remaining water, kneading until elastic. Break off walnut- (or larger) sized balls and pat out as thin as possible on a very well-greased tin. Spread the dough with more butter. If you wish, sprinkle with ground nuts or spread thinly with jam or cottage cheese, or leave plain. Fold over like a strudel, and then fold over again to form a sort of envelope. Pile the pastries in a pot. Melt the remaining butter (you should have about ⅓ pound for this) and add to the pot. Bring the butter to bubbling, so that it comes well up over all the pastries. Cover the pot firmly. Turn the heat down very low and let the pastries stew for about 2 hours, or until they are golden. Eat hot or cold. (Makes about 20.)

DOBOS TORTE   *Independence Day*

Dobos torte, the famous Hungarian cake, was brought to Israel in the past decade, but its quick-won popularity now gives it a place in every café, and in the kitchen of the most industrious housewives.

Layers for Cake

  8 *eggs, separated*
¾ *cup sugar*
  1 *cup flour, sifted*
     pinch of salt

Filling

  6 *eggs*
  1 *cup sugar*
  5 *ounces chocolate*
  4 *tablespoons strong coffee*
     or brandy
  1 *cup butter*

Glazed Frosting

⅔ *cup plus 7 tablespoons*
    sugar
½ *cup water*

The layers are of a very dry sponge. Beat the egg yolks with the sugar. Add the stiffly beaten whites and slowly add the sifted flour and salt, mixing at low speed. In Europe this cake is baked in 8 pans: in Israel we do it in two and then split each layer into four thin slices. Bake at 350° for about 15 minutes. When cool, spread with filling.

To make the filling, beat the eggs and sugar together and cook over hot water until the mixture thickens. Cool. Melt the chocolate, mix with the coffee or brandy and add to the egg mixture. Cream the butter and combine with the chocolate-egg mixture. Spread each layer and pile up.

After filling is well set, start the frosting. Melt and caramelize the 7 tablespoons sugar until golden, then stir in the remaining ⅔ cup of sugar and water and cook over low heat, stirring constantly. When thick, pour the glaze over the top of the cake and spread with a warm spatula. Mark off the slices at once, for the glaze hardens quickly and cannot later be cut.

BIENENSTICH—BEECOMB CAKE *Shabbat*

This cake came to Israel with the first large exodus of Jews from Germany in 1933, and before many months it was so much in demand that grocers had to get it for their eager customers every Friday, for the Sabbath. This is a cake that must be served very fresh: after the second day it loses all its appeal (but it never lasts that long!).

The Batter	The Topping
1¾ cups flour	1 cup slivered almonds
3 teaspoons baking powder	⅓ cup sugar
pinch of salt	¼ cup butter
⅔ cup sugar	1 tablespoon milk
½ cup butter	1 tablespoon flour
1 teaspoon vanilla	
2 eggs	
5 tablespoons milk	

The Filling

4 tablespoons cornstarch	2 cups hot milk
3 tablespoons sugar	¼ cup butter
pinch of salt	1 teaspoon vanilla
4 tablespoons cold milk	

For the batter, sift the dry ingredients into mixer bowl. Gradually add the butter and vanilla, then the eggs, one at a time, beating constantly. Add the milk. Pour into a buttered 9-inch springform pan.

For the topping, mix the almonds, sugar, butter, and milk. Heat just until the sugar dissolves. Sprinkle with the flour and mix. Gently spoon over the batter. Bake in a 375° oven 25 minutes.

For the filling (or use any custard you prefer), mix the cornstarch, sugar, and salt and dilute with the cold milk. Add to the hot milk and cook 15 minutes, stirring often. Remove from heat and beat in the butter. Add the vanilla. Cool while the cake cools.

Split the cake in two and spread the bottom half with the custard filling. Replace the top. Keep in the refrigerator until serving time.

COOKED HALVAH CAKE   *Independence Day*

Halvah is an Israeli confection made of peanuts or the nut-flavored sesame seed, and is usually eaten as a sweet or as a spread on bread. This cake is one of the very few dishes in which halvah is a cooking ingredient: quickly made and needing no baking, it is very delicious.

6 *wafer sheets, about 6 inches in diameter*	4 *tablespoons hot water*
1 *cup margarine*	2 *tablespoons cocoa*
4 *ounces halvah*	1 *teaspoon vanilla*
6 *tablespoons sugar*	1 *teaspoon honey (optional)*

Melt the margarine and crumble in the halvah, stir in the cocoa, sugar, and honey, and add the water. Cook for about ten minutes on medium heat, stirring constantly. When the mixture is thick, add the vanilla and spread at once on the wafer sheets, piling them up as you go along, and top with the same mixture. Serve chilled. (Serves 4.)

PASSOVER JELLY ROLL   *Passover*

Jerusalem has many faces, and one that my husband and I loved to see was the closing of the Sabbath in the ultra-Orthodox quarter of Mea Shearim. We once wandered into an old, very dilapidated synagogue that housed only a handful, but it was gloriously lit up with the setting sun, the Sabbath-enchanted faces of the bearded old men, and the singing of the "zmirot" at the Seudah Shlishit—the third meal—of the Sabbath. In this case the "meal" was a Passover jelly roll, for it was the week of the celebration of our exodus from Egypt. The Rebbe's wife, who had made it, proudly gave me the recipe.

4 *eggs, separated*	*juice and grated rind of*
½ *cup sugar*	½ *lemon*
½ *cup matzo meal*	*any preferred jam*

Beat the egg yolks and gradually add the sugar. Add lemon juice and rind. Sift the matzo meal at least three times and add to the first mixture. Fold in the stiffly beaten egg whites. Line a cake tin with waxed paper. Spread on the batter. Bake in a 350° oven for about 10 minutes. Sprinkle a dish towel with sugar and invert the cake onto it. Remove the waxed paper. Spread with jam and roll up at once, while the cake is still hot.

NON-BAKE SWEET POTATO CAKE *Rosh Hashana*

During the austerity years following the birth of the state of Israel, it was almost impossible to make cakes, since we had only two eggs a week, a pound or two of sugar a month, and a shortage of almost every other food. But the prolific sweet potato was not in short supply once we began its cultivation. I made up an unbaked sweet potato cake and very soon, through the Jerusalem Post, it was well known. This is the more glamorized version we still serve today.

2 pounds sweet potatoes	3 tablespoons rum or
1 cup margarine	brandy or curaçao
1/2 cup sugar (optional)	2 tablespoons cocoa
1/2 cup hot orange juice	4 tablespoons candied
grated orange and	citrus peels
lemon rind	

Cook the sweet potatoes in their skins. Peel and mash while hot and immediately stir in the margarine. Mix the sugar with the hot orange juice, rinds, and rum, brandy, or curaçao and stir into the potatoes. Separate 1/3 of the potato mixture from the rest. To the one-third add the cocoa, and to the remainder add the candied peels. Divide the candied-peel-and-potatoes section in two. With a spatula work the three into a layered cake. Although the cake will look very nice now, you can deck it out further with coconut topping and candied cherries. Refrigerate the cake to solidify it. Serve on small plates as you would any rich cake.

PASSOVER BUTTER CAKE *Passover*

3/4 cup sugar	1/2 cup melted margarine
3/4 cup matzo meal, sifted	or butter
pinch of salt	3/4 cup milk
3 teaspoons baking power *	1 teaspoon vanilla
3 eggs	

Sift the dry ingredients. Mix the eggs with the melted margarine or butter and add the milk and vanilla. Combine the two mixtures and mix well. Pour into greased cake pans and bake in a 350° oven for about 20 minutes. Put layers together with any desired filling or frosting.

* In Israel, kosher-for-Passover baking powder is available.

PASSOVER CHOCOLATE CAKE   *Passover*

*One of the easy things about living in Israel—even with still-
limited air-conditioning and push-buttons—is that when Passover comes we have everything available, even kosher baking
powder and soda! All one has to do, then, to make one's favorite
year-round cake, is to substitute one-half the amount of sifted
matzo meal for the full amount of flour and add one egg more.
You get a wonderful cake: a different cake, to be sure, but never
a failure and always a special surprise and delight.*

1 cup matzo meal	pinch of salt
6 tablespoons cocoa	3 eggs
1½ cups sugar	¾ cup butter (melted)
1 teaspoon baking soda	1 cup sour cream or milk
2 teaspoons baking powder	

Sift together the dry ingredients into a large bowl. Add the remaining ingredients all together and then beat very well. Bake
in two tins in a 350° oven 45 minutes. Fill and frost the cake as
desired.

ALMOND-POTATO TORTE   *Passover*

*Where does the Hebrew word "shaked" (almond) come from?
From "shakad"—to stand guard, be alert. For the almond tree
keeps a wakeful watch, ready to herald the appearance of spring
with its rosy blossoms, the first tree to bloom in Israel after
the winter.*

6 eggs, separated	1 cup cold mashed pota-
1 cup sugar	toes, put through a
1½ cups ground almonds	sieve (for lighter
1 lemon, grated rind and	texture)
juice	2 tablespoons potato flour

Beat the egg yolks with half the sugar until creamy. Add the
ground nuts, lemon rind and juice, and potatoes. Beat very well.
Beat the egg whites with the remaining sugar until stiff. Fold
into the other mixture. Dust the potato flour over an ungreased
cake pan and put in the batter. Bake in a 325° oven 50–60 minutes. This cake can be served as a dessert with any favorite sauce
or whipped cream.

PASSOVER NUT-DATE CAKE *Passover*

Unleavened cakes (ugah) were made out of unleavened dough (matzo) from the first Passover, as told in the Bible (Exodus 12:39). It seems likely that the ingredients were much like this cake, with honey in place of sugar and the citron or the golden apple providing juice.

½ cup chopped dates	rind and juice of
¾ cup matzo meal	1 lemon
6 eggs, separated	2 tablespoons honey
1 cup sugar	1 cup chopped nuts

Roll the dates in the matzo meal. Cream the egg yolks and sugar. Add the lemon juice mixed with the honey. Add the lemon rind and nuts and mix well. Fold in the stiffly beaten egg whites. Pour into a large pan. Bake in a 350° oven 35 minutes. As soon as you remove the cake from the oven, sprinkle with sugar and cut into squares.

MATZO APPLE TART *Passover*

4 matzos	1 or 2 tablespoons raisins
1 cup orange juice or water	2 tablespoons blanched
3 eggs, separated	chopped almonds
½ cup margarine	dash of favorite spices
1 or 2 tablespoons candied	sugar for sprinkling
peels	oil for sprinkling
2 cups chopped apples	4 matzos to cover (optional)
4 tablespoons sugar	

Dip the matzos in the orange juice or water (do not soak) and cover with a moist towel. Beat the egg whites stiff. Mix the remaining ingredients and fold in the egg whites. Lay the moist matzos on a very well oiled pie plate. Pour in the filling. Cover, if you wish, with moistened matzos sprinkled with a lot of oil and a little sugar, or leave uncovered. Bake in a 350° oven about 1 hour. Serve at once. (Serves 4–6.)

"CREME" CAKE FROSTING OR FILLING *Shabbat*

Icing sugar, or powdered sugar or confectioner's sugar, were unknown (and are still very expensive) in Israel until recent years. This filling or frosting (for which you can, of course—and with better success—use finer sugars) is the most used and the most loved, though it takes a lot of labor if you have no electric mixer.

1½ cups margarine or
     butter
  1 cup sugar (or 2 cups
     confectioner's sugar)
  4 egg yolks

4 tablespoons brandy or
     strong coffee
6 ounces unsweetened
     chocolate, melted

Cream the butter and sugar until fluffy. Alternately add the egg yolks and flavoring spoon by spoon and continue beating. Add the melted chocolate (it should not be hot) and keep whipping into the butter mixture. Spread on the cake. Keep refrigerated if the day is warm.

STRUESSEL CAKE TOPPING   *Shabbat*

Struessel is used to top yeast cakes and pies. It can also be used as a very fancy crust for a tart.

4 tablespoons flour, sifted
4 tablespoons butter or
     margarine
8 tablespoons sugar

dash of spice, if desired
ground almonds, if desired
     (a few)

With the fingers, rub all the ingredients together until they form into little balls. Sprinkle the top of buttered dough with the crumbs and bake, according to the cake or bun recipe you are using.

COOKIES

ORANGE NUT COOKIES

Tu Besh'vat

1 cup soft margarine
½ cup white sugar
½ cup brown sugar
2 eggs
1 tablespoon orange juice
2¾ cups flour, sifted

½ teaspoon soda
1 teaspoon salt
1 tablespoon grated orange
   rind
½ cup chopped nuts

Mix together the margarine, sugar, eggs, and juice. Sift together the flour, soda, and salt. Add to the first mixture, with the rind. Add the nuts. Mold into a long smooth roll and chill overnight in the refrigerator. With a sharp knife, cut in thin slices and bake until lightly browned (about 8 minutes in a 400° oven.) (Makes about 50.)

GINGERBREAD—LEBKUCHEN—BEAVERS *Rosh Hashana*

This Swiss honey cookie has many European relations and Israel variations, some requiring cider and kirsch and butter by the pound. Here is a simple version of the Rosh Hashana delight for Jews, and an all-year festive favorite for everyone. Children love them cut into animal shapes.

1 teaspoon cinnamon
1 teaspoon ground ginger
   dash of nutmeg
   dash of aniseed
6 cups self-rising flour,
   sifted
1 cup chopped citron peel

½ cup ground almonds
4 eggs
2 cups sugar
3 tablespoons rum or
   brandy
½ pound honey
   honey for brushing

Sift the spices with the flour. Add the peel and nuts and mix. Beat the eggs and add the sugar and remaining ingredients except the extra honey. Roll out to cookie thickness and cut into rectangles or any desired shape. Lay on a greased and well-floured baking sheet and set aside for about 24 hours. Next day, bake in a 350° oven 15–20 minutes. While the cookies are still hot, brush with a little honey diluted in water.

FLORENTINE ALMOND BISCUITS   *Rosh Hashana*

In 1680, in honor of the birth of the dauphin of France, a cele-
bration was held at the Hotel de Ville in Paris in which the
"buffets were furnished with almond biscuits, candied fruits,
cakes, sweetmeats, oranges, ices, sweet barley water, lemonade,
tea and wine." No wonder the Florentine almond biscuit was
born of these ingredients soon after, to outlive the prince. Today
one of the most popular café cookies in Israel, it is served as it is
in Paris, at little tables on the street, with coffee.

4 tablespoons butter	½ cup chopped almonds
4 tablespoons sugar	3 ounces milk chocolate
1 tablespoon honey	(if desired)
1 teaspoon lemon juice	3 ounces bitter chocolate
½ cup flour	(if desired)
1 cup chopped candied	
citrus peels	

Mix the butter, sugar, honey and lemon juice and melt over a low
heat. Remove from heat. Mix the flour, fruits, and nuts and add
to first mixture. On a buttered pan drop the batter from a teaspoon, leaving room for the Florentines to spread. Pat the
cookies down with a wet spatula. Bake 10 minutes in a 350°
oven (until the edges are lacy and crisp and the cookies are a
little brown). Lift the cookies off the pan and put them onto a
wire rack. Some people serve them like this (the cookies crisp up
quickly outside the stove) and others proceed to melt the two
chocolates together in a double boiler, over hot water, and ice the
bottom of the Florentines.

DATE COOKIES   *Yom Kippur*

1 cup margarine	2 teaspoons baking powder
3 cups brown sugar	1 cup broken nuts
2 eggs	1 cup chopped dates
4 cups flour, sifted	

Cream the margarine and sugar; add the eggs one at a time. Sift
the flour and baking powder and add to the margarine mixture.
Add the nuts and dates. Work the dough into six rolls. Freeze,
then slice the rolls very thin and bake in a 400° oven for 10
minutes.

ZIMSTERNE *Yom Kippur*

"Zimsterne" in Yiddish means "to the stars" and these cinnamon cookies are suited to breaking the fast after Yom Kippur, when the stars come out. Spicy biscuits and cakes are in the tradition of the event.

¾ cup butter	1½ cups sifted cornstarch
¾ cup sugar	1 teaspoon cinnamon
2 eggs	1 egg yolks, diluted with
1 cup self-rising flour, sifted	water

Cream the butter and sugar well. Beat in the eggs. Mix the flour, cornstarch, and cinnamon and sift. Add to the butter-sugar-egg mixture. Roll out on a floured board and cut with a star cutter. Brush with diluted egg yolk and bake in a 400° oven for about 15 minutes.

SUM-SUM SESAME COOKIES *Yom Kippur*

The aromatic sesame seed goes into much festive baking: on Yom Kippur night this flavorful cookie is served in many homes in Israel for increased fruitfulness. Eastern families have very many children, no matter what their financial status is, for this is a Biblical blessing.

2 eggs	½ teaspoon baking soda
½ cup sugar	½ cup flour, sifted
4 tablespoons olive oil	2 cups sesame seeds

Cream the eggs, sugar, and oil together. Sift the soda into the flour and add. Work in the sesame seed. Roll the mixture into small balls and spread them on a greased cookie sheet. Press each cookie down with your finger. Bake in a 350° oven about 20 minutes or until golden.

Yom Kippur—Purim

CHADJOOBABDAH—CARDAMOM CAKES

Cardamom seeds are celled "grains of paradise," and indeed— aromatic, tangy—they taste heavenly in many Oriental dishes, such as this one, which is an Iraqi Purim treat, or is served on Yom Kippur night after the fast.

2 cardamom seeds ("hale,"   2 eggs, separated
    in Arabic)   1 cup sugar
1 cup almonds   1 cup flour, sifted

Grind the cardamom seeds and almonds. Beat the egg whites
stiff. Mix the yolks and sugar, then add the flour, nuts, and spice.
Add the egg whites. Form into small balls and press flat. Bake in
a 350° oven about 20 minutes.

HONEY COOKIES   *Yom Kippur*

*These honey cookies can be made well before Rosh Hashana and
kept until after Yom Kippur without drying out. In many homes,
they are eaten to break the fast on Yom Kippur. You may add or
omit spices such as ginger, cinnamon, mace, cloves, to suit your
own taste.*

3 eggs   4 cups flour
1 to 1¼ cups sugar   ½ teaspoon baking soda
⅓ cup margarine   1 teaspoon cinnamon
1 cup honey   icing sugar for topping

Beat the eggs until light. Add the sugar gradually, beating well.
Melt the margarine and beat in with the honey. Add the dry
ingredients, sifted together, and mix well. Drop from a teaspoon
onto a cookie sheet that has been lined with waxed paper. Bake
in a 300° oven 15 minutes. When cool, cover with icing sugar.

PEANUT COOKIES   *Hanuka*

⅓ pound shelled peanuts   5 cups flour, sifted
1 pound margarine   1 teaspoon ginger
1 cup brown sugar   1 teaspoon cinnamon
1 cup white sugar   2 teaspoons baking soda
4 eggs

Break the nuts. Cream the margarine and the two sugars. Beat
in the eggs and nuts, then add the remaining ingredients. Roll
out the dough to a thickness of 1½ inches and chill in the refrigerator for a few hours. Cut into strips and bake in a 350° oven
until the cookies are golden and crisp (20–30 minutes).

SPECULAASJES ARE SANTA CLAUSES   *Hanuka*

One of the typical anomalies of life in Israel is that this Dutch Christmastime cookie was introduced to Israel by a baker from Holland who won prizes for the pastry in the Netherlands! Even Orthodox Jewish children in Amsterdam, like my husband, would put out their wooden shoes on St. Nicholas Night (twenty days before Christmas) and find them full of "Sinterklaasjes" (Santa Clauses—as the seasonal variation is called) in the morning. Today the treat is in all the best delicatessen shops, available for all Israelis. My sister-in-law, Rosine Kahn, makes the secret recipe in this wonderful way:

1½ cups sugar	½ teaspoon ground cloves
2¾ cups flour, sifted	dash of allspice
pinch of salt	1 cup butter or margarine
2 teaspoons cinnamon	grated rind of 1 lemon
2 teaspoons ground ginger	1 egg

Mix the dry ingredients. Work in the margarine and lemon rind. Add the egg. Knead together and roll out thin. Cut into any desired shape and chill. Bake on a greased tin in a 350° oven until brown (10–15 minutes). Keep the cookies in a jar, as they must be crisp.

QUEEN ESTHER GOODIES   *Purim*

More little girls in Israel will dress in a Queen Esther costume on Purim than in any other country. This year I was delighted to see a little Arab girl, helping her brother shepherd a flock, dressed in a crown and all the other doo-dads, including a white long dress, to be Queen Esther on Purim!

Children lick the sugar or icing on cookies cut into Queen Esther figures because they love the Queen—and the cookie!

½ pound butter	½ teaspoon baking soda
½ cup sugar	½ teaspoon vanilla
1 egg	1 teaspoon lemon juice
2½ cups flour	rind of ½ lemon
pinch of salt	

Cream the butter and sugar and add the egg. Sift the dry ingredients together and add, along with the vanilla, lemon juice and lemon rind. Roll out and cut into Queen Esther figures. Put into a pan and refrigerate overnight. Bake in a 325° oven until golden (8–10 minutes). Cool and ice with plain white icing sugar. Sprinkle confetti candy on the skirt and crown shaped into each cookie.

MOHN PLAETZHEN—POPPY SEED COOKIES   *Purim*

" 'Let us be merry,' said Mr. Pecksniff. And here he took a captain's biscuit." Charles Dickens had the right idea! Cookies are good helpers in having a good time. Maybe that's why these are called "plaetzhen," which sounds like German for a bursting belly laugh, for everyone must be gay on Purim.

2 cups flour, sifted	1 cup poppy seed
2 cups sugar	2 eggs, beaten
2 cups butter	white wine as needed

Rub the flour, sugar, and butter together to form pea-sized or smaller balls. Add the poppy seed, eggs, and enough wine to hold the dough together. Roll out on a floured board, to a thickness of about ½ inch, cut into rectangles, and bake in a 350° oven until golden (8–12 minutes).

HREYBEE—SHORTBREAD COOKIES   *Purim*

These butter cakes, very much like shortbread, are a delicacy brought to Israel by immigrants from Syria. A special cutter forms them into an "S" shape, but no one seems to know the reason why this figure is used for pastries of Purim, being neither like the hat, purse, or pockets of Haman.

1 cup butter	4 cups flour, sifted
½ cup sugar	blanched almonds

Cream the butter and sugar and gradually mix in the flour. This dough is too rich to roll and must be patted, into a thickness of about ½ inch, onto flour-dusted cookie sheets with one's hands. Run the cutter referred to above over the dough, then prick with a fork. Press blanched almonds into each cookie. Bake in a 350° oven for about 30 minutes. Remove from the pan and dust with icing sugar.

NOTE: If you haven't one of the special cutters, just cut the dough into bars.

PURIM TAHINA CAKES

Purim

Haman's hat (triangular in shape) and Haman's pockets (half-moons) come in for ridicule in these Turkish-type cookies.

½ cup sugar
1 teaspoon cinnamon

1 cup tahina (sesame paste)*
flour as needed
powdered sugar

Mix the sugar, cinnamon, and tahina and add just enough flour to make a dough that can be rolled. Cut into triangular or crescent shapes and bake in a 400° oven a few minutes. Cool before removing from pan. Sprinkle with powdered sugar.

PURIM STICKY SQUARES

Purim

In the Bible (Ezekiel 27), we learn how the merchants of yore traded in all manner of ingredients which were used in their cooking. Honey was the sweetening agent of their confections, so we have good reason to believe that their sweetmeats were sticky, spicy, nutty, and of a plain baked dough baked and then boiled in honey. Mediterranean cakes have indeed retained those characteristics until today.

2 cups flour, sifted
1 tablespoon sugar
4 eggs

3 tablespoons cooking oil
1 pound honey
¼ pound poppy seed

Mix the flour, sugar, eggs, and oil. Knead together and roll out very thin. Cut into squares and prick with a fork. Bake in a 375° oven until the dough is crisp (7–10 minutes). Boil the honey, and dip the squares in it for a few minutes. Remove and roll in the poppy seed.

MAAMOUL—NUT-FILLED CAKES

Purim

This nut-filled cake is shaped into triangles by Jews coming to Israel from Arab lands, to resemble Haman's hat. It is usually sprinkled with rose water or orange-flavored water to give it a highly aromatic perfume. Rum or vanilla diluted in a little syrup or honey can also be used.

* The tahina used here is the pure sesame paste, not the paste-and-garlic mixture used as an appetizer. See note under Tahina for preparation.

¼ cup margarine
3 cups milk, lukewarm
1 pound semolina
¼ cup butter, melted
flour as needed

2 cups finely minced nuts
½ cup (or more) powdered
sugar
2 tablespoons rose or
orange water

Melt the margarine and mix with the milk. Add the semolina, cover, and leave overnight. In the morning add the butter, and if necessary in order to make the dough pliable, add a little flour. Mix the nuts with the powdered sugar and rose water (or substitute) to make a paste. Make little balls of the semolina dough and then shape each one into a thick triangle. Make a dent in the middle of each and work out a cavity with your finger. Fill with the nut mixture and close. Place the maamouls on a floured baking sheet and bake in a 350° oven for about 15 minutes, or until light gold in color. While hot, sprinkle with a little powdered sugar.

BISQUOTTI MOSCELLIESS   *Shavuot*

This is the Italian for "Moses' Biscuits." The cookies are shaped like Ten Commandment Tablets and, like the injunctions themselves, are plain, hard, and good.

4 heaping cups flour, sifted
1 cup sugar
¼ cup margarine
3 teaspoons baking powder

½ cup lukewarm water
2 eggs
1 teaspoon vanilla

Mix all the ingredients together. Roll out to a thickness of ¼ inch and cut with a form of the Tablets. Sprinkle with sugar and bake in a 350° oven until the cookies are crisp (about 10 minutes).

PASSOVER COOKIES   *Passover*

1 cup matzo meal
½ cup potato flour
1 cup fine sugar

½ cup ground almonds
¼ teaspoon ground ginger
2 eggs

Mix the dry ingredients together. Add the eggs and mix well. Roll out, cut into oblong pieces, and bake on a greased tin in a 400° oven until golden (about 10 minutes).

PASSOVER MACAROONS   *Passover*

3 egg whites
⅔ cup fine sugar
1 cup blanched ground
    almonds

6 tablespoons sifted matzo
    meal

Beat the egg whites stiff, adding sugar gradually. Fold in nuts
and matzo meal. Drop from a teaspoon onto a greased cookie
sheet and bake in 300° oven for about 30 minutes, or until crisp.

NOTE: 1 cup shredded coconut may be substituted for the nuts.

PFEFFERNUESSE—PEPPERNUTS   *Purim*

*An old superstition about nutmegs is that you will dream of your
true love if you boil a nutmeg, drink up the liquor, and put the
nut under your pillow.*

4 cups flour, sifted
½ cup fine sugar
1 whole nutmeg, grated
1 tablespoon cinnamon
    dash of cloves and allspice
2 teaspoons baking powder
½ teaspoon baking soda

4 eggs
2 tablespoons grated candied
    peel
2 cups honey, syrup, or
    molasses (or mixed)
½ cup margarine

Sift all the dry ingredients together. Mix the remaining ingredients (if necessary, warm the honey and the margarine) and add
the dry mixture. Roll into little balls the size of nutmegs and
place on a buttered pan. Bake in a 325° oven 35 minutes.

MOUNT SINAI CAKES   *Shavuot*

*Jews who left Spain for Italy, Greece, Turkey, and now have
come to Israel, make the same pastry for Shavuot, the Mount
Sinai cake, baked to resemble a mountain. The walnut is symbolic
of the dark cloud over Sinai. There are many different recipes
for this cake, some are soft-textured, some cookie-hard, but the
shape is always the same.*

6 eggs
½ cup sugar
4 tablespoons melted butter
½ cup honey

dash of cinnamon
2 cups flour, sifted
walnut halves

Beat the eggs briskly, then add the sugar and butter. Mix well.
Add the honey and cinnamon and continue beating. Add the flour
to make a stiff dough. Shape into cones to look like a mountain.
Top each with half a walnut. Put in a buttered pan and bake in
a 350° oven 15 minutes.

SHAVUOT COOKIES—TUNISIAN   *Shavuot*

½ *pound flour, sifted*   ½ *pound cottage cheese*
½ *pound butter*   *jam, as needed*

Mix the flour, butter, and cheese and roll out on a floured board.
Cut into small rounds. Coat half the rounds with jam. Cover
each with another round. Bake 15 minutes in 400° oven.

SUGAR COOKIES   *Shabbat*

4 cups flour, sifted   *1 cup sugar*
3 teaspoons baking powder   *grated rind and juice of*
2 eggs   *½ lemon*
¾ cup oil   *dash of salt*
¼ cup orange juice

Mix all the ingredients together and knead well. Roll out thin.
Sprinkle with more sugar and run the rolling pin over the dough
once more. Cut into rounds and bake in a 350° oven until light
gold (about 20 minutes).

ALMOND BISCOTTINI   *Rosh Hashana*

*This is a very hard almond roll that is made in the Ghetto of
Rome (and now in Israel-Italian homes). It is the biscuit used
in all the chief festivals.*

8 cups flour   *4 cups whole unblanched*
1 teaspoon cinnamon   *almonds*
3 cups sugar   *water*

Mix the flour, cinnamon, and sugar. Throw in the almonds and
add enough water to make a firm dough. Knead, roll into a long
loaf shape, and bake in a 350° oven about 20 minutes. Cut while
the dough is still warm or you may have to use a saw-toothed
knife thereafter.

SHPRINGELEH—ANISE COOKIES   *Shabbat*

4 eggs   *2¼ cups flour, sifted*
1½ cups sugar   *½ teaspoon powdered anise*

Beat the eggs well and add the sugar. Mix until creamy. Mix the flour with the anise, add to the first mixture, and mix well. Set aside to rest for 3 hours. Stir the mixture up again and drop by spoonfuls onto well-buttered baking sheets. Bake in 350° oven 10–12 minutes.

KICHLACH—MAMA'S "NOTHINGS"   *Shabbat*

Kichlach are as Jewish as challah, and every good wife takes pride in how she makes them. Mama's were so airy that we children called them "Nothings" and they were so superior in taste that I still marvel at how she managed it. Her secret may have been that we always had our own chickens and the eggs she used came right from the nest. We also made our own butter from the milk of our cow.

3 tablespoons fine sugar   *3 eggs*
1¼ cups flour   *⅓ cup melted butter*
    pinch of salt

Sift the sugar, flour, and salt together. Beat the eggs thoroughly, then add with the butter to the dry ingredients until a smooth paste results. Drop the kichlach from a teaspoon onto a lightly buttered baking sheet and bake in a 325° oven for about 20 minutes, or until the kichlach are a light toasty color and nicely puffed.

ZWIEBACK   *Shabbat*

1 ounce fresh yeast   *½ teaspoon powder anise*
    (2 packages dry)   *or ¼ teaspoon ground*
½ cup lukewarm milk   *nutmeg*
¼ cup sugar   *3 eggs*
¼ cup melted butter   *2½ to 3 cups flour, sifted*
½ teaspoon salt

Dissolve the yeast in the milk. Add the sugar, butter, salt, anise or nutmeg, eggs, and flour (only enough so you can handle the dough). Mix and set to rise. Form into oblong shapes and put into buttered pans. Cover and set in a warm place to rise for 1 hour. Bake in a 400° oven for about 20 minutes. When cooled, cut into slices and toast the zwieback in a very slow oven until gilded and crisp.

SUSPENSE KICHALACH　　　　　　　　*Shabbat*

Often when our star amateur actress Rosalie Berman comes to our playreading gatherings in Savyon, she brings the hostess a tin of her mouth-melting kichalach. To achieve their fabulous taste and texture, the kichalach must be suspended in the air (by laying them on a grilling rack in the oven) during baking. As we have tea after the second act and reach, under suspense of what is to happen in the last act, for Rosalie's kichalach, we've come to cell her cookies not "suspended" but "suspense!"

4 *eggs*	8 *cups self-rising flour,*
¾ *cup cooking oil*	*sifted, plus*
¾ *cup sugar*	4 *tablespoons*
	(for board)

Beat the eggs lightly with a fork, add the oil, stir in the sugar, and then work in the sifted flour. The dough must be as soft as possible, just able to be rolled out. Sprinkle the board and rolling pin with the 4 tablespoons of flour. Roll out the dough as thin as possible. Cut into rounds. Place the biscuits on a heated grilling rack (one that is divided into small squares) and bake in a 450° oven until light gold (about 10 minutes).

Rosh Hashana — Hanuka
PIZZA EBRAICA ROMANA DOLCE—ITALIAN FRUIT BARS

These delicious fruit bars were to be found only in the Ghetto of Rome, but now on Rosh Hashana and Hanuka, Italian immigrant women nostalgically serve them to guests. The bar is rather hard and keeps very well.

1 *cup sugar*	1 *cup chopped almonds*
½ *cup butter or margarine*	1 *cup pine nuts*
8 *cups flour*	½ *cup raisins*
¾ *cup candied fruits*	1 *teaspoon salt*
1 *cup oil*	1 *cup sweet red wine*
2 *teaspoons vanilla*	

Cream the sugar and butter and work in the flour. Add the remaining ingredients. Pat out on a greased tin and cut into squares. Bake in a 375° oven until golden (about 30 minutes).

MANDELBRODT   *Rosh Hashana — Shabbat*

Hospitality—like visiting the sick, providing for a poor bride, and keeping the Sabbath—is a must-mitzvah. No matter how poor a family, to receive a guest is a good deed, almost a command, and ever a joy. To ensure that some good thing is always on hand for the purpose, Jewish housewives bake Mandelbrodt, which keeps well for weeks. A fresh batch, of course, is readied for Rosh Hashana.

1⅓ cups self-rising flour	4 tablespoons melted
pinch of salt	margarine
4 eggs	1 teaspoon vanilla
1 cup sugar	½ cup chopped almonds
	cinnamon for sprinkling

Sift the flour and salt. Beat the eggs well, add the sugar, and mix thoroughly. Stir in the melted margarine and vanilla. Work in the flour mixture and the almonds. Using a little of the dough, put a layer in the bottom of each of two 9-inch loaf pans. Sprinkle with cinnamon and repeat the layers until all the batter is used up. Bake in a 350° oven for about half an hour. Cool and cut into half-inch slices. Arrange these on a dry baking sheet and toast in a 400° oven for a few minutes.

GEILA'S FRUIT BARS   *Tu Besh'vat*

My daughter Geila is, like most nineteen-year-old Israeli girls, a soldierette. When she smells these cookies coming out of the oven, she warns me of her pending military raid upon them.

4 cups flour	pinch of salt
1 teaspoon baking powder	1 cup chopped dates
1½ cups brown sugar	½ cup raisins
2 teaspoons cinnamon	1 cup candied citrus peel
1 teaspoon ground or	½ cup broken nuts
candied ginger	⅔ cup margarine
½ teaspoon allspice	½ cup orange juice
½ teaspoon cloves	2 eggs

Mix the dry ingredients. Roll in the fruit and nuts. Melt the margarine and add, along with the orange juice. Beat the eggs and mix in. Pat out, about ½ inch thick, on greased cookie tins. Refrigerate the dough for about an hour. Bake in a 375° oven for about 15 minutes. Cut into bars while still hot.

BRASSADEL DI PURIM—PURIM CAKES   *Purim*

3 tablespoons cooking oil	*4 cups flour, sifted*
3 egg yolks	*3 ounces chocolate chips*
juice of 1 orange	*½ cup sugar*
grated rinds of 1 orange	*2 ounces candied orange*
and 1 lemon	*peel*

Mix the oil, egg yolks, orange juice, and grated rind. Add the flour to make a dough. Roll out and sprinkle with the remaining ingredients. Fold over and roll, then cut into pieces. Set in a 400° oven until done (about 12 minutes). (Baste with a little more orange juice from time to time during baking.)

MAARUT—CINNAMON DATE ROLLS   *Purim*

Cinnamon is probably one of the oldest spices used in baking in Israel, though its first mention in the Bible is as a perfume for anointing oil. The date, as a food, is nowhere mentioned in the Old Testament, but as the tamar—the date palm—is repeatedly spoken of, this fruit was undoubtedly one of the most common in use in ancient days. Maarut is a Purim date roll baked by Israelis who once lived in neighboring Syria.

The Pastry	*The Filling*
1 cup margarine	*½ pound pitted dates*
4 tablespoons sugar	*1 cup sugar*
3 cups flour, sifted	*1 cup water*
water as needed	*1½ teaspoons cinnamon*
	¼ cup chopped walnuts

For the pastry, cream the margarine and sugar, work in the flour, and add just enough water to hold the dough together. Roll out.

For the filling, cook the dates, sugar, water and cinnamon together over low heat for 10 minutes, stirring often. Remove from heat. Add the walnuts and mix well. Spread on the dough and roll up. Cut into slices and bake in a 300° oven 50–60 minutes. Sprinkle with sugar the moment you remove the cookies from the oven.

PISTACHIO DELIGHT BARS   *Shabbat*

*Pistachio nuts (the Botneh or Pistak in Hebrew) were among
the treats which Jacob sent to the governor of Egypt. These nuts
are still special in Israel today, though plentiful in surrounding
lands.*

2 eggs	1½ cups self-rising flour
1 cup sugar	½ cup soy flour
1 cup melted margarine	½ cup glazed cherries, cut
1 tablespoon ground	into small pieces
ginger	½ cup raisins
1 teaspoon cinnamon	½ cup (or more) pistachio
1 cup Turkish delight (see	or other nuts, chopped
Index), cut into small	
pieces	

Beat the eggs, add the sugar, margarine, and spices. Sift the
two flours together and roll the fruits and nuts in them. Combine
the two mixtures and the candy, and bake in a well-greased pan
(10″ x 13″) in a 300° oven until golden (about 10 minutes). Then
turn off the heat and let the bars remain in the oven until firm but
not hard. Cut into bars while still warm. Keep in a covered jar to
retain their "chewy" quality.

SUM-SUM PESTELLES—SESAME TURNOVERS   *Hanuka*

*In the days of Judas Maccabaeus, honey, white flour (although
a very great luxury), sesame seeds, and spices, as well as wine
and milk, went into the baking of cakes called "sweet varieties."
King Solomon sings of his nut trees, so nuts were not new. White
wheat holiday buns were flavored with myrtle and called "pastil-
lus," and one wonders whether the small festival pastries called
"pestelles," which Greek Jews make today, are the scion of the
Maccabean treat.*

The Filling

1 cup walnuts
1 cup almonds
1 cup sesame seed
½ cup Turkish delight
(see Index)
honey as required

The Pastry

¾ cup olive (or other)
oil
½ cup water
½ teaspoon baking powder
1 teaspoon salt
4 tablespoons sugar
juice of ½ lemon
4 tablespoons orange juice
1½ cups flour

To make the filling, grind the nuts and sesame seed fine. Cut up the Turkish delight. Mix together with enough honey to hold the mixture together. Set aside.

For the pastry, mix together all the ingredients, adding the flour slowly at the last, to make a dough. On a floured board, roll out to a thickness of less than ½ inch. Cut into rounds and place a teaspoon of the nut mixture in the center of each. Fold over and pinch the edges together. Bake in a greased pan in a 350° oven until lightly browned (about 20 minutes). Dust with icing sugar. (Serves 8.)

NOTE: These cakes are sometimes dipped in rose water while still warm and then dusted with icing sugar.

PIRISHKEHS—HONEYED PASTRIES   *Shabbat*

The Dough

4½ cups flour, sifted
 2 teaspoons baking powder
½ teaspoon baking soda
½ teaspoon salt
 4 eggs
¾ cup sugar
 4 tablespoons water
    grated rind of 1 lemon

The Filling

4 cups chopped apples
½ cup raisins
½ cup nuts
½ cup sugar

The Syrup

1½ cups honey or syrup
 2 teaspoons ground
     ginger
 1 cup sugar
 1 cup water
    shredded coconut
    (optional)

Mix all the dough ingredients and roll out very thin. Cut into small squares (about 2-inch). Mix all the filling ingredients and put a teaspoon of the mixture on each square. Take the four corners of each pastry and pinch together, leaving the sides open. Bake in a greased pan in 400° oven until golden (about 10 minutes). Boil the honey, ginger, sugar, and water and drop the baked pastries into the boiling syrup. Let them cook for about 20 minutes, or until they are glazed. Remove them from the syrup and either let them dry, or if you wish, roll them in shredded coconut and then let them dry.

BROWN BEDOUINS *Shabbat*

"Indian brownies" were (and still are!) my favorite cookie-cake when I was a child in Canada. In Israel, the costly chocolate and walnuts were unavailable during the austerity years, and so my children came to love this substitute, which they call "Brown Bedouins."

5 tablespoons margarine
1 cup brown sugar
1 egg
1 teaspoon vanilla
½ cup self-rising flour

pinch of salt
¾ cup freshly roasted
    peanuts
a few ground hazelnuts

Melt the margarine and stir in the brown sugar. Beat the egg and add with the vanilla. Sift the flour and salt and add to the moist mixture. Stir in the nuts. Pour into a 9" x 14" pan and bake in a 350° oven for 25 minutes. Cut into bars.

BOTERKOEK—DUTCH BUTTER CAKES *Shavuot*

2 cups butter
2 cups sugar
5 cups flour (self-rising),
    sifted

2 teaspoons vanilla
1 tablespoon ginger powder
4 tablespoons milk

Cream the butter and sugar. Work in the flour. Add the vanilla and ginger and knead. Pat the pastry into a well-buttered baking dish and then brush with milk (so it will glaze). Bake in a 400° oven until golden (about 35 minutes). Mark into rectangles or parallelograms while still hot. Remove boterkoeks only after they are cooled.

LITTLE FIBS—COOKIE TWISTS *Purim*

These fried twists are supposed to symbolize the little fibs one is said to hear in Romania. They taste so good that the Jewish immigrants adopted them from the Gentile cuisine in Europe.

4 egg yolks
4 tablespoons cream
1 egg white, stiffly beaten
    pinch of salt

2 tablespoons rum
2 cups flour, sifted
oil for deep frying

Mix the egg yolks and cream. Fold in the egg white. Add the salt and rum, then add the flour gradually and work together. Knead on a floured board until very thin. Cut into rectangles. Slit each rectangle in the center, and pull one end through the slit. Fry in deep hot oil, turning about during frying. When golden, remove and drain on paper. Cool and sprinkle with icing sugar.

MATRIMONY DATE BARS   Shabbat

The Filling	*The Crumb Mixture*
2 cups chopped dates	*2½ cups flour, sifted*
2 cups brown sugar	*½ cup soy flour*
2 cups water	*1 teaspoon baking soda*
1 teaspoon vanilla	*pinch of salt*
	2 cups brown sugar
	1 cup margarine
	3 cups rolled oats

For the filling, cook the dates, brown sugar, and water on low heat until thick. Cool the mixture and add the vanilla.

For the crumb mixture, sift together the flour, soy flour, soda, and salt and add the sugar. Cut in the margarine with a pastry blender or two knives and work together until the mixture is crumbly. Work in the rolled oats. Pat half the mixture into a well-buttered square pan. Pour the filling in and then pat down the other half of the crumb mixture. Bake in a 300° oven 1 hour. Cut into bars while the mixture is still warm.

EIRROHRLI—CARNIVAL CAKES   Purim

The Swiss eat this treat at all their carnivals, and the Jews of that land and Alsace-Lorraine adopted it, too. In many ways it is similar to the frittered "Haman's ears" that Jews have on Purim in many lands.

7 medium eggs	*4 tablespoons melted butter*
½ cup milk or cream	*flour as needed*
pinch of salt	*butter for frying*
3 tablespoons powdered	*powdered sugar*
sugar	

Beat the eggs, milk, salt, sugar, and butter until smooth. Slowly add enough flour to make a dough that can be rolled. Cut into balls as big as a small apple and roll each out as thin as possible, then pull very carefully, from the center (on the back of the hand), until they are as thin as paper. Fry in butter in a very small pan so that the edges crinkle, and sprinkle with powdered sugar.

HAMAN'S EARS—OZNEI HAMAN   *P*_{urim}

*The custom of chopping off a criminal's ears is the reason, ex-
plained in the Midrash, why Haman's head was covered before his
hanging. His ears must certainly be burning in hell if he can
hear how they are symbolically being fried to a fritter in so
many Jewish homes, all over the world, on Purim. Here is the
basic recipe, with some of the variations in Haman's ears from a
number of other lands:*

2 eggs	*lukewarm water*
2 cups flour, sifted	*powdered sugar*
1 teaspoon baking powder	*oil for deep frying*
pinch of salt	

Mix the eggs, flour, baking powder, and salt with just enough
warm water to make a dough that can be rolled. Roll thin and cut
into 2-inch squares. Fry in deep hot oil, then drain on paper.
While still warm, sprinkle with powdered sugar.

Hamansooren (*Dutch*) : As in basic recipe above, but cut into
long rectangles.

Hamman-Mutzen (*German*) : As in basic recipe above, but with
2 tablespoons sugar added to the dough.

Schunzuchen (*Swiss and French-Lorraine*) : As in basic recipe
above, but with 2 tablespoons sugar, 3 tablespoons melted butter,
and lemon rind added to the dough. Cut with a wheel edger,
make a slit in the rectangle, and pull the end out to make a bow-
knot.

Heizenblauzen (*Austrian*) : As in basic recipe above, but omit
the water and use 3 eggs. Add 1 tablespoon cinnamon. Shape like
the Swiss Schunzuchen.

Diples (*Greek*) : Shaped like the Swiss Schunzuchen above, but
the dough is made by mixing together 6 eggs, 2¾ cups flour, ⅓
cup olive oil and 1 teaspoon lemon juice. The bowknots are
sprinkled with cinnamon and powdered sugar.

Shamleya (*Turkish*) : As in basic recipe above, but with 1 teaspoon lemon juice added to the dough. The pastry is cut into
strips and twirled during frying to form odd ear shapes.

Orecchie de Aman (*Italian*) : As in basic recipe above, but with
½ cup sugar and 2 tablespoons olive oil added to the dough.
Twirl to form into muff shapes during frying.

Oznei Haman (*North African*) : As in basic recipe above, but cut the dough into strips, roll around the handle of a wooden spoon, and fry in deep hot fat, singly. Dip in warm honey.

SEMOLINA HAMAN'S EARS (TUNISIAN STYLE)   *Purim*

The mockery made of Haman at the Purim festival shows rather a touching side of Jewish character. Haman was a Hitler, but instead of being remembered in hate and with harrowing pain, his image is converted into that of a scarecrow of sorts. The escape from his hands is celebrated more with merrymaking than with prayers of gratefulness.

2 cups semolina	*oil for deep frying*
4 eggs	*honey*

Knead the semolina and eggs together and roll out on a floured board. Cut into narrow ribbons about 3 inches long. Roll each around the handle of a wooden spoon and fry in deep hot oil. Drop the fritter off the spoon and dip it in honey. Sticky but succulent!

YEAST KISHELISH   *Purim*

1 ounce fresh yeast	*pinch of salt*
(or 2 packages dry)	*½ cup sugar*
½ cup lukewarm milk	*½ cup melted margarine*
2 cups flour, sifted	*fat for deep frying*
dash of cinnamon	*powdered sugar*

Dissolve the yeast in the warm milk and add to all the remaining ingredients. Roll out, cover, and set to rise until double in bulk. Cut into triangles and fry in deep hot fat. Drain on brown paper and sprinkle with powdered sugar.

PURIM PUFFS   *Purim*

1 recipe dough for soof-	*oil for deep frying*
ganiyot (see Index)	*powdered sugar*

Roll out the dough, cover with a cloth, and let rise for an hour. Cut into triangles (the shape of Haman's hat) and drop into very hot oil. The pastry puffs up and crisps. Remove from the oil, drain on paper, and sprinkle with powdered sugar.

PIES & PASTRIES

LINZER TORTE *Shabbat*

1 cup butter
1 cup sugar
3 eggs, separated
1 tablespoon rum
   grated rind and juice of
    1 orange

1 cup chopped almonds
2 cups self-rising flour,
   sifted
jam as required

Cream the butter and sugar. Beat the egg yolks and add. Mix well. Add the rum, orange juice and rind, nuts, and flour, and then fold in the egg whites, stiffly beaten. Roll out ⅔ of the dough and fit into a shallow spring-form pan. Spread rather generously with jam. Cut the remaining dough into ribbons and lattice them over the jam. Fill the squares between the dough lattice with more jam. Bake in a 375° oven until golden (about 30 minutes). Fill the holes once more with jam after removing the torte from the oven.

PASSOVER FLANS OR PIES *Passover*

In making fillings for Passover flans or pies which require cornstarch or flour for thickening, just substitute an equal quantity of potato flour for cornstarch, and half the amount of potato flour for ordinary flour. One-crust pies are best when made of matzos or matzo meal.

2 matzos
½ cup margarine
½ cup sugar

2 eggs, lightly beaten
   grated rind of 1 lemon
1½ cups matzo meal

Soak the matzos in water, squeeze out the liquid and crumble. Cream the margarine, add the matzos, and mix very well. Add the sugar and eggs, then the grated rind and the matzo meal. Pat into a greased pie dish. Fill with any desired filling (fresh fruits with sugar, but without any syrup, are best) and bake in a medium oven for about 35 minutes. (Serves 4–6.)

LEMON MERINGUE PIE   *Shabbat*

dash of salt	grated rind of 1 lemon
1¾ cups (plus 5–6 table-	4 tablespoons margarine
spoons) sugar	⅔ cup lemon juice
6 tablespoons flour or	4 eggs, separated
cornstarch	1 pie shell (see Index)
2 cups hot water	

Mix together the salt, the 1¾ cups sugar, and flour or cornstarch. Add the hot water and rind and cook, stirring constantly, until thick, and until all taste of raw flour or cornstarch has been eliminated. Remove from heat and add the margarine and lemon juice. Then gradually add to the beaten egg yolks, stirring constantly. Pour into the pie shell and bake in a 375° oven for about 5 or 7 minutes. Meanwhile whip the egg whites and add the 5–6 tablespoons sugar to them. Spread on top of the pie. Reduce the heat to 350° and bake until the tips of the meringue are gilded (about 10 minutes).

MARZIPAN PASTRY
(PASTICCI DI PASTA FROLLA CON MARZAPANI)   *Succot*

Jews have lived in Italy from the time of Titus, and though they have kept their identity and their own festivals, their food has taken on more and more of the Italian flavor. In Israel today the Italian community serves delectable Roman, Florentine, and Leghorn pastries, which the rest of the populace is slowly learning.

1 pound almonds	8 cups flour, sifted
2 cups sugar	2 cups sugar
3 cups candied fruits, cut up	water
6 eggs	

Blanch the almonds and then grind them. Mix with the sugar and candied fruits, then set aside. Combine the eggs, flour, sugar, and enough water to make a dough that can be kneaded. Knead. Divide the dough in two and roll out. Sprinkle the fruit-nut mixture on one sheet of dough and cover with the other, if you are too busy to make the traditional form. If not, cut the dough into circles of two sizes (3-inch and 2-inch). Sprinkle the large circles with the fruit-nut mixture and cover with the smaller ones. Bake in a 400° oven until light gold (about 30 minutes). Ice the top and sprinkle with colored candy confetti. (Serves 8–10.)

MERGTAART—MARROW TART   *Rosh Hashana*

How little some dishes have changed in centuries! This English tart—baked in a "coffin," the term used for the pastry case of a pie—dates back 550 years! "Take and poke out the marrow of bones as whole as you may; then take the bones and boil them in water, until the broth be fat enough. Then take almonds and wash them clean and grind them and temper them up with the fat broth: thus will the (almond) milk be brown. Then take powdered cinnamon, ginger and sugar and cast thereon. Then take and raise fair coffins and let them harden in the oven. Then take raisins and currants and lay in the coffin along with stoned dates. Stick great and long gobbits of marrow upright on the bottom and let bake awhile. Then take eggs a few and swinge the yolks with the (almond) milk and pour into the coffin half full and let bake; and when it ariseth, it is enough; then serve forth."

Pastry	Filling
2 cups flour, sifted	1½ rusks
1 cup margarine or suet	¾ cup marrow
¾ cup sugar	4 eggs, separated
½ teaspoon salt	½ cup sugar
	1 teaspoon vanilla or spice
	1 cup ground almonds
	¾ cup candied peel or dates, currants, and raisins

Mix the ingredients for the pastry and line a casserole with ⅔ of the resulting dough. Grate the rusks and sprinkle half on the pastry. Melt the marrow and add beaten yolks, sugar, vanilla or spice, ground nuts, fruits, and the remaining rusk crumbs. Beat the egg whites until stiff, fold into the mixture, and pour the mixture into the pie shell. Roll out the remaining pastry and cut into strips to make a lattice on top of the filling. Bake in a 375° oven for one hour and serve warm. (Serves 6–8.)

THE BEST BANANA PIE   *Succot*

"Pyes" are an English creation and an American development. And with their liberation from the traditions of the Old World, the Yanks, who daringly introduced the banana into vegetable salads and into cooking as a meat accompaniment, put them even into the pies (no longer pyes, and not even "coffins," as pie shells were called in those days). Bananas are so abundant in Israel

that we have come to learn how to use them in cookery from the Americans.

The Pastry	The Filling
½ cup margarine	6 bananas
1½ cups flour, sifted	½ cup white sugar
½ teaspoon baking powder	⅓ cup ground nuts,
pinch of salt	preferably almonds
4 tablespoons cold water	1 tablespoon melted
	margarine
	¾ cup raisins
	dash of ginger, nutmeg,
	cinnamon
	3 egg whites, stiffly beaten

For the pastry, chop up the margarine and mix with the remaining ingredients. Divide the dough in half. Roll out each half on a floured board. Line a deep 9-inch pie plate with one half the dough, and prick with a fork.

For the filling, mash the bananas fine and add the sugar, nuts, margarine, raisins, and spices. Fold in the stiffly beaten egg whites. Pour into the lined pie dish and cover with the remaining pastry. Prick this pastry with a fork. Bake in a 425° oven for 30 minutes, or until golden. Cool the pie on a rack. (Serves 6.)

TART AUX PRUNES—PLUM PIE *Rosh Hashana*

From France came this dish. It is similar to a plum pie from Alsace, but different enough for identification. In Israel, the last plums of the orchards come onto the market at Rosh Hashana.

1 recipe any favorite pie	sugar to taste
pastry	½ cup dark jam or jelly
6 plums, halved and stoned	1 tablespoon water

Prepare the pie pastry and line a 7-inch pan with it. Fill the form with a single closely packed layer of plum halves. Sprinkle with sugar to taste and bake in a 375° oven 45 minutes. Mix the jam or jelly with the water. Immediately on taking the tart from the oven, glaze the plums with the jelly mixture. Or you can cool the cake and coat it with a dark jelly made of flavored gelatin from a package. But pour this on only after the tart is cold and the gelatin has already begun to thicken. (Serves 6.)

"HADAR" ORANGE CHIFFON PIE *Ju Besh'vat*

"Hadar" means "majestic, splendid," and it is perhaps for that reason that citrus fruits are called "hadarim" in Hebrew. While generally the American pie has not gone beyond the reaches of the small American-Jewish community in Israel, the citrus pie has crashed the cooking barrier of the land, because oranges and lemons are so plentiful.

¾ cup sugar
1 package lemon-flavored
   gelatin
1 cup orange juice
1 cup water
4 egg yolks, slightly beaten

1 tablespoon grated lemon
   rind
4 egg whites, beaten stiff
½ teaspoon cream of tartar
   any cooked pie shell,
   cooled
   whipped cream, if desired

In the top of a double boiler, blend together ¼ cup of the sugar, gelatin, orange juice, water and egg yolks. Cook over hot water, stirring constantly, until the mixture almost comes to a boil. Stir in the rind. Cool. Fold in the egg whites mixed and beaten with the remaining sugar and the cream of tartar. Pour into the cooled pastry shell and allow to set for a few hours. Top, if you wish, with whipped cream.

POPPY SEED PIE *Purim*

Legend relates that Queen Esther was a vegetarian because she would eat only kosher foods at the court of Ahasuerus. Poppy seed dishes were her favorites. And when you taste this poppy seed pie, you'll know why.

1¾ cups sugar
 ½ pound ground poppy
   seed
 1 tablespoon rum
 1 cup milk

6 eggs, separated
  butter and flour for pan
  rum-flavored, sugared
   whipped cream

Mix ¾ cup of the sugar with the poppy seed, rum, and milk. Cook for 20 minutes in a double boiler, over boiling water. Cool the mixture. Mix the egg yolks with ½ cup of the sugar and beat a little, and then beat into the poppy seed mixture. Beat the egg whites, until stiff, with the remaining sugar and fold in. Butter a large spring pan generously and sift enough flour on top to cover the butter. Gently pour in the filling and bake in a 350°

oven for about an hour. Cool and serve with a topping of rum-flavored, sugared whipped cream.

PASSOVER CRUMB PIE CRUSTS *Passover*

Cake or Cookie Crust

1½ cups cake or cookie
     crumbs
½ cup butter or margarine
2 tablespoons sugar

Matzo Meal Crust

1½ cups matzo meal, sifted
½ cup butter or margarine
4 tablespoons sugar

Mix the crumbs or matzo meal with the fat and sugar and pat into a pie pan. Bake for 5 minutes in a hot oven. Any everyday filling will do, but if it requires flour or cornstarch substitute potato flour (half the amount of flour called for, or the same amount as cornstarch).

APFELSTRUDEL—APPLE STRUDEL *Independence Day*

Apfelstrudel is on every festive board in Israel; it was a favorite here long before apples became the common crop they are now. There are as many recipes for apple strudel as there are good cooks; this one is a particularly succulent and rich concoction.

2½ cups flour
1 teaspoon salt
2 tablespoons margarine
2 eggs
⅔ cup lukewarm water
5 cups sliced apples
3 tablespoons oil

1 cup brown (or white)
    sugar
6 tablespoons raisins
6 tablespoons chopped
    almonds
lemon and orange rind
cinnamon and allspice

Mix the flour, salt, margarine, eggs, and water. Knead very well and beat with the rolling pin, or lift up and lash against table edge. Then allow the dough to rest for 15 minutes in a warm place. On a table (preferably a round one) put a cloth and dust it with flour. Roll out the dough and put it in the middle of the table, then stretch it on the backs of your hands until it is paper-thin. Cover the dough with the sliced apples, sprinkle with the oil, sugar, raisins, nuts, rinds, and spices. Roll up, folding in the edges. Bake for 10 minutes in a very hot oven (450°), continue to bake for another 20 minutes at 400°, then reduce heat to 350° and bake until done (about 20 minutes more). (Serves 8–10.)

SUCCOT STRUDELS

Succot

The strudels and strudel doughs that one can make are as many as there are pies and pie pastries. Today the busy Israel house-wife buys her favorite strudel dough (some so white and thin it looks like a roll of tissue paper) at the nearest bakeshop, but there are many who pride themselves in the pastry as much as in the filling. This Hungarian strudel dough, known as "rétes," is very good. Fill it with cherries or other fruit, as below, for a moist strudel. For a strudel that is to keep, use a filling of dates, glazed peels, shredded coconut, raisins, cookie crumbs, spices and a little jam with the fat and sugar.

The Pastry	Fresh Fruit Filling
2½ cups flour	⅓ cup melted margarine
1 teaspoon margarine	4 cups cherries or other
pinch of salt	fresh fruit
1 egg	1 cup sugar
½ cup water	dash of cinnamon
	½ cup chopped almonds
	½ cup cake or breadcrumbs

Sift the flour and knead with the fat, salt, egg, and water. Cover with a warm bowl and let stand for about 25 minutes. Cover a large table with a sheet and dust well with flour. Put the dough in the middle and roll it out as much as possible. Flour your hands and put them under the dough. As the dough gets thinner and thinner, keep lifting and pulling it gently towards the edges of the table. Remove any thick edges. Let the dough dry for a couple of minutes and then begin with the filling. Sprinkle the dough with the melted margarine, then sprinkle on the fruit, sugar, cinnamon, almonds, and crumbs. Roll up the strudel by lifting the tablecloth. Put into a lightly greased pan, brush with a little diluted egg if you wish or with oil, and bake in a 350° oven about an hour, or until golden. (Serves 8–10.)

HANUKA CHEESE STRUDEL

Hanuka

In the Middle Ages the favorite Hanuka food, like that for Shavuot, was cheese and dairy food generally, but for quite other reasons. The story of Judith, which was said to have inspired the Maccabees to fight more vigorously, was read during Hanuka week; it relates that she gave Holofernes milk to drink, which lulled him to sleep and thus led to his defeat. Cheese strudel and cheese pancakes are therefore still served in many Israel house-holds on this festival of victory.

The Pastry	*The Filling*
1½ cups flour, sifted	½ cup raisins
pinch of salt	2 pounds cottage cheese
1 egg	3 eggs
½ cup lukewarm water	pinch of salt
½ cup melted margarine	½ cup sugar
	¼ cup sour cream

Mix all the ingredients for the dough and knead on a floured board until elastic. Set to rest for an hour in a warm place. Roll out the dough as thin as possible and then, over a floured cloth on a tabletop, stretch it on the backs of your hands until it is very thin. Brush the dough with melted margarine and sprinkle with the raisins. Mix the remaining ingredients for the filling and spread over the dough. Roll up and bake in a 400° oven for about 30 minutes. For a good color, the strudel may be brushed with melted margarine during baking. The moment you remove the strudel from the oven, sprinkle generously with sugar. (Serves 8–10.)

PEACH NOODLE-STRUDEL　　　*Shabbat*

Mama didn't have time to stretch a strudel dough for every Sabbath when she knew full well that her seven children would devour most of it. So she used to make it quickly with a special noodle-type dough, like many another Jewish mother. I believe it tastes even better than the hard-labor variety.

4 eggs	sugar to taste
pinch of salt	6 medium peaches, sliced
4 tablespoons cooking oil	breadcrumbs
3 cups flour, sifted	egg diluted with water
¼ cup melted margarine	(optional)

Beat the eggs lightly, then add the salt and oil. Add enough flour to make a stiff dough. Roll out as thin as possible. Brush the dough with melted margarine and sprinkle with sugar. Cover generously with sliced peaches and sprinkle with more sugar and a few breadcrumbs. Fold over in a rather flat roll. Brush with more margarine or diluted egg and bake in 375° oven 30–40 minutes. Cut the strudel while hot but let it cool in the pan. (Serves 6–8.)

CHEESE STRUDEL   *Shavuot*

1 *cup cottage cheese*   1 *teaspoon vanilla*
⅓ *cup raisins*   1 *recipe strudel or Danish*
5 *tablespoons sugar*   *dough* (*see* Index)
2 *eggs*   4 *tablespoons melted*
   grated rind and juice   *margarine*
   of 1 lemon   3 *tablespoons crumbs*

Mix the cheese, raisins, sugar, eggs, lemon rind and juice, and
vanilla and spread on the dough. Drizzle on the melted margarine
and sprinkle with crumbs. Roll up. Brush the top of the strudel
with melted margarine and bake in a 375° oven until golden and
crisp (45–50 minutes). (Serves 4–6.)

DRIED FRUIT STRUDEL   *Tu Besh'vat*

*Strudel is festive pastry on all Jewish holidays, but on Tu Be-
sh' vat the dried fruit strudel is a must.*

The Pastry   *The Filling*

1 *tablespoon cooking oil*   ½ *cup brown sugar*
   plus oil for drizzling   ½ *cup shredded coconut*
1 *egg*   1 *cup raisins*
½ *cup lukewarm water*   1 *cup blanched almonds*
   pinch of salt   1 *cup chopped dates*
2 *cups flour, sifted*   ½ *cup candied cherries,*
                                     chopped
                                 1 *cup cake or breadcrumbs*
                                     rind (*grated*) *of one orange*
                                     and one lemon

To make the pastry, mix the 1 tablespoon of oil, beaten egg,
water, and salt. Add to the flour and form a ball of dough. Knead
until smooth and elastic. Stretch the dough as thin as possible.
(On a floured table top, the dough can be stretched on backs of
hands to paper thinness.) Drizzle oil over the whole surface.
Sprinkle with the brown sugar and the other filling ingredients.
Roll to desired thickness, cut off and put into a greased pan to
bake. Cut into serving sections while still warm. (Serves 6–8.)

RAHM STRUDEL *Shabbat*

1 recipe strudel dough
  (*see* Index)
4 cups yoghurt
1 cup bread or cookie
  crumbs

1 cup chopped nuts
1 cup raisins
2 cups sugar
2 teaspoons cinnamon
  margarine

Sprinkle the paper-thin strudel dough with yoghurt and then spread and sprinkle with the remaining ingredients (except margarine). Roll up and bake in a well-buttered pan in a 375° oven 30–40 minutes. Dab margarine on top of the strudel and baste with the liquid during baking. This strudel is served warm, generally as a dessert. (Serves 8.)

ALMOND STRUDEL *Shabbat*

1 recipe strudel dough
  (*see* Index)
½ cup melted margarine
2 cups blanched almonds

5 egg yolks, beaten
1 cup sugar
1 lemon rind, grated

Brush the strudel dough with melted margarine. Grind the nuts or chop fine. Mix with egg yolks, sugar, and rind and spread over the dough. Roll up and brush the top with more melted margarine. Bake in a 375° oven until golden on top (30–40 minutes.) (Serves 6.)

TOPFEN KIPFEL—CHEESE CRESCENTS *Shavuot*

2 cups flour, sifted
1 cup dry cottage cheese
1 cup butter

pinch of salt
egg yolk diluted with
  water

Sift the flour 3 times. Blend the cheese, butter, and salt together and work in the flour. Refrigerate the dough overnight. Working quickly, roll out on a floured board. Cut into triangles and roll up each triangle, beginning at the broad side. Turn in the edges to form a crescent. Brush the tops with diluted egg yolk and bake in a 350° oven until the crescents are golden (20–25 minutes). The crescents may be filled with a bit of jam mixed with crumbs, or ground nuts, sugar, and crumbs.

BAKLAVA

Succot

Greek and Turkish immigrants have introduced this rich pastry to Israel, where women make it on Succot for their husbands. It makes them feel very rich.

2½ cups butter or
    margarine
1 pound strudel pastry
    sheets *

3 cups nut meats (wal-
    nuts, pistachios, etc.)
2 cups sugar
¾ cup water
    lemon juice to taste

Melt the butter. Place a sheet of dough in a buttered baking pan and spread with butter, and repeat. Occasionally sprinkle a sheet with nuts (or save the lot for the top sheets). As you near the top, become a bit more generous with the sprinkling, so that the bottom part is flaky and the top fruity and nutty. Top with a few sheets of the dough, and butter well. Cut into diagonal sections and bake in a moderate oven for 45 minutes, or until golden. From time to time during baking, drain off the excess butter. Meanwhile cook the water and sugar to form a syrup and then add lemon juice to taste. When the baklava has been baked, but is still very hot, slowly pour the syrup over. Allow to cool and set. (Serves 8–10.)

    * The strudel dough, known as "yufka" or "borek" pastry in Turkey, is bought in pastry shops in Israel. You can use any thin strudel dough (*see* Index). Everything else in this recipe is very fattening, but worth the risk.

KINDLECH

Purim

An ancient Jewish legend relates that Haman was hanged on a thorn bush, which said: "I am fitted to do this service, because the ungodly are as prickling thorns." Then the following fruit trees cried out that they were symbolic of the people of Israel: the fig tree, the vine, the apple tree, the nut tree, the citron.
    The fruits of the symbolic trees are used in making kindlech.

1 ounce yeast
½ cup warm milk
4 cups flour, sifted
3 eggs, well beaten
½ cup butter, melted
¾ cup sugar
    pinch of salt
1½ cups lukewarm milk

½ cup margarine, melted
½ cup chopped dried figs
1 cup raisins
2 cups chopped apple
½ cup chopped nuts
½ cup candied citron peel
1 egg yolk, diluted in
    water

Dissolve the yeast in the ½ cup warm milk and add to the flour with the eggs, butter, sugar, salt, and the 1½ cups lukewarm milk. Knead into a smooth dough and roll out. Brush with the melted margarine and sprinkle half the dough with chopped fruits and nuts, then fold over. Brush the top of this fold with melted margarine and strew half with nuts and fruits and fold over once more. Continue this until all the dough is folded into a flat oblong. Brush the top with the diluted egg yolk and cut the dough into finger strips. Set aside in a warm place for about an hour to rise. Bake in a 325° oven about 1 hour.

KIPFEL—FILLED CRESCENTS OR RUGELACH   *Hanuka*

The Jews adopted kipfeln from the Viennese and called it "kipfel" or "rugelach." Its history goes back to the siege of Vienna in 1683, when King John III Sobieski of Poland arrived at the hungry, besieged city, to rescue it. To taunt the fleeing Turks, the bakers' guild used the last bit of flour to bake crescent-(kipfeln) shaped breads. Today they are filled with nuts, jam, or dried fruit.

The Pastry

⅔ cup milk plus 4 table-
    spoons
1 ounce fresh yeast
    (or 2 packages dry)
    pinch of salt
½ cup butter
3 tablespoons sugar
3 egg yolks
2½ cups flour, sifted
2 egg whites

The Nut Filling

1 cup walnuts
1 cup brown sugar
    juice of 1 lemon

For the pastry, scald the ⅔ cup milk. Cool to lukewarm. Add the yeast, then the salt. Cream the butter and sugar. Add the egg yolks one at a time, mixing well. Add flour alternately with the yeast mixture and knead well. Allow to rise until double in bulk (about 45 minutes). Roll out very thin and cut into triangles.

Combine the ingredients for the filling and put some of the mixture in the center of each triangle. Roll up, beginning at the broad side of the triangle. When rolled up, turn the ends in to form a crescent. Put on a buttered cookie sheet and allow to rise again for two hours. Beat the egg whites, mix with the 4 tablespoons milk, and brush on the kipfel. Bake in a 350° oven until slightly gilded (about 30 minutes). (Makes about 25–30.)

KINDEL   *Purim*

The favorite Purim pastry of Vienna Jews is the "kindel," which looks like a baby tied in a blanket, reminiscent of Haman's brood. The filling is of "mohn" (poppy seed)—because it sounds like "Haman"—and/or nuts.

The Pastry

¼ cup butter
1 tablespoon sugar
1 egg yolk
1 cup flour, sifted

The Poppy Seed Filling

(see Hamantaschen II, following)

Cream the butter and sugar and the egg yolk and flour. Pat out the dough and cut into rectangles. Put the filling onto one edge of the dough and roll up like a strudel. Mark with a fork like strings tied around a blanket. Bake in a 350° oven until golden (12–15 minutes).

HAMANTASCHEN I (COFFEE-TIME TYPE)   *Purim*

This recipe has a povidle—plum jam—filling, the most popular among Jews hailing from Bohemia.

The Pastry

1 cake compressed yeast
    (or 2 packages dry)
¼ cup lukewarm milk
½ cup sugar
½ cup butter
    pinch of salt
1 cup hot milk
2 eggs
4 cups flour, sifted
    oil, or egg yolk diluted in
    water (for topping)

The Povidle Filling

1½ cups plum jam
    rind and juice of
    1 lemon
½ cup chopped nuts
½ cup bread or cake
    crumbs

For the pastry, dissolve the yeast in the lukewarm milk and add sugar. Mix the butter, salt, and hot milk. Cool. Add the yeast mixture. Add the eggs and flour, a little at a time, to make a soft dough. Knead and place in a warm bowl to rise until doubled in bulk. Knead again and roll out to a thickness of ¼ inch. Cut into rounds.

Mix the filling ingredients and place some of the mixture on each round. Pinch the edges of each circle to form triangles (the shape of Haman's purse). Put on a baking sheet, cover, and put to rise until again doubled in bulk. Brush the tops with oil, or egg yolk diluted with water. Bake for about 25 minutes in a 350° oven.

TOPFEN PASTRY   *Shavuot*

This is a Viennese pastry folded over like an envelope to hold a filling. When filled, its shape is like that of a mountain, and so was eaten by Jews in Germanic countries on Shavuot as a symbol of Mount Sinai. It is topped with povidle—plum jam—to represent the dark cloud that hovered over the mountain at the time the Tablets of the Law were given. You can use any good rich yeast dough, but Danish pastry is the favorite dough for this.

Danish Pastry

 4 cups flour, sifted
 1 cup margarine
 ½ cup milk
 3 tablespoons sugar
 1 ounce yeast
 2 eggs
   plus (or any dark) jam,
     for topping

The Filling

 1½ cups cottage cheese
  3 tablespoons sour cream
  2 tablespoons flour
  2 eggs, beaten
  ¾ cup sugar
  ½ cup chopped blanched
     almonds
  2 tablespoons melted
     margarine
  1 teaspoon vanilla

The puff pastry is complicated, but worth the effort. Take a third of the flour and work into a paste with the margarine. Warm the milk slightly and dissolve the sugar and yeast in it. Beat the eggs and add (reserve a spoonful for glazing the pastry later on). Mix the remaining flour with the egg mixture. Roll out the egg dough, thinning at the edges. Roll the butter dough into a small circle and put on top of the egg dough. Overlap the butter dough with the thin edges of the egg dough. Put the dough in the bottom of the refrigerator for 10 minutes and then roll out, fold over and roll out again. Refrigerate again for a few minutes and roll out again thinly, folding over as before. Cut into 3-inch squares.

For the filling, mix all the ingredients to a smooth paste. Place a spoonful of filling on each pastry square. Fold corners into the center and pinch together tightly. Set aside to ferment in a cool place for as much as 6 hours. Brush the pastry with the leftover beaten egg, top with a little plum or other dark jam. Bake in a very hot oven (450°) for 15 minutes.

HAMANTASCHEN II (TEATIME TYPE)   *Purim*

What the bulging cheeks enclosed, what the jaws were chewing and the throats swallowing, he could not see from the window, but he felt fairly certain that it must be those sweet and fresh and wonderful triangular hamantaschen, stuffed with honeyed poppy seed that melted in your mouth and tasted like something in Eden.

—SHOLOM ALEICHEM

The Pastry

2 cups flour, sifted
2 teaspoons baking powder
½ cup sugar
   pinch of salt
2 eggs, well beaten
3 tablespoons oil
   grated rind of 1 lemon

The Filling

2 cups ground poppy seed
⅓ cup honey
1 egg
1 tablespoon lemon juice
4 tablespoons chopped nuts

For the pastry, sift the dry ingredients together. Add the eggs, oil, and lemon rind. Mix well and roll out on a floured board to a thickness of ¼ inch. Cut into 3-inch squares.

To make the filling, wash the poppy seed in hot water, and if not purchased ground, put through the meat chopper or pound with a mortar. Mix with the honey and cook over very low heat for 5 minutes. Remove from heat and add the remaining ingredients. Place a spoonful of filling on each square and fold over to form triangles. Then press the edges together. Bake in a 375° oven for 20 minutes.

Independence Day
SAVARINS LEAVENED—RUM CUP CAKES

This French yeast cake was created by Brillat-Savarin, the French gastronome. It is made in individual forms, one of the most popular treats bought in cafés. On Independence Day, countless thousands of savarins will be consumed in Tel Aviv, as holiday makers sip coffee and watch the crowds go by.

2 ounces dry yeast
    (4 packages)
1 cup lukewarm water
4 cups flour
1¾ cups sugar
1 cup margarine

1 teaspoon salt
6 eggs, separated
1 teaspoon vanilla
6 tablespoons rum or
    brandy
   whipped cream

Put the yeast in the water and then stir in 1 cup of the flour. Cream 1 cup of the sugar and the margarine. Add the salt, half the egg whites, all the yolks, and the vanilla. Stir in the remaining flour and the yeast mixture. Fold in the three remaining egg whites, stiffly beaten. Butter muffin tins, and if you wish, sprinkle with brown sugar. Divide the dough into balls, to half-fill individual muffin tins. Cover with a cloth and let rise until doubled in bulk. Bake for about 10 minutes in a 375° oven, then reduce heat to 350° and bake about 15 minutes more. Remove the cakes from the tins. Boil the remaining ¾ cup of sugar with ½ cup water until thick, and then add the rum or brandy. Pour the hot syrup into the muffin tins and put the warm savarins back into the tins to soak up the syrup. Spoon some of the syrup over the top of the cakes, too. Cool, then chill. Cut a cap halfway through the savarin and fill with whipped cream. Serve very cold. (Makes about 24 cakes.)

CREME SCHNITTE (NAPOLEONS)   *Shabbat*

The Millefeuille Pastry

3 cups flour
½ cup margarine
1 tablespoon vinegar
¾ cup lukewarm water
1 cup butter

The Custard Filling

3 eggs, separated
7 tablespoons sugar
2½ tablespoons flour
2 cups milk
½ cup butter
1 teaspoon vanilla

For the pastry, mix the flour, margarine, vinegar, and lukewarm water and knead very well. Divide the butter into 3 parts. Roll out the dough, spread with one third of the butter, fold over, and put to rest in the refrigerator for 3 hours. Roll out again, spread with the second third of the butter and fold over. Refrigerate overnight. Next day roll the dough out again, spread with the remaining third of the butter, fold over, and put to rest in refrigerator for 3 minutes. Roll out, prick with a fork, and bake in a 350° oven about 55 minutes. Cut into rectangles.

To make the custard filling, beat the egg yolks and sugar. Add the flour and milk and cook in the top of a double boiler. Remove from heat, add the butter and vanilla and fold in the egg whites, stiffly beaten. Cool and fill the split millefeuille pastry thickly (1 inch or more).

MANDARIN (ORANGE) MUFFINS

Tu Besh'vat

The orange, especially the mandarin—often called the Japanese orange—was held in such esteem centuries ago that a Japanese princess born in the year 712 was named "Younger Daughter of the Mandarin Tree." The following recipe can be made with sliced mandarins or other oranges.

2 eggs	2 teaspoons baking
½ cup milk or orange juice	powder
4 tablespoons melted	½ teaspoon salt
butter	12 teaspoons honey
1½ cups flour, sifted	12 slices unpeeled mandarin
½ cup sugar	oranges

Beat the eggs slightly with a fork and stir in the milk (or orange juice) and butter. Sift together the flour, sugar, baking powder, and salt and add. Place in the bottom of each of 12 greased muffin tins 1 teaspoon honey, then an orange slice. Pour batter on top. Bake and turn out so that the orange slice is on top. (Makes 12 muffins.)

ECLAIRS

Shavuot

The Pastry

½ cup margarine
1 cup water
1 cup flour, sifted
3 eggs

The Filling

3 teaspoons cornstarch
½ cup sugar
1 cup hot milk
2 egg yolks, slightly beaten
1 teaspoon vanilla

For the pastry, put the margarine and water into a pot, and when the margarine has melted, add the flour all at once. Stir briskly until the mixture no longer sticks to the side of the pan. Cool somewhat and add the eggs, one at a time, beating after each addition. Put the mixture into a pastry tube and squeeze it out onto greased tins, into oblong shapes about 1 inch wide and 4 inches long. Bake in a 450° oven 20 minutes. Cool.

For the filling, mix the cornstarch and sugar, add the hot milk, and pour gradually over the slightly beaten egg yolks. Cook in a double boiler, stirring often, until thick. Cool and add the vanilla. Open the pastries at one side and fill with custard. Frost the tops with any favorite chocolate icing.

LA FLOGNARDE (PUFF)   *Hanuka*

Tereska Torres, French novelist, told me she could cook only one thing, the quick-puff-cookie (giant size) which her colleague Colette publicized. It is a pastry dating back to the time when transport was by carriage, and could be made by the innkeeper's wife at the posting stations in the time it took to change horses.

1 cup self-rising flour, sifted	1 cup milk
salt	2 eggs
	3 teaspoons sugar

Put the flour and salt on a board and make a cavity in the middle. Put the milk and eggs into this. Mix well into a smooth dough. Allow the dough to rest 10 minutes. Put into a greased pan and place in a cold oven. Turn on the oven to 350°. In 25 minutes the flognarde will be puffed and golden. Sugar it and serve at once. (Serves 4–6.)

SARAH-LEAH PASTRY   *Rosh Hashana*

These honey-soaked sweets are named for two of the Biblical mothers of Israel—one who was childless until her old age, and another who had to share her husband with a woman he loved more than he did her. Sarah is known for the cakes she baked, and Leah for the love apples she got but didn't use (maybe that's why they aren't in this recipe!).

10 sheets baklava pastry (paper-thin strudel dough)	1/4 teaspoon cinnamon
	1/2 teaspoon grated lemon rind
1/4 pound butter or margarine, melted	1/2 pound honey
cake crumbs	1 cup water
1/4 pounds walnuts or pecans, chopped	1 teaspoon vanilla

Take 2 sheets of pastry at a time (one over the other) and brush with melted margarine. Put crumbs over 1/8 of the dough at the edge nearest to you. Fold the edges over. Sprinkle on the nuts, cinnamon, and rind. Roll up over a rod (thickness of a pencil) and then squeeze together like an accordion. Bake in a 250° oven until golden (about one hour). Boil honey and water for a minute. Pour this mixture over the pastry as soon as it is taken out of the oven. This makes 5 Sarah-Leahs.

JUDY'S PETITS FOURS   *Shavuot*

Judith Zuckerman is famous in the land of Israel as a creative cook and outstanding hostess. This treat is her invention, which is worthy of a patent.

The Pastry

6 tablespoons soy flour
2 tablespoons icing sugar
2 tablespoons cornstarch
   pinch of salt
9 tablespoons butter

The Filling

4 tablespoons sugar
1 cup heavy cream,
   whipped
½ cup walnuts, chopped

For the pastry, mix the soy flour, icing sugar, cornstarch, and salt and cut in the butter. Pat into two pans and pierce with a fork. Bake for 30 minutes in a 300° oven.

For the filling, melt the sugar until golden, and while still warm, work into the cream. Spread over one layer of pastry. Break up the other layer and sprinkle the pieces and chopped nuts over the whipped cream filling. Cut into squares and put into paper holders.

Yom Kippur
CIAMBELLE DI KIPPUR—ITALIAN DOUGHNUTS

Ciambelle are akin to the filled raised doughnuts of America, except that they are not filled and are not crusty, but are soft and spongy. The double round form is typical in foods of Yom Kippur, for good luck all year round, all around the world.

1 ounce fresh yeast
   (2 packages dry)
¼ cup lukewarm water
6 cups flour (about),
   sifted
1 cup milk

4 eggs
1 cup cooking oil
¾ cup sugar
1 lemon rind, grated
1 teaspoon vanilla
   dash of cinnamon

Dissolve the yeast in lukewarm water, add 2 cups of the flour, and set aside to rise. When risen, add the milk and mix well. Add the eggs, oil, sugar, lemon rind, vanilla, cinnamon, and as much flour as is needed to make a soft dough. Cut with a doughnut cutter and allow to rise for about 2 hours. Fry in deep fat and sprinkle with sugar or honey. (Makes 50.)

SOOFGANIYOT (PUNCHIKOT, PFANNKUCHEN, FILLED DOUGHNUTS)   *Hanuka*

2½ cups flour
 2 cups hot milk
 1 ounce compressed yeast
      (or 2 packages dry)
 ¼ cup lukewarm milk
 6 egg yolks
 ⅔ cup sugar

 1 teaspoon vanilla
      rind of 1 lemon or
      orange
 ½ cup butter
      jam for filling
      oil for frying
      icing sugar

Sift one cup of flour into the hot milk and beat until smooth, then allow to cool. Dissolve the yeast in the lukewarm milk, add to the flour mixture, and set aside for about half an hour. Mix the egg yolks and sugar with the vanilla and rind and add to the dough. Then add the remaining flour and the butter and knead. Allow to rise until double in bulk (about 45 minutes). Roll out on a floured board to a thickness of ½ inch and cut into rounds. Put a teaspoon of jam in the center of one round and cover with another round. Press the edges together and allow to rise again in a warm place. Fry in hot oil, drain, and dust with icing sugar.

PASSOVER STRAWBERRY CREAM PUFFS   *Passover*

½ cup margarine
      pinch of salt
 1 cup cold water
 1 cup matzo meal
 4 eggs

 2 cups whipping cream
 2 tablespoons sugar
 1 teaspoon vanilla
      strawberries

Combine the margarine, salt, and water and bring to the boil. Add the matzo meal all at once. Reduce the heat and keep stirring the mixture until the batter leaves the side of the pot and forms into a ball. Remove from heat and add the eggs, one at a time, beating very well after each addition. Drop from a small spoon onto a greased baking sheet. Begin baking in a 450° oven for 30 minutes, then reduce the heat to 325° and bake about 35 minutes more. Remove the puffs to a cooling rack. When cool, cut a slit in each. Whip the cream and add the sugar and vanilla. Fill the puffs with this and tuck in one or two fresh strawberries.

Hanuka

TULUMBAS OR LOUKOUMADES—GREEK HONEY SPONGES

This pastry is also served as a night breakfast after one returns home in the early hours from the Selihot prayers.

2 cups water	8 eggs
1/3 cup butter	oil for deep frying
rind of 1 lemon	1 1/2 cups honey
2 cups flour, sifted	juice of 1 lemon
1 teaspoon salt	cinnamon

Boil the water, butter, and rind for a minute. Remove from heat and discard the rind. Add the flour and salt all at once and beat well. Cook over medium heat, stirring constantly, until the mixture forms a large ball which keeps its shape (this takes about 5 minutes). Remove from heat and cool to lukewarm. Add the eggs, one at a time, beating well after each. Continue beating until the mixture is smooth. Drop from a tablespoon into very hot olive or other oil and cook until golden brown. Remove and drain on paper. Dilute the honey with the lemon juice and pour over the puffed sponges. Sprinkle with cinnamon and serve hot. (Makes 30–40 loukoumades.)

NOTE: Tulumbas are long and ribbed, being put through a special squeezer to shape them.

TUNISIAN BEIGNETS OR PASSOVER BEOLAS   *Passover*

Honey, one of the world's oldest foods, originally had to be taken from wild hives. Besides being an exquisite food, it has many wonderful associations. Even the Bible is compared to milk and honey. It is a name of endearment to one beloved. And what wisdom and biting satire it helps convey in proverbs such as: "Who has no honey in his pot, let him have it in his mouth."

1/2 cup matzo meal	few drops orange essence
8 eggs	or grated rind of
oil for frying	1 orange
	1/4 cup honey

Mix the matzo meal with the well-beaten eggs. Drop by spoonfuls into hot oil and fry until golden. Drain on absorbent paper. Add the orange essence or grated rind to the honey. Impale each beignet on a toothpick and dip it in the honey mixture. (Serves 8.)

ZINGZOOLA OR ZELEBI FOR HANUKA   *Hanuka*

As a reporter at the Eichmann trial in Jerusalem, my place in the press room was next to Larry Fellows of The New York Times. *Larry's task was a serious one, involving political commentary; mine was easy—just to radio photographs with flash captions. In between I'd write recipes for my own paper.*

But one day I had a serious political piece to do and noticed that Larry was also very tense about his job. He suggested we change places, for The New York Times *had cabled him for Hanuka recipes. After a long interview he was able to report on zelebi (a snail-shaped honey confection that is seen on a tomb drawing of Ramses III, with details of how it is made) exactly as the giggly, bashful housewife had given the recipe to him, thus:*

> *A few handfuls of flour, a lot of water and a little oil so that dough is liquid. Pour through a funnel into a pot of boiling oil, and pour so as to curl into snail shape—and stop funnel with forefinger after each snail. Fry long enough to go to the window and call a proper Hanuka greeting to your neighbor, and get back to the pot. By this time the dough should be golden brown. Scoop up and throw for a minute only into another pot of hot honey. Remove and cool.*

And the dish always comes out right!

Zingzoola is the Iraqi name of this fritter, and it is made as above, using 1 cup flour, 1 cup semolina, and 1 cup cornstarch. Hot water is used in the recipe, but no oil.

PRESERVES

Rosh Hashana

METTIKA-GLEECOA APPLE OR QUINCE CONFITURE

This confiture is symbolic of the sweet year and the first fruits, and it is served in Greece on Rosh Hashana eve. A similar dish, made of cooked quinces, is eaten on this occasion by the Jews from Iraq. "Mettika" means "sweet" in Hebrew.

2 pounds apples or quinces	*1 teaspoon vanilla*
1 cup sugar	*juice of 1 lemon*
1 cup honey	

Parboil the apples or quinces, then peel and dice them. Add the remaining ingredients. Cook very gently until apples or quinces are done (about 15–20 minutes). (Serves 6.)

NOTE: It takes much longer to parboil quinces than apples, so this must be taken into consideration as far as the cooking time goes.

ORANGE AND GRAPEFRUIT JAM   *Hanuka*

According to Through the Looking-Glass, *"The rule is, jam to-morrow and jam yesterday—but never jam today." In Israel, however, almost every housewife makes homemade orange jam and has it today and every day.*

8 oranges	*2 cups sugar*
2 grapefruits, juice only	

With a fine grater, scrape the outer rind (zest) off the oranges. Peel the oranges and cut the peel into small pieces. Boil the peel three times, in changes of fresh water, for about 2 minutes each time. Put the peel through the meat chopper together with the pulp of the orange, from which the seeds have been removed. Add the grapefruit juice and the sugar. Boil together on low heat until the mixture becomes syrupy and thick. Pour into sterilized jars, seal, and store.

ETROG (CITRON) CONFITURE   *Succot*

*The citron—or etrog or Median apple—is as aromatic as the
headiest perfume. It is the oldest citrus fruit grown in Israel,
having been produced there since the time of Alexander the
Great. Jewish folklore relates that the citron was the apple that
tempted Eve, and since then has been considered a food to increase fertility. Even today, barren Middle Eastern women bite
off the pistil of the citron after Succot, the Feast of Tabernacles,
as many of its rites deal essentially with the fertility of agricultural crops. This custom was also taken on by Christians, and
King Frederick William IV of Prussia was conceived only after
his mother, the queen, bit the stalk off the Succot citron!*

*In former times, the citron was held as such a delicacy that
its use, as in the following recipe, was limited almost entirely to
royalty. There is an entry, dated Friday, July 5, 1539, in the ac-
counts of the Treasury of the King of France as follows: "Four
pounds of citrons were brought to King John the Good for a
conserve . . . a very great luxury, more than the price of cloves
per weight measure."*

1 etrog	1 lemon, if desired
1 orange, if desired	sugar
1 grapefruit, if desired	water

The citron may be used alone, or in company with any of the
other citrus fruits above. Wash the fruit and cut into halves in
order to remove the seeds. Cut into very thin slices, then cut
through each slice twice. Soak the fruit overnight. Bring the
fruit to a boil and change the water twice. Pour off the water.
For every cup of fruit add one cup sugar and cook until the fruit
jells (about 30 minutes).

GRAPE VARENJE (PRESERVES)   *Succot*

*Varenje is served in little dishes with lemon tea. It is eaten with
a small spoon and a dry biscuit. As a rule, the seeds are left in
the whole grapes.*

5 pounds dark grapes	5 pounds sugar

Cook the fruit and sugar together (no water needed) on low
heat for about 30 minutes. Stir only occasionally to make sure
the sugar does not burn. When the preserve is thick, pour it into
jars.

Yom Kippur — Succot
GELATINA DE COTOGNE—QUINCE CONFITURE

*It is amazing how long food traditions cling. During the Spanish
Inquisition, Jews from Spain fled to North Africa, western Asia,
Holland, and the lands of southern Europe. For generations there
was no contact between these groups, and they developed into
separate communities. Yet almost without exception, this confiture, which they must have made in Spain, is served by Sephardic Jews either at the close of the Yom Kippur fast, as a Rosh
Hashana sweet, or as a harvest symbol on Succot. This is the
Italian version.*

quinces   *whole cloves or stick cinnamon*
equal weight of sugar   *water*

Peel and core the quinces and then quarter. Weigh the quinces.
Add an equal weight of sugar and just enough water to keep the
confiture from burning during cooking. (Usual proportions in
bulk are one cup sugar to 2 cups raw fruit.) Add a few cloves or
cinnamon sticks (which will later be removed) and cook until the
quinces are rosy and the syrup thick. Pour into jars and seal.

GOLDA'S PRESERVES   *Hanuka*

*An aspiring young Israel politician, who loves to cook as a hobby,
held up a glowing golden jar of orange preserves and said to me,
"I'm calling this 'Golda's Preserves.'"*
"Because of the color? Golda for golden?" I asked.
*"No," he said, "because when Golda Meir became Israel's for-
eign minister I felt she was getting into a man's preserves, and
I'm darned if I won't get into a woman's to show her!"*

1 or 2 large oranges   *sugar as required*
1 or 2 lemons   *broken walnuts, as desired*
*   water as required*

Wash and quarter the fruit and remove the seeds. Do not peel.
Cut the fruit into 1/4-inch slices. Measure the fruit, without pack-
ing it down, and cover with an equal quantity of water. Soak for
24 hours. Cook the fruit in this water for 10 minutes and then
soak in the same liquid for another 24 hours. Measure the fruit
and liquid and add an equal amount of sugar, in volume. Cook
over low heat for about 2 hours, until the fruit syrup begins to
have a jelly-like consistency. Add broken walnuts as desired (1/2
cup for the above is ample) and cook two minutes more. Pour
into sterilized jars and seal.

BITTER POMELO (SHADDOCK) OR OTHER CITRUS MARMALADE

*4 pomelos (shaddocks), or   4 quarts water
8 oranges (or part   12 cups sugar
lemons), or 5 grapefruit,
or citrus fruits combined*

Wash, brush, and peel the fruit. Prepare two pots, each to cook different parts of the citrus fruits at the initial stage. Cut up the peel into slivers and cook it separately, with 8 cups of water, for 1 to 1½ hours, until the peel is soft. Meanwhile, cut up and boil the pulp of the fruit in another pot with 8 cups water. Both pots should be uncovered, and the water should boil briskly. After the fruit has cooked for 1½ hours, strain it through a very fine sieve. The fruit is now only tasteless mush, and should be thrown out. The liquid from the fruit is transferred to the big pot, with the peels. Boil for 5 minutes and then add the 12 cups of sugar. Continue to cook on moderate heat until the mixture begins to jell—from ½ hour to about 1 hour, or more, depending on the age of the fruit and the amount of natural pectin in it. Pour into hot sterilized jars and seal. (Makes about 8 pounds marmalade.)

RADISH EINGEMACHTES (PRESERVES)   *Passover*

The Talmud refers to the radish as an elixir of life. And yet it recognized this vegetable as having certain drawbacks, for it states: "To nullify the harmful effects of lettuce, eat radishes; to nullify the harmful effects of radishes, eat leeks; to nullify the harmful effects of leeks, drink hot water."

*2 cups black radishes   1 teaspoon ground ginger
½ cup water   ¼ cup blanched almonds
½ cup honey   or broken walnuts
1½ cups sugar*

Peel the radishes and cut into cubes or strips. Cook for 5 minutes in plenty of water. Drain. Put into fresh water and cook for another five minutes. Drain again. Mix the water, honey, sugar, and ginger. Bring to the boil and add the radishes. Cook over very low heat until the radishes are almost transparent. Add blanched almonds or broken walnuts and continue cooking until the confiture is quite thick.

KUMQUAT PRESERVES   *Succot*

An ancient Chinese writing has this to say of kumquats: "These fruits are eaten without peeling off their golden coats. When preserved in honey the flavor is still better. . . . The Empress Wen Cheng (1023) manifested a liking for the fruit, and it became popular and expensive in the capitol."

4 cups kumquats	*1 cup sugar*
1½ cups water	*½ cup honey*

After washing the kumquats, make a small slit across the top of each one so the syrup will penetrate. Bring the water, sugar and honey to the boil. Add the kumquats. Cook over very low heat until the fruit is somewhat transparent (about 1 hour). Cool in the pot and then put into jars. Serve as a "varenje" confiture with lemon tea, or as a jam or garnish for special dishes.

ROSE CONFITURE   *Rosh Hashana*

The time to make rose confiture is just before Rosh Hashana. In Afghanistan Jewish women also make rose water, with which to flavor their sweets, at this time of year. Moreover, fragrant rose water is now prepared for the Yom Kippur prayers; the Kohanim dip their fingers in it before singing the priestly blessings. The women thereafter drink this rose water for favor in God's eyes. This symbolic superstition is no longer practiced in Israel by immigrants from Asia but the women are adept in making the confiture.

1 pound rose petals	*1 pound lemons*
(red are best)	*1 pound sugar*
water to cover	*2 tablespoons water*

Cut off the white peaks at the heart of the rose petals (if they have them). Cut the lemons very thin, cover with water, and bring to a boil. Throw away the first water. Add the sugar, rose petals, and the 2 tablespoons water to the lemons and cook until thick enough to make a soft ball in cold water (234°–240° on candy thermometer).

SQUASH OR EGGPLANT CONFITURE   *Purim*

Ashdod is the brand-new city in the desert, planned and set up to receive, house, and employ thousands of people at one go. We drove to see this wondrous miracle and four times passed by the town without seeing it, for it hid in the sand like a marauding Bedouin. Finally we gave a new immigrant a lift to Ashdod, and lo and behold, there was the town—a whole town, to be sure. We gasped with the expected surprise.

Our "trempist" (the hitch-hiker) invited us to his home, and his wife offered us this North African confiture, now widely made in Israel.

2 pounds baby eggplants or squash	*orange essence or scented herbs such as aromatic*
2 pounds sugar	*geranium or nasturtium*
½ cup pistachio nuts or walnuts	*or mint*

Use only very small (in fact, tiny) eggplants or squash. Put them, whole, into a heavy pot with the sugar and simmer until the syrup is thick (about 2 hours). Break up the nuts and add. Cook with the herbs, but remove these before bottling. (Makes about 25.)

STRAWBERRY VARENJE (PRESERVES)   *Passover*

4 cups strawberries   juice of 2 lemons
4 cups sugar

Hull and wash the berries and then layer them with sugar. Let the berries stand overnight. Pour off the liquid and cook it over high heat for about 3 or 4 minutes. Add the berries and cook for 5 minutes more. Add the lemon juice and cook for another 2 or 3 minutes. Pour into sterilized jars and seal.

MAMA'S CHOCOLATE BUTTER   *Shavuot*

1 pound butter   ½ cup hot water
3 cups sugar   2 teaspoons vanilla
1½ cups cocoa

In a heavy pot, melt the butter mixed with the sugar and bring very slowly to the boil. Add the cocoa dissolved in the hot water. Simmer gently for 15 minutes, stirring occasionally. Add the vanilla. Remove from heat and keep stirring until cool (it thickens as it cools) to ensure that the butter does not rise to the top. Store in a crock, preferably in a cool place.

CANDY

Rosh Hashana — Passover
PLETZLACH CONFECTION

2 pounds dried apricots   5 cups sugar
water to cover

Soak the apricots overnight. Put to boil in the same water, adding more if necessary to cover the fruit. Cook until soft (15–20 minutes). Mash up the fruit with whatever liquid is left. Add the sugar and cook on low heat, stirring often, about 20 minutes. When the mixture forms a ball in cold water, it is ready. Pour out on a wet board. Cool. Cut into candies.

TAYGLACH—HONEY CONFECTION   Rosh Hashana

This dish, so popular on Rosh Hashana in England and the United States, was probably brought there from Russia or Poland. Nonetheless, it much resembles the type of confection the ancient Greeks made, and which was introduced into Israel with their Hellenic culture centuries ago. Being made with honey, it has become a traditional Rosh Hashana sweet.

2 tablespoons cooking oil   1 cup honey
2 eggs   ½ cup sugar
1¾ cups flour   1 teaspoon ground ginger
1 teaspoon salt   1 cup chopped nuts
1 teaspoon baking powder

Mix the oil, eggs, and dry ingredients together and then roll out the dough on a floured board to a thickness of about half an inch. Cut into half-inch squares. Or make ropes of the dough and cut into half-inch pieces. Put the squares or pieces into a shallow baking dish. Bring the honey, sugar and spice to a rolling boil. Pour over the pieces of dough. Bake for about 20 minutes in a 350° oven without opening the oven. Add the nuts and stir. Bake 30–40 minutes longer. The tayglach are done when the mixture sounds hollow during stirring. Pour onto a wet board and pat into an even thickness of ½ inch. Cool and cut into rectangles.

384

Independence Day
CANDIED ALMONDS OR OTHER NUTS (GRILLAGE)

"Rozinkis and mandlen"—raisins and almonds—have always been an Ashkenazic festive treat. The Sephardic Jews, most of whom dispersed after the Spanish Inquisition to countries where almonds happen to be a main fruit crop, seem to have followed the Biblical cue (Genesis 43:11) for the following recipe:

3 tablespoons honey	*dash of ginger or*
¾ cup sugar	*cinnamon*
1 cup blanched almonds	

Put the honey and sugar into a saucepan over low heat to caramelize. Be careful not to scorch. Toss in the almonds and the spice. Stir occasionally. When the candy forms a hard ball in cold water, remove from heat. Pour the mixture on a marble slab or cookie tin and cut into squares or break up into pieces.

ORANGE CANDIED NUTS   *Passover*

Turkish and Greek immigrants have introduced candied nuts, particularly the almond and walnut, to the cuisine of Israel. With the orange so bountiful in Israel, this recipe has come into popularity in their homes. Candied nuts were a special confection in seventeenth-century England, when coffee houses were opened for the first time and where they were allowed to sell such other delicacies as "lemonade, candied nuts, fruits in brandy and the like."

2 cups nuts (almonds or walnuts	*dash of salt*
2⅔ cups orange juice (water may be substituted for 2 cups of the orange juice)	*1 teaspoon grated orange rind*
	2 cups sugar

Cook the nuts in 2 cups of the orange juice or 2 cups water for 2 minutes. (If almonds, blanch them thereafter.) Put the nuts in a pan to dry and toast in a 350° oven for about 15 minutes. Mix the ⅔ cup orange juice, orange rind, salt, and sugar and cook until the mixture forms a soft ball when dropped in a glass of cold water (234°–240° on a candy thermometer). Remove from heat and stir in the nuts. The syrup will turn sugary, as in fudge. When it does, take out the nuts and scatter them on a sheet of waxed paper or buttered pan to dry.

SUKARIYOT SUM-SUM—SESAME SWEETS

Honey and seeds are often mentioned in the Bible among the good things to eat, but sugar cane is a rare treat that had to be brought by travelers from some distant land (Isaiah 43:24). This confection seems to have its source in an ancient recipe.

1 cup honey	2 cups sesame seeds
1 cup sugar	1 cup broken unblanched
½ cup water	almonds

Mix the honey, sugar, and water and bring to boil over low heat. Cook gently until a drop of the syrup forms a ball in cold water (234°–240° on a candy thermometer). Stir in the sesame seeds and nuts and cook until the seeds begin to gild. Pour the candy onto a marble slab or wet board. Cut into squares and let the mixture cool and harden.

MOHNLACH—POPPY SEED CANDIES *Purim*

½ pound poppy seed	¼ pound whole blanched
½ pound honey	almonds

Pour boiling water two or three times over the poppy seeds and drain. Boil the honey and add the poppy seeds and nuts. When a soft ball is formed by dropping a bit of candy from the end of a spoon into a glass of cold water (234°–240° on candy thermometer), the candy is ready. Stir well to prevent burning. Pour on a wet board or marble slab. Pat with a spoon into a thickness of ½ inch. Cut into squares and let harden.

SIMHAT TORAH BRIDAL SWEETS *Succot*

2 tablespoons margarine	1 teaspoon vanilla
1 cup warm milk	½ cup blanched almonds,
3 cups white sugar	slivered

Add the margarine to the warm milk and stir into the sugar. Cook on medium heat until a few drops of the candy form a soft ball when dropped into a glass of cold water (234°–240° on a candy thermometer). Remove from heat. Add the vanilla and the nuts. Cool for a few minutes and then beat until the mixture is thick and smooth. Pour onto a buttered pan and cut into squares.

PAULA'S PEANUT BRITTLE   *Ju Besh'vat*

2 cups sugar   *1 cup shelled peanuts*

Blanch the peanuts and cover a greased platter with them. Heat
the sugar in a pan until it melts and becomes golden brown. Stir
well. Pour over the nuts and cut into squares before it hardens.
Break the pieces after the candy hardens.

CARROT INGBERLACH   *Passover*

*For most of two thousand years the carrot was scorned as a
lowly weed. Then, in Elizabethan times, a Dutchman realized
their value as cattle fodder. The French were next to develop the
vegetable, and today it goes into the making even of cakes and
confections. Ingberlach are a grandma candy served particularly
on Passover.*

1½ pounds carrots   *1 cup (or less) blanched*
  2 cups sugar   *almonds*
  1 teaspoon ginger   *juice of 2 lemons*

Cook, mash, and strain the carrots. Add the sugar, ginger, and
chopped (or ground) almonds. Cook over low heat until very
thick, stirring often. Add the lemon juice. Sprinkle some sugar
and a dash of ginger on a board and pour the thick carrot mixture over it. Sprinkle the top with more sugar and ginger, and
before the mixture gets too hard, cut it into diamond shapes or
squares.

NOTE: If you wish, some of the almonds (about one-fourth) may
be bitter almonds for a particularly piquant taste.

PUNCH BALLS   *Purim*

2 teaspoons cocoa   *5 cups cake or cookie*
2 tablespoons grated milk   *crumbs*
    chocolate   *½ cup brandy*
2 tablespoons milk or water   *sugar and coconut for*
1 cup icing sugar   *rolling*

Put the cocoa, chocolate, and milk or water over low heat until
the chocolate melts. Stir in the icing sugar. Pour the brandy over
the crumbs and then add the icing mixture. Shape into walnut-
sized balls and roll in a plate of coconut mixed with sugar.

PURIM SWEETS—MUSTACHINONI OR ESCRAVANIYA *Purim*

Mustachioni is made by immigrants from Italy. The same recipe is used by Greek newcomers, except that they flatten out the mixture and cut it with a form of a pen and inkpot. The marzipan is then called "escravaniya" to recall Mordecai, who was a scholar and a scribe.

2 egg whites	1 tablespoon cocoa
3 cups blanched almonds,	1 egg yolk
ground	6 tablespoons icing.sugar
2½ cups sugar	juice of ¼ lemon, if
1 teaspoon brandy	needed
1 teaspoon cinnamon	colored confetti candy

Add 1 egg white to the ground almonds. Add the sugar. Put over very low heat to melt and thicken slightly, but not so long that it sticks to the pot. Into half the mixture put the brandy, and into the other half the cinnamon and cocoa. Add the egg yolk to the brandy-nut mixture. Form into three rounds and top with rounds of the cinnamon-cocoa mixture. Bake five minutes in a 400° oven. Cool. Mix the icing sugar with the second egg white, adding a few dops of lemon juice if the mixture is too stiff. Glaze the sweets with this. Sprinkle with colored confetti candy.

Rosh Hashana
RAHAT EL HALKUM—TURKISH DELIGHT

To view a sampling of the confections and pastries introduced from seventy lands into Israel, one has only to go to the Central Bus Station in Tel Aviv and see them for sale in bake shops and from carts, kiosks, and even piled up on the sidewalk. For at this travel mecca, people going to visit friends buy an old home treat. Turkish delight, which comes in many qualities, is usually flavored with rose water.

5 tablespoons cornstarch	1 teaspoon rose water or
½ cup cold water	vanilla
½ cup hot water	½ cup pistachios or other
2 cups sugar	nuts
½ cup orange juice	powdered sugar
2 tablespoons lemon juice	

Mix the cornstarch with the cold water. Bring the hot water, sugar, and orange juice to the boil. Add the cornstarch mixture and simmer for about 15 minutes, stirring often. Remove from

fire and add the lemon juice and flavoring. Stir in the nuts. Pour
into a buttered pan. When mixture has cooled and thickened, cut
the candy into 1-inch cubes with a knife dipped into hot water
and roll the cubes in powdered sugar.

FISTOOKIS—GARINIM—TOASTED SEEDS   *Purim*

*Cinemas in Israel flash a notice on the screen—"No cracking of
seeds allowed"—and in the cities a fine is imposed if you are
caught in the act. But in immigrant villages the notice is utterly
ignored. A lusty laugh goes up when the sign comes on, and the
sound of seeds cracking in the grip of six hundred sets of jaws is
like a rat-tat-tat orchestration. And when the film is over, the
floor is snowflaked with seed pods.*

sunflower, melon, watermelon, *water*
* or pumpkin seeds* *salt*

Cover the seeds with water and add salt (2 teaspoons to 1 cup
water). Bring to a boil, reduce heat to very low, and simmer
about 1½ hours. Drain on paper. Toast the seeds in a pan in a
250° oven, until crisp (about 45–75 minutes, depending on seed).
Stir from time to time.

OATMEAL "MARZIPAN"   *Shavuot*

*In the austerity days in Israel, sweets of any kind were unavail-
able. It was then that industrious and creative mothers made
new confections out of common fare. This mock marzipan has
the texture and nutty flavor of the real thing. You can, if you
wish, add a few ground almonds to make the candy indistinguishable from its expensive counterpart.*

1 cup oatmeal *2 tablespoons margarine*
3 tablespoons sugar * ground almonds, if desired*
2 tablespoons milk * icing sugar or cocoa*
1 teaspoon rum *1 teaspoon cocoa, if desired*
1 teaspoon almond flavoring

Grind the oatmeal in the meat chopper. Dissolve the sugar in the
milk. Mix the oats with the rum, almond essence, milk, margarine, and a few ground almonds, if desired. Knead into a
dough. Form into balls. Roll in icing sugar or cocoa. If you wish,
the marzipan can be chocolate-flavored by adding 1 teaspoon of
cocoa to the above mixture.

NOVEEGUS—GREEK PURIM MARZIPANS   *Purim*

*Dante's friend Immanuel of Rome wrote that in many houses in
the papal city the foods eaten on Purim included marzipan.
Kalonymos wrote much the same in the fourteenth century, adding also that meat was too common. Food among the Jews in
Greece was very similar at the time. Marzipan is called the "bread
of Mordecai" ("pat Mordecai," in Hebrew), for the Purim hero.*

2 cups margarine	4 cups flour, sifted
2 cups powdered sugar	2 tablespoons lemon juice
4 cups ground almonds	2 tablespoons water

Cream the margarine with the sugar. Mix the nuts and flour and
work into the margarine mixture. Add the lemon juice and
water to make a dough that can be rolled (if necessary add a
little more water). Roll to cookie thickness and cut with cookie
cutters in Queen Esther or other shapes. Bake in a 275° oven for
about 30 minutes. Dust with more powdered sugar.

MOUNT SINAI MARZIPAN   *Shavuot*

*The Italians make Mount Sinai as a marzipan confection, filling
a shell shaped like an ice cream cone (you can use a cone, cut
down, for the purpose), covering it with white icing and tipping
it with colored candy confetti to symbolize the snow-covered
mountain. This the Italians eat with a marmalade of green
squash as a symbol of the first fruits brought to the Temple, and
as a sign of spring.*

1¼ pounds almonds	1 cup icing sugar
3½ cups sugar	2 tablespoons hot water
6 egg whites	1 teaspoon lemon juice
3 egg yolks	candy confetti or glazed
rind of 2 oranges	green citron peel
ice cream cones, cut	
down to about 2 inches	
in height	

Blanch and grind the almonds and mix with the sugar. Beat in
the egg whites to make a paste, then add the egg yolks and the
grated rind. Cook the mixture in the top of a double boiler, stirring constantly, until thick. Cool. Fill the cones with the mixture.
Mix the icing sugar with the hot water and lemon juice and ice
the cones with this. Decorate the top with colored candy confetti
or a piece of green citron peel. (Makes about 25.)

SEMOLINA MARZIPAN *Shabbat*

½ cup fine semolina	1 teaspoon almond essence
¼ cup sugar	¼ teaspoon lemon juice
1 cup confectioner's sugar	3 tablespoons ground
pinch of salt	almonds (optional)
1 egg white	cocoa (optional)

Mix the dry ingredients, then work in the egg white to make a heavy paste. Add the almond essence and lemon juice. As the size of egg whites differ, you may have to add a little more confectioner's sugar. Pat on to a buttered plate and cut into squares, or roll into marble-sized balls and then in cocoa for a coating.

NOTE: I made this up without almonds, but a few (or even a lot) do add to the positive conviction that this fake marzipan is the real thing.

TUNISIAN SEMOLINA SWEETS *Purim*

1½ cups semolina	½ cup pine nuts (or
¼ teaspoon salt	walnuts and almonds)
2 eggs	4 tablespoons icing sugar
½ cup water	oil for deep frying
	honey for dipping

Make a dough of the semolina, salt, eggs, and water. Roll out very thin and cut into 2-inch squares. Pound the nuts with the icing sugar and put a teaspoonful of nut mixture in the center of each square. Fold over and pinch the edges together. Fry in deep hot oil until golden, then remove and drain. Dip in warm honey.

PASTINE DI SCHIUMA DI GERUSALEMME—MARZIPAN CONFECTION *Yom Kippur*

In the synagogues on Yom Kippur men wear white robes, and all the coverings and draperies are changed for white hangings and cloths. White, the color of purity, goes even into the cooking of Yom Kippur.

1 cup blanched almonds	1 egg white, stiffly beaten
½ cup powdered sugar	

Grind the almonds and mix with the sugar and egg white. Roll out like dough and cut into rounds. Put these rounds on a buttered pan and bake in a 375° oven 10 minutes. The marzipans will be soft inside.

BEVERAGES

Until the German immigration, Israelis drank tea, and this they took from a glass with a slice of lemon and a lump of sugar to bite on. Today Israel's cafés, or coffee houses, have their regulars as much as those in Vienna. Chess is played, newspapers are read, and friends meet to talk in the restful atmosphere of the café. But tea is no longer the beverage (except for the faithful Second Aliya immigrants who came from Russia and Poland): coffee is the thing.

But don't be bewildered when you order a cup of coffee. The waiter will first ask you: "Espresso, Nes, or Rawghil?" "Espresso" is the powerfully concentrated demitasse of Italian origin. "Nes" is the term used for Israel's Elite instant coffee. "Rawghil" is "regular," and this may be percolated, boiled, or dripped. When you make your choice you still have to decide whether to have it black, with milk, or "upside down." "Upside down" means a glass of milk with a few tablespoons of coffee. Or you may take it with a topping of "kozefette"—whipped cream. You may also insist on the concentrated sterilized milk known as "coffee milk" or just normal pasteurized milk. And if you want your milk hot, don't forget to say so.

Of course you may want none of these coffees, but prefer the popular Turkish coffee, which is a sweet heavy brew, with half the cup full of the pounded coffee grains. This coffee is never taken with milk, but you may want it bitter, and then you must say so. Or if you want a Middle Eastern touch, you have the coffee with hale (cardamom). If you are with a Yemenite, you'll also have ginger added to your brew. Cappuccino coffee, mocha-colored like the cloaks of the Capuchin monks and topped with whipped cream and a grating of chocolate, is also much loved in Israel, even by the most Orthodox religious Jewish zealot. And in the army camps a new ritual has begun: instant coffee is put in cups and water is added, drop by drop; all the while a spoon is beaten against the side of the cup, until the drink is total froth and creamy. You can almost locate an army camp in the dark by the sound of the rhythmic beating of spoons against cups, like some ancient drummed message echoing from hill to hill.

The after-dinner demitasse served in the hotels has several very exotic names. If it's not called "mocha," then the name is "pearls of Istanbul" or "perfume of Yemen."

If all this confuses you, ask for good strong American coffee, and you can even have it with a nip of brandy thrown in.

Don't forget to tell the waiter if you want it in a cup or glass!

TURKISH COFFEE   *Yom Kippur*

The making of Turkish or Arabic coffee is quite a ceremony in a Bedouin tent. The beans are hammered in a wooden mortar beautifully ornamented in brass, with a rhythmic rap-tap-tap like music. The coffee is roasted and then brewed in a magnificent long-handled brass or copper finjan coffee pot, with a rigid protocol of so many bitter and so many sweet cups. Good Arab manners demand that after duly hiccoughing to show satisfaction with the meal one sips the coffee slowly with very loud and elegant noises (much as Western boors unrefinedly drink their soup). Turkish coffee is served as a demitasse after fine meals everywhere in Israel.

1½ cups water
  3 tablespoons sugar
  2 tablespoons pulverized
       coffee

pinch of hale
  (cardamom)
1 tablespoon cold water

Put the water in a finjan or other coffee pot. Add the sugar and stir well. Add the coffee mixed with the hale (cardamom). Place on low heat and bring to a rising boil. Remove from heat and add the 1 tablespoon cold water without stirring. Return to heat and bring to a slow boil. Remove from heat and pour froth into each cup. Bring to a boil a third time, remove from heat, and serve in small cups. The pulverized coffee will sink like mud to the bottom, the syrupy liquid remaining above it. This is the coffee with which most Middle Eastern families will break the fast, after the usual almond or herb drink.

ICED MINT TEA   *Shabbat*

Saladin's Jewish doctor, Ibn-Jamiya, wrote (in the twelfth century) recipes of lemon drinks to which quinces and other fruits, as well as scented herbs such as mint, were added. The beverage enjoyed on hot summer days in Israel has not altered much.

3 sprigs mint
3 tablespoons lemon juice
8 teaspoons sugar
3 teaspoons tea leaves

4 cups boiling water
2 cups ice cubes, crushed

Put the sprigs of mint, lemon juice, and sugar into a teapot. Put the tea leaves in a strainer and pour the boiling water through them, and over the mint sprigs. Pour into a pitcher and add the ice and lemon slices. Chill further. Serve very cold.

ICE COFFEE   *Shavuot*

1 cup strong coffee
2 teaspoons fine sugar or
     syrup

1 tablespoon sweet cream
     or milk
1 ball of mocha, vanilla or
     chocolate ice cream

Serve the coffee, mixed with sugar and cream, in a tall glass, with a ball of ice cream in it. (One twirls the ice cream around as he imbibes the ice coffee.) (Serves 1.)

CITRUS TEA   *Purim*

In the fourth century the Chinese made a tea drink, the recipe of which read as follows: "Steam tea leaves crushed in a mortar and made into a cake which was boiled with rice, ginger, salt, orange peel, spices, milk, and onions." Perhaps the Russian lemon tea is a survival of this dish. In any case, during the acute rationing in the early days of the state of Israel, a good strong cup of tea with sugar was out of the question, and I would serve this beverage, which has remained as a delight to my guests:

1 cup boiling water
1 teaspoon tea leaves
3 cups grapefruit juice
3 cups orange juice

dash of ginger
sugar (optional)
sliver of lemon rind
     (optional)

Pour boiling water over the tea leaves. Heat the juices (do not boil them) and add to the tea with the ginger and sugar, if desired. Add a sliver of lemon rind, if you wish.

Yom Kippur
POST-FAST ALMOND DRINK: MIZO, SOUBYA, SOUMADA

This drink for breaking the fast is traditional among Jews from Turkey, Greece, Iraq and many other lands where Jews have resided since their escape from the Spanish Inquisition. It is snow white as a symbol of purity after all the confessional prayers: it is also light yet very nourishing. Each land has a different name for this drink, such as "mizo," "soubya," "soumada."

This almond milk is made by pounding blanched almonds until they are smooth and thick as syrup. A little water may be added. It can be made in a blender, in which case use 2 cups blanched almonds and 1 cup water.

In some countries white melon seeds are used instead of, or along with, the almonds.

SPECIAL LEMONADE   *Shavuot*

*Lemonade began to penetrate to the public palate by the four-
teenth century. Indeed, the Italian rabbis of the period had to
decide whether the making of lemonade was considered cooking,
and therefore not to be done on the Sabbath. But the final ruling
was that squeezing lemons for lemonade was merely the seasoning of water and therefore permitted. Lemonades are so much
used in Israel that the syrup comes ready bottled and a huge
variety of iced drinks are concocted on the spot, such as this one:*

6 tablespoons lemon syrup   6 cups water
    or juice of 3 lemons and   crushed ice
    6 tablespoons sugar   6 lemon slices with rind
6 tablespoons white wine   6 preserved cherries or
    juice of 6 granadillas   pitangas
    or other fruit   6 melon cubes
                           6 sprigs of mint

Mix the lemon syrup (or juice and sugar), wine and granadilla
(or other fruit juice) with the water. Fill 6 glasses with crushed
ice and add lemon slices, cherries, and melon cubes to each glass.
Pour the lemonade over. Garnish with the mint. (Serves 6.)

NOTE: You can use other fruits in season if you wish.

MULLED WINE   *Hanuka*

2 bottles dry red wine   3 threads of saffron
2 cups pomegranate juice   thin peel of 1/2 lemon
1 cup sugar   orange slices
8 cloves   sprigs of mint
    pinch of cinnamon

Pour the wine and juice into a pot, stir in the sugar, cloves,
cinnamon, saffron, and lemon peel. Cover and bring to the boiling point, but do not boil (for the alcohol evaporates first). Serve
hot, with a thin slice of orange topped with a sprig of mint in
each glass.

NOTE: Other juices, such as grape, may be substituted for
pomegranate.

SPECIAL ORANGEADE   *Shavuot*

*About 1600, when sugar cane became plentiful, orangeades rose
to popularity. They were made highly aromatic by the addition
of flowers such as jasmine and carnations for perfume. Spices
such as coriander seed, cinnamon, mace, and essences of rose
water made the drink even more heady. The aphrosidiac musk
was sometimes added, so that the drink had much more than
taste appeal as an aim. Orangeades are everyday drinks in Israel,
the squash coming bottled in mandarin, orange, lemon or mixed
syrups. But every housewife makes her own specialties, and here
is mine:*

sugar for frosting	1 tablespoon ginger syrup
crushed ice	or dash of ginger powder
6 tablespoons mandarin syrup	6 cups water
or juice of 3 oranges,	6 orange slices, unpeeled
mixed with 6 tablespoons	and studded with a clove
sugar	each, for garnish
2 tablespoons lemon juice	6 sour cherries and 6 sprigs
6 tablespoons light wine	mint for garnish

Wet the tops of 6 glasses and dip in sugar to "frost" the rims.
Half-fill with crushed ice. Mix all the ingredients except the garnishes and pour into the glasses. Garnish with the orange slices
studded with cloves, cherries, and mint sprigs. (Serves 6.)

MITZPEH RIMON   *Passover*

*We were traveling through the desert to Elath. The day was hot
and dry and the sight of the village of Mitzpeh Rimon heartened
us, for there we could refresh ourselves with a cold drink. I
asked my five-year-old Sherry what she wanted, and in Hebrew
she gave me the answer, the name of the village broken into
three words: Mitz (juice—usually referring to citrus); Peh
(pointing to her mouth—a drink); Rimon (pomegranate). This
was concocted for her on the spot and named for the isolated
village of Mitzpeh Rimon:*

2 oranges	1 cup ice-cold sparkling
1 pomegranate	water

Squeeze the juice out of the pomegranate and oranges. Pour on
the icy soda water and drink 'er down.

POMEGRANATE NECTAR   *Rosh Hashana*

*The ancient Romans knew the pomegranate very well and re-
ferred to its as the* malum punicum (*Punic apple*), *referring perhaps to their finding it in the Tunisian area. To the Greeks its
juice was fit for the gods, and perhaps they prepared it much as
the Arabs and Jews from Arab lands do today:*

10 *pomegranates*   *juice of 1 lemon*
 6 *tablespoons sugar*   *rose water*

Cut the pomegranate in two and extract the juice with a lemon
squeezer. Add the sugar, lemon juice, and a sprinkling of the
rose water and chill thoroughly. Serve with a sprig of mint.

INDEX

A